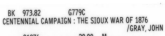

973.82 G779c
GRAY   M
 CENTENNIAL CAMPAIGN : THE
 SIOUX WAR OF 1876
                              20.00

St. Louis Community
College

Library

5801 Wilson Avenue
St. Louis, Missouri 63110

CENTENNIAL CAMPAIGN

The Sioux War of 1876

CENTENNIAL CAMPAIGN

The Sioux War of 1876

by John S. Gray

Maps by John A. Popovich

THE OLD ARMY PRESS

Library of Congress Catalog Card No. 76-47160

ISBN 0-88342-049-X

VOLUME NO. 8 IN THE SOURCE CUSTERIANA SERIES

THE OLD ARMY PRESS
1513 WELCH
FT. COLLINS, COLORADO 80521

CONTENTS

PART I. THE NARRATIVE

PART II. FACETS

PREFACE

Over twenty-five years ago an ever-increasing burden of university administrative duties began threatening my deepest love — research, then conducted in bio-medical science. As a countermeasure I looked for an auxiliary area of research that could be pursued in spare moments without elaborate facilities and government funding. I found it in American frontier history.

Initial investigations focused on the fascinating careers of a number of those unsung frontiersmen who scouted for the Indian fighting army. Inevitably, some of these subjects scouted for Custer and served or died at the Battle of the Little Big Horn.

That was when I balked. The reams of melodramatic and partisan verbiage written from derivative sources and confined to a single hour in a year of warfare offended my scientific training. I vowed to steer clear of that example of caricaturized history.

Like the bicycle rider who concentrates so hard on avoiding an obstacle that he inevitably runs into it, I found that Custer battle constantly in my road. So I tried to read *around* it in order to learn what had happened before and after. So little was available, however, that a search began for new and unused primary sources. To my surprise, they proved both rich and extensive and revealed a fascinating story that had never been told.

The problems of presenting so large a story, especially when parts were already buried deep in controversy, seemed overwhelming, but one by one possible solutions came to mind. The first decision was to work entirely from the wealth of primary sources and avoid voluminous refutations by paying minimal heed to derivative material. The second decision was to present the material in two parts, designated "The Narrative" and "Facets." The latter consists of analytical solutions to problems long unresolved and some deemed unresolvable, while the former narrates the actions without interruption by taking for granted the solutions reached in the analytical part.

Another problem was documentation, which in the field of history is fast becoming pedantic ritual. The solution, described in a note that precedes the bibliography, is based on a simple principle — that the purpose of documentation is to enable the interested scholar to find the sources used, and not to lead others to isolated words so that they need not read or learn.

The book attempts for the first time to narrate the full story of the Sioux War of 1876, which epitomizes racial conflicts that began millenia ago and continue unabated today. It covers the genesis of the war and the concealed maneuvers that became necessary to disguise unpalatable features. It follows the strategy and tactics of all the army columns and Indian forces as they campaigned in 1876 to achieve their incompatible goals. It carries the conflict to its dramatic and tragic conclusion.

It is hoped that the reader will recognize the determined effort, if not full success, to achieve two self-imposed objectives. I have tried my best not to be a partisan of only the white man or only the Indian, but to be bi-partisan, i.e., to portray the attitudes of each and thereby reveal the tragedy of their incompatibility. The result often proved uncomfortable to me, as it may to the reader.

I have also tried my best to avoid the popular melodramatic fallacy that forces characters into either of two non-existent molds — the invariably good or the invariably bad. If each of the chief actors in the drama do not display both virtues and faults, then the portrayal must be false.

It would be tedious to name the myriad of persons who have aided in the search for and the providing of sources, or have encouraged my efforts to become a historian, or have discussed issues with me by the hour. But I must express my debt to a master historian and congenial friend who encouraged me as well as thousands of others, and introduced me to the Chicago Corral of Westerners — Ray A. Billington, then a fellow professor at Northwestern University. And I gratefully acknowledge years of stimulating association with that Corral, especially with friends Don Russell, Harry H. Anderson, and Father Peter J. Powell.

John S. Gray, Ph.D., M.D.
Fort Collins, Colorado

PART I. THE NARRATIVE

Chapter 1
Cultures in Conflict

When two air masses collide, action at their interface generates a front, whose turbulence is proportional to the dissimilarities in the air masses and the forces driving them to collision. When two civilizations collide, action at their interface generates a frontier, whose turbulence is proportional to the dissimilarities in the two civilizations and the forces driving them to collision.

The continental United States is the perpetual scene of air mass collisions, whose eastward rolling fronts mark the stormy progress of the displacement of one air mass by another. It has also been the scene of a grand cultural collision, whose westward moving frontier has marked the stormy displacement of the Indian civilization by the white. The confrontation between two such different cultures, each driven by the will to survive, generated a violent conflict that could end only in victory for the stronger and defeat for the weaker.

Rarely has either side appreciated the differences between the white and Indian civilizations, and no more today than in the past. The differences, so profound as to make the two mutually exclusive, were not in degree but in kind. The Indian was never a primitive, ignorant, and shiftless exponent of the white culture. He was an advanced, educated, and responsible exponent of the Indian culture. Nothing can generate such tragic human consequences as to judge one culture by the arbitrary standards of another. Yet this is probably the most wide spread and rarely surmounted of all human failings. Its name is cultural bigotry.

Even differences so superficial as to be meaningless can bring incredible friction between peoples. To prove the point, we need

1

only cite the ultimate in superficial differences — the color of the skin! Innumerable, but equally superficial, pseudo-differences characterize cultures. A typical example is the oriental delight in eggs long subjected to bacterial action, versus the occidental delight in milk solids similarly treated. However intense the cross-repugnances toward cheese and ancient eggs, the superficial differences masks a profound similarity — the shared delight of gourmet delicacies. Such pseudo-differences between white and Indian cultures are legion. Witness the missionary who found Indian magic so abhorrent that he instinctively made the sign of the cross! And countered Indian ritual with a pious mass! Behold white women fainting at the appearance of warriors with artificial coloring applied to their cheeks! Even bank-robbers protested righteously against Indian thievery!

The real differences that rendered the white and red cultures so utterly incompatible were far deeper — so profound as to remain hidden in the subconscious. The red man's ideal was to make himself a part of nature, while the white man's was to exploit nature. A subconscious compulsion to blend with the ecology drove the first, but a like compulsion to bend the ecology to his own use drove the second. The white man prided himself on his mastery over nature, but the Indian on his adaptation to nature. The Great Spirit made the red man and nature one, but God made nature the servant of the white man. From these bone-deep, but opposite, poles stemmed a thousand incompatibilities.

Since the naturalistic red culture found little need to differentiate matter from spirit, the Indian thought and acted largely in terms of an all-pervading spirit. The exploitative nature of the white culture, however, compelled a distinction between spirit and exploitable matter, and so the white man thinks and acts largely in terms of material considerations. Exploitation demands acquisition and ownership, i.e., the exclusive possession and use of real property, for one man cannot operate a strip-mine where another farms. But life as a part of nature demands no hard acquisition and ownership. Nor must it strive to make a virture of toil and labor.

The Indian society, having little need for a controlling government, retained extraordinary freedom for the individual. Chiefs wielded little more than the power of persuasion in open council; when disagreements developed, the individuals or factions simply went their separate ways. But white society, pious protestations to the contrary notwithstanding, is compelled to organize, regiment, and control its members to a high degree, using force, if necessary. Voluntary sharing comes naturally to the Indian, but requires a

2

denial of the acquisitive principle for the white man. Material wealth, technology, science, growth, power, and conquest come naturally to the white man, but require the denial of the naturalistic principle for the red man.

Our object in ferreting out the deeper and unconscious characteristics of the two cultures is not to pronounce an Olympian judgement as to their relative merits. There are no impersonal, nonpartisan criteria for reaching such judgements, for each of us is steeped in his own culture. The simple fact is that each cherishes his own and tends to despise all others. Our real object is to expose the utter incompatibilities of the two cultures. They could not possibly exist in the same place at the same time. Put simply, one cannot live by the chase in another's fenced corn patch.

The forces that drove the two cultures into inevitable and violent collision stemmed from these same profound differences. The naturalism of the Indian society held it essentially stable in population and material power. The Indian and nature operated as a regulator with negative, i.e., stabilizing, feedback. Should the population increase, its relative food supply necessarily diminishes, thereby curbing growth by malnutrition and reduced fertility. A significant degree of stability was thus automatic, and the society could flourish within such limits indefinitely, barring cataclysms of nature.

This is in striking contrast to the expansionist and aggressive white society, which operates with unstabilizing, i.e., positive feedback, as a vicious cycle of growth that must bring ultimate disaster — as past history seems so clearly to demonstrate. Success in the exploitation of nature force-feeds the explosion of both population and material power. These, in turn, fuel the demand for more territory and the more efficient exploitation of more natural resources. By its fundamental nature it is automatically expansionist, both in numbers and power, and therefore aggressive.

The arrival of the expansionist white civilization on the North American continent spelled doom for the stabile Indian civilization. White society could not commingle and coexist with the incompatible red society. Accordingly, the white fought aggressively for the survivial of his expansionist civilization. This forced the Indian to fight defensively for his static civilization. The ultimate outcome of a desperate push from an organized and powerful many against an unorganized and impotent few could not long remain in doubt.

It cannot be emphasized enough that we have been speaking of *cultures* and *civilizations*, not *persons*. The distinction is of the essence. The former are attributes of populations more than of

3

individuals. Two cultures may differ profoundly, even though the attributes of the individuals composing each may be very much alike. We hold no more brief for the "nobility" of an Indian than for the "nobility" of a white man. The same spectrum of vices and virtues characterizes the individuals of both races. A few of each stand out because they are wise, tolerant, honest, generous, and even noble. Most of each, at times, can be extraordinarily vicious, cruel, treacherous, and selfish. When acting as populations, guided by different cultural heritages, the white race represented disaster for the Indian race, regardless of the similarity of the vices and virtues of their individual members.

The white frontier, advancing and displacing the Indian, took centuries to run its course across the continent. The process exterminated many of the eastern tribes, while others fled to contest for hunting grounds with their neighbors to the west. The whites banished still others to trans-Mississippi territory. With the passage of time and distance, zeal for extermination began to fade in favor of establishing enclaves, or reservations, where the survivors, no longer able to support themselves, could be confined and fed, and around which the tide of white expansion could flow — unless the reservation lands proved exploitable. Today, shrunken reservations dot the western states, where the majority of surviving Indians struggle to keep alive. Though the Indian race is far from extinct, its original culture has been shattered. Only the deepest of cultural traits survive to clash with others acquired from the white man.

Dispossession from a homeland is disaster enough, but the disintegration of a culture brings the ultimate in tragedy. Nothing so devastates the spirit of a people as the destruction of its cultural heritage, which alone gives meaning and guidance to life. Only a myth, born of bigotry and nurtured by guilt, can pretend that the imposition of a "superior" culture confers a welcome blessing on the "benighted." Culture is not inherited through the genes but taught by one generation to the next. If one generation is demoralized, lost, and groping, so are the children for generations to come. A compelling and ennobling culture is centuries in the building.

The cultural conflict had moral and humane aspects that can neither be ignored nor evaded. These aspects strike highly emotional sparks from partisans of both sides, but more often than not the charges and counter-charges becloud rather than clarify the issues. The justification, or lack there of, for the displacement of the Indian by the white is largely a spurious moral issue, for it was scarcely a matter of choice. Neither white nor red had any alternative

4

save to fight for the survival of their respective civilizations. Without choice there can be no morality; homo sapiens, being unable to survive on minerals, is not immoral for feeding on other life forms. The cultural collision seems more akin to the disaster of an ice age, earthquake, flood, or plague. Though this makes guilt irrelevant to the *fact* of displacement, it in no way mitigates the tragedy visited upon the victims. Neither does it justify the cultural chauvinism that twists subconscious and uncontrollable forces for human destruction into proud virtues.

The true moral issues concern the *manner* of displacement and the *treatment* accorded the victims. In these matters a whole gamut of alternatives were open, and the choices made are subject to moral evaluation. It is no news that "civilized" peoples have barbarously treated "savages," and then ignored all responsibility for the plight of the vanquished. The record of the American frontier abounds in such incidents. These aspects afford grist enough for anyone's moral mill.

From the broad spectrum of white attitudes toward the Indian, we may single out three special patterns. For a scattered few, intimate association with the red man transformed cultural bigotry into respect and admiration for the Indian way of life, even to the degree of marrying and living within the tribe. Fellow whites usually despised them as "renegades" and "squawmen", and some, who were the dregs of white society, may have deserved such epithets. But a surprising number were sensitive and educated persons, who found the Indian culture more satisfying than their own — a manifestation of the "back to nature" yearning that strikes sporadically among "civilized" people. Many of these men served their new hosts well in their difficult dealings with predatory whites, to the indignation and resentment of the latter.

The attitude of the majority of whites largely reflected their proximity in time and space to the frontier, where active displacement was in progress. All too commonly, the pioneer resented the Indian's aversion to labor and to the exploitation of his land for material gain. By white criteria he was, therefore, shiftless and of no account. And he had the effrontery to stand in the way of his betters! His refusal to adopt on the instant the invader's values made him a criminal outlaw with no rights whatever. They branded every defensive reaction of the Indian an aggressive "depredation." that justified punitive retaliation and happy confiscation of more of his land. They chose to ignore the fact that the country, originally all Indian, ended up all white, thus leaving no ambiguity whatsoever as to the identity of the agressors.

Recognizing that the Indian was powerless to stand against the white, the pioneer often salved his conscience with the convenient moral fallacy that the inevitability of the end justifies any means of achieving it. At its worst, this attitude made the Indian fair game for everything from chicanery to genocide. At its best, it held that the agony for all concerned was least when the conquest was swift, on the principle that if decapitation is inevitable, it is humanely (not just more humanely) accomplished by the single stroke of the guillotine rather than the many strokes of the bologna-slicer. This was the attitude of the army command, as exemplified by Generals Sherman and Sheridan. They took for granted the ultimate conquest of the Indian and deemed their responsibility to consist of serving their nation's interests by accomplishing its objective efficiently. For this they were praised by some and damned by others.

Far from the scene of action, the descendants of the first exterminators became known as "Indian sympathizers" for protesting the continuing mistreatment, though milder, of the now distant Indian. But their intervention often aggravated what it was intended to ameliorate. They inveighed against the immutable end, instead of the mutable means, and attempted to block it by fair means or foul. This was tilting at windmills while Rome was burning — a policy as confused as the metaphors. Any success they met with in stemming the tide merely dammed back the pressure until it erupted in even more vicious and destructive forms.

These well-intentioned people sympathised with the Indian, but not, alas, with his culture. They devoted themselves to misdirected attempts to reform the Indian overnight into the image of the white man; not, of course, into wealthy industrialists like themselves, but into the more virtuous ideal of the bucolic toiler. The soul of the savage infidel must be saved by converting him to an honest, Christian farmer, even where there was no reservation land from which an expert white farmer could wrest a living. When the Indian proved so ungrateful as to hang back, they piously starved him into it — for his own good. And when his miserable crops failed, it was God's doing, not man's.

It is no wonder that greedy aggression, teamed with intolerant sympathy, made the manner of Indian displacement and his subsequent treatment something less than admirable. Nor is it any wonder that the Indian has not come to respect a culture that covers exploitation and aggression, greed and dishonesty, arrogance and violence, with a righteous cloak of hypocrisy. Of course, the Indian was no winged angel, but neither was he more devilish than the white man; and at best his society did not live for massive exploitation and aggression.

The "Indian problem," as the white so loves to call the white-Indian problem, is still with us, and for the same reason — cultural insight and respect are still in woefully short supply. But the problem today does not really consist of the sins of our forefathers; it consists of the sins of today, some even sanctioned by law. Wrongs of the past can never be corrected, for the flow of time is irreversible. No event can be erased, much less replaced by a better one. Retaliation, so dear to the heart of all mankind, leads to the self-perpetuating vendetta, and so becomes a cause, not a cure, of wrongs.

Restitution and compensation can work wonders for a wronged person. But common sense, the rights of the innocent, and the compelling necessity of breaking the vendetta chain dictate that the eligibility for compensation expire with the life of the wronged person. If my ancestor stole your ancestor's cow, I am not the thief, and you are not the victim of thievery. But if I steal your car, while my generation and yours are fighting over your ancestor's cow, the situation is reduced to a farce. Though the dead have no problems, the living do. Only the redress of *present* wrongs can do anything for the living and the unborn. But even this taxes all the insight, understanding, and patience that both sides can muster, even without the hindrance of emotional red herrings.

The Sioux-Cheyenne War of 1876, in which General George Armstrong Custer figured so prominently and disastrously, epitomizes in a brief span of time all the facets, both good and bad, that characterized the centuries-long conflict between the two cultures. It was an aggressive war launched by the executive branch of the Government, with neither consultation nor consent of the legislative branch. It was a violation of a solemn treaty designed to permit further violations of the same treaty. It was forced in part by an earlier successful intervention by misguided Indian sympathizers. Although a disastrous and humiliating military failure in its early phases, it nevertheless spelled final tragedy for the Sioux-Cheyenne way of life.

The high point (or low, depending upon the point of view) of the war came on June 25, 1876, in the form of the Battle of the Little Big Horn, which has so captivated the popular fancy as to obliterate the war and its significance. Although more has been written about these few hours than any similar number in American history, the light thus shed scarcely matches that of a lightning bug. The battle has generally been treated, not as an insignificant episode in the meaningful stream of history, but as a discrete flash

7

of high drama, isolated from context the better to free the poet's license. Explanations have been invented in terms of personalities, grotesquely caricatured to feed the melodramatic fallacy. This is the stuff of fiction, folklore, and myth, but not history, and certainly not reality.

This unhappy trend has focussed all eyes precisely where there is least to see. Reams have been written on how the battle could have been so incredibly lost, when it is obvious that Custer's scattered regiment suffered a classic defeat in detail at the hands of a superior force of Indians. There are speculations galore on the detailed maneuvers of Custer's own annihilated battalion, though little can ever be known on this score. Lost in this astigmatic flash are all the chronic problems of white-red relations, the forces that moved the antagonists, the strategy and tactics they adopted in the struggle, and how and why they went awry. This is the proper stuff of history and far more fascinating and instructive than cheap mellerdramer.

Chapter 2
The President's Dilemma

In the fall of 1875 the inexorable march of events on the northern plains brought President Ulysses S. Grant face to face with a dilemma. The surge of frontier pressure to seize the gold-bearing Black Hills of Dakota, the very heart of the permanent reservation of the Sioux and Cheyenne tribes, was growing utterly irresistable. Yet solemn treaty obligations made such a seizure patently illegal. The President was powerless to prevent the rape of the Hills, yet could scarcely sanction an act that violated the law of the land and the conscience of half the nation. It was a painful dilemma.

The seeds of the problem had been sown ten years earlier, when the close of the Civil War had released a vast tide of white emigration to the plains and mountains. Unlike previous westward movements, this one would have the support of three railroads. The Union Pacific was building toward California along the Platte River; its Eastern Division was about to take the Smoky Hill route across Kansas to Denver. The Northern Pacific would ultimately follow the Yellowstone through Montana and beyond. These, and the rapidly multiplying wagon roads, must inevitably criss-cross Indian country.

No one understood better than the Indian how surely wagon trails and railroads drove off the buffalo herds, the very foundation of the Indian economy, and how surely miners and settlers would follow to destroy the land for Indian use, while robbing and killing the Indian himself. Desperate and bitter resistance was the only recourse open to the threatened tribes.

In June of 1866 a government commission arrived at Fort Laramie to wheedle the consent of the Sioux to a new emigrant trail from the upper Platte River to the gold diggings of Montana. Skirting the eastern foot of the majestic Big Horn range of Wyoming, this Montana Road, or Bozeman Trail, cut through the favorite hunting grounds of the Sioux. At the very moment the commissioners were dickering for advance consent, in marched Colonel Henry B. Carrington's army under orders to garrison along the trail three military posts, Forts Reno, Phil Kearney, and C.F. Smith. At this crude proof of bad faith, Red Cloud, the chief of the powerful Oglala band, stalked from the council, vowing to make the trail run red with blood. He was as good as his word. The climax of Red Cloud's War came on December 21, 1866, when Captain William Fetterman stormed out of Fort Phil Kearney with over eighty troops in pursuit of a Sioux decoy party that drew him into ambush from which not one man returned.

The Fetterman disaster shocked the nation, and like all overwhelming defeats was instantly branded a "massacre." General William T. Sherman, then commanding the Division of Missouri, bluntly revealed the truculent reaction of the military just one week after the battle in an official letter to his subordinate, General Phillip St. George Cooke, commanding the Department of Missouri: "Of course, this massacre should be treated as an act of war and should be punished with vindictive earnestness, until at least ten Indians are killed for each white life lost." (M-58)*

Rejecting Sherman's blood-thirstiness, Congress merely empowered President Andrew Jackson to appoint a commission to investigate the causes of the trouble. On February 18, 1867, he appointed the so-called Sanborn Commission, which promptly launched its inquiry. By June, it reported the obvious — that the cause of the hostility was the military occupation of the Bozeman trail across unceded Indian country. It went on to recommend that aggressive warfare against the wronged Indians be terminated in favor of negotiations designed to induce the Sioux to accept a special reservation. (O-5,1867)

Army bungling that spring broadened the area of trouble and at the same time reinforced Congress in its more temperate position. General Winfield S. Hancock, whose ignorance of matters Indian made him a bull in the china closet, led a formidable body of troops, including General George A. Custer's new 7th Cavalry, out on the Kansas prairies, cryptically flourishing an olive branch in one hand and a bloody sword in the other. The Cheyenne Indians, well

*References are to a bibliography at the end of the book; its organization and use are explained in a note preceding the bibliography.

indoctrinated in the white man's treachery by the infamous Chivington affair of 1864, promptly concluded that Hancock was slyly maneuvering for an encore. The General never quite understood why the Indians faded away to hit the war path.

In the light of these developments, Congress, by an act of July 20, 1867, authorized the President to appoint a Peace Commission to negotiate treaties with all the plains tribes in order to remove their just causes of complaint, to secure peace and safety for the whites, not only in their settlements but along their trails and railroads, and to institute plans for civilizing the Indians. This inaugurated what was to become known as the Indian Peace Policy, so heralded by one half of the nation and so reviled by the other half.

The Commission was directed to achieve its objectives by treaty, the means then so popular of dealing with indigenous tribes. It was so exclusively a white man's device, however, that it served primarily as an instrument of chicanery and a weapon of aggression. A treaty is a *written* agreement reached between *sovereign* nations by *legal* means. Written in legal English, they were selectively translated for the ear of the Indian. In a white man's legal confrontation, each party strives to take advantage of the other while exerting equal effort to prevent being taken advantage of; such a contest of legal wits hopefully ends in a tie, with justice all around. But the Indian was not only ignorant of these rules of the game, he was not even allowed legal counsel. Furthermore, the United States was a sovereign nation, boasting a government empowered to act for its people and to enforce the observance of its obligations. But the Indian had no need for a sovereign government, not even for leaders authorized to speak for the tribe or to control the acts of its members. It was just these grotesqueries that kept the treaty popular, for the least Indian violation neatly justified unlimited white violations.

President Johnson promptly appointed to the Peace Commission four proponents of the new Peace Policy and four opponents. The former included N.G. Taylor, the current Indian Commissioner, J.B. Henderson, chairman of the Senate committee on Indian affairs, S.S. Tappan, a former Indian agent, and General J.B. Sanborn, who had headed the preceding commission to investigate the Fetterman disaster. The opponents were Generals W.T. Sherman, commanding the army, A.H. Terry, commanding the Department of Dakota, C.C. Augur, the new commander of the Department of the Platte, and W.S. Harney, a famous retired Indian fighter.

In its early deliberations (O-5,1868) the Peace Commission concluded that the only alternative to extermination was to confine the southern tribes to a large reservation south of Kansas, and the

11

northern tribes to another north of Nebraska. This would secure the peace and safety of the whites and Indians alike, for neither area was yet occupied by settlers nor lay in the path of planned railroads. Within these reservations, the government could support the tribes while transforming them into civilized farmers. The proponents of the Peace Policy were sanguine that negotiations could win immediate consent of the tribes to this plan. The more realistic opponents, however, recognized that few of the friendly Indians and none of the hostiles were yet ready for such abject surrender of all they had been fighting for. They were convinced that negotiations would prove futile until the army could soundly thrash the hostiles and thoroughly subdue the remainder.

Since Red Cloud and his desperate Oglalas were still effectively defending their hunting grounds along the Bozeman trail, the Commission could not even make contact with them in 1867. Accordingly, the army received orders to retreat from the trail, abandon its three protective forts, and restore the Powder River country to the Sioux. Red Cloud put the torch to the posts the minute their garrisons retreated out of sight in the summer of 1868. The doughty chief had won a complete victory — for the moment at least. The "hawks" on the Commission seethed with resentment at this self-imposed defeat, while the "doves" welcomed it, perhaps without realizing that it compromised their key objective of confining the tribes to reservations.

However great the obstacles, the Commission simply could not tolerate a failure to negotiate a treaty of some sort with the Sioux, the most powerful and disaffected tribe on the northern plains. It proceeded, therefore, to devise compromises, accept contradictions, and foster misrepresentations to fashion the Sioux treaty of 1868. In the course of six months the "signatures" of 159 chiefs from ten Sioux bands were procured at places as distant as Fort Laramie on the Platte and Fort Rice on the upper Missouri, some in the absence of any commissioner. Most revealing, however, are the gross contradictions in the treaty's six, over-sized, printed pages, parts of which would drive a supreme court judge insane. The mass of Indians must have remained largely ignorant of its contents, and it is inconceivable that any Indian was truthfully informed of all its provisions.

The original plan of the treaty is easily discerned in the text (O-22). Article 2 "set apart for the absolute and undisturbed use and occupation of the Indians" a reservation covering the whole of present South Dakota west of the Missouri River, where "no unauthorized person shall ever be permitted to pass over, settle upon, or reside in." The Indians were bound by Article 15 to "regard said reservation their permanent home" and to "make no permanent settlement elsewhere," and by Article 11 "to relinquish all right to occupy permanently the territory outside their reservation."

In short, the Sioux were asked to relinquish the vast area over which they were accustomed to roam and to confine themselves to a part too small to support living by the chase. The only selling point was the permanency of the reservation and the exclusion of whites. By an impulse of mis-guided sympathy the Commission attempted to guarantee perpetuity by adding a fatal rider in Article 12: "Cession of any portion or part of the reservation" shall be invalid "unless executed and signed by at least three-quarters of all the adult male Indians occupying or interested in the same." Even the white citizenry has never been exempted from forced sale of land by the right of eminent domain! The rider merely served to block any future *legal* cession when the inevitable day came, and thereby eliminated any possibility of just compensation. This rider perfectly fashioned the first horn of President Grant's dilemma.

Other treaty articles spelled out the government's obligations to civilize the Indian and convert him to an industrious farmer. Reservation Indians would be provided with schools and teachers and with articles of clothing and trinkets for thirty years. Any male Indian wishing to farm could select a 320 acre tract, to be recorded in the Sioux Land-Book, and would then receive one cow, a yoke of oxen, and farming instruction. Seeds and farming implements would be supplied for four years. All reservation Indians were promised daily rations of one pound each of meat and flour (unsuitable and inadequate), but again for only four years. The clear implication is that each brave was to be allowed four years in which to transform himself from a roaming buffalo-hunter into a self-supporting farmer!

Unfortunately for this original plan, it was not only completely unacceptable to the Indian, it had already been sabotaged by restoring to the Oglalas the Powder River country, located outside the reservation. Confinement to a small reservation to live on the white man's alms was unthinkable to the still proud Sioux nation. The warrior and hunter despised manual labor in general and detested the woman's work of farming in particular. Even if any reservation land could grow crops, the meat-loving red man would not eat them. To him the white civilization was a greedy abomination that epitomized everything evil and abhorrent.

The Commission "hawks" were right. The Sioux were in no mood to submit. The "doves" were forced to compromise, which certainly can not be held against them. But they compromised, not by altering the original provisions of the treaty, but by merely adding utterly incompatible concessions that reduced the melange to legal gibberish, beautifully susceptible to sly misrepresentation! Though this subterfuge succeeded for the moment, it set the fuse for a devastating time-bomb. And the "hawks," who held military jurisdiction over the plains, simply countermanded the concessions, as we shall see.

The incompatible concessons are also easily discerned in the treaty text. Note that the above-quoted Article 11 relinquished the Indian right to occupy "permanently" any extra-reservation lands. The implication is that this relinquishment was agreed to then, but to become effective at some later unspecified date, obviously not to be set by the Indian. Was it so explained to them? Another concession in the same article reserved to the Indian "the right to hunt on any lands north of the North Platte River and on the Republican Fork of the Smoky Hill River, so long as the buffalo range thereon." Just how were these unbounded lands bounded for Indian ears? Was the phrase, "as long as the buffalo range," translated as an Indian figure of speech meaning "forever?"

The Machiavellian Article 16 reads: "The country north of the North Platte River and east of the summits of the Big Horn Mountains shall be held and considered unceded Indian territory, and . . . no white person shall be permitted to settle upon or occupy any portion of the same; or without the consent of the Indians first had and obtained, to pass through the same; . . . the military posts now established in the territory of this article named, shall be abandoned, and . . . the road . . . to . . . Montana . . . shall be closed." What could have pleased Red Cloud more? But was he also told that Article 11 had already lag-ceded this territory? And just how extensive was it? The Commission was not so naive as to bound an area with only west and south borders. The possibility that this was a careless oversight goes aglimmering when it is remembered that besides Red Cloud's Oglalas the Commission had to conciliate many other Sioux bands that roamed over North Dakota and the whole expanse of Wyoming and Montana east of the Rockies. How was the unceded territory bounded in talks with these bands?

Even the guarantee of the unceded territory against trespass was incompatible with other clauses. Article 11, for example, pledged that the Indians "will not in future object to the construction of railroads, wagon-roads, mail-stations, or other works of utility or necessity, which may be ordered or permitted by the laws of the United States." This refers to unceded as well as reservation lands, for the next sentence provides for damages, exclusively in the case of such trespass on the reservation. Were the Oglalas informed that they had agreed to the immediate reopening of the Bozeman trail, or the Hunkpapas to the passage of the Northern Pacific through their favorite hunting grounds?

Here is a solemn treaty that cedes territory admittedly unceded; that confines the Indian to a reservation while allowing him to roam elsewhere; and that guarantees against trespass, unless a trespasser appears! The Indian was given to understand that he retained his full right to live in the old way in a vast unceded territory without trespass or molestation from whites. The treaty does indeed say precisely this. The fact that it also denies it, was no fault of the Indian. It was the Commission that wrote in the contradictions. There can be only one explanation — they designed one set of provisions to beguile and another to enforce.

Proof of this came on June 29, 1869, only four months after the retiring President Johnson had proclaimed the treaty. On this date General Sheridan issued a general order, under a directive from General Sherman, the most prominent signer of the treaty. The simple stroke of a military pen unilaterally nullified all the concessions and restored the treaty to its original, unacceptable form: "All Indians, when on their proper reservations, are under the exclusive control and jurisdiction of their agents . . . Outside the well-defined limits of their reservations they are under the original and exclusive jurisdiction of the military authority, *and as a rule will be considered hostile.*" (Italics added.) As of that moment the unceded Indian territory became white territory, and Indians who continued to roam there were officially labeled "hostiles," no matter how peaceful, nor how insistent on avoiding all contact with whites. And Generals Sherman and Sheridan would soon lead the white chorus of protests against Indian violations of the treaty!

The Peace Commission had been a creation of President Johnson's administration. Grant had scarcely assumed office as his successor when an act of Congress of April 10, 1869, further strengthened the Peace Policy by authorizing the appointment of prominent and public-spirited citizens to a new Board of Indian Commissioners (O-2,1869) to advise and oversee the regular Indian bureau in its conduct of Indian affairs. It was given the responsibility of evaluating current and recommending new policies to insure justice to the Indians. It was to counsel with them in their lodges over grievances and to devise the means for righting them. It assigned the agencies to various Christian sects for recommending honest agents from their own memberships and for fostering religious

15

education on the reservations. It supervised the purchase and inspected the quality of Indian supplies. It had access to all bureau records and the power to investigate fraud. It soon became an influential group with some sense of Indian justice, to the future discomfiture of the President.

General Sherman's unilateral edict, however, had beaten the Board to the punch, and trespass on the expropriated unceded territory became the order of the day. By the summer of 1871 the government itself sponsored systematic trespass in the interests of the Northern Pacific Railroad. Surveying parties with army escorts began exploring a right of way along the Yellowstone, bisecting the unceded hunting grounds of the northern Sioux. The next summer angry "hostiles," led by Sitting Bull's roaming Hunkpapas, harrassed and battled the surveyors from both east and west on the Yellowstone. Accordingly, Board Commissioners, aided by agency chiefs, journeyed to Fort Peck to seek an audience with Sitting Bull to gain his consent to the railroad; this at the very time the surveyors were in the field! To their chagrin, the Chief sent his brother-in-law in with blunt instructions that "whenever he found a white man who would tell the truth to return and he would go see him." (O-5,1872). Needless to say, Sitting Bull never deemed his conditions to have been met.

In 1873 General David S. Stanley escorted the surveyors with an enlarged army including General Custer and the 7th Cavalry, newly dispatched to Dakota to keep the restless Sioux in check. Custer fought two lively engagements with the waiting hostiles on the Yellowstone, August 4th and 11th. Then to the complete satisfaction of Sitting Bull, the progress of the railroad abruptly stopped. It was not Indian resistance, however, but the financial panic of 1873 that halted the creeping tracks at Bismarck. The 7th Cavalry took permanent station across the Missouri at the newly built Fort Abraham Lincoln.

The panic did not check the army, however. General Phillip H. Sheridan, now commanding the Military Division of the Missouri, which included the Departments of Dakota and the Platte, had been itching to establish a major post in the Black Hills "so that, holding an interior point in the heart of Indian country, we could threaten the villages and stock of the Indians, if they made raids on our settlements." In the fall of 1873, President Grant and his Secretaries of War and Interior freed Sheridan to scratch his itch. A prompt visit to Fort Laramie, however, convinced him that a reconnaissance of the unknown Hills from that post would "probably provoke hostilities." The following spring, therefore, he settled upon more

16

distant Fort Abraham Lincoln as a more favorable staging post and General Custer as a highly suitable commander. (O-39,1874).

In response to a directive from Sheridan, General Alfred H. Terry, commanding the Department of Dakota, ordered Custer on June 8, 1874, to organize a reconnaissance of the Black Hills "to obtain the most information in regard to the character of the country and the possible routes of communication through it." (O-23). Accordingly, Custer marched twelve companies of cavalry and infantry supported by a great fleet of white-topped wagons west from Fort Abraham Lincoln on July 2nd. He soon turned south toward the Hills, sacred to the Sioux and Cheyennes. In the van and on the flanks rode Arikara scouts from Fort Berthold, the hereditary enemies of the Sioux. The enraged Indians offered no resistance whatever, but promptly dubbed Custer's trail "The Thieves' Road."

What makes this expedition puzzling is not its scientific staff, nor its topographers, but two eager and experienced gold prospectors who accompanied the column, apparently as unofficial hangers-on. The army-financed expedition served the interests of these two prospectors far better than it did those of Sheridan, for by early August the nation's newspapers were headlining sensational reports that the Hills had proved a veritable paradise with "gold in the grass roots."

If there is any purpose a financial depression can serve well, it is to escalate rumors of a gold strike into a full-blown rush. In no time, a strong party of adventurous gold-seekers had violated the Sioux reservation by sneaking into the heart of the Hills to stake out mining claims and build a winter stockade in Custer Gulch. Orders came for the army to drive these illegal trespassers from the reservation, but the troops did not accomplish this until April 7, 1875, just as hordes of other adventurers from all points of the compass were organizing for a mass invasion. The army suddenly faced the unpleasant duty of warring against its own citizenry. It was this that fashioned the other horn of the President's dilemma.

Washington was not slow to recognize that the tide of gold-seekers would grow uncontrollable, and that the only solution was to induce the Sioux to cede the Black Hills portion of their "permanent" reservation. The prospects of success were anything but encouraging, in view of the legal necessity of obtaining the consent of three-fourths of the adult male Sioux. There was no alternative, however, save to persuade to the point of coercion. The only ready legal persuader was the curious clause of the 1868 treaty that had promised rations for only four years, a dead-line

17

long since passed. Congress had continued to appropriate funds for rations, however, for the compelling reason that to withold them in the face of disappearing buffalo and inability to grow crops would bring starvation and provoke a bloody outbreak.

The administration delivered its first salvo in the campaign of coercion on April 13, 1875, when Indian Commissioner E.P. Smith circularized all the Sioux agents with a reminder that Indian rations were now a "gratuity" from Congress, subject to termination without violation of the treaty. Starting immediately, the agents were to issue no more rations to squaw-men and half-breeds, except for equivalent "return in labor." They were further admonished to warn all full-blooded Indians that sooner or later the same obligation would be imposed upon them. (M-46)

Since Sherman's unilateral abrogation of Sioux hunting rights enjoyed no legal status, Congress had appropriated $25,000 to be paid the southern Sioux for a legal relinquishment of their right to hunt on the Republican River. Accordingly, in mid-May a large delegation of chiefs treked to Washington to negotiate this relinquishment. The officials also seized this opportunity to soften up the chiefs in regard to ceding the Black Hills and their vast unceded territory. But the delegates indignantly refused even to discuss such questions.

President Grant then personally addressed the delegates, asking them to ponder deeply some brutal facts, viz.: that rations were simply gratuities that "could be taken from them at any time," and that the "white people outnumber the Indians now at least two hundred to one." He told them that since nothing could prevent swarms of miners from invading the Hills, they must cede them; in the meantime, any resort to hostilities "would necessarily lead to witholding" rations. He even asked them to consider vacating their traditional homeland and moving far south to Indian Territory. These naked threats shocked the chiefs. After some weeks of fruitless and irritating disputations, the delegation returned to the agencies, promising no more than to ask their people to accept the $25,000 for the hunting rights already denied them. Consent to this agreement was formally obtained on the reservation on June 23rd. (M-46).

This fiasco in Washington prompted Bishop William H. Hare, long a friend of the Sioux, to pen a lengthy protest on June 25th to the New York *Tribune*. He pointed out that "the only plea which the proposed effort to obtain the [Black Hills] country from the unwilling Indians can make with any force, is this: that civilization having driven the game from the plains, the Indians have been made

18

dependent for their food upon the bounty of the white man's government, and that being 'beggars,' they cannot be 'choosers.' " His conscience-pricking letter ended with a dire prophecy destined to be fulfilled to the letter: "We should not be surprised if, insisting now upon buying with money what the Indian does not wish to sell, we drive him to frenzy, our covetousness end in massacre, and we pay for the Indians' land less in money than in blood." (M-46)

In the meantime, the Interior Department had ordered another intrusion into the Hills to confirm Custer's glowing reports. Professor Walter P. Jenney headed a staff of scientists and an official party of prospectors and miners, which left Fort Laramie on May 25th, escorted by eight companies of troops under command of Colonel Richard I. Dodge. On reaching the Hills, they encountered trespassing miners by the hundreds and promptly invited them to assist in the prospecting! They combed the Hills for three months, again with no resistance from their outraged owners. Their confirming reports soon convinced the last sceptic that the Black Hills abounded in treasure too valuable to leave unexploited in red hands.

While the Interior Department was thus probing the tender sores of the southern Sioux, General Sheridan was challenging the northern Sioux. He had also been itching to erect two new posts on the Yellowstone River in the heart of the unceded Sioux territory. Accordingly, on May 19, 1875, he ordered Lt.Col. James W. Forsyth, his military aide, accompanied by Lt. Fred D. Grant, the President's son, to conduct a steamboat reconnaissance far up the Yellowstone, because "it may be necessary, at some time in the immediate future, to occupy by a military force the country in and about the mouths of Tongue River and the Big Horn. You will therefore make especial examination of these points with this view." (M-34). The steamboat *Josephine*, skippered by Captain Grant Marsh, left Fort Buford with Forsyth and Grant and a military guard on May 26th, and returned there on June 10th, having made a pioneering ascent of the river to its head of navigation near present Billings, Montana, with neither fluvial nor aboriginal misadventure. But this excursion helped entice a strong party of traders and wolfers from Bozeman, Montana, to set out that summer for the mouth of the Big Horn to establish Fort Pease, an irritating thorn in the side of the northern Sioux.

All this time, of course, the Black Hills invasion continued to flourish. The principal burden of cordoning off the reservation fell upon General George Crook, the new commander of the Department of the Platte. Although an exceptionally dogged Indian fighter, his incredible annual reports for 1875 and 1876 brand him as a man who fed his Indian prejudices on a steady diet of home-cooked fiction. To place him in charge of driving trespassers from the Hills, was to appoint a gang leader as commissioner of police.

General Crook proceeded in person to the Hills, where on July 29th he issued a proclamation to the droves of trespassers he found there. This document "whereas'd" that the President forbade such illegal trespass, and had appointed Crook to evict them; accordingly, he ordered them to leave the reservation by August 15th. Realizing that fully to enforce this order was impossible, the General resorted to a ruse, forgiveable because unavoidable. The proclamation directed the trespassers to hold a mass meeting on August 10th for the purpose of duly recording their claims, in order "to secure to each, *when the country shall have been opened*, the benefit of his discovery and the labor he has already expended." (Italics added.) (M-46)

With such explicit guidance, 169 miners did in fact assemble at Custer Creek on August 10th. They passed resolutions, duly recorded their claims, drew lots for town-sites, and elected a committee to remain and guard their interests until June 1, 1876. Crook agreed to intercede with General Sheridan in favor of the latter violation of his orders. Crook did not even supervise the miners as they scattered out of sight. Some even left the reservation! But few tarried long before returning. In short, Crook made little effort to keep trespassers out until such time as a legal cession could extinguish the Indian title.

Incredibly enough, the people who kept their heads and exhibited angelic restraint were the Sioux, the very victims of these numerous, provocative, and threatening invasions! On November 1, 1875, the Indian Commissioner would be able to report that, despite unusual provocation of the Sioux "during the year passing in review there has been less conflict with the Indians than for many previous years . . . and complaint of marauding has been much less than usual." (O-5,1875) The Board of Indian Commissioners seconded this on the next January 1st by reporting that "during the past year there have been no organized acts of hostility by any tribe or band of Indians. This is the more noteworthy from the fact that two years ago all the bands of Sioux threatened to wage war upon any individuals or parties who might visit the Black Hills." (O-2,1875)

One might suspect bias in views expressed by these "Indian-sympathizing" sources, but their claims are amply supported by frontier newspapers for the year 1875. Stories of Indian "depredations" figured as their most salable news, but editors found

20

remarkably few opportunities to exploit that market. Less than a year later, the military would be attempting desperately to paint an opposite picture, but their own official records refute their propaganda. General Sheridan's *Record of Engagements with Hostile Indians* could list for 1875 only one trivial incident involving the Sioux, and that occurred in the remote and unsettled Judith Basin of Montana!

Beneath the surface, however, the peace was exceedingly fragile. Hoping to forestall any serious clash following the dismal failure to seduce the delegation of chiefs in Washington, a special Commission set out to negotiate with the stubborn Sioux for the cession of both the Hills and unceded territory. In September of 1875, the Indians treked to the chosen council grounds, midway between Red Cloud's and Spotted Tail's camps, from every Sioux agency and from the unceded lands. The confrontations were stormy in their best moments and life-threatening in their worst. But scarcely a Sioux, to say nothing of three-fourths of the adult males, could be bribed, cajoled, or threatened into ceding anything. The Commissioners managed to escape with their lives, but not their dignity. Their report of November explored every devious loop-hole without finding any legal means of seizing the coveted Hills. Lamely, and "with hesitation," they recommended that Congress determine a fair price and offer it to the Indians, thereby implying that the price they had offered was unfair. (O-5,1875)

The dismay of the harassed President at being thus forcibly impaled on the horns of a dilemma can easily be imagined. The clamor for seizing the Hills was overpowering. But his administration was pledged to maintain the reservation inviolate as long as the Indians refused to entertain a legal cession. Grant would be damned by the white population if he enforced the Sioux treaty rights; he would be damned by the Indian Board, the courts, and every citizen with a conscience if he didn't. There seemed no avenue of escape.

Sensing the approaching crisis, delegations of apprehensive citizens appealed to the President. A dispatch from Washington, dated November 1st, to the New York *Herald* informed its readers:

> Several pastors in this city of different denominations, who were apprehensive that the Government was about to abandon its peace policy toward the Indians, called upon the President today to express their conviction that such a course would greatly disappoint Christian people... The President replied with great promptness and precision that he did not regard the peace policy as a failure, and that it would not only not be abandoned while he occupied that place, but that it was his hope that

during his administration it would become so firmly established as to be the necessary policy of his successors.

To this, the prophetic reporter added his own comment: "In that, he might possibly be mistaken."

Chapter 3
The President's Escape

As President Grant mulled, worried, and pondered his growing dilemma, the inspiration of escaping it by a resort to war must have early crossed his military mind.

To reap the full advantages of such a solution, the war would need to be directed, not against the docile agency Sioux, but against the unreconstructed roamers of the unceded territory, whom Sheridan had long since branded "hostiles" in his unilateral abrogation of the Sioux treaty. A punishing, terrifying campaign against these wild bands would certainly subdue them, and at the same time so intimidate their agency relatives that a legal three-fourths might panic and sign away the Black Hills. And failing that, the nation could seize the Black Hills as the spoils of war without legal hindrance.

The more Grant pondered, the more attractive the scheme must have become. The punitive campaign would drive the "hostiles" in to the reservation, where they could be Christianly civilized — certainly a laudable result! At one stroke the war would open up the vast unceded territory to white use, legally open the Black Hills, terminate the chronic red-white friction in both areas, and remove all resistance to the coming advance of the Northern Pacific Railroad. Indeed, such a war would qualify as a veritable panacea; it would cure all the white problems and accelerate the "civilization" of the red man. It would also resolve the President's own immediate and painful dilemma.

Furthermore, military action was now feasible for the first time in years. The army was at last reasonably recovering from its enforced over-demobilization following the Civil War. The diversion of most of the troops to the Southern states on reconstruction duty was no longer necessary. Even the lively Indian war that had been raging on the southern plains was largely won and subsiding. And fewer troops would now be required, since the majority of Sioux had become docile agency Indians. The time was indeed ripe.

It would be advisable, however, to devise some smoke-screen to cloak such naked aggression from political opponents and the public. It would be imperative somehow to shift the onus to the Indians, especially the "hostile" bands. This would demand a little ingenious conniving, inasmuch as the Sioux had chosen to remain so peaceful in the face of outrageous provocation. But the War Department could be counted on to cooperate fully. General William W. Belknap, Secretary of War, was an old war crony of the President. General of the Army, William T. Sherman, would be more than sympathetic to a plan he had advocated for years, even if he was still sulking in self-imposed exile in his provincial St. Louis head-quarters. There could be no question of the support of General Sheridan, who would have to carry the brunt of the action in his military division. Even the man in the street could predict that he would propose his favorite tactic — an immediate winter campaign.

But the Secretary of the Interior, Columbus Delano, and his subordinate, the Commissioner of Indian Affairs, E.P. Smith, presented a problem. And then fate intervened at the crucial moment. A long series of scandals had been shaking Grant's admin-istration. One of these was triggered by the prominent American paleontologist, Professor Othniel C. Marsh, who had chanced to meet Red Cloud on an expedition and had lent a sympathetic ear to his many complaints. The professor's intervention led to an extensive investigation of affairs at Red Cloud's Agency in August of 1875 (O-35). Although the inquiry failed to turn up evidence adequate to support prosecution, it raised a pungent odor of sus-picion that the opposition newspapers delighted in wafting under the noses of the nation. Partly as a result of this, Columbus Delano resigned under a cloud on October 1, 1875.

President Grant lost no time in seeking a replacement more adaptable to his budding war policy. While on a trip west, from which he did not return to Washington until October 16th, Grant recruited a new Secretary of the Interior in the person of ex-Senator Zachariah Chandler of Michigan. Grant's only distinguished cabinet member, Secretary of State Hamilton Fish, confided to his diary that contrary to custom the President in this instance acted without the advice or consent of the remainder of his cabinet, and went so far as to make a secret offer some weeks before disclosing the fact

24

(M-56). A Washington dispatch of October 19th to the New York *Herald* announced that Chandler had accepted the appointment, adding that the selection had occasioned considerable surprise, accompanied by rumors that the offer had been made secretly two weeks earlier while the President was on his western tour.

The public, not privy to Grant's design had reason to be surprised. For many years, Chandler (M-16) had been the powerful boss of the Republican machine that controlled Michigan politics. His organization had recently cracked enough to deprive him of yet another term in the Senate, but he had openly aired his militant views on Indian affairs before that legislative body. He had consistantly championed the return of Indian affairs to the Army, which had exercised this function until the establishment of the Interior Department back in 1848 — incidentally, with no more success nor freedom from scandal than its successor.

The secret choice of the like-minded Chandler indicates that Grant was turning toward a war policy in early October. This is well confirmed by a telegraphic summons he issued to General Sheridan at about the same time. Sheridan, then in San Francisco, answered the summons on October 8th, stating that he would be leaving shortly for his Chicago headquarters and he would then "go to Washington to see the Secretary and President on the subject of the Black Hills (C-69)." On November 2nd Sheridan, accompanied by his belligerent subordinate, General George Crook, appeared in Washington and proceeded directly to the White House. Either that night or the next morning Secretary Chandler arrived to assume the duties of his new office.

An innocent-appearing, but highly significant, syndicated dispatch, dated at Washington, November 3rd, appeared in most of the nation's newspapers:

> Secretary Chandler, accompanied by Assistant Secretary [Benjamin R.] Cowen, called at the Executive Mansion today and had a long talk with the President, mainly in regard to Indian affairs. Secretary of War Belknap and Generals Sheridan and Crook participated in the conference and gave expression to their well-known opinions concerning the Indian question, besides furnishing much information respecting the practical administration of the peace policy within the limits of their past and present commands.

It was at this conference, planned in early October, that Grant divulged to a select few his decision to resort to war. He had chosen his men well — there was no dissent. At this meeting two phases of the strategy were worked out. The first consisted of serving public notice that the orders forbidding trespass into the Black Hills would no longer be enforced, though they would not be rescinded. The resulting acceleration of the invasion would keep the Sioux under pressure to cede the land. Sporadic hostilities would probably break out, but even these would serve a useful purpose. They would justify further coercion in the form of witholding rations, as the President had already threatened. They would also provoke white clamor for punitive retaliation. The second phase, to be kept secret, was to initiate preparations for a punitive campaign against the winter roamers in order to subdue them before hostilities in the Hills could get out of control. To prepare the public for such drastic action, the Indian bureau was to fabricate complaints against the winter roamers of so serious a nature as to justify punitive measures. Later, as the plan began to unfold, the conspirators would find it desirable to invent an additional gimmick to win public acceptance.

We can follow the unfolding of Phase One in successive documents. A Washington dispatch of November 4th, the day after the conference, read as follows:

> The President, Secretary Belknap, Generals Sheridan and Crook had a private interview yesterday regarding matters in general and the Black Hills in particular. At the close, Secretary Chandler and General Cowen were sent for, and the subject was further discussed. The result of the conference is that the government will preserve a neutral position toward the miners who are crowding into the Black Hills in great numbers. Four hundred men left Cheyenne a few days ago for the gold fields, and it may be said positively that they will not be molested by troops. General Crook says that the miners are crowding in from all directions and it is impossible to keep them out . . .

Sheridan and Crook left the capitol the next day. From his headquarters in Chicago, Sheridan informed General Terry of some of the results of the conference in a letter, dated November 9th and marked "Confidential":

> At a meeting . . . in Washington on the 3rd of November . . . the President decided that the orders heretofore issued forbidding the occupation of the Black Hills country by miners should not be rescinded, still no fixed resistance should be made to the miners' going in, it being his belief that such resistance only increased their desire and complicated the troubles. Will you therefore quietly cause the troops in your Department to assume such attitude as will meet the views of the President in this respect. (C-69).

Phase One of the President's plan had been set in motion. The official record would be kept pure by not rescinding orders, but the rape of the Hills would be left to "uncontrollable" citizens. But reporters, apparently more perceptive than Sherman, suspected there was more to the iceberg than appeared above water, and kept diving for more information about the White House conference. Especially active was William E. Curtis, of the Chicago *Inter-Ocean* (M-16), who had been a correspondent with Custer on the Black Hills expedition and was now chief of the Washington bureau. A November 7th dispatch from Curtis revealed that he was closing in on the secret and that Indian Commissioner E.P. Smith was scheduled for replacement (by J.Q. Smith):

> The recent visits of Generals Sheridan and Crook and their private consultation with the President and Secretary Chandler, which it is known was in reference to Indian affairs, gives rise to rumors that the military are to have more to do with Indian matters in the future than they have had in the past. It is quite certain that a new Commissioner of Indian Affairs will soon be selected, Commissioner Smith having stated his willingness to retire any time Secretary Chandler wished to place a person of his own choice in charge.

Curtis sent a dispatch of November 8th that hit the jackpot in one sentence: "*The roving tribes and those who are known as wild Indians will probably be given over entirely to the military until they are subdued* enough to remain on their reservations and adopt civilized modes of life." (Italics added.) This was the naked secret, unclothed in justification to hide its illegality. It was precisely what Sherman and Sheridan had been advocating for years. That this Phase Two of the President's plan had also been decided upon at the White House conference of November 3rd is supported by ample evidence.

George W. Manypenny, a former Indian Commissioner, in writing his history of Indian affairs up to 1880, either knew from personal knowledge, or strongly suspected, that this decision had been reached at the White House conference, although he failed to document the fact (M-53). But Lt. John G. Bourke, General Crook's faithful aide, recorded that "General Crook said that at the council where General Grant had decided that the Northern Sioux [i.e. roving bands] should go upon their reservation or be whipped, there were present Secretary Chandler, Assistant Secretary Cowen, Commissioner Smith, and Secretary Belknap. (C-7)" And certainly the series of current news dispatches leaves little doubt in the matter.

It is highly significant that Curtis' revelation of the secret is dated November 8th, one day earlier than the notorious Watkins' report, which is usually cited as the genesis of the war policy. But the dates imply, instead, that the war policy generated the Watkins' report. The latter was a heavy propaganda document engineered to produce a specious justification for the aggression earlier decided upon. Manypenny recognized this from the facts that Watkins was in Washington at the time of the conference, and that the report contained pure "fiction" of the sort reflecting the influence, perhaps even the authorship, of Sheridan and Crook. But there is independent evidence to support Manypenny's suspicions.

Erwin Curtis Watkins had just completed a second year of service as one of three Indian Inspectors. These bureau officials made annual inspection tours to audit agent's accounts, check their administrative procedures, and investigate irregularities. Inspector Watkins had just returned from a routine tour of all the Dakota and Montana agencies. He was induced to prepare, or perhaps only sign, an extraordinary report that had nothing to do with his inspection duties and for the composing of which his brief service qualified him as no better than a novice.

There are certain aspects of Watkins' background that are relevant (M-23). Although a native of New York, he had spent his adult life in and around Grand Rapids, Michigan, as a business man with legal training. A Republican politician, he had served three terms in the State Legislature as a cog in Zachariah Chandler's political machine. Furthermore, he had risen to the rank of Captain in the 1st New York Volunteers during the Civil War. In May of 1864 General David Hunter, commanding Union troops in the Shenandoah Valley, appointed Watkins as his adjutant. Hunter's most valuable and intimate subordinate at this time was none other than General George Crook. When General Sheridan took over this command in August of the same year, he promptly assigned Watkins to the adjutancy of one of his cavalry corps.

It seems like Providence that a green Indian Inspector, fresh from a tour of the Sioux country, a political henchman of Secretary Chandler and a former war crony of Sheridan and Crook, should arrive on the scene at the same moment these gentlemen were searching for a means to camouflage a war against the Sioux. Just how providential is revealed by a careful reading of the verbose and propagandistic report to Commissioner E.P. Smith which Watkins signed on November 9th at Washington, D.C. (O-27)*

The report is as remarkable for its silence as for its noise. It makes no reference to the Black Hills, least of all to their invasion by greedy whites. It makes no mention of the treaty of 1868, to say

---

*The rest of this chapter is based on this same reference.

nothing of its guarantee of an inviolable reservation and the right to roam in unceded territory without trespass by whites. It thereby conceals the real issues that forced the resort to war and led to the White House conference.

But with most righteous indignation it levels a series of charges, not against the agency Sioux who refused to cede their reservation, but exclusively against "a few hundred warriors" under Sitting Bull and lesser chiefs. First, they are *disrespectful* of white authority (the string of pejorative adjectives includes hostile, lofty, independent, contemptuous, defiant, boastful, scornful, savage, untamable, and uncivilized!). Second, they claim *sovereignty* over their own country (as guaranteed by treaty!). Third, they *plunder and murder* frontier settlers, hunters, and emigrants (i.e., plundering and murdering trespassers!); significantly, they are claimed to strike only north, east and west (to the south was Crook's department and the Black Hills!). Fourth, their attacks on *submissive tribes* are injurious to the latter (intertribal strife was reciprocal and not limited to "hostiles!"); coupled with this charge was an inadvertent revelation that submissive Indians "complained bitterly" that their submission earned them "no consideration or reward" from the "humane policy" of an "enlightened, Christian nation." This was a boomerang charge, if there ever was one.

Having concealed the true issues by leveling trumped-up charges against a handful of unpopular scape-goats, our bureau underling proceeded to recommend Sheridan's military strategy and to enunciate a national policy for the President:

> In my judgement, one thousand men under the command of an experienced officer, sent into their country in the winter, when the Indians are nearly always in camp, and at which season of the year they are the most helpless, would be amply sufficient for their capture or punishment . . .
> The true policy in my judgement, is to send troops against them in the winter, the sooner the better, and *whip* them into subjection. They richly merit the punishment for their incessant warfare on friendly tribes, their continuous thieving, and their numerous murders of white settlers and their families, or white men found unarmed.
> The Government owes it, too, to these friendly tribes, in fulfillment of treaty stipulations. It owes it to the agents and employees, whom it has sent to labor among the Indians at remote and almost inaccessable places, beyond reach in time to save. It owes it to the frontier settlers who have, with their families, braved the dangers and hardships incident to frontier life. It owes it to civilization and the common cause of humanity."

There it is in a nutshell: the Government owes it to civilization and humanity to wage a winter campaign to whip scapegoats into subjection!

Manypenny labeled these fictions "humorous," which they might have been, had they served a less tragic purpose. Even the plotters must have recognized that so sudden a dose of overdrawn and gamey propaganda might prove counterproductive, for they withheld it from publication. It was leaked, however, on November 17th, to reporter Curtis, who quoted from it generously and verbatim, but in the discrete guise of a personal interview with Watkins. The next July, when a new Secretary of War responded to a request from Congress, then shocked by the news of the Custer disaster, for all documents bearing on the causes of the war (O-27), he cited the Watkins' reports as its sole justification, thus proving that the Black Hills crisis had nothing to do with it! This official "line" fooled the gullible then and still does today.

Non-hawkish Commissioner E.P. Smith procrastinated for nearly three weeks before he could bring himself to forward Watkins' report and thereby hand over his wards to the mercy of a bloodthirsty War Department. On November 27th he sent it to Secretary Chandler, but with the recommendation that it be "referred to the War Department for consideration and such action as may be deemed best by Lt. Gen. Sheridan, who is personally conversant with the situation on the Upper Missouri and with the relations of Sitting Bull's band to the other Sioux tribes." Does this referral to subordinate Sheridan instead of superior Sherman mean that the Commissioner knew of the former's involvement in the production of the report? In any case, it took only two days for Chandler to forward it to Secretary Belknap, endorsed simply "for the consideration and action of the Hon. Secretary of War."

Someone was sharp enough to perceive that both endorsements blew the cover from the President's deception by leaving the responsibility for punitive intervention up to the War Department! Undoubtedly in some hasty, stormy, and off-the-record conference it was explained that the Interior Department had sole responsibility for Indian management and that only on its direct request could the military intervene. Probably this same conference gave birth to the final gimmick of having the Commissioner issue an ultimatum to the hostiles to surrender at their agencies by a given deadline, or the army would come after them. This device neatly shifted the onus of military action to the rebellious hostiles, should they choose to ignore the ultimatum, even in the eyes of the public.

At any rate, this is precisely what was done. After a suspicious lull, Chandler, under date of December 3rd, *initiated* the following communication to Belknap:

> Referring to my letter of transmittal of the 29th ult. . . . requesting [Sic!] that steps be taken to compel the hostile Sioux to go upon a reservation and cease their depredations, I have the honor to inform you that I have this day directed the Commissioner of Indian Affairs to notify said Indians that they must remove to a reservation before the 31st of January next; that if they neglect or refuse so to move, they will be reported to the War Department as hostile Indians and that a military force will be sent to compel them to obey the orders of the Indian Office.
>
> You will be notified of the compliance or non-compliance of the Indians with this order; and if said Indians shall neglect or refuse to comply with said order, I have the honor to request that the proper military officer be directed to compel their removal to and residence within the bounds of their reservation.

In accordance with this refined plan, Commissioner E.P. Smith, on December 6th, directed his Indian agents at Red Cloud, Spotted Tail, Standing Rock, Cheyenne River, Fort Peck, Lower Brule, Crow Creek, and Devil's Lake Agencies to communicate to Sitting Bull and other hostile chiefs the ultimatum to surrender at their agencies by January 31, 1876, or be driven in by military force. The notice, of course, did not reach the Standing Rock Agency until December 22nd, nor the remote Fort Peck Agency until January 21st! The various agents, knowing full well that their charges for the past year had been exceptionally peaceful and restrained, registered all degrees of surprise and concern at the sudden threat of military subjugation, but dutifully dispatched runners to seek out the winter camps and deliver the ultimatum.

In the meantime, the Watkins' report, with its growing tail of endorsements, finally reached Sheridan's headquarters on December 14th. On the 20th he forwarded copies to his departmental commanders, Terry and Crook, requesting reports on the feasibility of winter campaigns. General Crook, the eager and experienced Indian campaigner, had been making secret preparations ever since the White House conference. He promptly replied on December 22nd, and in the best military tradition, that "military operations may be commenced . . . whenever in the opinion of the War Department such action becomes necessary." But Terry faced a different situation in his winter-bound department. His reply, delayed until December 28th, was neither so laconic nor so confident:

> . . . information from various sources tends to show that these Indians [Sitting Bull's band] are now encamped for the winter on the Little

Missouri; it is believed that they are near the mouth. If this information is correct, it will be possible, in ordinary winter weather, to reach their camp by a rapid march from Fort A. Lincoln. For such an operation there are available five well-mounted companies of cavalry at Lincoln and two at Fort Rice, a force which I think would be sufficient. Such an operation must, of course, be conducted with secrecy and rapidity, for it would not be possible for cavalry to follow the Indians for any considerable distance, should they receive notice of the approach of troops and seek safety in dispersion and flight. It would be impracticable to carry supplies of food and forage for more than a very few days.

In view of the conversation which I had with the Lieutenant General upon this subject when I was in Chicago week before last, I have not felt at liberty to communicate, even to any of my staff, that such operations have been contemplated, nor have I felt at liberty to take any steps to ascertain the precise location of Sitting Bull's camp . . .

Terry, clearly torn between military duty and common sense, made the mistake of using a subtle approach to the blunt Sheridan. He did reveal that secrecy orders had prevented any preparations, but failed to point out that his hibernating Dakota posts could undertake no extensive operations for which they had not been supplied in the fall before railroad and steamship lines closed down. He did remind Sheridan that a Major commanded the 7th Cavalry while Custer was on leave in New York. But he betrayed uncertainty regarding the whereabouts of Sitting Bull, and certainly hedged on the matter of the cavalry sortie. The Little Missouri lay a hundred miles from the fort; even in ordinary winter weather, the week of marching required for a round trip would place inordinate demands on horses without forage and on shelterless troopers carrying rations and rounds only on their persons.

Sheridan, however, remained oblivious to Terry's signals, and obtuse regarding the special problems of a winter-bound department. On January 3rd he advised General Sherman that both his department commanders were ready for "decisive" winter movements, and requested only that "should operations be determined upon, that directions to that effect be communicated to me as speedily as possible, so that the enemy may be taken at the greatest possible disadvantage." Sheridan thereby invited the first of many frustrations that the war would bring him.

The snow-balling Watkins' report, reversing its transit through channels, finally arrived at the desk of the newly-appointed Indian Commissioner, J.Q. Smith, who may have caught his first glimpse of what had been going on before he arrived on the scene. In a curious letter to Chandler, dated January 21st, he reminded his superior that not he himself, but his predecessor, had initiated this call for military intervention. But he was forced to admit that events had progressed to the point of irreversibility. This reluctant document likewise made the rounds, and on February 4th the impatient Sheridan endorsed it back to Sherman with the cynical comment:

> It is now for the Indian Bureau to make its decision on the subject. The matter of notifying the Indians to come in is perhaps well to put on paper, but it will in all probability be regarded as a good joke by the Indians. If it is intended that the military should operate against these Indians, I may safely say that every possibility of success will vanish unless directions are immediately given. I fully comprehend the difficulties of the country inhabited by these hostile bands, and unless they are caught before early spring, they cannot be caught at all. Generals Terry and Crook should be notified, one way or the other, without delay.

Neither Sitting Bull, nor Crazy Horse, nor any other chiefs of the scattered villages of winter roamers were impressed by the pompous ultimatum from Washington that so casually erased treaty obligations. Had they chosen to surrender, few could have reached the agencies in time because of slow travel on winter-poor ponies. But this was purely academic; having the right to roam, they had no intention of committing cultural suicide. The few runners that returned before or after the deadline carried polite but cool responses from the chiefs.

In truth, during this critical winter, the reservations were more repellant than attractive. Life there depended upon agency rations, a precarious existence at best because of delinquencies in ordering, delivering and paying for beef herds, even when spared the drain of a grafting agent. But the preceding autumn the grand council over the cession of the Black Hills had thrown the rationing machinery into chaos. Beef herds had been speeded up and shuffled between agencies to meet the emergency. By mid-winter, famine had struck. And then came dismaying rumors of the removal of all the Platte Sioux eastward to the detested Missouri in order to save a few dollars in freight charges.

As a last straw, on January 18th, the new Commissioners, acting in response to army pressure, ordered all Sioux agents to impose an embargo on the sale of arms and ammunition, to be enforced by the military. This would seem only prudent in the face of the coming campaign, but there is more to the matter than this. Since agency rations were neither satisfying to the Indian palate nor sufficient in quantity, the recipients were compelled to supplement them with hunted game, for which arms and ammunition were indispensable. All licensed Indian traders were therefore allowed to deal in these necessities, but with restrictions on quantity and quality. To the agency Indians the sudden embargo, especially in the face of famine, amounted to a grave threat and an alarming omen of whiteman evils to come. The predictable effect was to drive unusual numbers of Indians from the agencies that spring. Ironically, the army would soon be attributing its failures in the campaign to the agents, who sent all the Indians from the agencies armed with new repeating rifles — just as though it had not imposed and enforced an embargo!

The January 31st deadline came in due course, but no "hostiles" had come in to surrender at the agencies. On that very day, the reluctant Commissioner recommended that "hostilities be commenced." The next day Chandler forwarded the recommendation to Belknap with the comment that "the said Indians are hereby turned over to the War Department for such action on the part of the army as you deem proper under the circumstances." The irritated Belknap had to adjust the record once more by replying on February 3rd that the "Adjutant General has directed the General of the Army to take immediate measures to compel these Indians to return to and remain upon their reservation, *as requested by your department*." (italics added)

The President had indeed found an escape from his dilemma. However tragic for the Indian and however repugnant to an honest conscience, it must be admitted that no other escape was open to him. Circumstances compelled him to resort to force, the only means available for controlling determined resistance to law, on the one hand, or for crushing legal obstructions, on the other. His freedom was limited to choosing the enemy — his own constituents, or the Indians. Could you or I have chosen differently, if faced with the responsibility?

But war must be justified — by illusion, if reality will not do. Behind the scenes the props had all been marshalled to set the stage for a grand illusion. When the time came, a benevolent government would be able to show the people that it had given the nation's openly rebellious wards still another gracious chance to become peace-loving, Christian farmers. It was only their defiant rejection of this handsome offer that compelled a sympathetic Indian Office to request disciplinary action from a reluctant army. The nobility of the charade almost brings tears to white eyes!

34

Chapter 4
Mobilization in Secret

While machinations were proceeding in Washington, the roving bands of "hostiles" were wintering, more or less peacefully as usual, in the fastnesses of their unceded lands, isolated by distance and weather from the despised white man. But who, and how many, were these people whom the President had been compelled to sentence to a whipping?

They were the western division of the Sioux Nation, known to themselves as Lakota, but to the white man as Teton Sioux, and the Northern Cheyennes. The former were divided into seven bands. The Oglala band, together with their friends, the Northern Cheyennes, had long frequented the Platte River and were now served by the Red Cloud Agency, located on the Nebraska-Dakota line. The Spotted Tail Agency, just to the east, and the Lower Brule Agency, further east on the Missouri, served the Brule band. The Hunkpapa, Mineconjou, Blackfoot Sioux, and Cut-Head bands were often called Northern Tetons, for they circulated on the Yellowstone and as far north as the Montana reaches of the Missouri. Their agencies were on the river, the Cheyenne River Agency in South Dakota and the Standing Rock Agency in North Dakota. A few resorted to the Fort Peck Agency in Montana, near the mouth of Milk River.

During the decades in question, the population of these tribes was remarkably static.* The Teton Sioux totaled about 18,190 men, women, and children, while the Northern Cheyennes numbered some 1520. Their strength, however, was commonly expressed in

*Chapter 26 presents an analysis of Indian populations and factions.

terms of lodges. The Sioux lodge averaged seven persons, made up of 1.75 men, 2.45 women, and 2.80 children. Whites reckoned the number of warriors at two per lodge, since they were concerned with all potential fighters, including old men and older boys. The true warriors, in the Indian sense, however, ran even less than the number of men. The Teton Sioux thus numbered about 2600 lodges and 5200 potential warriors. The Northern Cheyennes, who ran eight to the lodge, but with an identical distribution of age and sex, numbered about 190 lodges and 380 potential warriors.

Although the punitive campaign was aimed to influence all these people, the direct target was a small minority. Most had already forsaken their ancient roving ways and remained the year around on their reservation, struggling to adopt alien and repugnant white ways. These 11,000 "agency" Indians were only an indirect target. The same was largely true of a transitional group, numbering perhaps 5000, whom we may call "summer" roamers. They spent the hard winters on agency rations, but the easy summers eating fat buffalo in unceded territory. Their annual migration was a festering irritation to the impatient and unsympathetic army officer, but the Indian agent recognized it as the encouraging sign of transition from "wild" to "tame" state.

The real target for punishment consisted of a small minority, numbering about 3400 persons, equivalent to about 480 lodges and less than 1000 potential warriors, who clung desperately to their traditional ways, living by the chase in unceded territory the year around. No matter how distant or peaceful, they were invariably called "hostiles," though a better designation is "winter" roamers. They included representatives of the Northern Cheyennes and all seven Teton bands, but the larger contingents were Hunkpapas, led by Sitting Bull, and Oglalas led by Crazy Horse. As these were the only chiefs known to most whites, their names, especially that of Sitting Bull, served as popular symbols for any and all winter roamers — a source of constant confusion. As Sheridan well knew, the advantages of a winter campaign were that the target village was less mobile, more easily surprised, and more likely to contain the numerically few, but dedicated, hold-outs.

It was February 8th when General Sheridan sent confidential wires to both Terry and Crook, notifying them that "the War Department has ordered operations against hostile Indians (O-29)." He knew that Crook, whose preparations were already far advanced, was planning to operate in the direction of the headwaters of Powder, Tongue, Rosebud, and Big Horn Rivers, where Crazy Horse was thought most likely to be found. He asked Terry to mature and submit his plans.

These instructions signaled only too painfully to Terry that his feasibility report had failed to register properly on his superior. He wired back the same day, admitting that he could do nothing and calling for Custer's return to duty:

> Letters from Fort Stevenson show conclusively that Sitting Bull has left the Little Missouri for the Yellowstone, probably as high up as Powder River. I report this not for the purpose of making objection to any orders I may receive, but to put the Lieutenant General in possession of all the information which I have. I suggest that Colonel Custer be directed to report here on his return to Lincoln. (O-28)

Sheridan's displeasure showed through his reply of the next day:

> I have no specific instructions to give you about Indian hostilities. If Sitting Bull is not on the Little Missouri, as heretofore supposed to be, and cannot be reached by a quick march, as you formerly contemplated, I am afraid that little can be done by you at the present time. I am not well enough acquainted with the character of the winters and early springs in your lattitude to give any instructions, and you will have to use your judgement as to what you may be able to accomplish at the present time or early spring. (O-29)

Terry must have winced at this reply, but his message had at last gotten through; Sheridan now realized that a Fort Lincoln column could not get into action before spring.

Contrary to popular belief, Custer involved himself early and deeply in the planning for the Fort Lincoln column. His long leave of five months terminated as of February 15th, at which date he was to report to Terry in St. Paul before proceeding to Fort Abraham Lincoln to resume command of the Middle District of the Department of Dakota. He returned with his wife from New York in time to report on the morning of the 15th, and spent the next two weeks on duty at Terry's headquarters. There is no indication that any planning had been initiated prior to that date, but the wires began to hum the day after Custer arrived.

Terry was still keeping the campaign a close secret — just how close Custer learned to his embarrassment on reaching St. Paul. Between trains in Chicago on Febraury 13th he had told a reporter of the Chicago *Tribune* that he understood the frontier was already apprehensive because the Sioux "have lately been stirred up considerably by the irruption of whites into the Black Hills." When asked if a general Indian war would interfere with settling the Black

Hills, he replied, "I can't tell where the field of operations will be. Probably they will cover a large territory. However, I don't think that an Indian war, no matter how serious, will prevent people from rushing to the Hills." Terry instantly ordered Custer to deny this implication of a coming campaign in a letter published in the St. Paul *Pioneer-Press* of February 16th. Custer lamely wrote that the Chicago reporter had heard rumors of an Indian campaign, but that he himself had known nothing of it and would not have divulged it if he had!

Aside from this minor contretemps, Terry heartily welcomed the arrival of the most experienced Indian campaigner in his department. He undoubtedly revealed Sheridan's displeasure at his inability to conjure a winter campaign out of a hat, and emphasized the urgency of getting into action as soon as possible. The expedition force would have to be built around the only cavalry in the Department east of Montana — the 7th Regiment. Custer would have the command of the expedition as well as of his cavalry. The real problem was that the concentration of men and supplies would have to await the opening of the railroad, if not also the river. Custer, delighted at the prospect of action after the eventless year of 1875, responded eagerly to the challenge.

Both officers knew that a major campaign against the powerful Sioux in their vast roving lands would prove extensive both in duration and distance. This would demand a strong nucleus of combat cavalry to operate from infantry-guarded supply bases deep in the field. Infantry could be made available by transfer within the Department, but there were only nine of the 7th Cavalry companies within Terry's jurisdiction. It was probably Terry who suggested beefing up Custer's fire power with Gatling guns, and accordingly ordered the transfer of such a battery and a detachment of 20th Infantry to serve it. It may have been Custer who suggested that the three absent companies of his regiment be restored to his command. Terry made this request of Sheridan on February 16th:

> I earnestly request that the three companies of the 7th Cavalry now serving in the Department of the Gulf may be ordered to rejoin their regiment in this Department. The orders which have been given recently render indispensably necessary a larger mounted force than the nine companies of the 7th now in this Department. These nine companies comprise about 620 men all told, and of these 550 could be put in the field for active operations. This number is not sufficient for the end in view. For if the Indians who pass the winter in the Yellowstone and Powder River country should be found in one camp (and they usually are so gathered) they could not be attacked by that number without great risk of defeat. (R-26)

Terry was more prescient than he knew; in June, Custer would actually attack a consolidated village with only 566 troopers!

On February 20th Sheridan wired back that Secretary Belknap had refused to transfer the requested companies (O-29). But they reckoned without Custer! When the latter passed through St. Paul again on March 24th, he prevailed upon Terry to repeat the request, adding that "the most trustworthy scout on the Missouri, recently in hostile camp, reports not less than 2000 lodges, and that the Indians are loaded down with ammunition (R-26)." Even this exaggeration failed to elicit a response, but on reaching Washington Custer made an urgent appeal in person. He was able to write his wife on April 10th that he had been "instrumental in getting the four [sic!] companies up from the south (C-23)." The transfer orders were written on April 11th, but the three companies would not reach Bismarck until May 1st. They were enabled to join the expedition only because of other delays.

The 7th Cavalry was also understrength in officers, some companies having no officer on duty. Custer wrote to the Adjutant General on February 19th recommending remedial changes and suggesting that an officer be transferred to Company E, inasmuch as he deemed its only duty officer unqualified for the command. Sheridan disapproved with the endorsement that such transfers "are generally attended with injustice to some one, and it is only a short time since we had a clear illustration in the case of Lt. Weston."* Sheridan must have succumbed to malicious gossip, for Lt. John F. Weston had transferred to the Commissary Department at his own request. He had already thanked Custer for his excellent recommendation by writing him that he was "very fortunate in getting the appointment — which is solely due to your kind interest in my behalf (M-54)." Weston would vindicate Custer's judgement by rising to Commissary-General of the Army!

Custer also induced Terry to ask on March 2nd for the delivery of recruits to replace the 70 troopers of his nine companies scheduled for discharge by May 1st (O-28). Nothing came of this request, either, until Custer interceded personally in Washington. The order for recruits was written on April 15th, but again the 63 men would not reach Bismarck until May 1st, and then two-thirds would be assigned to two of the southern companies. Since they were unmounted, they would contribute nothing to the strength of the expedition.

Custer was sparing in the use of quartermaster scouts, but

*Copy in Mss. Files, Custer Battlefield National Monument.

relied heavily on Enlisted Indian Scouts. The latter were locally mustered into the service, usually for six-month hitches, paid the regular $13 per month, uniformed, armed, and rationed like regulars, and subjected to a modified discipline. White men were ineligible, though this regulation was not always honored (M-24). Probably again at Custer's suggestion, Terry requested authorization on February 20th to enlist additional Indian scouts. Sheridan's reply the next day authorized only twenty additional recruits, and suggested that those already in service be concentrated (O-29). Unfortunately, the limited number in service were not idle in their present assignments. It would seem likely that Terry and Custer were beginning to feel that they were enjoying something less than whole-hearted support from higher up!

Despite these set-backs, on February 21st Terry was able to outline to Sheridan the plans for Custer's column: "I think my only plan will be to give Custer a secure base well up on the Yellowstone from which he can operate, at which he can find supplies, and to which he can retire at any time the Indians gather in too great numbers for the small force he will have (R-26)." More details were supplied by Custer himself in a statement that appeared in the Bismarck *Tribune* for March 15th:

> The General returns to take command of the expedition which will move on Sitting Bull about April 5th ... General Custer's command will consist of eight [sic!] companies of 7th Cavalry, six companies of infantry, and detachments from several other companies and a battery of Gatling guns. It will cross the Little Missouri and then be governed by circumstances, probably establishing a base of supplies at the mouth of the Big Horn, or at Glendive Creek. The expedition will be out all summer, probably.

While Terry and Custer were formulating these plans, there came an interuption that may well have triggered a new train of thought in their minds. Back on June 24th, 1875, a party of some forty adventurers from Bozeman had erected Fort Pease on the Yellowstone some 200 miles out at the mouth of the Big Horn (M-52). Two of the principal entrepreneurs were Fellows D. Pease, a former Indian trader and Crow Indian agent, and Paul W. McCormick, an enterprising local merchant. They were hoping that Sheridan's reconnaissance of the Yellowstone and the construction of two new posts on its banks, would bring regular steamboat service and a profitable trade to the river. McCormick would later figure as a free-lance sutler to Gibbon's column, and four of the hands would serve as quartermaster scouts: George B. Herendeen, H.M.

("Muggins") Taylor, John W. Williamson, and Zed H. Daniels.

The river traffic failed to materialize and as the isolated stockade became a tempting target for resentful Mineconjou war parties, the prospects for profit began to vanish. The augmented crew, however, remained to prospect, trap, and wolf, although several were soon killed or wounded. The climax came on January 2nd, when five men were wounded, one mortally. Bear Wolf, a friendly Crow chief, then joined the fray by leading a party of his braves against the Mineconjou village on Tongue River and running off a prize herd of ponies. As the Crows neared Fort Pease on their return, January 8th, they ambushed eight Sioux, killing all but one. When another wolfer was killed on January 29th, and the stockade appeared to fall under seige, its promoters sought a way out of their profitless venture. On February 14th, Paul McCormick left the fort under cover of a blizzard and reached Bozeman four days later. There he swore out an affidavit that exaggerated the plight of the garrison. He then hastened to Major James S. Brisbin, 2nd Cavalry, commanding the adjacent Fort Ellis, demanding that troops rescue his endangered men.

It was Major Brisbin's telegraphic report of these events that interupted Terry's planning. The latter could scarcely have failed to recognize that sending even a relief column into Indian country at this moment would look better than nothing. It might be able to get in a lick against the hostiles harrassing Fort Pease, and even cooperate with Crook's winter campaign headed in the same direction. Promptly on February 19th, Terry wired Major Brisbin to relieve Fort Pease.

The Major left his post on February 22nd, a week before Crook got off from Fort Fetterman, taking four companies of 2nd Cavalry, a detachment of ragged but enthusiastic volunteers from Bozeman, and a contingent of Crow Indians picked up en route. He reached Fort Pease on March 4th, now tranquil ever since McCormick had left; on the 6th he started back with the entire garrison of nineteen men, against the wishes of the hands, since they were no longer being molested, but to the entire satisfaction of the entrepreneurs, whose trade goods were being salvaged by the army free of charge. Brisbin saw no Indians and his scouts failed to find any sign of them on the Big or Little Horn streams. The returning procession, its initial cargo of whiskey undergoing merry depletion as the weather turned bitterly cold, marched in to Fort Ellis on March 17th (O-27).

Perhaps this relief sortie prompted Terry to explore the possibilities for a more substantial contribution to the campaign from this distant part of his Department. The District of Montana was

41

commanded by General John Gibbon, Colonel of the 7th Infantry, with headquarters at Fort Shaw, north of Helena. He had but four companies of 2nd Cavalry and ten companies of 7th Infantry in his entire District, distributed among four widely-scattered posts. But perhaps Brisbin's column could be supported by infantry and kept in the field to operate in conjunction with Crook and make a winter campaign possible after all.

On February 25th Terry directed Gibbon to plan "a campaign down the Yellowstone valley on the theory that Crook is coming up from the south and that you and Custer must prevent the Sioux from getting away to the northward, and then turn in and help Crook give them a whipping (R-26)." On the 29th Terry could assure Gibbon of Sheridan's approval and request for prompt execution, with authorization to enlist twenty-five Indian scouts and two interpreters. Terry added, "I think it would be best for Brisbin to remain out until you can join him with the infantry, you supplying him in the meantime; but I submit this to your discretion (O-28)."

Logistical problems prevented Gibbon from maintaining Brisbin in the field, but by leaving one company of infantry to garrison each of his posts, he could concentrate under his own command the four companies of cavalry and six of infantry at Fort Ellis by about April 1st. On March 8th he outlined his plan of operation to Terry:

> . . . My first objective will be Fort C.F. Smith, *or*, the mouth of the Big Horn, dependent on whether we can cross the stream at its mouth. After crossing the Big Horn, my next objective will be any camps of Indians I can hear of in that vicinity. To get there I may have to go down the Big Horn from C.F. Smith and then down the Yellowstone; and this I understand will conform to what you expect in the programme from my command. The route to be finally adopted will depend upon the information to be derived from guides, which I expect to employ at the Agency, and there, too, I expect to enlist my Indian scouts (Crows), and can possibly induce a good many more to join us with the hope of sharing in the plunder. I would like to know beforehand, if possible, General Crook's probable course . . . It ought not to take long to finish up this matter satisfactorily . . . (O-29)

A telegraphic exchange with Crook at Fort Fetterman on February 27th had advised Terry that Crook's twelve companies would depart March 1st on a 40-day campaign into Indian territory. By that time Terry had already gotten Brisbin's relief column into the field, and was expecting Gibbon's Montana force of ten companies to get off no later than April 5th, about the time Crook should be returning. What had looked so hopeless to Terry only a few weeks earlier was now far more encouraging. Even the

42

Northern Pacific Railroad was preparing to send a special train over its snow-bound Dakota division to deliver Custer to Bismarck.

On March 6th, General Custer, his wife, servant girl, and hounds reached Fargo, on the Dakota border, where the special train, equipped with three engines and two snow-plows, would attempt to open the 200-mile line to Bismarck. The Custers settled themselves in a private car, while a throng of hopeful Black Hillers and the detachment of 20th Infantry crowded into four passenger coaches. A flat car had been fitted up as a dining room for the crew of forty shovellers, and eight freight cars carried fuel, provisions, live-stock, and the Gatling guns. Among the passengers was Mark H. Kellogg, reporter and former telegraph operator, who thought he was bound for the Black Hills, but whom destiny would attach to the fatal expedition.

At 8 a.m. of March 7th, the special pulled out under an ominous sky. By late afternoon the heaviest blizzard of the year was raging, and on approaching Crystal Springs, some 65 miles from Bismarck, the train stuck fast in enormous drifts, despite bucking by the plows and shovelling by relays of crew, soldiers, and miners. It lay marooned in a cheerless white expanse for two weeks, smothered by the same storm and cold wave that would inflict such misery on Crook's winter campaigners. Eventually a telegraph hand-set was discovered and Mark Kellogg spliced it into the line to contact Bismarck. After nearly a week of lonely confinement, Captain Tom Custer dashed up in a mule-drawn sleigh, into which he bundled the Custers and their hounds, and whisked them off to reach Bismarck on March 13th. The train, and most of its passengers, having to await a thaw, did not get through until the evening of March 20th. (M-48 and M-14).

At Fort Abraham Lincoln, Custer learned that Major Marcus A. Reno, commanding in his absence, had put a few key personnel on the quartermaster's pay-roll, but had failed to recruit any Indian scouts. Of course, neither troops nor expedition supplies had yet been delivered. It was only too clear that the late winter had made a joke of the April 5th target date. It was promptly postponed to April 15th, but this, too, would prove overly optimistic. In fact, regular railroad service would not begin until April 14th, and the first steamboat would not reach Bismarck until April 24th. Even the first overland wagon train would not pull in until April 29th.

But Custer would not be present to fret over the delays. He had to leave on March 21st, under subpoena, to testify in Washington. Neither he nor Terry could forsee that politics would join forces with the weather to delay the expedition until May 17th, and then

43

bring a shocking shake-up in its command.

General Sheridan had been quick to realize that his double winter campaign had shrunk to one cylinder proportions, and promptly began to take out insurance against its likely failure. In a letter of February 26th (New York *Herald*, March 2) he urged the House Military Committee to support his request for the two new posts on the Yellowstone. His plea clearly discloses the scope of land coveted and the means chosen to wrest it from the Indians, as planned at the secret White House conference:

> The necessity for the military posts on the Yellowstone has been apparent to me for two years past . . . So strongly have I been convinced of this necessity that I have, at little expense to the government, made an examination of the Yellowstone River and selected the points at which they should be built. The Indian question in the Black Hills must now be settled by the establishments of posts . . . one at or near the mouth of the Big Horn, the other at or near the mouth of Tongue River . . .
>
> The Black Hills country will probably be covered with towns and villages during the next five or six years. Its value will cause the extension of the Northern Pacific Railroad on the south side of the Yellowstone . . . and will also build another railroad to the Black Hills. I am of the belief that the largest deposits of gold are further west than where the mines are now working . . . Besides this, the Black Hills have abundance of good timber for the treeless country south of them and west of the Missouri. The success of all these interests depends upon the establishment of the two posts named.
>
> Military operations have now been commenced against the hostile bands of Sioux by request of the Indian Department, and I consider this appropriation necessary . . .

*   *   *

General Crook, undaunted by the prospect of a solo operation, was preparing to launch his winterized column from Fort Fetterman, far up the North Platte River in Wyoming. He had left his headquarters in Omaha on February 17th, accompanied by his personal aide, Lt. John G. Bourke, an inveterate diarist and author of a book on Crook's campaigns. At Cheyenne, on February 22nd, Robert A. Strahorn ("Alter Ego") of the Denver *Rocky Mountain News*, the only professional journalist to join the expedition, found his first chance to pump the General. So did Major Thaddeus H. Stanton, Paymaster, whom Crook would soon appoint as his Chief of Scouts; he would send a stream of dispatches to the New York *Tribune*.

Crook realized that secrecy could no longer be maintained, and that the time had come to begin staging the grand illusion for the people. Both reporters reveal just how faithfully the General

44

hewed to the official line. Here is the relevant portion of Strahorn's interview:

Cheyenne, Wyo., Feb. 23. — Although there is still a tantalizing air of mysteriousness about some of the details and objects of Gen. Crook's suddenly organized expedition, enough is now known by the military circles to at least foreshadow its earlier operations and some of its results.

As early as last December an order was issued by proper authorities, the disobeyance of which by the Indians was the direct cause of this campaign. The order was to the effect that all the tribes of the Sioux then off their reservations should immediately repair thereto, and that if they failed to obey by the 31st of January, they would be considered enemies and thoroughly chastised.

Lying north and northwest of Fort Fetterman is a vast scope of country known as the "unceded lands," to which the Indians have no right or title [sic!], but in which the most warlike of them have sought refuge, rest, and succor ever since the general abandonment of that region by the military and settlers during the massacre of 1866. Since that date, those bands of Sioux who bid defiance to our attempts at reconciliation, have marauded north, south, and east of this, their natural stronghold . . . These tribes were included in the order referred to above; but not only have they treated the order with a supreme contempt, they have made redoubled efforts in the way of replenishing their supplies of arms and ammunition, etc.

This, then, is one of the secrets of Gen. Crook's movements. The reason given for the hasty and quiet manner in which he has thus far proceeded, are simply, first, that he is determined to strike a blow at once which will demoralize the savages from the start; second, that a winter campaign, although terribly arduous in that region, will have thrice the terror of one two months later; third, because everything points to a general Indian war in the section adjacent to the Black Hills, even in the advance of the advent of spring, and to make the small force at his command adequate to the demands of next summer's tasks, Gen. Crook sees the prime necessity of immediately crushing out the more western tribes, at the same time showing all others that the Black Hills and Powder River regions are not to be made the hiding place of the whole Sioux nation, in case of its general defeat.

The next day Strahorn and Major Stanton left for Fort Fetterman. Their first night out they put up at the ranch of Portugee Philips, a prominent frontiersman who had brought the harrowing news of the Fetterman disaster to civilization in December of 1866. Both reporters questioned him about the hostiles and their strength. As Strahorn reported it, they learned that the Indians scattered over the unceded territory would number at least 18,000 to 20,000 and could muster nearly 4000 warriors willing to fight. "Unless the savages were thoroughly demoralized at the first encounter . . . he [Mr. Phillips] was of the opinion that it would require more than

45

one campaign to force them to the extreme of suing for peace." These extravagant numbers could only have referred to the entire Teton Sioux, but they soon became the accepted estimate of the enemy strength the winter campaign would face!

The two reporters reached Fort Fetterman on February 27th to find General Crook completing his final preparations. They also found that several bands of Arapahoes, who shared the Red Cloud Agency, were frightened by the ultimatum and the promised punitive campaign, and were fleeing to the agency to avoid trouble. Except for half a dozen braves, this tribe would not figure in the coming war. But these little bands reported that hostile Sioux, especially the Mineconjous, were swarming on the Powder, Tongue, and Big Horn Rivers, and there committing depredations. Although none seemed to know it, these "depredations" consisted of harrassing the trespassing wolfers at Fort Pease.

About this time Lt. Bourke confided to his diary that "we are now on the eve of the bloodiest Indian war the government has ever been called upon to wage. The war with a tribe that has waxed fat and insolent on government bounty and has been armed and equipped with the most improved weapons by the commissioners or the carelessness of the Indian agent . . ." The first sentence was right on target, but the second was empty spite.

Chapter 5
First Check on Powder River

Snow-blanketed Fort Fetterman nestled at the mouth of LaPrele Creek on the south bank of the North Platte River eighty miles above Fort Laramie. It was then the take-off point for the old Bozeman trail to Montana that veered off to the northwest to skirt the Big Horn Mountains. From this post General Crook, long experienced in chasing small parties of Apaches over the sun-baked deserts of Arizona, was about to get his first taste of campaigning against the powerful Sioux in the blizzards of Wyoming and Montana. But the General decided to accompany the column with his aide, Lieutenant Bourke, only as observer, for on February 27th he turned over the immediate command of the Big Horn Expediton to General Joseph J. Reynolds, Colonel of the 3rd Cavalry, an elderly officer of Civil War fame.

The expedition consisted of twelve companies, five each of the 2nd and 3rd Cavalry and two of the 4th Infantry, making a total, including staff, of thirty officers and 662 enlisted men (M-66). Each of the six battalions of two companies was supported by its own pack train of fifty mules, requiring a total of 62 civilian packers. Crook deserved his fame as the father of the military pack train, and it was these superbly disciplined and civilian-tended trains that made his winter campaign possible. In addition, however, he took a supply train of eighty wagons with eighty-four civilian teamsters, and five light ambulances with an equal number of drivers. He rationed the column for forty days, one third of the meat ration in the form of bacon and two-thirds in the form of forty-five beeves on the hoof, tended by three civilian herders. The heavy wagons carried 200,000 pounds of grain, amounting to about one-third forage for the cavlary horses and mule teams.

The most indispensable civilians hired by the quartermaster were a corps of thirty-one frontiersmen and half-breeds who served as guides and scouts, all under the command of Major Stanton, now Chief of Scouts. These men provided the eyes, ears, trackers, geographers, and Indian psychologists for the otherwise nearly helpless military command. The best known were Frank Grouard, Big Bat Pourier, and Louis Richard. The first, though least known and trusted at the outset, soon proved to be the star performer and henceforth enjoyed a well-deserved reputation as Crook's most competent and dependable scout. Grouard had been born in the South Sea Islands as the son of a Mormon missionary and his Polynesian wife (M-25). He had only just returned from some eight years of living among the winter roamers, first with Sitting Bull's band and then with Crazy Horse's. Big Bat Pourier, an experienced frontiersman, was a Frenchman from St. Charles, Missouri (M-20). Louis Richard (pronounced Reeshaw on the frontier) was a half-breed Sioux, the son of an old French trader on the Platte River (M-44).

Crook's command of less than seven hundred fighting men was expecting to tackle four to five thousand warriors "depredating" near the mouth of the Big Horn River. Their only hopes were the innovative nature of winter campaigning, and the likelihood that the foe would be scattered at that season in small villages. But they were grossly exaggerating the enemy strength and were dead wrong in placing them so far west. All the winter roamers, including the Mineconjous who had earlier been harrassing Fort Pease, had moved eastward to the sheltering valleys of Powder River and the Little Missouri, in accordance with their usual migratory pattern.* All this Frank Grouard knew perfectly well, having so long lived with these bands, but he would not speak up until he became more at ease with these alien officers and they with him.

Although the troops were outfitted in heavy winter gear, a forty-day winter campaign was a novelty fraught with apprehension. The very eve of departure brought a heavy snow storm, but if anyone hoped for a delay on that account, General Crook promptly disabused them by circulating a dictum: "The worse it gets, the better; always hunt Indians in bad weather." Happily, the next morning, March 1st, dawned crystal clear with bright sunshine glinting on the blanket of fresh snow. Crossing the river on the ice without mishap, the column stretched out on the trail to the north-

*Capter 27 analyzes the movements of the winter hostiles.

west. It made a motley procession of muffled figures — riding cavalry, tramping infantry, trotting pack mules, straining wagon-teams, lowing beeves, and scurrying scouts.

Covering twenty-nine barren miles northwest in two days, the command encamped the night of March 2nd on the headwaters of the South Cheyenne River. At some time after midnight, a sudden tumultuous roar of pounding hooves startled the troops from their snug beds. They learned that an impudent party of braves was stampeding the beef herd from under the frosty noses of sentries and herders! One of the three herders, Jim Wright, had spied two or three Indians creeping toward him, fired, and received an ultimately fatal ball through his lungs. Pickets rushed up in time to hear the rattle of the herd as it faded into the distance. Immediate pursuit was futile, but at first dawn a company of cavalry and scouts took up the trail. They soon returned empty-handed, reporting the herd far distant and making for Fort Fetterman. But it was never seen again, there or elsewhere. Thus by the wave of an Indian blanket, the expedition meat rations were magically diminished to one-third bacon for thirty-eight days! Crook intervened with orders to beef up camp security in future.

Three more days of travel carried the column another sixty miles to encamp, March 5th, on the bank of Powder River near the ruins of old Fort Reno within full sight of the Big Horn range. They had forged ahead this day into the teeth of a blowing snow storm. Both in camps and on the march signs of Indian spies had abounded, and the sight of repeated smoke signals and of a few watching braves convinced the troops that the enemy was keeping them under close surveillance. Although they had crossed a few lodge pole trails of moving small villages, Crook chose to ignore such small fry, hoping thereby to relax enemy vigilance.

According to Lt. Bourke, on this evening of March 5th, Crook ordered a party of picked scouts, mounted on unshod ponies so as to leave an "Indian" trail, to begin a three-day scout in advance toward Tongue River; if they found the enemy in force, they were to await the arrival of the main column, otherwise they were to capture any stray Indians for interrogation as to the whereabouts of their villages. Grouard named the party of six as consisting of himself, Louis Richard, Big Bat Pourier, Little Bat Garnier, John Shangrau (Gingras), and Charlie Jennesse (LaJeunesse). That evening the scouts rode quietly out of camp in the moonlight.

Shortly after their departure, the infantry pickets spotted several Indians nearing the camp, where tent lanterns and camp fires still burned merrily. The pickets opened fire, only to be answered by unexpectedly heavy fusillades from both sides of camp. "Lights were snuffed out in a twinkling, camp fires were kicked to smithereens, men were in their ranks, and rifle pits were sunk in an incredibly short time," wrote reporter Strahorn. But already having the range, the attackers laid on a deliberate provoking fire from shifting positions of concealment for over half an hour. Restrained by their officers, the resentful soldiers could retaliate only by loosing an occasional, futile shot at gun-flashes.

When the attackers finally withdrew into the darkness, infantry Corporal Slavey, with a ball through his cheeks. proved to be the sole known casualty of the affair. Throughout the fight, General Crook had reclined on a blanket with bullets whistling around him, calmly explaining to excited junior officers that the raiders were only a small party, whose bold approach with yelling and firing was simply designed to stampede the horses and mules, but since the tightened security precautions would foil them, they would retire and not return. He proved a prophet in his own command, thus impressing everyone with his coolness and perspicacity. But the distant gun-flashes had brought Grouard's scouting party back on the run, thereby aborting their mission.

The next morning the column and scouts resumed the trail, crossing Powder River and proceeding twenty-seven miles west of north to Crazy Woman's Fork. All day in the clear spring-like weather the troops had noted smoke columns rising on the horizon and even mirror signals flashing from point to point around them. As the significance of all this began to sink in, the ranks started to worry and question. How could they hope to overtake and surprise a hostile village when the enemy so minutely followed their progress and broadcast the news for miles in every direction? They even began to pray for bad weather as a necessary ally.

Crook may fully have intended to remain unobtrusive as a silent observer, but all accounts make it abundantly clear that he took full command of the campaign, relegating General Reynolds to the role of expedition house-keeper. At sundown of March 6th, Crook held an officers' call to issue instructions to prepare the next day for an offensive to be launched after nightfall. The ten companies of cavalry would strip down for a fast move against whatever hostile force the scouts could locate; this would begin with a night march to elude Indian watchers. On the following morning, the two infantry companies would ostentatiously escort the wagon train back to a waiting camp at old Fort Reno, thereby hopefully misleading the enemy spies.

The General then bluntly spelled out what he meant by stripped down cavalry. They could take one buffalo robe, or two blankets, for each man — no more. They could not carry a spare sock — only the clothes on their backs. They could take no tents — only one piece of shelter cloth shared by two men. Cooking paraphernalia must be cut to the bone, requiring officers to mess with their men. Each trooper would carry one hundred rounds of ammunition on his person. The pack trains would carry an equivalent amount, as well as fifteen days' rations — full rations of hardtack, sugar and coffee, but only half-rations of bacon. This, with one-sixth forage of grain for the cavalry horses for fifteen days, would make full loads for the pack mules.

At 7 p.m. of March 7th, the cavalry stretched out on its rugged moonlight march, guided by Frank Grouard. After riding thirty-five punishing miles north, the weary column bivouacked at 5 a.m. on the Clear Fork of Powder River, just as Frank had predicted. Within a few hours the troops awakened to find a blizzard was answering their ill-considered prayers for bad weather. They shivered in the biting cold and whirling snowfall, but at least they could see no sign of spying Indians. That day they plowed only five miles north down the Clear Fork to the mouth of Piney Creek, near present Ucross, Wyoming. On the morning of the 9th, Crook again sent Grouard with seven scouts to look for Indians on Tongue River, while the main column followed their trail fourteen miles to the head of Prairie Dog Creek, where they bivouacked a little north of old Fort Phil Kearny.

On March 10th the command descended the north-flowing Prairie Dog Creek for twenty-two miles, passing just east of present Sheridan, Wyoming, and camping four miles from where the creek joins Tongue River at the Wyoming-Montana border. By this time the continuous snowfall and wintry temperature had turned the trail treacherous with ice; Corporal Moore, 3rd Cavalry, was badly hurt when his horse fell on the ice. At this camp Grouard's scouting party returned to report that they had found nothing but a deserted campsite of sixty lodges ten miles west, where Goose Creek joins Tongue River. Stanton, Strahorn, and Bourke all recorded that the site was fresh, but Grouard recalled that it had been deserted a month.

The skies finally cleared on the morning of the 11th, but the mercury hid below the last graduation mark on the thermometer at 25 degrees below zero! Having abandoned the idea of heading for the Big Horn valley, Crook moved to, and then four miles down, Tongue River, whose narrow, winding valley coursed northeast for another 115 miles to join the Yellowstone. Because of the cold and the need to graze the under-grained horses, the column bivouacked early, but the scouts made a frigid ride westward to Rosebud Creek in a futile search for traces of the enemy. The next day was still colder, but Crook drove his men another twenty miles, crossing the tortuous stream eighteen times on the solid ice. Again Louis Richard scouted to the Rosebud and Grouard down the Tongue, with no success. The 12-mile march of the 13th passed the mouth of Hanging Woman's Fork, as well as several deserted village sites, and discovered a stray mule, presumed to have wandered from some nearby village.

Crook was beginning to grow impatient. The hostiles were eluding him as successfully as he had eluded their spies. That night he ordered the scouts to advance down the Tongue all the way to the Yellowstone, if necessary, while the main column would proceed only a short distance and wait. Accordingly, on the 14th the command marched only ten miles to the mouth of present O'Dell Creek, ten miles above the larger Otter Creek. As an indication of how dependent the officers were on the scouts, many of the former thought they were nearing the Yellowstone, actually some seventy miles distant. On the march the men had noted some old Indian camp sites, in one of which they found the amputated arm of an Indian, frozen and pierced with buckshot; the scouts pronounced it to be that of a horse-stealing Crow, whom the Sioux had caught and dismembered.

On the afternoon of March 15th the scouting party returned, having found neither Indian nor village, but reporting that the freshest trails led eastward toward Powder River. In the time available they could not have made the 150-mile round-trip to the Yellowstone, and Lt. Bourke in fact recorded that they had gone but twenty-five miles downstream. Some suspected that the scouts were getting cold feet in proportion as they neared the enemy, but they were merely beginning to agree with Grouard. A careful reading of the trail for twenty-five miles downstream would have been enough to reveal whether it headed for the lower crossing to Powder River, or to the upper crossings that started from Otter Creek. Having found the latter to be the case, it was more important to report it promptly than to waste time continuing on to the Yellowstone.

The cavalry column had now been out since March 7th — eight days — over half the time for which it had been so meagerly rationed and foraged. Crook knew he would have to make a strike very soon, or return to his wagon train in frustrated failure. He therefore held a long conference with his scouts, hoping to extract some useful information. According to Grouard, Louis Richard still insisted that the hostiles were west on the Little Big Horn, but Frank at last spoke up in contradiction. He told Crook he knew they were on Powder River, which lay only 35 to 40 miles to the east, and insisted that he could find them within three days. He offered to scout Otter Creek and find which of the trails leading east the hostiles had taken. By the time the marching column could reach him on Otter Creek, he would be able to tell Crook exactly where the hostiles were. The General adopted the plan then and there.

The next morning, March 16th, Crook turned his back on Tongue River to follow Grouard's trail southeast for eighteen miles, winding up O'Dell's Creek, crossing the rugged divide, and descending Cow Creek to its junction with Otter Creek. In the van, Grouard had improved his luck by spotting a pair of hostiles out hunting. Having glimpsed the Indian-like scouts but not the troops, they made a successful escape, but left a back-trail from their village. On receiving this encouraging news, Crook called a halt while the scouts followed the back-trail. They soon traced it two miles up Otter Creek, when it turned southeast up Indian Creek, one of the regular Indian routes that told Grouard where the village must be located, within a night's march on Powder River.

Events were finally breaking right for General Crook, who promptly ordered a mobile force to make the night march and strike the village at dawn. As this was his last chance to fulfill his intention to act as observer, he assigned to General Reynolds the command of the strike force, sending Lt. Bourke as his representative. He gave Reynolds three of the two-company battalions, which totalled 15 officers and 359 men, including staff. Major Stanton went in command of the scouts, taking Grouard, now generally referred to as principal scout, and about half of the others. The troops would carry nothing but ammunition and one day's ration of hardtack. Crook, retaining command of the two remaining cavalry battalions and the pack train, would proceed up Otter Creek to rendezvous with the strike force after the battle higher up Powder River at the mouth of Lodgepole Creek (present Clear Creek).

General Reynolds led his force out shortly after 5 P.M., the weather cold and cloudy, but the troops eager and keyed up. Only the prospect of action could temper the cavalryman's aversion to night marching. They had scarcely turned southeast to ascend Indian Creek when it grew pitch black and snow flurries fell to obscure the back-trail of the hostile hunters. Grouard took the lead on foot, often forced to grope on hands and knees for the faint trail and occasionally striking a match to see by. Every recorder of this march sang his praises as a tracker of uncanny, unbelievable skill. Despite the difficulties, he proceeded with consummate assurance, even faster than the cavalry could follow on the dark and rough trail. Each battalion had its own guides, in case of a disastrous separation, but nevertheless frequent halts were called to allow the rear to close up. After midnight, the sky cleared, but the temperature steadily plummeted, adding the danger of frostbite to the hazards of the trail.

Having covered some twelve miles, it was about 4 A.M. of March 17th, when the column broke out on top of the divide, where they caught a glimpse of the chaotic breaks below that continued to Powder River, some six miles east. Here the scouts went ahead, while the column halted in a concealing ravine. The march had been hard, but the halt was worse. The troops waited, silent, nearly motionless, without fire or coffee. They could only shiver and freeze in the coldest night of their lives. Officers circulated among the men, arousing them from fatal drowsiness. Dr. Charles E. Munn won everyone's gratitude by his tireless attention to anyone threatened with frostbite. At 6 A.M., Grouard reappeared to report that they had found a heavy, fresh trail leading down to the river and a sure village. With universal relief, the stiffened men and horses began the rough descent in the early light of dawn.

Within an hour Grouard again returned from the front with the electrifying news that they had sighted a sleeping village of about one hundred lodges in the river bottom on the near bank, some thousand feet below. It nestled at the foot of high bluffs, with timber and brush close by and the pony herd grazing on the grassy bottomland. With blood warming at the prospect of sailing into the surprised camp, the troops began checking their horses, equipment, and arms, while General Reynolds questioned Grouard and formulated his plan of attack. The descent must cover unknown and badly broken country, necessitating a general plan that would demand resourcefulness and judgement from the company commanders for effective execution.

The General chose Captain Henry E. Noyes' battalion to make the first attack; it would descend to the river by the right and attack from that direction, i.e., from the south, or upstream, side. Captain James Egan's company (the only one which had retained its side arms) would charge alone directly into the village, mounted and using their pistols; unfortunately, 47 pistols fired from the backs of running horses would create more noise than execution. Captain Noyes' own company would cut out the pony herd and drive it back upstream to hold it out of reach of its owners. Captain Alexander Moore's supporting battalion was to descend by the left and take position, dismounted, on the bluffs overlooking the village, where they could cover the Indians flying before the charge. Captain Anson Mills' reserve battalion would descend by the center and move in behind Egan's charge to secure and hold the village. All were to remain concealed until Egan launched his opening charge.

It was broad daylight by the time the three battalions, each with its assigned guides, started down the mountain side by their separate, but uncertain, paths. The difficulties of the terrain exceeded expectations, so that 9 o'clock came before Captain Noyes' attack battalion reached its launching point on the river bottom. Captain Moore's support battalion completely failed to reach its assigned position on the bluffs commanding the village, and despite this calamity General Reynolds was slow to order Mills' reserve battalion into action. Incredible though it seems, the rattling of troops on the rocks failed to alert the villagers, buried deep in their robes against the unseasonable cold wave. But the officers could see that the village was a sizeable one, ultimately found to harbor 105 lodges, representing about 735 persons and 210 braves.

Captain Egan, accompanied by Lieutenant Bourke and reporter Strahorn, led his forty-seven pistoleers in as rapid a charge as their exhausted steeds could carry them. Sheridan himself could have asked for no more perfect surprise. In yelling, firing, and trampling confusion the company swept through the array of tight-closed lodges. Naked Indians burst in terror from the tepees, scattering in every direction, but otherwise unhurt. They instinctively grabbed their arms and ammunition, and having herded the women and children into concealing brush and timber, rallied quickly to pour in a heavy return fire. In no time they were seizing vantage points on the nearby bluffs, which the troops had failed to occupy. Desperate to save their families, and aroused at the sight of half their pony herd vanishing up the bottom in control of Captain Noyes' company, the two hundred braves quickly forced Egan's men to dismount, take cover, and unlimber their more effective carbines. Their noisy charge had driven the Indians, as expected, but not into any devastating fire. Where Moore's dismounted riflemen should have lain in ambush, Egan could see only hard-fighting Indians.

Before disaster could overtake Egan's lonely company, Captain Mills' reserve battalion rode in to help hold off the enemy skirmishers and to secure the lodge area. Eventually, Captain Moore's belated support battalion tramped in to join the command in the village. By then, however, events had reversed the roles of attackers and defenders. The 375 uniformed soldiers were under seige by

200 naked Indians, whose ardor disdained the frigid air. They even launched a strong counterattack that failed, although the officers' calls for reinforcements met with slow or no answers. They smarted under the realization that neither General Reynolds nor themselves had handled their troops efficiently. The Indian casualties, though never countable, were incredibly light, for they had fought from cover after the non-lethal pistol charge. But there were four soldiers lying dead, and Dr. Munn was working over six wounded men in his make-shift hospital on a hill upstream.

The troops were in no immediate danger of being over-run, but neither were they able to vanquish the Indians. Their success had been limited to the surprise and capture of the village and half the pony herd. The longer they remained the more this success would be diluted by continuing casualties and the possible loss of their own horses, many of which were still held on the mountain side. Pressing for an early withdrawal, General Reynolds ordered the horses brought down and the lodges, with all their contents, destroyed by fire. The horses were slow in getting down through the cordon of Indians, and the General grew exasperated at the delay occasioned by troopers trying to salvage meat and robes from the tepees for their own dire needs.

Grouard, recognizing many familiar Oglala ponies, pronounced the village of 105 lodges to be that of the notorious Crazy Horse in person. He was mistaken, however, for that chief was with another Oglala village some 35 miles distant on the East Fork of Little Powder River. The scouts questioned an old squaw found lying wounded in one of the tepees. Although interpreted to confirm that Crazy Horse was the village chief, she must have said that she and a portion of the villagers were Oglalas of Crazy Horse's following. She identified forty of the lodges as belonging to the Northern Cheyennes, and others to the Mineconjous. She disclosed that Sitting Bull's Hunkpapa band was camped some sixty miles down the valley near the Blue Earth Hills (present Chalk Buttes).

At 1:30 P.M., the command, still under a hot fire, began evacuating the smoking village. General Reynolds apparently managed the withdrawal no better than the attack. He assigned no responsibility for the captured herd of 700 ponies, although some one fortunately herded them along in the rear. The ranks were angry and disgusted at the failure to bury their dead comrades, and rumors flew that one wounded soldier was abandoned to the merciless villagers. But the command did disengage, and then made a hard march of twenty miles up Powder River to reach the rendezvous point at the mouth of Clear Creek by nightfall. The exhausted, cold, and hungry troops fell into troubled sleep. In one frigid period of 36 hours they had marched about 56 miles and fought a difficult battle, mostly on one lunch of hardtack!

On awakening on the morning of March 18th, the command found that a handful of triumphant warriors from the village were recovering about 550 of their captured ponies, which had been left unguarded during the night! Worst of all, Reynolds vetoed all urgings to attempt their recapture. Instead, he sent a party of scouts to find General Crook's still-missing command and ordered his own column to prepare to move out that afternoon. The scouts missed Crook's detachment, but he rode in about noon, driving some fifty Indian ponies he had recaptured. The united command then made a cold eight mile march upriver to camp in another snow storm.

Crook had at first been delighted to learn that the strike force had found, surprised, and destroyed a sizeable hostile village. But he soon discovered that officers and men were engaged in acrimonious debate over the mismanaged attack, over the stupid burning of needed robes and provisions, the hasty and inept withdrawal, and finally, the careless loss of the pony herd. The more Crook listened the more disappointed he grew. He eventually convinced himself that Reynolds' bungling and Moore's delinquency had robbed his winter campaign of a decisive victory over the hostiles, had demoralized the ranks, and even aborted all hope of striking other nearby villages. The newspaper dispatches of Strahorn and Major Stanton were outspoken in their condemnation of General Reynolds. Lieutenant Bourke's diary was even more severe on the aged general.

Partly to supplement the seriously short rations, some 110 Indian ponies were shot, leaving less than a hundred for eventual distribution among the scouts. The bickering command then started up Powder River again to rejoin the infantry and wagon train awaiting them at old Fort Reno, still seventy miles distant. Not until March 20th did the temperature finally begin to moderate, and the trails the next day turned viscous with mud, but the column reached Fort Reno to lay over for a day. On March 26th, the Big Horn Expedition straggled into Fort Fetterman on scare-crow horses, the men weary, hungry and disgruntled. General Crook promptly preferred court-martial charges against General Reynolds and Captain Moore, as the denouement of the great winter campaign.

What had the expedition developed in regard to the strength and location of the winter roamers? It had found the Indian country west of Powder River completely deserted. It had found a Cheyenne, Oglala, and Mineconjou village of 105 lodges on Powder River, and heard of a Hunkpapa village further downstream. By some process of clairvoyance, Crook concluded that the destroyed village represented exactly half of all the hostiles out, thus implying a total of 210 lodges. Major Stanton revised his original claim of 3000 lodges down to 300! These mysterious estimates were better, however, than the 150 to 160 lodges that Sheridan officially reported as out in February of 1876. In the preceding fall the Indian Commissioner had reported them at 430 lodges, with uncanny accuracy, but the military were destined never to come close.

What about the Indians? Although their casualties had been negligible in Reynolds' attack, they did lose their lodges, robes, provisions, personal effects, and about two hundred ponies. The destitute refugees were compelled to flee across frozen country to find sanctuary in the villages of other winter roamers. Most important of all, the attack convinced all that the ultimatum from Washington meant that they were marked for extermination and their lands for seizure by the relentless and greedy white man. The dreaded day had come when they must fight for survival. In bitter desperation they began gathering into one powerful camp for self-preservation.

The arrival of the news of the inconclusive winter campaign at Chicago shattered Sheridan's dream. He must have recalled in dismay his earlier prophecy that if he did not catch the hostiles by spring, he could not catch them at all. Spring was now here. One half of his expected winter campaign had never materialized, and the other half had shrunk from a forty-day triumph to a twenty-six day fizzle that ended in recriminations. Instead of putting a glorious finish to the war, it had merely started one. And the enemy was now thoroughly alerted and aroused. The President's scheme had worked to perfection — until the army had taken the stage. It was exasperating.

Chapter 6
Tempers Flare in Washington

It 'was the investigation into the malfeasance in office of Secretary of War Belknap that summoned Custer to Washington and held him there for six weeks while he and Terry fretted over the delay. The Belknap affair was one more scandal in a series of malodorous revelations, that rocked the Grant administration to its foundations. But this particular scandal especially nettled the President, for it reflected not only on his administration and war cronies, but on his own brother, Orvil Grant.

It all originated in 1870, when Secretary Belknap converted the traditional army sutler into a post trader. A board of local officers had appointed the army sutler and supervised his operations at their post. But the new post trader was appointed by the Secretary of War and subject to supervision only through his office. This opened the door to corruption in appointments and to exploitation of garrisons by unscrupulous appointees. A general howl went up from the army, but one of the first to lodge a formal protest was General William B. Hazen, Colonel of the 6th Infantry, who would soon be assigned to the command of distant Fort Buford. In 1873 the Secretary found it necessary to issue a military "gag" order to prevent any officer from speaking out on any military matter save through the Secretary's office (O-1).

Since many army posts were located at or near Indian agencies, traders sometimes served both soldier and native customers. This brought a tendency to lump army post traders with Indian agency traders, although the latter were licensed independently by the Indian office. Orvil L. Grant, the unemployed brother of the President and an "influence man," used his intimacy with the President to peddle trading licenses for a suitable compensation. In the fall of 1874 all trading licenses on the upper Missouri had been abruptly revoked without cause or warning. Orvil then promptly appeared, traveling from post to post to haggle over the price of a new license. Those who offered suitable bribes got the licenses; those who refused found themselves facing a ruinous forced sale of their property. The Bismarck *Tribune* assiduously followed the peregrinations of Orvil, dubbed "The Christian Capitalist," noting the consternation left in his wake.

The graft in army and Indian traderships was thus an open secret on the frontier. It became nationally known in 1875, when the New York *Herald* sent reporter Ralph Meeker to investigate such transactions on the upper Missouri. He operated there under the alias of J.D. Thompson, and relied on the help of a few local persons privy to his secret, namely, General Custer, Clement A. Lounsberry, editor of the local *Tribune*, and Mrs. Linda B. Slaughter, the local post-mistress (M-11). From July through October of 1875 the *Herald* featured a series of Meeker's articles on the trading scandals. A modern reader finds these "exposés" rather rambling and wanting in discrimination between convincing facts and rumors or personal animosities, but they served their purpose.

On September 3, 1875, while Meeker was still engaged in his amateur sleuthing, Secretary Belknap and party, who were returning from an inspection tour and gala outing at the Yellowstone National Park, arrived in Bismarck (M-64). The distinguished party spent two hours at Fort A. Lincoln. Custer, convinced that Belknap was a willing party to the tradership graft, received him with military courtesy, but personal coolness. He sent brother Tom Custer to meet the party at the boat landing and conduct it around the post, while he waited to receive it at his quarters (C-23). He left the extension of social amenities to his wife, Elizabeth, a natural-born charmer, who so mesmerized the guests that they failed to note her husband's coolness.

However pleasant the Secretary found his stay at Custer's post, he was less than charmed by one feature of his reception at Bismarck, as deplored in the local *Tribune*. At every turn in the rowdy town some wag had posted insulting handbills, and copies were rudely thrust in the Secretary's face at every opportunity. These handbills took the form of a circus program, which billed "Bilk-knap, Grant & Co." and their aggregation of "acrobats" as having nothing but the most costly jewels and (Indian) rings" — and more in the same vein.

Editor Lounsberry named the author of this handbill as one

James A. Emmons, a local steamboat agent, whom he had characterized only a month earlier as "one of our oldest settlers," but "the irrepressible . . . who loves to initiate and lead opposition to almost anything as well as a hungry turkey-gobbler loves young grasshoppers." Since the offending instrument had been printed in Lounsberry's own job-shop, albeit in his absence, the next issue of his weekly carried a public apology for having been an unwitting party to such a "gratuitous insult."

Although Custer had not written the *Herald* exposés, nor been involved in the handbill incident, and his charming wife had camouflaged his coolness toward Belknap, all three counts would be used against him in Washington. Some even insisted that he had personally inspired the Belknap investigation. It is easy to identify the true instigator, however, as George A. Armes, an ex-Captain of the 2nd Cavalry, who was either the most injured of men, or the most paranoid, but in either case a devious and persistent cuss (M-4). Having been cashiered from the army for obscenity in March of 1870, he became a claim agent and purveyor of real estate to Washington politicians and officials.

Armes dedicated himself to the destruction of Belknap and all his other real or fancied enemies. On January 11th he talked with General Hazen, then in Washington, who supplied "the names of witnesses and evidence enough to impeach Belknap." On February 9th Armes made the New York *Herald* with his charges and evidence, and an editorial of the following day called for the impeachment of the Secretary. On March 9th, the *Herald* published a lengthy letter, signed George A. Armes, which spelled out the charges, the evidence, and his own role in accomplishing the downfall of Belknap.

Back on February 1st Armes had persuaded Heister Clymer, Chairman of the House Committee on Military Expenditures, to launch a quiet investigation. A month later Clymer, appalled at his findings, became anxious to spare Belknap the disgrace of a formal impeachment. Armes wrote in his diary-like autobiography:

> He [Clymer] called on Belknap last evening [March 1st] with the information that the charges I had made were so strong that if he appeared before his committee he would have to be impeached, and in order to save impeachment he advised him to tender his resignation as promptly as possible . . . Belknap went to President Grant this morning before nine o'clock and tendered his resignation as Secretary of War. Great excitement prevails this evening all over the city, and I have been congratulated by hundreds of people during the afternoon who give me credit for exposing him (M-4).

All this had transpired, incidentally, without participation from Custer, who was far distant in New York or St. Paul. But Custer had known Armes, having befriended him in one of his numerous court-martials, and this, too, would bring more trouble.

Custer has also been charged with eagerly seeking to testify. But Clymer found Custer's name on Hazen's list of witnesses. This alone prompted the *subpoena* that Custer received on March 15th at Bismarck. He promptly queried Terry, a lawyer in civil life, as to what course to pursue. Terry replied that the subpoena authorized his going without official orders, but to avoid delaying the campaign, he suggested that if he could give only hearsay evidence, he might request permission to submit it by telegraph. Custer so wired Clymer early on March 16th, but later in the day changed his mind, wiring Terry: "After further consideration, fearing my request to be relieved from obeying summons may be construed into a desire to avoid testifying, I have concluded to prefer no request to that effect (R-26)." In short Custer did not actively volunteer; he refused to dodge a summons.

It has been commonly charged that it was dishonorable of Custer to have testified against "fellow officers," even under subpoena. But neither Belknap nor Orvil Grant were officers. It was Custer's moral duty to testify to corruption that exploited enlisted men by forcing them to buy dearly of the post trader what they could buy cheaply of others. If Custer had volunteered to testify to graft in the Indian Department, his accusers would have hailed him as a courageous hero! This charge, therefore, degenerates to one of violating a "code of the mafia!" Personal malice was probably involved, for the "brethren" failed to charge General Hazen with dishonor. As a matter of justifying fact, the investigation did lead to the correction of some of the abuses, known to every army officer, but about which very few had the moral courage to speak out.

Custer left Bismarck on March 21st, taking a special stage to Fargo to get beyond the railroad blockade. Having spent a few busy hours at Terry's headquarters on the 24th, he reached Washington on the 28th. He testified before the Clymer committee on March 29th and again on April 4th. His hearsay testimony dealt as much with Orvil Grant as it did with Belknap, but what he could only imply was fully established by the direct testimony of post traders, including the one at Fort A. Lincoln. Most devastating was Orvil Grant's own admission, back on March 9th, that he had no profession, that he had been interested in Indian traderships on notice from his brother of openings to be made, and that from a number of traderships he drew money out but had put none in (O-1). It was such confessions under oath by participants, not Custer's testimony, that established the graft.

During his initial week in Washington, Custer made two rejected efforts to pay a duty call on the President. On March 31st he breakfasted with General Sherman and the two made a call on Alphonso Taft, the new Secretary of War. Custer wrote his wife (M-54) that Sherman complimented him highly to Taft, who received him very cordially and returned his call. Right after being sworn into office on March 11th, Taft had invited Sherman to come and discuss the anomalous army procedures that had driven him into self-imposed exile. Sherman arrived on March 23rd, and receiving assurances that he would no longer be subordinate to the Adjutant-General and Inspector-General, he re-established his headquarters in Washington on April 5th. It was in this new, amicable atmosphere that Custer succeeded in having his three companies sent north with fresh recruits.

The Belknap inquiry carried more than intrinsic significance, for it was part of a vicious power struggle then raging between bitter political factions in an election year. Grant's administration faced violent attacks on numerous fronts. Political considerations therefore demanded retaliation and discrediting of an adverse witness of Custer's prominence. They were not long in coming, but were mighty long on innuendo. The Merrill affair provided the first opening.

Lewis Merrill, Major of the 7th Cavalry, was not overly popular with the duty officers of the regiment, for he had spent much of the preceding eight years on detached service. He had been enjoying a plush assignment to the Centennial in Philadelphia, until recently recalled to answer charges of accepting a $20,000 reward from the State of South Carolina for aiding in the conviction of Ku Klux Klansmen a few years earlier. Although not illegal, this was widely condemned, since the work was in the line of duty, and the troopers who presumably did the leg-work did not share in the reward. It was again George A. Armes who initiated this investigation, for Merrill had been Judge Advocate of the court-martial that had cashiered him.

On March 30th Armes called on Custer, ostensibly to renew acquaintance, but hoping to find more evidence against Merrill (M-4). Apparently Custer disclosed that in 1870 Merrill had been Judge Advocate of the court-martial of one Samuel B. Lauffer, of the Quartermaster Department. Here Armes must have pricked up his ears, for Lauffer had once pressed unsuccessful charges against him! Custer related that he had heard rumors that Merrill had accepted a $500 bribe from Lauffer to engineer an acquittal. Both by letter and in person the General had contacted Lauffer, who had resigned

January 1st, 1871, and was destined to die June 15th, 1876. Lauffer claimed to have paid part of the bribe and exhibited a letter from Merrill asking for additional money due him; he insisted he could prove the charge in court (M-40). Custer submitted these weak accusations to the regimental colonel, Samuel D. Sturgis, but when no action resulted, he dropped the matter. Whether Custer realized it or not, he had armed Armes with just what he wanted.

On March 31st Custer discussed a new bill for the reorganization of the army with Representative Banning of the Military Affairs Committee, suggesting that non-commissioned officers deserved a significant pay raise. Unfortunately, Armes accompanied him and again pressed his request for an investigation of Merrill, undoubtedly adding the Lauffer bribery charge to his indictment. After talking with Custer again the next day, Armes recorded his impression that the General was anxious, also, to have Merrill brought to trial. That very evening Custer wrote his wife, stating that "Merrill seeks to gain sympathy by intimating that I am persecuting him. I have neither suggested nor instigated any steps against him." The letter further revealed that the reward issue, not the Lauffer issue, was his only concern:

> Am also summoned before the Manning committee on military affairs, and next week am to testify concerning Merrill. He will be put on the stand to tell all he knows about how the South Carolina Legislature passed a Bill by which he drew $20,000 from the State Treasury. He has been released from duty at the Centennial, in consequence of an article in the N.Y. "Herald," in which he tried to make his fall easier through having been made to suffer by being caught in bad company. He went to Sherman and tried to have the order set aside, but Sherman said, "Merrill, in your ascending scale you chose to ignore me. Now in your descending scale I do not propose to interfere." This Sherman told me himself when I breakfasted with him yesterday. (M-54)

On April 3rd Merrill testified before the Manning Committee that he had indeed accepted $21,400 from Governor Scott of South Carolina as a reward officially proclaimed and open to all who should secure the arrest and conviction of Klansmen. He had earned the reward by submitting affidavits of witnesses and not by conducting the prosecution himself (he had been admitted to the bar). He did not think the acceptance improper simply because he was an officer. When confronted with the Lauffer bribe, he flatly denied it — undoubtedly truthfully (his letter had asked payment of a gambling debt, not a bribe). But the ubiquitous and vindictive Armes apparently leaked to reporters that Custer could substantiate the bribery charge.

The next day's papers carried a long interview in which Merrill insisted that General Sherman himself had absolved him of the charge trumped up by Lauffer, and bitterly attacked Custer for repeatedly spreading this malicious slander against him. The next day, Custer, in a brief and restrained interview (and Custer was a master at making every phrase bite twice when he wanted to) denied that he ever had had proof of Lauffer's bribe and stated that he had long ago investigated the rumor and dropped the matter when his superiors took no action. He pointed out that not he, but Armes, had initiated the investigation of Merrill, a fact subsequently confirmed by the Committee itself.

Not until April 18th was Custer called to testify before Banning's Committee. He told of his early investigation of the Lauffer charge. Unable to tell whether this charge or Merrill's denials were false, he had believed that a trial should have been held to exonerate one or the other. But Colonel Sturgis had not seen it that way. The final salvo in the contest was fired by Merrill in the form of a lengthy letter to the *Army and Navy Journal* of May 6th, in which he denied all charges and loosed a shockingly intemperate tirade against Custer.

Colonel Sturgis was the superior officer who had neglected to ascertain whether Merrill or Lauffer was innocent, and thus reconcile his subordinate officers. The obvious result was persistent hard feelings between Custer and Merrill. But it was Merrill, not Custer, who spewed out public vituperation on a fellow officer. The affair was petty indeed, as the Banning Committee admitted by dropping it completely.

The Belknap faction promptly seized the opportunity to discredit Custer's Belknap testimony by dragging in the Merrill-Lauffer affair. As an example, we quote, with added italics, a typical press release of April 13th: "Gen. Custer's action before the Clymer Committee *and elsewhere* in giving points against Secretary Belknap *and his brother officers* has not been regarded favorably by the latter, and they will not be very reluctant to give points on him . . . and he may be investigated himself."

On April 13th an attempt was made in the Clymer Committee to incriminate Custer as the author of the notorious "Belknap's Anaconda" article in the New York *Herald* of March 31st, but dated at Bismarck, March 21st, while Custer was there. It began: "Last summer when your correspondent [Ralph Meeker] first visited this country . . . and engaged in ferreting out and making public through the columns of the *Herald* the corruption and fraudulent management of the Indian Department, as regulated by the Delano-Orvil Grant ring, the working of the latter was described as that of an anaconda, whose head was in Washington and whose tail was on the upper Missouri." Significantly, this article flaunted a facsimile of the handbill that had so annoyed Belknap in Bismarck.

Robert C. Seip, post trader at Fort A. Lincoln, testified that he suspected Custer of writing this article, and told of cashing drafts for Custer against the *Herald*. At Custer's request, Ralph Meeker then testified that not one cent of this money went to Custer, who was merely the intermediary through whom he received his pay while operating incognito out of Bismarck, *back in 1875*. He, too, was curious about the identity of the author, but even if he were to find out, his editor would not allow him to disclose it (O-1). Custer felt that this disproved the allegation of authorship, and so wrote his wife, but since the real author was not established, suspicion has continued to cling to him.

It is highly improbable, however, that Custer authored the article. Priding himself on his literary style, he strove to achieve an aristocratic dignity and authority. But this article was written by a man who felt himself to be a self-righteous underdog. Although proof is lacking, the most obvious suspect is the "irrepressible" James A. Emmons, who may well have seized this means of giving national circulation to his lampooning handbill.

A Washington dispatch of April 18th revealed that the attacks on Custer were increasing in venom:

> Ex-Secretary Belknap and his friends are collecting material to make out a case against Gen. Custer with a veiw to having him tried by court martial before Gen. Terry at St. Paul. Belknap . . . is collecting the testimony given by Gen. Custer concerning the post trading and Indian frauds of the upper Missouri River. It is charged that Custer swore falsely and it is on this ground that an attempt is to be made to court martial him.

Belknap failed to disclose the precise nature of Custer's alleged perjury, but it was not just coincidence that on the preceding day he had received a letter, dated April 15th at Chicago, from Major James W. Forsyth of Sheridan's staff (published April 22nd in the *Army and Navy Journal*). Having been a member of Belknap's party when it had visited Custer's post the previous fall, Forsyth attempted to refute Custer's testimony about receiving Belknap cooly. He wrote: "In fact, you were, in my opinion, treated by General George A. Custer during your visit at his post (Fort Lincoln) last summer with all the politeness, courtesy, and distinguished consideration that he was capable of, or could think of." No wonder Belknap had concealed the nature of Custer's perjury! It is absurd to charge perjury when a man conceals his inner feelings with military correctness. Since the matter bore not one iota on Belknap's guilt or innocence, it can only be considered an attempt to discredit by innuendo.

Custer was amused, but the very emptiness of the charge would soon trigger disaster.

By this time a Board of Managers was preparing to conduct impeachment proceedings against Belknap, although his resignation had undermined the jurisdiction of Congress in the matter. Having no more stomach for capitol politics, Custer easily won a release from the Board, for the indictment contained no charges related to his own testimony. With everyone's blessing, he left Washington on April 20th, but stopped off at the Philadelphia Centennial and dallied with his publishers in New York, where a puzzling summons from the Board overtook him on the 24th. Since he could contribute nothing to the trial, it must have been Grant who pressured the Board into this summons. Reporting to the Board on the 27th, the next morning Custer consulted Sherman, who promptly induced Secretary Taft to intercede in the matter.

Up to a cataclysmic instant on the afternoon of April 28th, Custer was clearly in the best graces of Taft and Sherman. But how they switched rather than fight when the President suddenly blew his cool! Of course, Grant was unstrung by the appalling series of scandals and took umbrage at those who exposed the corruption, especially when it stained his own family. His refusals to accept Custer's courtesy calls indicate that he was nursing a grudge. Then something prompted him to strike out blindly at Custer without a thought as to his key role in the plan to whip the hostiles.

The circumstances of Grant's eruption are revealed in a confidential wire Custer sent Terry on April 29th:

> I telegraphed you yesterday that Secretary Taft would address a communication to impeachment managers looking to my early return to my command. The suggestion was made to Secretary through General Sherman. The Secretary stated to Sherman he would write the letter after cabinet meeting, but at the latter he mentioned his intention to the President, who directed him not to write the impeachment managers requesting my discharge, but to substitute some other officer to command expedition. I saw Sherman's dispatch and the reply to Sheridan. I at once sought an interview with the managers and obtained authority from them to leave. Would have started this evening, but General Sherman suggested that I delay until Monday [May 1] in order to see the President. (R-26)

Although it is abundantly clear that the President's blow-up stemmed from Custer's testimony against his brother and Belknap, why was the explosion delayed a full month? It is obvious that the precipitating cause was not in operation on April 20th when Custer had left the capitol with universal blessings. At that time, however, plans were afoot to court-martial him at his destination, St. Paul. It is probable that the charges had become recognized as futile by April 28th, and that this is what triggered the delayed blow-up.

If Custer were allowed to retain command of a major campaign, it would amount to a public admission that he retained the confidence of the administration and that his testimony was unimpeachable. This was simply too much for the harrassed President to swallow, and political suicide to boot. Personal inclination and political necessity demanded that Grant depose Custer from command, and if he could not punish him legally, he could humiliate him personally. And these real motives could be fogged over by charges of "derogation of fellow officers" by recourse to the Merrill affair.

Once Grant's trigger was pulled, the resulting discharge set a record for fast action through military channels. Within hours, orders sped from Taft to Sherman to Sheridan and to Terry, directing the latter "to send someone other than Custer in charge of the expedition from Fort Lincoln." Terry rejected Major Reno for insufficient rank and proposed three of his infantry Colonels. Unsatisfied, Sheridan expressed the conviction that "the command will be better satisfied in having the Department Commander in charge." Terry replied, "I will go myself." All this was settled within twenty-four hours! (R-26)

Summary dismissal from command of the expedition that he had been so active in planning came as a blow to Custer. He could scarcely have considered it anything but a mistake arising from some misunderstanding, or a foul blow. On Saturday, April 29th, he talked the matter over with his friend Sherman, who advised him to wait until Monday, when he could see the President, explain himself, and perhaps regain his command. Custer agreed and obtained Sherman's authorization to leave for his post on Monday evening, May 1st. He then spent a miserable Sunday in agitated, but helpless, idleness.

Promptly at 10 a.m. on Monday morning, Custer appeared at the President's ante-room and presented his card. He sat there in surprise as others were invited in while his presence was ignored. His dismay mounted when hour after hour passed with recognition to everyone but himself. Finally, General Rufus Ingalls, Acting Quartermaster-General, found him sitting there in anger and humiliation and offered to intercede in his behalf. But this merely provoked the President, who sent out curt word that he would not admit Custer to his presence. (M-70)

Convinced that his case was hopeless, Custer penned the following note to Grant:

> Today for the third time I have sought an interview with the President — not to solicit a favor, except to be granted a brief hearing — but to remove from his mind certain unjust impressions concerning myself,

which I have reason to believe are entertained against me. I desire this opportunity simply as a matter of justice, and I regret that the President has declined to give me an opportunity to submit to him a brief statement, which justice to him, as well as to me, demanded. (M-70)

Since Sherman was in New York, the dejected Custer proceeded to the War Department, where the Adjutant-General and Inspector-General granted him permission to leave directly for his post. Expecting Sherman back that evening, he delayed as long as possible before calling at the hotel to say his farewell. Finding Sherman still absent, he dashed to the station to board his 7 o'clock train.

The next day Sherman wired Sheridan as follows:

I am this moment advised that General Custer started last night for St. Paul and Fort A. Lincoln. He was not justified in leaving without seeing the President or myself. Please intercept him at Chicago or St. Paul, and order him to halt and await further orders. Meanwhile, let the expedition from Fort Lincoln proceed without him. (M-70)

When Custer stepped off the train at Chicago on the morning of May 4th, he was greeted with this order and held in detention. It had been bad enough to have been deposed from command of the expedition, but this new order barred him from any service on the campaign. And it appeared to emanate from his friend, Sherman! It had probably been imposed on Sherman by Grant, but Custer had no way of knowing this. He was stunned, hurt, and baffled. He fired three telegrams to Sherman that day, the first explaining his actions and defending his good faith, the second reminding Sherman that he had agreed to let him retain command of the regiment, and the last begging to be detained at Fort Lincoln with his wife, instead of in Chicago. After consultation with Grant, Sherman relented to the extent of granting the last boon. (M-70)

Deeply humiliated, Custer proceeded to St. Paul, where he beseeched Terry for help. The latter not only needed Custer, he liked and had confidence in him. Faced with the disastrous prospect of seeing the command of his main attack force devolve upon a major, Terry coached the humbled Custer in composing a diplomatic letter, dated May 6th and directed through channels to the President:

. . . As my entire regiment forms a part of the expedition and I am the senior officer of the regiment on duty in this department, I respectfully but most earnestly request that while not allowed to go in command of the expedition I may be permitted to serve with my regiment in the field. I appeal to you as a soldier to spare me the humiliation of seeing my regiment march to meet the enemy and I not share its dangers. (R-26)

General Terry forwarded this letter with a tactful endorsement, indicating that "Custer's services would be very valuable with his regiment." General Sheridan also added his endorsement, but in what seems to be a churlish and irrelevant vein:

> . . . I am sorry Lieutenant Colonel Custer did not manifest as much interest in staying at his post to organize and get ready his regiment and the expedition as he now does to accompany it. On a previous occasion in 1868 I asked executive clemency for Colonel Custer to enable him to accompany his regiment against the Indians, and I sincerely hope if granted this time it may have sufficient effect to prevent him from again attempting to throw discredit on his profession and his brother officers.

The answer came to Terry from Sherman on May 8th: ". . . The President . . . sent me word that if you want General Custer along he withdraws his objections. Advise Custer to be prudent, not to take along any newspaper men, who always make mischief, and to abstain from personalities in the future . . " (R-26) This note fully confirms the fact that the object all along had been to humiliate Custer. Indulgence in "personalities" is the only specified offense. Mitigation of punishment is granted on simple request. And as a parting barb, Custer himself, instead of the responsible commander of the expedition, is enjoined from taking correspondents along, because they always make mischief — except when a dozen accompany Crook's command! When spite rules, there is no room for logic.

This unhappy affair certainly shook Custer to his cavalry boots, but it is the rankest speculation to assume, as melodramatic tradition has it, that it so unnerved the soldier that he promptly abandoned his successful flair for battle command in favor of suicidal impetuosity. He had not the slightest reason to expect that the President's personal and political ire would be magically wiped out by a daring military success. Nor did he have any need to restore himself in the public eye, for it was Grant, not Custer, who suffered in the national esteem.

The New York *Herald* on May 6th castigated the President in both a news article on Custer's arrest and in an editorial that observed that "no formal charges are preferred against Custer, and he is disgraced simply because he did not 'crook the pregnant hinges of the knee' to this modern Caesar." On May 8th the Chicago *Times* ran a detailed narrative of the entire affair, concluding that "the facts in the case present the President of the U.S. in one of the most humiliating and disreputable of the many humiliating and disreputable plights he has been put in this winter."

Those who attempted to defend Grant's actions had a hard time of it. A Washington dispatch of May 6th to the Chicago *Inter-Ocean* "officially denied the statement that the President relieved General Custer from his command because he was a witness in the Belknap impeachment trial. On the contrary, it was the wish of the President that General Custer, having been subpoenaed as a witness, should remain until he had testified." This disclaimer fooled no one, for the impeachment managers bore the responsibility for judging the necessity of Custer's testimony, not the President, and they had released him.

A dispatch of the next day tried a bizarre new tack, which we quote with bracketed interjections of our own:

The reasons why Custer was sent back to his post [a neat evasion of explaining why he was relieved of command] were: (1) because he has been absent from it nearly two months without leave [Terry gave him leave], having come here voluntarily [yesterday his subpoena had been admitted] to testify before Clymer's Committee regarding alleged misdemeanors [sic!] of brother officers [sic!], when the Secretary of War and General Sherman [?] think [a month after the fact] whatever charges Custer has against brother officers [here it is again] should be presented to a military court rather than a Congressional committee [neither Belknap nor Orvil Grant were army officers] ; (2) because charges already have been, or soon will be, made against him [no official charges had been nor would be made] for falsehood in statements in his testimony regarding the visit of Belknap to Fort Lincoln, which General Forsyth of Sheridan's staff has positively denied [how silly can you get?], and for conduct unbecoming an officer [honesty?] ; (3) because the impeachment managers informed General Sherman they would probably have no need of Custer as a witness [that's why he left, not why he was relieved of command] ; and (4) because nearly all the officers in the northwest have gone on expedition and Custer is needed at his post [his prolonged absence was Grant's doing].

The resort to such specious double-talk is the most convincing proof that no one could invent a valid defense of Grant's action.

The tempest in a teapot merely led to bad feelings all around and another unfortuante delay in launching the Dakota column.

Chapter 7
All Alone on the Yellowstone

Even while General Crook had been marching into Montana, General Gibbon was struggling against weather, distance, and supply problems to launch his Montana column. By the time he had pushed his small force out to dangerous Indian country, however, he would find himself all alone and compelled to remain so for a month. Although this gave him a unique opportunity to gather indispensable enemy intelligence, he muffed the job.

Gibbon chose Fort Ellis, only three miles from Bozeman, as the place to assemble his troops for the expedition. Here Major Brisbin's four companies of 2nd Cavalry returned from the relief of Fort Pease on March 17th, the day General Reynolds attacked the village on Powder River. Here Captain Clifford's Company E of 7th Infantry arrived on March 22nd, having tramped through snow-drifts for eight days and 120 miles from its home post of Camp Baker. On the 28th, five more companies of 7th Infantry marched in from Fort Shaw, 180 miles and 11 days distant, having lost a few officers and men from snow-blindness.

At Fort Ellis Gibbon first received the news of Reynolds' attack. He was disconcerted to learn that Crook had veered east toward Powder River, and dismayed to find that he had prematurely retired from the field. Since this might call for a revision of strategy, he wired Terry on March 30th:

> In view of the information from General Crook, am I not operating in a wrong line by going south of the Yellowstone, instead of north of it? Brisbin reports a large fresh lodgepole trail leading north from the mouth of the Rosebud. He thinks Sitting Bull is on the Big Dry Fork, toward which this trail leads. Must I limit my offensive operations to

Indian reservation lines, or may I strike Sitting Bull wherever I can find him? (O-9).

Recognizing the altered circumstances, Terry wired back the next day:

> Until I learn what General Crook's further movements may be and until Custer starts, I think you ought not to go south of the Yellowstone, but should direct your efforts to preventing the Indians from getting away to the north. I doubt that Sitting Bull is on the Dry Fork. All information here points to the Powder River as his present location, and General Crook is positive that such is the fact. I think that if you move to the mouth of the Big Horn, by the time that you reach it I shall be able to send you information of the movements of Crook and Custer, upon which you will be able to determine your course. If, however, you find that you can strike a hostile band anywhere, do it without regard to reservations; but in doing it, be careful not to neglect the great object of keeping between the Indians and the Missouri. Custer has been delayed by the blockade of the Northern Pacific road. We have not yet been able to send up his train or his supplies. I hope that the road will be open next week. Make ample arrangements to communicate with Ellis. (O-28)

On April 3rd, Gibbon wired Terry that he was off from Fort Ellis with 27 officers and 409 men (O-31). The majority had already forged ahead to escort a quartermaster supply train and a civilian wagon train contracted to Thomas C. Powers. Although delayed by snow and mud, the separate detachments united to establish Camp Supply at Horace Countryman's ranch, 110 miles out on the north bank of the Yellowstone opposite the mouth of Stillwater River (present Columbus). About fifteen miles south up the latter stream was the Crow Agency (present Absarokee), where the General planned to secure more scouts.

The expedition quartermaster, Lt. Joshua W. Jacobs, 7th Infantry, had brought along as guide, Henry S. Bostwick, the post interpreter at Fort Shaw. At Fort Ellis he had hired John W. Williamson, formerly of the 2nd Cavalry and a Fort Pease hand, as scout from April 3rd to September 30th. At the Crow Agency he now added H.M. ("Muggins") Taylor, also a Fort Pease hand, as scout from April 8th to September 30th. On the same day he also employed as guide the famous half-breed Sioux, Michael ("Mitch") Boyer, who was now living with the Crows; Gibbon reckoned him the best guide in the country, next to the late Jim Bridger. When the General offered George B. Herendeen (M-41), another Fort Pease hand, only $50 a month, that competent and respectable frontiersman declined the offer. He soon, however, joined trader Paul McCormick in navigating a load of trade wares down the river to cheer the troops. He then remained to scout without pay, until Lt. Jacobs finally enrolled him as scout from June 21st to September 30th at $100 a month. (O-34)

Gibbon, accompanied by his adjutant, Lt. Levi F. Burnett, and his Chief of Scouts, Lt. James H. Bradley, both of the 7th Infantry, proceeded on April 9th to the Crow Agency to recruit Indian scouts. They held an embarrassing two-hour council with the assembled chiefs of the Mountain Crows, using as interpreter the aged Pierre Shane (Chêne), a French-Canadian with execrable English. Although the Sioux were their bitter enemies, the chiefs expressed reluctance to help the expedition, for lack of faith in white soldiers. They pointed out that when Indians went on the warpath, they traveled light and fast and struck quickly; but the soldiers marched with heavy wagons, slowly out and slowly back, without finding the enemy.

Fortunately, the young braves were less perceptive, for the next day Lt. Bradley was able to muster in his full quota of 25 Crows. These included two interpreters, although neither was eligible for such enlistment, unless marriage to Crow women made them so. One was Bernard ("Barney") Bravo, another discharged soldier of the 27th Infantry, who had lived with the Crows for nine years. The other was young Thomas H. LeForge, whose reminiscences have been recorded by Dr. Thomas B. Marquis. Tom was later transferred to the quartermaster roll as interpreter from July 10th to September 30th.

The General had failed to persuade a host of braves to fight the Sioux for sport and plunder, although some did move out on the Bozeman trail. But the Bozeman *Times* reveals that he did interview William Langston, the leader of a party of nearly 200 Montana prospectors, including future scout, Zed H. Daniels, and several women and children. Leaving the Agency on April 10th, this party prospected every creek along the Bozeman trail from Fort C.F. Smith on the Big Horn to Fort Reno on the Powder. There they split into two parties to make their way to the Black Hills. Gibbon was hoping this party would flush some hostiles northward toward his force on the Yellowstone.

The addition of the twenty-five Crows, four quartermaster scouts, ten teamsters, and two packers gave Gibbon an aggregate of 477 persons. This included a battery of one Napoleon gun and two Gatling guns in charge of Lt. Charles A. Woodruff, 7th Infantry. Lt. Bradley commanded not only the Crows but a detachment of mounted infantrymen. He would prove to be the most enterprising and effective intelligence officer in the field that summer, but would find his heroic accomplishments largely ignored and sometimes spurned.

Not a single newspaper reporter accompanied Gibbon's command, but Lt. Bradley and Captain Clifford both kept superb journals, and the Engineering Officer, 2nd Lt. Edward J. McClernand, 2nd Cavalry, kept a detailed official itinerary. A number of others preserved brief diaries: Captain Henry B. Freeman and Lt. William L. English, 7th Infantry, Assistant Surgeon Holmes O. Paulding, Sgt. William H. White of Company F, 2nd Cavalry, and Matthew Carroll, in charge of a later supply train contracted to his Diamond R firm. In addition to his official annual report, General Gibbon wrote a lengthy popular account of the campaign, and Montana newspapers published scattered anonymous letters from expedition members.

Leaving infantry Captain William Logan's Company A to guard Camp Supply, the Montana column on April 13th marched down the north bank of the Yellowstone. Lt. Bradley kept his Crow scouts scouring the country for hostiles, but the quietly grazing buffalo gave assurance that not even far-ranging hunting parties were about. On April 20th the column encamped opposite the mouth of the Big Horn, 200 miles from Fort Ellis. This stream marked the western limit for roving Sioux villages, although war parties often penetrated deep into Crow country. But only two miles from camp stood deserted Fort Pease, with its flag still fluttering in the breeze to prove that no Sioux had approached it since its relief in early March.

The next morning came news that let down the entire command. Couriers galloped in from Camp Supply with dispatches from General Terry dated April 15th. In his popular account, Gibbon wrote that Terry had "directed that I proceed no farther than the mouth of the Big Horn, unless sure of striking a successful blow . . . and for three weeks we were engaged in what to a soldier is the hardest of all duties — *waiting.*" Lt. Bradley painted a fuller picture:

> It appears that General Crook has not yet retaken the field and will not before the middle of May, and that General Custer will not start from Fort Abraham Lincoln until after the same time. We were to have acted in conjunction with these forces, but we are now, when well advanced in the Sioux country, left unsupported. General Crook's victory was not so decisive as we have regarded it, while the fighting seems to have demonstrated that there are heavier forces of warriors to encounter than had been counted on. General Terry fears that the Indians may combine and get the better of us.

At the very moment Terry's dispatch arrived on April 21st, Gibbon was penning a long letter to him recounting his supply problems. He then resumed:

> 10:40 a.m. I had just got this far when a courier arrived with your dispatches of the 15th. I have in accordance with the directions moved

my camp alongside Fort Pease, where I am strong enough to defy the whole Sioux nation, should they feel inclined to come this way, but I think they will be felt in the direction of the Black Hills mines first, whatever they do afterwards. The position here is so strong that one company can easily hold it and let all the rest loose in case we see a chance to strike. In the meantime I will send back for Logan's company and the supplies left with him, and make requisition on McClay & Co. [the Diamond R firm] for freighting another month's supplies down and make this my depot.

I have today sent scouts to the *north* of us where some sign was seen yesterday. Will keep my scouts busy every day in various directions and think also I will send a company of cavalry with good scouts in the direction of [Fort] C.F. Smith to communicate with that citizen party [Langston's Montana prospectors] on the road. If there are any Sioux in that direction, I imagine I shall soon hear of it. Hoping we shall be able to definitely settle this Sitting Bull matter, I am . . . (O-9)

Gibbon would indeed wait, but with blinders on! For a month he would be the only commander in the field where he could gather enemy intelligence, so indispensable to the successful prosecution of the campaign. His indefatigable Chief of Scouts would secure just the information needed, but Gibbon would ignore or misrepresent it. Even at this time he had useful evidence that the hostiles were nowhere near his route and had not been since March, in confirmation of Crook's findings. Yet this letter to Terry dwelt at length on house-keeping chores and reported only the false clue of Indian sign to the north, which Lt. Bradley had already identified as the tracks of "a couple of wild horses in the neighborhood; so no Sioux yet."

In the ensuing week Gibbon did send out parties in various directions, though none to the north. On April 23rd Captain Freeman's Company H, guided by Mitch Boyer, left with the empty wagons of the Powers Contract train for Camp Supply, there to load all the stores and return with Captain Logan's company. During the return, on April 30th and May 1st, Captain Freeman recorded that they encountered a war party of Crows returning from a sortie "nearly to Powder River." The disappointed braves had found no trace of Sioux even that far down river. There is no proof, however, that this information was passed on to Gibbon when they returned to Fort Pease on May 8th.

In the meantime, Captain Edward Ball and Lt. Roe, with Companies H and F, 2nd Cavalry, and Lt. McClernand as scribe, had left camp on April 24th for a week's scout to the south. Tom LeForge and Jack Rabbit Bull guided the force as it made its way 78 miles up the easy west bank of the Big Horn to the adobe remains of old Fort C.F. Smith at the mouth of the Big Horn Canyon. Then taking the Bozeman road southeast to the head of the Little Big Horn, the cavalry descended the latter to camp at noon of April 29th just below the tranquil site of the future Custer battle. Only a few miles back they had found a deserted sundance camp of the preceding summer. With uncanny accuracy in position, if not in prophecy, Jack Rabbit Bull built an elaborate sign to tell passing Sioux that a force of soldiers would wipe them out this summer. The column then crossed the divide and descended the rugged valley of Tullock's Fork to reach the base camp on May 1st. Not a sign of Indians had been seen.

While this reconnaissance had been out, Lt. Bradley, on April 27th, had sent six Crows on a scout down the river as far as the Rosebud. Returning on the 30th, they reported the country teeming with buffalo but barren of Sioux. Faithfully this time, Gibbon reported to Terry on May 1st:

> Captain Ball just in with two companies from Fort C.F. Smith. Went out on Phil Kearney road as far as Rotten Grass, thence over on Little Big Horn and Tullock's Fork and down that. He saw no sign of Indians. My scouts report none on Rosebud. As soon as my supplies reach here, say in ten days, I propose, if no news comes from you, to move down the river. (O-9)

Ten days of idle peace had set the camp buzzing with speculations regarding the whereabouts of the hostiles. Lt. Bradley asked on May 2nd, "Where are they? The question is answered in different ways, but the general impression seems to be that having learned, as they undoubtedly have, the extensive preparations making for waging war on them, they have become frightened and resorted to the agencies." Even General Gibbon held to this view. Within hours, however, over-confident speculations gave way to embarrassing events.

The prolonged tranquility abruptly ended on the morning of May 3rd, when scout Bostwick sheepishly reported that he could find no trace of his horse and mule save two picket-pins with attached stubs of knife-cut ropes! In utter consternation the Crows dashed to the island where they had left their horses — to find nothing but the moccasin tracks of fifty of the hated Sioux! An anonymous author wrote on May 9th that the hostiles "had waltzed off with the herd — 35 in number — leaving our scouts without a single head of stock." The Crows were not only dismounted but humiliated before the jeering troops. After a good cry over the ignominious loss, the Crows started out afoot to trail the impudent thieves, but some eight miles downstream the crack of shots rang out to turn them back empty-handed.

Where had these sudden raiders come from? It would take two

weeks to find out, but Lt. Bradley would prove equal to the challenge. On the 5th he prevailed upon the Crows to make another attempt to trail the thieves on foot, but this likewise proved abortive. The next day he loaned good mounts to Jack Rabbit Bull and Half Yellow Face, who, thus encouraged, followed the trail some fifteen miles down the north bank. On spotting three careless Sioux, the two Crows charged them headlong, heedless of the possibility of others lurking near. The startled trio fled incontinently, abandoning their own mounts to the bold scouts. The pair returned to camp in triumph with their prizes.

Bradley finally won Gibbon's consent to lead a larger scouting party after the miscreants. Foolhardy in the eyes of his fellow officers, Bradley took Bostwick, LeForge, four Crows, and seventeen of his mounted infantrymen and left camp at dusk of May 7th. At the point where the two Crows had captured the enemy ponies they found three war lodges sheltering perhaps thirty braves, abandoned only twenty-four hours earlier. They followed the trail a few miles down to where it crossed to the south bank. From a high point they saw thousands of quiet buffalo, but neither smoke nor other sign of a village. Continuing downstream Bostwick soon cut the sign of his stolen mule, indicating that an advance squad of raiders had herded the stolen stock even further down before crossing. On approaching the Big Porcupine, nearly forty miles from camp, they discovered a campsite of size and age to accommodate the entire raiding party on its way up to the soldier camp. Now convinced that the thieves had come from south of the river and considerably farther down, Bradley turned back to reach Gibbon's camp on May 8th.

The return of Captain Freeman's detachment having now resupplied and re-united his command, Gibbon decided to move downstream, where he could better prevent the hostiles from crossing to the north side. This he reported to Terry on May 9th:

> Leave here tomorrow with my whole command. Small war parties have been in our vicinity and this place is too far upriver to produce any effect. A scouting party under Lt. Bradley, just in from the Porcupine, 40 miles below, saw no Indians, but found the fresh trail of a war party of thirty Indians leading down the river. This party ran off some Crow ponies from the vicinity of this camp on the night of the second. We shall be short of rations before our next train can reach us, but buffalo are plenty and we shall not suffer. (O-9)

Back on May 2nd, a mackinaw boat dubbed "Fleetfoot" had left Benson's Landing (present Livingston) in charge of Paul McCormick and George Herendeen. It floated in to the Fort Pease camp on May 6th with a welcome cargo of nectar and ambrosia for the troops. On the 9th McCormick turned back overland to Fort Ellis, bearing the mail and Gibbon's above dispatch, leaving Herendeen behind. The latter found Gibbon about to commandeer a few small boats abandoned at Fort Pease. As a boat-building member of the Fort Pease company, he convinced the nettled General that the boats were rightfully his. Having won his point, he volunteered to use them in the service of the expedition without hire or pay. Accordingly, when the command moved out on May 10th, Herendeen skippered Captain Clifford's Company E in his flotilla of boats, from which they could readily scout the south bank and yet tie up at night near the camp of the main force. The infantrymen welcomed this chance to spare their shoes at the expense of their pants.

Marching only on alternate days because of the rain, the column made 53 miles to reach the mouth of the Little Porcupine on the afternoon of May 14th, Herendeen's flotilla noting signs of Sioux on the south bank en route. Here the command remained mudbound for nearly a week, while the scouts found that hostile spies were sneaking close in to camp. Four dismounted Crows, who had set out on a two-day horse-stealing sortie, returned on May 15th to report that some distance below on the south bank they had struck and followed the trail of a war party of thirty Sioux coming upstream. Just as they were about to realize their ambition of running off the coveted pony herd, a violent hail and thunderstorm scattered their quarry.

Suspecting that this party had also come from the village perhaps as far down as Tongue River, Lt. Bradley again won permission to conduct a reinforced scout in that direction. His party, consisting of Barney Bravo, five Crows, and twenty-six infantrymen, crossed the river at dusk of May 15th in Herendeen's boats. Riding five miles southeast, they forded the Rosebud and proceeded another 14 miles to reach the Wolf Mountains by the next morning, May 16th. Hiding their horses, they climbed a high peak which exposed to view the Rosebud valley for thirty miles above its mouth — clearly empty of Indians. They then rode about ten miles east to a ridge that parallels Tongue River flowing in its valley five to six miles beyond. On the way they came across the trail, now a day or two old, of thirty warriors, presumably the same party followed by the frustrated Crow horse-raiders. It appeared to come from a point on Tongue River some fifteen to eighteen miles above its mouth.

Spying from the ridge, Bradley was elated to see a heavy blanket of smoke rising from an Indian village hidden in the river bottom. The Crows dampened his eagerness to approach close

79

enough to count the lodges, insisting that it would be fatal for clumsy soldiers, and wholly unnecessary besides. The smoke alone told them that it was a large village of "no less than 2-300 lodges." Reluctantly, Bradley led his party back to the command on the morning of May 17th, and there reported the large hostile village on the Tongue, only thirty-five miles away.

It should be emphasized that Bradley was an exceptionally accurate observer and faithful reporter. When checked against modern topographical maps, his terrain, locations, and distances are uncannily accurate. For example, his Wolf Mountain look-out, nineteen miles southeast of the mouth of the Little Porcupine, is readily identifiable as the highest point (3072 feet) at the very head of present Sweeney Creek. He sighted the hostile village on the Tongue from the ridge and thirty-five miles from camp, and these bearings unmistakably define a point very near present Garland, thirty miles above the mouth of the Tongue. Bradley was not peddling guesses, but reliable facts.

After more than a month in the field, the persistent and daring Chief of Scouts had at last located a large hostile camp and could lead a force directly to it. This gave the chance to strike the blow of which Gibbon had been talking. A fast overnight march could take him to the unsuspecting village in time for a dawn attack. Gibbon promptly ordered such a movement. The Crows were jubilant as the camp sprang to life. The quartermaster issued rations for three days and chief packer Jack Bean readied 30 pack mules. Leaving Captain James M.J. Sanno's Company K to guard the camp, the striking force would number thirty-four officers and 350 men, including the Crows. The odds would be at least two to one against them, if the scouts were right in their estimate, but everyone considered these sufficiently favorable.

By mid-morning of that May 17th, Herendeen's flotilla began ferrying the cavalry across the Yellowstone, the led horses swimming behind the boats. But the craft were small and few, the horses panicky, and the troopers excited. An hour's cursing struggle crossed no more than ten horses! So the mounts were tied in tandem and choused into the river by shouting troopers. Chaos immediately erupted and four horses were drowned in the first trial. Hours of exhausting and risky work having yielded such meager progress, Gibbon countermanded the movement.

General Gibbon was not the first to fail in crossing cavalry over a stream that Indian women and children took in stride. Custer had the identical experience on the Yellowstone in August of 1873. But Gibbon's counterorder was influenced by another factor. That very morning a party of Sioux, apparently following the trail of Bradley's scouts, had been sighted on the bluffs watching the crossing attempt. Delay would thus rob the attack of the essential element of surprise; the alerted village could either evaporate or lay an ambush. However wise Gibbon's reluctant decision may have been, the Crows could not help remembering what their chiefs had said in council about the way soldiers campaigned.

It is hard to believe, but Gibbon did not bother to report to Terry that he had precisely located a large hostile village on Tongue River, nor that his attempt to cross and strike it had failed.

The next day, May 18th, rain and muddy trails held the command in camp at the mouth of the Little Porcupine. Nevertheless, at noon Captain Thompson with two companies of 2nd Cavalry, guided by Mitch Boyer and two Crows, rode down toward the mouth of Tongue River on a three-day reconnaissance. A few hours later another quartet of Crows set out on foot to steal Sioux ponies, or to sight the village again, whichever came first.

The next day, while these parties were still out, couriers brought an important dispatch from General Terry, written from St. Paul about May 8th. It told that two steamboats had been chartered for service on the river to support both columns in the field; that Custer, now in some sort of trouble, had been demoted to the command of only his own regiment; that Terry himself would lead the expedition scheduled to depart about May 10th and to reach Glendive Creek on the lower Yellowstone about May 28th — only nine days hence. Terry again cautioned Gibbon to patrol the north bank to prevent any hostiles from crossing the river.

Early on the morning of the 20th, the four horse-seeking Crows returned to camp, still afoot, but bearing startling news. At noon of the preceding day they had been examining the country from the Wolf Mountain look-out, when they sighted several hundred Sioux warriors approaching from the direction of the Tongue. The quartet remained concealed as the war party crossed the divide perilously close, and then disappeared into the lower valley of the Rosebud. This is Bradley's version, but others imply that the Sioux were heading for a crossing of the river at the mouth of Rosebud Creek. Dr. Paulding added that the Crows reported firing down river all day — from the direction that Thompson's reconnaissance had taken.

Fearing that Thompson might be under attack, Gibbon promptly organized a relief force. Captain Kirtland's Company B was left to guard the wagon train, while the remainder rode out in a mid-morning downpour. After making a slow nine miles they went into camp opposite and two miles below the mouth of the Rosebud. No Indians had been seen, nor any evidence of a crossing. But Bradley, with his Crows, continued thirteen miles farther, where he found an old bivouac of Thompson's missing command. Unable to decipher the trail in the rain and darkness, he returned to camp just before midnight. Thompson's fate remained as mysterious as before, but all concern vanished when no Sioux crossing had been detected.

The Rosebud site proved so superior that on May 21st the wagon train and escort were brought down to make a new base camp, where the command would remain for the next two weeks. That afternoon Thompson's battalion rode in from below, unaware of the brief flurry of excitement it had caused. The Captain reported that on the morning of the 19th, just as they were leaving the bivouac Bradley had found, they saw forty to fifty Sioux approaching the opposite bank, apparently intending to cross. Thompson deployed his troopers in ambush at the expected landing point, but the tantalizing war party merely tested the water and faded back into the timber. Eyeing their nice horses, Mitch Boyer and the two Crows stripped, and sans arms, swam across to purloin the ponies. As they were stealthily stalking the herd in the timber, they ran into the guards, and friend and foe alike skedaddled, the scouts swimming safely back to the command. The reconnaissance then continued down to Tongue River and returned without seeing any more of the enemy. It was concluded that the war party they had seen was the same the Crow quartet had seen later that same day. But since Thompson had heard no firing, the Crows must have heard the Sioux hunting buffalo south of the river.

The next morning, May 22nd, eight or ten Sioux fired on a party of three soldiers hunting near camp. Bradley's mounted infantry, a flock of dismounted Crows, and Lt. Whelan's cavalry company all dashed out in different directions in hot pursuit, only to see the trail scatter, as usual, and peter out. This kind of sortie did considerable damage to the cavalry horses, but none to the enemy.

While these wild geese were being chased, General Gibbon turned his attention to more prosaic matters. Having now been out for fifty-two days on two months' rations, supplies were running so low that he ordered half-rations for the men, hoping that hunters could make up the difference. He was expecting new supplies by the Diamond R contract train of twenty-four wagons in charge of Matt Carroll, but the latter was now only approaching the old Camp Supply. Gibbon ordered the Powers contract train, now empty, back to the settlements for discharge. It left the Rosebud camp under escort on May 23rd, accompanied by Barney Bravo and two

Crows, assigned the humiliating mission of finding the Crow village and begging ponies to replace those stolen by the Sioux.

At noon of that same day, George Herendeen galloped in from a hunt reporting Indians and firing in the direction of another hunting party. Three cavalry companies quickly mounted and sped to the rescue. Only three miles from camp they came upon the badly mutilated bodies of Pvts. Henry Raymeyer and Augustus Stoker of Company H, 2nd Cavalry, and citizen teamster James Quinn. Only Stoker had been scalped, but all were riddled with bullets, as Dr. Paulding recorded in clinical detail. The bodies were wrapped in blankets for burial that evening in a common tree-shaded grave. The most demonstrative mourner was an elderly Crow, Shows-His-Face, whose grief prompted him to cover the bodies with a green blanket far better than the one he was wearing. Sorrow was soon forgotten, however, for that very afternoon "Colonel" J.D. Chesnut, of Bozeman, had arrived by mackinaw with a cargo of vegetables, butter and eggs, and a grief-banishing keg of beer.

In view of the growing boldness of the hostiles, who watched the funeral services from across the bluffs, Gibbon instituted special precautions for camp security that evening. Then on May 24th a lone Sioux was flushed from cover practically inside the camp.

This was the last. Just as abruptly as the hostiles had appeared, they completely vanished. Not a trace was seen of them for days. Dr. Pauling's curiosity prompted him to make inquiries among the Crow scouts. They told him that the Sioux had probably left for their camp on the Tongue to dance over the scalp of Pvt. Stoker. The ominous lull, however, only drove Bradley to gather thirteen of his infantry, Tom LeForge, and five Crows for another dangerous scout across the river to determine what had become of the village.

Early on May 27th Bradley's detail crossed to the south bank a mile below the mouth of the Rosebud. On riding for some miles south up a concealing ravine, they debouched onto the open plain, now unexpectedly dotted with week-old carcasses of buffalo and criss-crossed by innumerable pony tracks. As they mounted into the hills, they crossed a week-old beaten trail of many Indians. Fourteen miles from camp they reached the familiar look-out. This time they instantly spotted a heavy smoke, some lodges, and a vast pony herd some eight or ten miles south up the valley of the Rosebud, only eighteen miles from Gibbon's camp.

Bradley watched for half an hour, sobered by the realization that to have moved so close meant that the villagers stood in little awe of the Montana column. He was anxious to bring every one of his infantrymen up to where they could see the village and vouch for its presence to sceptical brother officers, but discretion won out and the party beat a hasty retreat to the river. By noon, Bradley was reporting his crucial findings to Gibbon.

The lieutenant realized that this village must be the one he had seen eleven days earlier on the Tongue, and concluded that it had moved west on the 19th behind the screen of warriors seen that day by Thompson as well as the Crows. But what he reported to Gibbon as to its size is unfortunately not of record; he merely characterized it as "immense." Others said it was "large," or "in strong force," but someone wrote the Helena *Herald* on May 28th under the sobriquet of "Long Horse": "Yesterday Lt. Bradley . . . discovered a camp of 500 lodges of Sioux on the Rosebud . . ." But Bradley had not been mistaken in fearing scepticism. Captain Freeman recorded that Bradley "came in saying he had seen a big smoke on the Rosebud 18 to 20 miles off, also a large band of horses — thinks it a village."

The most indifferent of all proved to be General Gibbon. His lack of response to the momentous news of an immense village only eighteen miles away baffled the industrious Chief of Scouts, who confided to his journal that "everybody wondered why we were not ordered over to attack the village; but the General probably had good reasons." The less diplomatic Dr. Paulding, who was no admirer of Gibbon's military genius, recorded: "Don't know whether Gibbon's instructions or disposition will allow us to go for them . . . I suppose we will wait for Crook and Terry, hoping our untutored friends across the river will await their arrival. In the meantime Bradley can go over and take a look every day or so to see that they are still there. His party will be accommodated in a small grave 30x8x4 ft. some day."

The real puzzle is not Gibbon's failure to attempt another river crossing and attack on so strong a village, but his complete suppression of the crucial intelligence his expert Chief of Scouts had brought him. Neither in his annual report nor in his popular account did Gibbon even so much as admit the discovery of the village so near on the Rosebud. He began this suppression immediately. Only a couple of hours after Bradley reported to him, he sat down to write General Terry, stating that no camps had been seen! In an after-thought postscript, he mentioned that the scouts had reported one, but an "if" betrays his scepticism:

> I have reached this point [opposite the mouth of Rosebud] and have scouted the country on both sides of the Yellowstone. No camps have been seen, but war parties of from twenty to fifty have been seen to the south of the river and a few on the north side. One of these latter murdered three of our men whilst out hunting on the 23rd inst.

84

As soon as my train arrives from Fort Ellis, which is expected about the first of June, I will resume the march down the Yellowstone with supplies which will last till about July 10th, and I can draw no more from there, the supply being nearly exhausted. In the meantime I will keep scouting parties out, up and down the river, and watch closely for any movement of the Indians to the northward.

A steamboat, if you have one at your disposal, will be of great assistance in passing troops across the river for effective cooperation if necessary. I have a few small boats which can be used, but they require, of course, a good deal of time. I send this by men in one of them. The three are Pvts. Evans and Stewart, Co. E., 7th Infantry (volunteers), and Williamson, a citizen scout, and if they get through successfully will deserve commendation. The danger by river is less than by land . . .

P.S. A camp some distance up the Rosebud was reported this morning by our scouts. If this proves true, I may not start down the Yellowstone so soon. (O-9)

Gibbon's letter defies belief. His command had seen numerous and sizeable war parties, or their sign, almost daily for some weeks. His daring scouts had precisely located their home village, first on the lower Tongue on May 16th, and again on the lower Rosebud that very day. The village was estimated at no less than hundreds of lodges, enough to contain the major portion of all the winter roamers. Locating these Indians in order to whip them was the very goal of the campaign. Yet Gibbon had made no report of the first discovery, and after the second still reported that no camps had been seen, except for a doubtful recent claim! And later, he refused even to admit this much! Was Gibbon too preoccupied with logistics to remember what he was there for? Was he the kind who believed nothing his own eyes had not seen? Whatever the explanation, the damage was done.

The General's dispatch was scarcely worth sending, but he risked men's lives to deliver it. Scout John Williamson undertook the mission in the regular line of duty, but Pvts. Benjamin F. Stewart and William Evans, both of Clifford's flotilla company, recieved $100 each for volunteering. As darkness fell on the evening of May 27th, the daring trio stepped into one of Herendeen's skiffs to float down the river in search of the Dakota column, or a steamboat, or failing these, Fort Buford.

Chapter 8
Crook and Terry Reorganize

As the month of April slipped by, General Terry found it necessary to postpone the target date for the departure of Custer's column from April 5th to the 15th, and then May. His only consolation was that General Crook's Wyoming column was meeting with similar delays. Terry's preparations, however, did begin to gather momentum in the last half of April when the weather embargo began to lift. Troops, supplies, and trains began flooding in to Fort Abraham Lincoln, where their local supervision fell on the shoulders of Major Marcus A. Reno.

As early as February 23rd, Reno had sent Lt. John A. Carland, 6th Infantry, some sixty miles upriver to the Fort Berthold Agency to recruit scouts from among the Arikara, or Ree, tribe, which supplied the most eager and reliable Indian scouts. But he returned on March 3rd without a single Indian. It would take later appeals from Rees already in service to bring seven recruits on April 26th, and twenty-three more on May 9th.

But Lt. Carland did bring back two prizes in the persons of Charles A. ("Lonesome Charley") Reynolds, and Bloody Knife. The enigmatic Charley, a silent and educated gentleman, who had served Custer so well since 1873, was considered the best scout, guide, and hunter in Dakota (M-29). Corporal Bloody Knife, half Ree and half Sioux, had also given many years of excellent service as an enlisted scout here and at Fort Buford (M-39). On March 3rd, Lt. Henry J. Nowlan, 7th Cavalry, the expedition quartermaster, hired Reynolds as guide and Bloody Knife as scout. The latter was proud of his promotion to quartermaster scout. But neither was impressed by the simultaneous hiring of Boston Custer, the young

86

brother of the General, as a guide. Only nepotism can explain this appointment, for Boston's frontier experience consisted of eight months at the post as foragemaster!

Since the enlisted scouts would include a few Sioux among the Rees, interpreters were indispensable. The best Ree interpreter in the country was Frederic F. Gerard, an Indian trader since 1848, but now post interpreter at Fort Lincoln (M-19). Major Reno would fire Gerard in a fit of temper on May 6th, making for bad blood between the two, but Custer would promptly reverse his subordinate's ill-considered action. A Sioux interpreter was not procured until May 15th, when Isaiah Dorman, a negro long-married to a Sioux woman, was hired (M-50). He had been a daring and reliable courier and interpreter at nearby Fort Rice for many years.

Overly impressed with his weighty duties, Major Reno had developed a proprietary interest in the expedition by April. With considerable presumption he wired Terry: "From Custer's telegrams and the papers it seems he will not soon be back. In the meantime the expedition here is making large expenses and Sitting Bull waiting on the Little Missouri. Why not give me a chance, as I feel I will do credit to the army? (M-60)" Terry rejected this offer, but with more diplomacy than discipline. The Major then bypassed channels to importune Sheridan on April 16th: "Expedition ready when transportation from Abercrombie and cavalry companies from Rice arrive. Why not give me a chance, sending instructions what to do with Sitting Bull if I catch him. He is waiting for us on the Little Missouri (O-28)." With uncharacteristic gentleness Sheridan replied the next day that "General Terry has entire charge of the expedition. I do not feel like interfering with him in his plans (O-29)."

Terry had expected Custer's column to depart before navigation opened, thus requiring all troops and supplies to move overland, consuming precious provisions en route. He was now able, however, to capitalize on delays by delivering both supporting infantry and supplies to a field depot by steamboat. He chartered two boats for exclusive service to the campaign, the *Josephine*, Captain Mart Coulson, and the *Far West*, Captain Grant Marsh, both operated by the Coulson Line. Then on April 21st he had the following instructions sent to Fort Buford, commanded by Major Orlando H. Moore, 6th Infantry, in the temporary absence of General Hazen:

> The Commanding General directs that upon the arrival at your post of steamer, probably the Josephine, especially designated to carry troops and supplies to the depot on the Yellowstone River, Major Moore and Companies C, D, and I, 6th Infantry, will embark on board of her and proceed up the Yellowstone River until they shall meet the expedition under command of Lt. Col. Custer, to whom Major Moore will then report

for duty. Should Major Moore and his command fail to meet Lt. Col. Custer, or to receive orders from him before reaching the mouth of Powder River, they will halt at that point and there await instructions from Lt. Col. Custer. As soon as this, or other point of debarkation fixed by Lt. Col. Custer, shall have been reached, the men and freight destined therefor will be landed with all possible dispatch in order that the boat may return for additional supplies. Assistant Surgeon G.E. Lord will accompany the troops. (O-17)

A week after sending these instructions Terry learned that he would have to command the expedition, without certainty of retaining the indispensable services of Custer. Accordingly, on May 4th, he modified these original instructions. Major Moore was no longer to proceed to Powder River unless Custer met him and ordered differently; instead, he was to locate the depot in advance at the mouth of Glendive Creek, to which the overland column, to be commanded by General Terry, would march by the 1873 surveying trail of General David S. Stanley. Major Moore was to open communications with the overland column as soon as possible, for which purpose he was authorized to take enlisted Indian scouts from Fort Buford, or hire suitable frontiersmen. The General emphasized the importance of the supply depot, since the marching column could carry only enough stores to reach it. He also cautioned vigilance against possible Indian attack (O-28).

In accordance with this revised plan, the *Josephine* pushed off from Bismarck on May 9th, loaded with expedition supplies. Reaching Fort Buford in four days, she partially unloaded to accommodate Major Moore's battalion and Dr. George E. Lord, the force totalling seven officers, 120 men, and three scouts (O-33). The latter included George P. Mulligan, detached from duty as post interpreter, Crow Bear, an enlisted Gros Ventre Indian, and Charles Sargent, hired from May 14th to August 2nd by Lt. Bernard A. Byrne, Company C, Moore's quartermaster (O-34). Neither reporter nor diarist accompanied the command, but an officer, undoubtedly Lt. Byrne, submitted frequent dispatches to the New York *Times*.

The *Josephine* nosed into the Yellowstone at 3:30 p.m. of May 14th and reached Stanley's Stockade, opposite the mouth of Glendive Creek on the morning of the 18th, a trip of 126 river-miles, but only about 72 by road. Having unloaded the troops and supplies, she turned back, carrying a note from the Major to Terry's adjutant announcing her safe arrival. On May 21st she headed back up the river with her temporarily unloaded supplies, as well as the party of the expedition sutler, "Captain" John W. Smith, and his wares. Unloading at the rapidly organizing supply depot on the 24th, the *Josephine* headed back for the States (O-16).

General Terry and the humbled Custer left St. Paul by rail to reach Fort Abraham Lincoln on the evening of May 10th, finding all the troops assembled and preparations nearly completed. Terry assumed formal command of the expedition on May 14th, and then informed Sheridan of his plans and prospects in a letter dated May 15th:

> Information from several independent sources seems to establish the fact that the Sioux are collected in camps on the Little Missouri and between that and the Powder River. I have already ordered Colonel Gibbon to move eastward and suggest that it would be very desirable for General Crook's column to move up as soon as possible. It is represented that they have 1500 lodges, are confident, and intend to make a stand. Should they do so, and should the three columns be able to act simultaneously, I should expect great success. We start tomorrow morning. (O-28)

At the same time, actually May 14th, Terry telegraphed Gibbon, via Fort Ellis, to move down the Yellowstone to Stanley's Stockade and then east on Stanley's trail to meet the Dakota column where he expected the hostiles to concentrate.

Every dispatch from Fort A. Lincoln at this time carried this story of Sitting Bull having gathered 1500 lodges and 3000 warriors on the Little Missouri due west of the Fort, near present Medora. Unfortunately, it was a myth, whose origin reveals how poorly Terry's staff was processing the generous flow of Indian intelligence from its own and other sources.

That the winter roamers had been concentrating since General Reynolds' attack in mid-March had been correctly reported to Terry's headquarters about mid-April.* So had the gathering of northern Sioux near the mouth of the Little Missouri to send in trading parties at Fort Berthold late in March and early in April. In fact, Charley Reynolds had been sent to Fort Berthold to tap this fountain of intelligence. Before April 1st, he had reported to Custer in Washington that these trading parties amounted to 3-400 lodges, enough to represent most of the winter roamers. Shortly after this the local newspapers picked up the rumors that Sitting Bull would fight Custer in the badlands of the Little Missouri. Major Reno reported this on April 16th, but sent Reynolds again to check it out.

On April 30th, Agent Darling reported to Reno that 1500 Sioux lodges were camped a few days' ride from his Berthold Agency, and that Reynolds, who carried the letter, could give further particulars. Reno forwarded this letter May 2nd with a covering wire, undoubtedly based on Reynolds' information, that read: "Twelve lodges of Uncapapas at Berthold, trading, report several hundred lodges between here and the Yellowstone waiting for the expedition (O-28)." Charley had obviously deflated the lodge count and extended its possible location, but these corrections got lost in the shuffle.

About this time several reports came in that the young Sioux were leaving the river agencies, especially Standing Rock. These, of course, were the van of the summer roamers, who were edging out on their reservation to hunt and feed up their ponies before venturing farther. On May 8th, Louis Agard, a former reliable scout then farming at Standing Rock, arrived with a report that appeared in the Bismarck *Tribune* for May 10th — the very day Terry arrived: "Agard reports the hostiles 1500 lodges strong in camp on the forks of the Little Missouri, waiting anxiously for the long-haired chief." The number of lodges is again grossly exaggerated, but the reference is to *summer roamers*, who would not consolidate with the winter roamers for another month. The forks of the Little Missouri referred to the junction with Box Elder Creek, some seventy-five miles south of Medora, but due west of the river agencies.

It is axiomatic that raw intelligence demands careful processing. But Terry and his staff would reveal ineptness in interpreting Indian intelligence throughout the summer.

Although Terry had wired Sheridan that the Dakota Column would get off on May 15th, one more delay occurred, as revealed by another telegram of May 16th:

*Chapter 27 details the movements of the winter roamers.

> The storm was very severe yesterday, making the plain below the post on which we are encamped almost impossible for wagons loaded as ours are. It has not rained now since sunrise and I am very confident that we shall be able to pull out and make a short march tomorrow. I have no doubt of the ability of my column to whip all the Sioux whom we can find. I suggest Crook's immediate movement with the idea that if he moved up he would force them toward us and enable us to get at them more easily. (O-28)

Sheridan replied the same day, cautioning Terry not to rely too much on cooperation from the distant Wyoming column:

> I will hurry up Crook, but you must rely on the ability of your own column for your best success. I believe it to be fully equal to all the Sioux which can be brought against it, and only hope they will hold fast to meet it. Keep me as well posted as you can, and depend upon my full assistance in every respect. You know the impossibility of any large number of Indians keeping together as a hostile body for even one week. (O-28)

Future events would make a mockery of Sheridan's predictions, but nevertheless, the Dakota column would indeed march out of Fort Abraham Lincoln on May 17th.

* * *

After the close of his winter campaign, General Crook resolved to wait for the new spring grass as support for his cavalry before resuming the campaign. The new grass sprang up in late April that year, but still another month would pass before the General could get his second expedition into the field. In the meantime spring would entice summer roamers to the plains and miners to the Black Hills, and violence would erupt primarily in Crook's own department.

The Oglalas and Brules of the Red Cloud and Spotted Tail Agencies were especially restless that season. They were closest to the Black Hills threat. They had heard the rumors of a removal to the detested Missouri River. Above all they were so hungry that even Congress, on February 3rd, called for an investigation. Lt. Col. Wesley Merritt, 9th Cavalry, conducted the inquiry and reported on March 17th that an extra appropriation of $135,000 would be needed to feed these Indians for the remainder of the fiscal year (O-26). But bureaucracy moves slowly.

As late as April 27th, Captain W.H. Jordan, 9th Infantry, the commander of Camp Robinson at Red Cloud's Agency, reported that the Indians were stormy and would be compelled to raid, or join the hostiles, unless beef rations arrived quickly. He felt confident that no Oglalas had yet left the reservation, although a few Cheyennes, upset by Reynolds' attack on their Powder River village, had been sneaking away (O-28). James S. Hastings, the Red Cloud Agent, indignantly denied on May 5th that his Indians were starving, and contended that they had never been more peaceful (O-36). But there was, in fact, a ration shortage, the Cheyennes had been slipping away in small parties, and the Oglalas were beginning to drift out on their reservation.

The paths of the hunting Sioux and the trespassing Black Hillers began to cross, with inevitable clashes. The predictable cry for military protection rang out so loud and clear that Governor John M. Thayer of Wyoming Territory petitioned General Crook for aid. The latter responded on May 7th by detailing Captain James Egan, 2nd Cavalry, to patrol the Cheyenne-Black Hills trail with a troop of cavalry and a company of infantry. The Captain set up a base camp by May 16th, and the very next day while on patrol he rescued a wagon train that had been beseiged by a war party too large for his company to pursue and punish (O-28). Despite the efforts of his forlorn patrol, a veritable rash of Indian attacks nearly paralyzed traffic on the trail during May. It should be noted, however, that these reacting Indians were still within their reservation.

Governor Thayer carried his plea for protection all the way to the White House, and in person. The President temporized, placing his faith on the punitive campaign and a removal of the offending tribes to the Missouri or even Indian Territory. In a transparent bit of hair-splitting, the White House Solomon refused protection for miners illegally entering the Hills, but authorized protection for supply trains illegally entering, and for miners leaving! This is revealed in a letter of May 25th from Sherman to Sheridan:

> Have just been to the President with Governor Thayer. After reading the papers and some discussion, the President said that the people who had gone to the Black Hills of Dakota, inside the reservation, and who may hereafter go there, are there wrongfully, and they should be notified of the fact, but the Government is engaged in certain measures that will probably result in opening up the country to occupation and settlement, and meantime the Indians should not be allowed to kill and scalp anybody, and you are authorized to afford protection to all persons who are coming away, or are conveying food or stores for those already there . . . (*Bismarck Tribune, June 7, 1876*)

In the meantime, General Crook was stripping his department of troops by ordering them to Fort Fetterman to join his expedition, hopefully scheduled to depart on May 15th. Either for reasons of economy or choice, he would rehire only three of the thirty-two quartermaster scouts he had used on his winter campaign. Although they were the best — Frank Grouard, Big Bat Pourier, and Louis Richard — they were far too few. Crook preferred large numbers of Indian volunteer allies, as he had used in his Apache campaigns, because of his conviction that nothing so demoralized hostiles as to have their brothers defect to the army side.

Accordingly, Crook left his Omaha headquarters for the Red Cloud Agency to secure at least three hundred Sioux as volunteer allies for glory and loot. He reached the agency post, Camp Robinson, on May 14th, accompanied by Lt. Bourke, Grouard and Richard. On the morning of the next day he conferred with a few minor chiefs; that evening he held a formal council in the presence of chief Red Cloud and Agent Hastings. The results proved consistent — not an Oglala would volunteer! Agent Hastings permitted the Sioux to volunteer if they chose, but he would not encourage or force them to. Red Cloud was brutally blunt — the agency Indians were fighting no more, least of all for the very general whom Washington had illegally ordered to whip the Sioux and Cheyennes (C-7).

Now worried, Crook left the agency on May 16th, fortunately in the company of the military inspector and paymaster with their sizeable escort. As they rode off, they noted mysterious smoke signals rising from behind the Indian village. While taking their noon-rest, the Cheyenne mail-carrier, Charles Clark, passed them in his light wagon bound for the agency. Lt. Bourke later learned that the smoke signals had been made to inform the party of discontented Sioux, waiting to ambush the General, that the latter had left the agency. When the assassins found their quarry so well escorted, they took out their fatal spite on the luckless mail-carrier (C-7).

Although Crook escaped with his hair, he had secured no scouts, without whom his campaign was doomed. He therefore wired, probably from Camp Robinson on May 16th, to Camp Brown on the Shoshone reservation in western Wyoming, and Fort Ellis, a hundred miles west of the Crow Agency in Montana; he asked that a few hundred each of Shoshone and Crow volunteers be sent to join his column out on the Bozeman trail crossing of Powder River, the site of old Fort Reno. He did not know that his wire was not delivered to Fort Ellis until May 24th, nor that its commander, Captain Daniel W. Benham, 7th Infantry, set out for the agency that afternoon, only to be turned back by floods; the Captain probably made no further attempt, since he was aware of Gibbon's failure to secure voluntary allies from the Crows. Although a contingent of Shoshones volunteered, they did not leave Camp Brown until June 4th. Crook was destined to suffer acute anxiety over his Indian allies.

At Fort Fetterman on May 21st, Crook ordered Sgt. John A. Carr, Company A, 2nd Cavalry, and a squad of nine men to accompany Frank Grouard on an advance scout to Powder River, some ninety miles distant, ostensibly to locate a better trail and crossing of the stream. The party had not gone far when Frank discovered they were under hostile surveillance. He had the squad construct a sham camp with dummies and hearty camp fires, and then led them on a circuitous night ride to elude the spies. But on approaching within twenty miles of Powder River, he spotted Sioux gathering for an ambush. He sent the squad back, while he advanced alone to draw off the enemy, then circled back to lead his party on a run for Fort Fetterman. Keeping only one jump ahead of their pursuers, they returned safely on May 26th. Frank nominated this adventure as the closest call he ever had.

Although other sources identify Frank's mission as locating a better trail and crossing, he remembered his assignment was to meet the expected Crow allies. Furthermore, on May 27th, Crook dispatched Captain Frederick VanVliet with two companies of 3rd Cavalry to old Fort Reno, with the admitted purpose of meeting and holding the Crow allies. We suspect that Frank was right about his own assignment, and that both missions betray Crook's anxiety about his essential allies.

On May 28th Captain Egan reported from Fort Laramie on his patrol of the Black Hills trail (O-28). As revealed by a supplementary news dispatch (Chicago *Inter-Ocean*, May 30, 1876) from his own lips, he figured *seven* warriors to the lodge to make hash of his intelligence, as so many officers did, despite years on the plains. Correcting the ratio to two, we find that on May 17th he had rescued a wagon train from an attack by two hundred warriors; on his return via Red Cloud's Agency he learned that 120 lodges of Oglalas and 50 of Brules had already departed. The report claimed the agency was almost deserted, but the dispatch limited this to the Cheyenne and Arapahoe camps. Both versions, however, were dead wrong, for the agency served vastly more than 120 lodges of Oglalas and many Cheyennes were still present, while the Arapahoes never joined the hostiles. But however faulty in detail, the spirit of Egan's report was correct — the Indians were drifting out from the agency and many of them would eventually swell the ranks of the hostile camp.

This report prompted Crook to wire Sheridan on May 29th that the diversion of nearly all the departmental troops to his expedition had left the settlements little protection against Indians. The same day Sheridan wired back:

> Have already anticipated movement of Indians from agencies and have made application to General Sherman to be permitted to control Indians at all agencies, so that none can go out and no hostiles or families come in, except on unconditional surrender. What say you to my running up the majority of the 5th Cavalry to Red Cloud's and Spotted Tails? (O-29)

Following his own suggestion, on June 2nd Sheridan ordered eight companies of 5th Cavalry transferred from Kansas to the army posts at the two Nebraska agencies. In the meantime, Crook's Big Horn and Yellowstone Expedition would march out of Fort Fetterman on May 29th.

*   *   *

By the end of May, Sheridan could finally say that three offensive forces, the Montana, Dakota, and Wyoming columns had taken the field to whip the hostiles into subjection. He reviewed the present status and future prospects for the benefit of General Sherman in a letter of May 29th:

> . . . As no very accurate information can be obtained as to the location of the hostile Indians, and as there would be no telling how long they would stay at any one place, if it was known, I have given no instructions to Generals Crook or Terry, preferring that they should do the best they

can under the circumstances and under what they may develop, as I think it would be unwise to make any combinations in such country as they will have to operate in. As hostile Indians in any great numbers can not keep the field as a body for a week, or at most ten days, I therefore consider — and so do Terry and Crook — that each column will be able to take care of itself and of chastising the Indians should it have the opportunity.

The organization of these commands and what they expect to accomplish has been as yet left to the Department Commanders. I presume the following will occur: General Terry will drive the Indians toward the Big Horn valley, and General Crook will drive them back toward Terry, Colonel Gibbon moving down on the north side of the Yellowstone to intercept, if possible, such as may want to go north of the Missouri to the Milk River.

The result of the movements of the three columns may force many of the hostiles back to the agencies on the Missouri and to the Red Cloud and Spotted Tail agencies on the northern line of Nebraska, where nearly every Indian man, woman, and child, is at heart a friend. It is easy to foresee the result of this condition, that as soon as the troops return in the fall, the Indians will go out again, and another campaign with all its expenses will be required, as was the case with the Cheyennes, Arapahoes, Comanches, and Kiowas of the Indian Territory.

To obviate this, I advise that the two posts recommended by me be established on the Yellowstone, and that the military be allowed to exercise control over the Indians at the agencies to such an extent as to prevent any friendly Indians from leaving to join the hostiles, and the latter, or any of their families, from coming in, except by unconditional surrender — the ringleaders to be punished, as were the Southern Indians, by having them sent to some distant point until they and their people are willing to behave themselves.

I hope that good results may be obtained by the troops in the field, but am not at all sanguine, unless what I have above suggested be carried out. We might just as well settle the Sioux question now; it will be better for all concerned. (O-29)

This letter establishes Sheridan as a prophet of mixed genius. The hostiles in a large body, in fact, would remain in the field for months. The separate army columns would prove unequal to handling the Indians they would encounter. Instead of the hostiles fleeing to the agencies, the agency Indians would flee to join the hostiles. But he was only too right in predicting that the campaign would probably fail to achieve its purpose, unless the military were given free reign at the agencies.

When he received Crook's report of deserted agencies, as claimed by Captain Egan, Sheridan sent another letter to Sherman on May 30th, escalating his previous suggestions to requests:

I wrote you yesterday about the Sioux Indian troubles, making suggestions. Since writing, the information from Crook goes to show that all the agency Indians capable of taking the field are now, or will be, on the warpath. And if this intelligence is confirmed, I will order eight companies of 5th Cavalry to the Red Cloud Agency and will ask you to let the Indian Department give the military the same control as was done at Fort Sill and at the Cheyenne Agency in the Indian Territory during the troubles there. (O-29)

These requests lay dormant — until disaster brought panic.

Chapter 9
Junction on the Yellowstone

The day so long anticipated, but so often postponed, finally arrived. On the foggy morning of May 17th, Terry's column assembled on the plain adjacent to Fort Abraham Lincoln, awaiting the command to march. It was good to exchange barracks boredom for field action. Proud and confident, officers and men alike were eager to drive straight to the badlands of the Little Missouri and show Sitting Bull's rabble of savages what it meant to challenge Custer's invincibles.

Terry's force of twelve companies of cavalry and three and a half of infantry totalled only 52 officers (including four contract surgeons and one veterinary surgeon) and 879 men, appreciably fewer than Crook's force.* An elaborate headquarters comprised not only General Terry and staff (nine officers and three men), but Captain Stephen Baker's Company B, 6th Infantry (two officers and forty men). The nucleus of the force was Lt. Col. Custer's 7th Cavalry (32 officers and 718 men), but this included the regimental band. The remainder consisted of Captain Louis H. Sanger's battalion of 17th Infantry (7 officers and 89 men), and Lt. William H. Low's detachment of 20th Infantry (2 officers and 29 men) serving the Gatling battery.

Custer's Chief of Scouts, Lt. Charles A. Varnum, 7th Cavalry, commanded thirty-nine enlisted Indian scouts, whose number would fluctuate by interchange with six others left at Fort Lincoln (M-24). As quartermaster employees, there were three scouts, the silent

*Chapter 24 analyzes 7th Cavalry campaign and battle strengths, detachments and recruits.

Charley Reynolds, the volatile Bloody Knife, and the larking Boston Custer, as well as two interpreters, Fred F. Gerard and Isaiah Dorman. The column also trailed a large wagon train under Charles C. Brown, a token pack train under John C. Wagoner, and the usual beef herd in charge of J.M. Ayers.

Since the injunction against reporters applied to Custer, but not Terry, the Bismarck *Tribune* sent Mark H. Kellogg and passed his dispatches on to the New York *Herald*, which published only his last. Custer got around the injunction by submitting three anonymous dispatches to the New York *Herald*; he also wrote frequent letters to his wife. It was undoubtedly Terry's adjutant, Captain Edward W. Smith, 18th Infantry, who furnished a series of dispatches to the St. Paul *Pioneer-Press*. Terry's engineering officer, Lt. Edward Maguire, kept the official itinerary, and expedition diarists included General Terry, Mark Kellogg, Lt. Edward S. Godfrey, Dr. James M. DeWolf (also a letter writer), and even Lonesome Charley Reynolds.

As the command to march rang out, the band burst into spirited song, while the troops paraded past a throng of wives and children waving their last goodbyes. The rising sun soon burned off the fog to reveal a gala picnic party in the lead. With Custer rode his devoted wife, Elizabeth, his sister Margaret Calhoun, his younger brother Boston, and his still younger nephew, Autie Reed. The ladies would ride along this first day, stay the night, and return home the next morning with the paymaster, who was serving the troops virtuously far from the saloons, brothels, and gambling dens of Bismarck. Camp was made that afternoon thirteen miles out on Heart River.

For the next four days rain and a pelting hail storm turned the trail to gumbo and the ravines to torrents. The heavy wagons bogged down in the mire and the troops assigned to pioneer, or engineering, duty labored to build bridges, cut down the banks of gullies, and lay brush and logs in sloughs. Terry's diary, which records every halt and start, reads like a railway time-table. But as the column inched its way out on the butte-studded plains, game became plentiful. Charley Reynolds, a consummate hunter, brought in antelope and mountain sheep to spice the officers' mess, while the Rees did a thriving business hawking game to anyone willing to buy.

It took days of monotonous marching to make 135 miles west to the head of the east-flowing Heart River. Surmounting the divide on May 27th, the command approached the picturesque badlands that skirt the canyon of the north-flowing Little Missouri. Reynolds was relying on his memory of General David S. Stanley's surveying trail of 1873 to guide the command to the head of Davis Creek, the only route down to the river. When the trail dimmed at a critical point, however, he lost his way. His laconic diary carries the simple confession: "Went south to the head of Davis Cr., 7 miles, but by mistake crossed Stanley's trail and followed the ridge 3 miles too far and had to return, losing six miles."

Terry's diary, for once, fills in more details: "Custer in the advance with scouts and Weir's company looking for the trail . . . Bearing of hills supposed to be Sentinel Buttes shows us far south of Davis Creek. Our course plotted on the map agrees with bearing. Turned back at 1 o'clock, scout having reported that he had found Stanley's trail to the northward." Reporter Kellogg made Custer and his "fine memory" the hero of the day; "what is known as Sentinel buttes . . . were pronounced so at once and emphatically by him."

For two days the swearing teamsters maneuvered their ponderous wagons down the breaks to a point on the Little Missouri, about five miles above (south) present Medora. The sweating pioneers had to bridge the tortuous creek again and again, but not even they could close out the colorful scenery. Especially inviting were the shady cottonwoods and the clear running water in the bottom, where a pleasant camp was made on May 29th. The expedition had now struggled 166 miles in thirteen days.

But what of Sitting Bull's belligerent braves who were to make a desperate stand at this point? Twice they had seen signs suggesting spying, but nothing to sustain hopes that resistance was gathering. Apprehension flared briefly during the vulnerable descent into the canyon, but it quickly subsided when the hard-riding Rees found no trace of hostiles, to say nothing of a village of 1500 lodges. It became abundantly clear to all that Sitting Bull had not gathered his forces here to contest the crossing.

This was a let-down to the command and an embarrassment to its commander, for Terry had not only advised Sheridan of his expectations, but had summoned Gibbon's column to help trap the enemy. The natural reaction was to indulge in contemptuous scoffing at rumor-mongering scouts and frontiersmen. Then Custer offered a suggestion to replace chagrin with action. He proposed that a scouting column be sent out to make a bold pretense of looking for Sitting Bull. Terry agreed, and as Custer wrote his wife, "left the matter to me."

That night Terry ordered Custer to leave at daybreak "with four companies of his regiment . . . to make a reconnaissance to the" south. Leaving both route and distance "to the discretion" of Custer, he specified that "his absence will not extend beyond 7 a.m. of the 31st inst." (O-8). These orders gave Custer his first independent command of the campaign. Terry revealed his faith by leaving everything to Custer's discretion, save the hour of his return — and Custer more than kept that faith by returning half a day early. But there is another significant message in these orders. Since the force amounted to only four companies, neither officer could have entertained the remotest expectation of finding a village of 1500 lodges. They planned no more than a diversionary excercise.

As supporting actors for his skit, Custer selected twelve Rees in charge of Lt. Varnum and five forage-laden pack mules in charge of J.C. Wagoner. The curtain rose at 5 a.m. and fell at 6 p.m. of May 30th, the little column having loped twenty-five miles up the canyon bottom and back again on the same trail. There is no hint that the Rees were sent beyond earshot. Writing his wife that night, Custer confessed that the day had been nothing but a frolic: "When we lunched, all the officers got together and we had a jolly time. Only think, we found the Little Missouri so crooked and the Bad Lands so impassable that in marching fifty miles today we forded the river thirty-four times. The bottom is quicksand. Many of the horses went down, frequently tumbling their riders into the water but all were in good spirits, and everyone laughed at everyone else's mishaps."

Dr. DeWolf confirmed the spirit, if not the statistics, in a letter to his own wife: "Went up the Little Missouri 24 or 5 miles, crossed it 13 times each way — 26 in all. Had a great time. Lots of fun seeing the horses mire and throw their riders. The General's nephew got thrown over his horse's head into a mudhole. My old steed made them all." The troopers, anxious to nurse one horse through the entire campaign, found the picnic less amusing.

Terry's intelligence had not been false, only misinterpreted. It referred not to Sitting Bull's winter roamers, who had long since moved west to Rosebud Creek, but to some summer roamers gathering at the very time on the Little Missouri fifty miles south of Custer's farthest penetration.* Perhaps the scouts succeeded in correcting Terry's misinterpretations, for he decided to conduct heavy sweeps to the south before reaching the expected supply depot at Glendive Creek, as he revealed in a dispatch of May 30th to his St. Paul headquarters:

> . . . Contrary to all the predictions of the guides and scouts, no Indians have been found here, and there are no signs that they have been in this neighborhood within six months or a year. I intend to push on about two marches, halt, and again push a party well to the south, hoping to find trails, and if none are found, I may halt once more for the same purpose before reaching the Yellowstone . . . (O-27)

*The movements of the summer roamers are detailed in Chapter 30.

On May 31st the column began the hard climb up through the badlands on the west side of the river. Custer at first lagged behind to direct the wagons over the ford, or, as Terry dubbed it, "to play wagon-master." Then gathering brothers Tom and Boston, he sallied far ahead. He and Tom managed to shake Boston in the breaks, then circled around to fire a salvo of frightening shots over his head. This proved so effective that they had a hard ride to overtake the terror-stricken "scout" before he false-alarmed the main column. Despite the horse-play, the brothers all reached the evening's camp-site on a branch of Andrew's creek, near the edge of the badlands that morning. During their absence, and that of Charley Reynolds, who was out bagging mountain sheep, the column managed to get lost again.

Custer's larking in the van had not gone unnoticed, for Terry entered in his diary that "a message was received from Lt. Col. Custer, who left the column early in the day without any authority whatever, that we were not on Stanley's trail but Whistler's [1871 trail]. Turned back and examined the ground. Found that to return would take too much time, and marched on." That Terry rebuked his subordinate is revealed by the following note addressed to Terry by Custer under date of May 31st:

> At the time I proposed to accompany the advance battalion I was under the impression that it would probably be sufficiently far in advance of the main column to constitute a separate command, and that I could be of more service to you and to the expedition acting with the advance than elsewhere. Since such is not the case, I will, with your permission, remain with, and exercise command of, the main portion of my regiment. (O-9)

Not a word of this appears in the published portion of the letter Custer wrote his wife that night. Instead, he tells of the horse-play with Boston, and adds: "This is the second time I have left the main command and both times they have lost their way; so you see my 'bump of locality' is of some use out here . . . When they found they were lost, the officers all assembled at the head of the column to consult together and try and find the right way." It was apparently Varnum and the Rees who found the way, for there are three notes, all dated May 31st, from this officer to Adjutant Smith, sending back advice as to the trail (O-9).

After this rebuke, Custer became contrite and cooperative. Despite their contrasting temperaments, the two officers, over the several years of their association, had found complementary talents in one another, and developed a strong mutual regard and respect. Occasionally Custer, the boy, would test Terry, the father, to probe for the limits of his freedom, but once these were established, the two operated with less friction than prevailed in most other commands.

That night a cold rain swept the bivouac and by morning of June 1st flying flakes of snow filled the air and covered the ground to a depth of several inches. Since this would retard the wagons and make the feet of the animals "ball," Terry decided to remain in camp. The snowfall continued all day and part of the next. On the advice of Chief Medical Officer, Dr. John W. Williams, that to march in such untoward and changeable weather would risk colds and diarrhea, the command remained in camp the second day. But Charley Reynolds and wagonmaster Brown went out to examine the trail and the pioneers did a little work on the bad places.

On the bright morning of June 3rd the column climbed the last few miles out of the badlands to strike across an open and rolling country. After a good march of twenty-five miles they camped on the north-flowing Beaver Creek, a major tributary of the Little Missouri. On the march that morning, three couriers had met the advance of the column, bearing news that would bring a revision in Terry's plans.

It will be recalled that Gibbon had sent three scouts downriver in a skiff on the night of May 27th to deliver his meaningless dispatch to Terry. They had reached the Glendive post probably on May 30th, where the local correspondent, Lt. Byrne, faithfully reported the meager contents of Gibbon's note, but not one item more. Either the couriers were spontaneously tight-lipped, or Gibbon had ordered them so. For some reason, Major Moore had then sent the trio on downriver, where they soon met Captain Grant Marsh's *Far West*. She had left Bismarck on May 26th, laden with expedition stores, but at Fort Buford had partially unloaded to make room for Lt. Nelson Bronson's escort of 6th Infantry, and then pushed off for Glendive on May 30th. When Gibbon's couriers met her, they learned that Terry was marching overland with the Dakota column. Happy to trade their skiff for the luxury of the *Far West*, the trio sailed back to Glendive through a snow-storm, arriving at 10 p.m. of June 1st.

Writing a covering letter of his own, Major Moore gave both dispatches to three couriers for delivery overland. Since Terry's Rees identified one of them as Crow Bear, and Williamson later implied that he completed the delivery himself, the original brace of soldiers were replaced by either Mulligan or Sargent. This new trio were the ones who met Terry on the march on the morning of June 3rd. But again they added not one word to Gibbon's unrevealing dispatch.

The letter from Major Moore, dated June 1st at Stanley's Crossing, assured Terry that the depot was in operation, that the river was safe for steamboats, and that no Indians had been seen:

> I have the honor to forward dispatches from General Gibbon, which I had sent down the river in anticipation of reaching General Terry on the Far West.
>
> The steamer Far West arrived this evening at 10 p.m., bringing back the dispatches. I now start them by scouts this morning (the 2nd) to meet the expedition. The freight of the Josephine entire is at this camp, and all but 100 tons of forage on the Far West, which was left at Buford, is received. I detain the Far West at this point in accordance with instructions until the command arrives. The river is in fine condition, the stage of water being such that the boat can proceed higher without difficulty and serve the interests of General Gibbon's command now near the mouth of the Rosebud.
>
> I have no news of hostile Indians in addition to what General Gibbon gives in his dispatches. If you deem it proper for the Far West to return to Fort Buford for the balance of her freight before the command arrives at this point, please inform me, and the boat will be dispatched at once. (O-9)

Gibbon's uninformative dispatch of May 27th, already quoted in full, must have annoyed Terry. What had Gibbon been doing for over a month on the Yellowstone? Had he really been unable to gather any useful intelligence in all that time? And what about this village? Was there one or not? Was it large or small? Where was it on the hundred mile course of that stream? Terry searched in vain for anything definite or useful. Neither he, nor anyone else in his command, learned that Lt. Bradley had been keeping track of an immense village as it moved from the distant Tongue to the nearby Rosebud, and that the swollen river had thwarted an attempt to cross and attack the camp.

Since there was no evidence of hostiles anywhere along the Yellowstone, Terry could only search for them himself to the south. He therefore changed his plans, as revealed in his annual report:

> From the scouts I learned that there were no traces of Indians between Stanley's stockade and Beaver Creek; by the dispatches I was informed that the steamers with supplies had reached their destinations, and that Col. Gibbon, having received the dispatch sent him from Fort Lincoln [this was a false inference], was marching down the Yellowstone. Upon this information I determined to move up Beaver Creek [south], and thence march directly [west] to Powder River. Orders were therefore sent to Colonel Gibbon to suspend his movements and to Major Moore to send one boatload of supplies to the mouth of Powder River. (O-39, 1876)

From the evening's camp on Beaver Creek, the three couriers left with Terry's orders for Major Moore to send the *Far West* to the mouth of Powder River; Williamson and the other white scout were promised $200 apiece if they succeeded in reaching Gibbon with Terry's orders to halt wherever the orders might reach him. The next morning the Dakota column began its 92 mile march to Powder River. On the 4th and 5th it covered about 20 miles south up Beaver Creek, then swung west across the headwaters of Cabin and O'Fallon's Creeks. Terry thus made a strong sweep to the south, but found no Indian sign. The command was now blazing its own trail through unknown country, which became daily rougher.

On the march of June 6th, Reynolds again became confused by the numerous heads of O'Fallon's Creek, and the prospects for the next day were worse. The train would have to descend the badlands to the Powder, a region none had set eyes on. That night Custer proposed to Terry that he take the lead the next morning, promising to find a suitable trail to the river by 3 o'clock in the afternoon. Few believed he could make good his boast, but Terry had the faith to grant permission, probably to Reynolds' relief, since the route would be rough and the General, unlike himself, would be spared open criticism.

Early on June 7th, Custer set out in the lead. He rode hard and fast that day, some fifty miles, probing for a passable route. He found it — 32 miles of rugged trail — and watered his horse in the river, 24 miles above its mouth (near present Locate) at 3:30 that afternoon. He came so close to his boast that none was disposed to quibble. While his companions fell into exhausted sleep, the tireless Custer penned the following note to Terry, headed at Powder River, 3:45 p.m., June 7th:

> We arrived here at 3:30. Considering the character of the country, the road is good, but will require some work. The valley of the Powder is over a mile in width, well timbered and well grassed. The river is about 100 yards wide and fordable. The scouts report the trail of four Indians made since the rain. No other signs. A few buffalo. If you can find camp grounds, it would be best not to march here tonight, as we will bivouac in preference to going back, as our horses have ridden hard. I believe we came by the only practicable route within several miles. (O-9)

Weary of delays, Terry rejected the advice to camp on the trail and kept the column moving. He even got down to swing a pick and shovel with the engineers laboring on the trail. When he reached the river at 7 p.m., he was more than satisfied with Custer's feat. Reporter Kellogg, completely overwhelmed by his dazzling ride in the van, elaborated at length on Custer's triumph.

The trail-weary command failed to record the arrival of another courier bearing a dispatch from Major Moore, dated at Stanley's Crossing, June 5th:

> I have the honor to acknowledge the receipt of your communication by the scouts. Today the Far West starts for Powder River in compliance with your instructions.
>
> The boat is loaded as directed with 75 tons of forage and 15 days'

subsistence stores for 1200 men, hospital stores, private packages for the officers, and I have taken the responsibility, trusting that it will meet with your approval, to place upon the boat the ammunition, including the 10,000 rounds of half-inch Gatling, which I brought from Buford. I am aware of your appreciation of plenty of ammunition.

Captain Grant Marsh is fully assured that the Far West can make the trip with his present freight without difficulty. I send Captain [James W.] Powell with his Comapny C, 6th Infantry, on the boat with orders to report as soon as practicable. I forward your dispatches to General Gibbon by two scouts, giving them the benefit of the authorized extra pay for the trip. They will make it with dispatches at all hazards. One of the scouts [Williamson] belongs to General Gibbon's command, who came down with the late dispatches which you received forwarded by me.

I have no information of Indians in this vicinity and the scouts report no Indians seen on their return from your command. (O-9)

In response to this communication Terry at 10 p.m. of the evening he arrived at Powder River sent a party of Rees down to the Yellowstone to contact the *Far West*. They reached the boat the next morning and were promptly sent back to Terry. Arriving at 11 a.m. of June 8th, they brought some welcome mail and a dispatch from Captain Powell, dated 8:45 a.m., June 8, on board the *Far West* near the mouth of Powder River:

Your scouts just arrived here. The Far West is cutting wood a mile below Powder River — will be at the mouth of Powder River in an hour. Have not seen any Indians or any trace of Indians.

The two civilian scouts who were disembarked on the north side of the Yellowstone on the evening of June 6th at Custer's Creek with your dispatches to General Gibbon, returned here this morning at 6 o'clock, reporting that they proceeded to within a couple of miles of Tongue River yesterday afternoon,that they there observed a party of about forty Indians, on the same side of the river, and claiming to have been discovered, determined to return here.

Believing this information of importance to the command, General, I immediately sent a small boat down the river, anticipating that your command would be met near O'Fallon's Creek.

This boat with the supplies ordered left the stockade June 5th, 1:05 p.m.; arrived at Powder River June 6, 9:15 p.m. Running time, 14 hours and 38 minutes. No trouble at Powder River rapids. Minimum water, 5½ feet. River rising rapidly. (O-9)

Although pleased to learn that the supply-laden boat was in position, Terry was distressed to read that the couriers sent to halt Gibbon upriver had been turned back by hostiles. He was growing more anxious daily to contact the Montana column. He needed Indian intelligence, and he wanted to bring the two forces into concerted action as quickly as possible. There had already been enough costly delays. He decided to make a trip to the Yellowstone that very afternoon and commandeer the *Far West* to make personal contact with Gibbon.

Before leaving camp, however, Terry ordered the three infantry companies to prepare to escort the wagon train down to the Yellowstone, and the entire 7th Cavalry to prepare to take pack mules on an eight-day reconnaissance south up Powder River in search of the exasperating enemy. Eleven pack mules having been assigned to each company, the troopers turned out for instruction in the art of packing by the civilian packers. Since the mules were as green as the troopers, the combination generated more bruises and hilarity than progress.

At 12:30 on the afternoon of June 8th, Terry started for the Yellowstone, escorted by Companies A and I, 7th Cavalry. This gave Custer the opportunity to insert the following coy sentence in his second letter to the New York *Herald*; "Terry's brief absence left Custer in temporary command of the expedition, Grant's positive orders to the contrary notwithstanding." Of course, since Custer was the second ranking officer, Terry had no choice, but neither is there any reason to believe that he had any qualms in the matter.

Terry's ride was a tiring one, the more so because he felt duty-bound to extend it beyond the minimum 24 miles by prospecting for a trail suitable for wagons. Reporter Kellogg had remarked that Terry, in contrast to Custer, did not thrive on heroic exertions. One day he had suffered a sun-stroke and had to take to the ambulance for the rest of the day. On reaching the *Far West* at 8 o'clock that night, a pleasant surprise banished some of the General's fatigue. On board he found a detachment from Gibbon's command that had arrived by Herendeen's boats only a few hours before. This party included Captain Clifford and his company, as well as Major Brisbin and Lt. G.C. Doane, who had joined the mariners for the day. With them were three Crows and George Herendeen, still an unpaid volunteer.

Knowing that his latest orders to Gibbon had not been delivered, Terry undoubtedly interrogated the Montana officers and scouts to learn of Gibbon's whereabouts and operations. The results must have appalled the Department Commander.

*   *   *

We must now resume Gibbon's story from the evening of May 27th, when he had sent his three couriers downriver by skiff. The very next morning the enterprising Paul McCormick docked his mackinaw at the camp opposite the Rosebud, bringing more trade goods and the mail from Fort Ellis. The mail included Terry's orders of May 15th directing Gibbon to march to Glendive and on east to help trap Sitting Bull on the Little Missouri. These orders disturbed Lt. Bradley, for he well knew that the hostiles had already moved west from the Tongue to the Rosebud and were far from Terry's assumed location. To march downriver now would leave the village free to move where it pleased, even across into the wild north country. Captain Freeman also commented unhappily that "I'm afraid our work will all be for naught, unless the different columns cooperate more intelligently than heretofore."

General Gibbon, however, voiced no misgivings at moving far from the long-sought quarry. This may have contributed to a flare-up of friction in the command at this time. Dr. Paulding had a tiff with the General over the management of medical supplies; the frustrated Bradley discharged some indignation at camp-bound officers who questioned his scouting findings.

Despite his new orders, Gibbon idled in camp for over a week, ignoring the hostile village and a party of ten Sioux seen on the north bank on May 28th. The next day he detailed two companies to escort his now-empty train of wagons back upstream to meet the expected Diamond R train and share its load. On the 31st Captain Whelan's company, guided by Tom LeForge and five Crows, made a meaningless scout seventeen miles upriver and back. The only move in the direction of the village came on the 30th, when two Crows set out on their own hook to steal horses, but were driven back by thirty Sioux. Captain Freeman understood these Crows to report that the village was moving closer, but they actually moved farther up the Rosebud that day.

On June 1st and 2nd the vegetating troops huddled in their tents under a blanket of snow. Dr. Paulding took the opportunity to record in his diary: "I dare say the village up Rosebud has left — anyhow there is nothing to prevent, if they want to go." Finally on June 4th, the Diamond R train under diarist Matt Carroll pulled into camp bringing in all the detached units to restore the command to full strength. Even Barney Bravo and the two Crows returned with the train, having secured enough ponies from the Crow village to remount all of Bradley's Indian scouts.

On June 5th, the column began its march downstream to meet General Terry, Clifford's company again taking the small boats. Four days of liesurely travel took them fifty-seven miles to a point opposite and seventeen miles below the mouth of Tongue River. Early on the last day, June 8th, Bradley's Crows found the trail of two shod horses and picked up a whiteman knapsack. The sign revealed that the pair had been coming upstream, but had abruptly fled down again. These were, in fact, scout Williamson and companion bringing Terry's orders to halt his march. Just as they were about to win their $200 bonuses, the Crow scouts, whom they mistook for Sioux, had scared them off.

That same morning Major Brisbin and Lt. Doane joined Clifford's boat company, and because of a mistake in the delivery of Gibbon's orders, they proceeded all the way to Powder River in one day, much to the General's irritation. Clifford's narrative reveals that he was unaware of Gibbon's real intentions:

> On the evening of June 7th, I was notified that, being in the boats, I must take care of myself for two days . . . The main column was not expected to strike the river again until opposite the mouth of Powder River, on account of the broken country that bordered that stream . . . Ran to Powder River, where, instead of a large body of Indians, as had been surmised, found the steamer Far West, Captain Grant Marsh. On the boat were Captain Powell, and Lt. Bronson, 6th Infantry, in command of the guard. They had heard exaggerated reports of our being in a starving condition.

That evening of June 8th on the *Far West* Terry probably first learned that Lt. Bradley had kept track of a village large enough to harbor the majority of winter roamers as it moved from the Tongue to the Rosebud; that an attempt to cross and attack it had been aborted; that Gibbon had ignored it while idling a week nearby before unconcernedly marching away from it. There is no record of Terry's reactions, but that very night he dispatched couriers with orders for Gibbon to hold his force in camp and come down in person to report.

The couriers selected to carry these orders were George Herendeen, whom Clifford had found to be exceptionally capable and reliable, and one of the Crows. They slipped off the boat that night and reported to Gibbon at 2 a.m. Only then did Gibbon learn what had become of his flotilla and that others than himself had been the first to contact Terry. Dr. Paulding recorded that "Brisbin, of course, accomplished his object in getting in the first word with Terry, and Gibbon is very hot about it apparently." Perhaps Gibbon was also smarting from the tone of Terry's summons, although the latter has not been found.

On the morning of June 9th, Terry started upriver on the boat, while Gibbon marched down with a small escort. At 11 a.m. they met, and conferred on the boat until 12:30, when it reached Gibbon's camp and Terry devoted half an hour to a courtesy reception of all the Montana officers. At 1 p.m. he cast off for Powder River. Lacking any record of the long conference, we can only point out that although Terry was ordinarily gracious and diplomatic, he had also been a lawyer in civil life. He may have cross-examined his subordinate as a hostile witness in order to wring him dry of useful information otherwise left unmentioned. It may have been a painful session for Gibbon.

Terry at last could replace a vacuum with tangible intelligence to guide the formulation of a plan of operations. He instantly ordered Gibbon to hike back on the double to his former camp opposite the Rosebud, sending the cavalry ahead that very afternoon and the infantry no later than the next morning. On arrival he was to prevent the Rosebud village from crossing to the north, presuming it had not already taken advantage of his neglect. He was to prepare to take the offensive as soon as Terry could return on the steamboat, approximately a week hence. During that week Terry would have his own force scout the Powder River to make sure there were no hostiles that far east and south, for which purpose he commandeered the services of Mitch Boyer, Gibbon's scout most familiar with the country.

In his annual report (O-39,1876), Gibbon mentions meeting Terry on the boat and adds that "in accordance with his instructions the command at once prepared to move up the river again, but a furious rain-storm that afternoon delayed the movement." In his popular account he gave a version that defies credulity:

> The existence of any large camps of hostile Indians in this region was now more than ever a matter of doubt . . . [But he was sent back to Bradley's village]. He [Terry] intended on his return to Powder River to send a cavalry command on a scout up the river and across it west to the Tongue and Rosebud. [Terry planned to shun the Rosebud.] If no Indians should be discovered there, the only remaining chance would be higher up the Yellowstone, where from my observations there must be some Indians [he had seen none above the Rosebud], and if General Crook should strike them from the south, it would be all the more necessary for us to guard the line of the river and prevent any escape northward. He therefore instructed me to retrace my steps and await his arrival at the mouth of the Rosebud, and as dispatch was now more important than ever, I agreed to start the cavalry part of my command that afternoon [but failed to do so].

In composing these passages, Gibbon seems to reveal himself as a very disoriented intelligence officer, or a very inept dissembler. Maybe his recollection of the conference was still painful.

Chapter 10
Second Check on the Rosebud

Having come to regret that he had turned over the command of his winter campaign to a subordinate, General Crook assumed personal command of the Big Horn and Yellowstone Expedition at Fort Fetterman on May 28th. Sobered by the realization that two hundred hostile warriors had proved a match for General Reynolds' four hundred cavalrymen, he had this time stripped his Department of troops to fashion a stronger force. But he had also gambled by trading thirty-two scouts in the hand for hundreds of Indian allies still in the bush. He bore this nagging worry alone, however, for he was practised at concealing his inner feelings from even those closest to him.

Crook's Wyoming column was as strong as Terry's Fort Lincoln and Fort Buford units combined. Colonel William B. Royall, 3rd Cavalry, commanded fifteen companies of cavalry (ten of the 3rd, and 5 of the 2nd), while Colonel Alexander Chambers, 4th Infantry, commanded five companies of infantry (three of the 9th, two of the 4th). Including command and staff, the total came to 51 officers and 1000 men. Veteran Thomas Moore took charge of the efficient pack train of 81 men and 250 mules, and Charles Russell controlled the wagon train of 116 men and 106 wagons. But the sole quartermaster scouts were Frank Grouard, Big Bat Pourier, and Louis Richard.

The column was sufficiently supplied with correspondents to prove that President Grant's injunction against reporters, "who always make trouble," applied only to Custer. The press corps boasted Reuben H. Davenport (New York *Herald*), John F. Finerty (Chicago *Times*), Thomas B. Macmillan (Chicago *Inter-Ocean*),

110

Robert A. Strahorn (Denver *Rocky Mountain News* and Cheyenne *Sun*), and Joseph Wasson (San Franciso *Alta California*). A number of expedition officers contributed even more useful chronicles. Lt. John G. Bourke maintained his diary and Captain William Stanton, engineering officer, kept an official itinerary. Captain Gerhard L. Luhn, 4th Infantry, and Lt. Thaddeus H. Capron, 9th Infantry, also preserved diaries and letters, while 2nd Lt. James E.H. Foster, 3rd Cavalry, submitted his journal to the Chicago *Tribune* and supplied sketches to *Harper's Weekly*.

At noon of May 29th, a bright spring day, the Big Horn and Yellowstone Expedition stretched out from Fort Fetterman on the dusty Bozeman trail, now familiar to the few who had also served on the winter campaign. All were aware that their immediate destination was old Fort Reno on Powder River, where they would pick up their Crow and Shoshone allies. Beyond that they knew nothing, but they had swallowed the rumors that all the agency Indians were flocking out to give them battle. The afternoon march of ten miles took them to a barren camp on Sage Creek.

What Crook's tight lips and poker face concealed, his actions betrayed. He had earlier sent Grouard with a squad, and then Captain van Vliet with a battalion, to old Fort Reno to greet the Crows. And now, on the morning of the 30th, from this first camp on Sage Creek, he ordered Captain Meinhold to take Grouard and two companies of 3rd Cavalry, rationed for four days, on still another reconnaissance to the west of the main column. Sources differ as to its objective, but all agreed that its mission was unsuccessful. Some thought it was to seek a better crossing of Powder River, though it seems not to have ventured that far, and it would have been superfluous, since van Vliet's battalion was already there. Others thought it was to patrol on the left flank in search of hostile trails, although the hostiles were to the east and friendly Shoshones to the west. It was Grouard who revealed that they were looking for Indian allies, undoubtedly the Shoshones.

That night the main column camped at the site where the Indians had stampeded the rations-on-the-hoof of the winter campaign. The irrepressible Lt. Foster noted that the herders were particularly apprehensive that night, and as poet-laureate of the expedition he composed the following couplet:

> If Sitting Bull doth steal our meat,
> What shall we do for grub to eat?

The balmy spring weather fled in the face of a chill northern blast during the next day's march, and the troops awakened on June 1st to a hard snow-storm. But on they pushed into the driving snow and sleet. Reporter Strahorn painted a capsule sketch of General Crook, who "rode at the head of the column, his long blond side-whiskers wrapped in twine after the manner of an Indian scalp-lock . . . He is a strange man. Singularly quiet and reticent, he is thought cold and perhaps heartless by many. Certainly his face indicates ambition, determination, and a crafty — almost fox-like — shrewdness . . . One who knows him well said, 'He's just like an Indian. He can live on acorns and slippery elm bark,' — and I believe it." The campaign would validate all these observations, save the General's crafty shrewdness.

Grouard and Captain Meinhold's patrol rejoined Crook that evening in camp on the Dry Fork of Powder River, having found no sign of Indians, friendly or hostile. To Crook, this signalled that the Shoshones were delayed or reluctant to join, but reporter Finerty, with Irish impatience, was already crying, "Where are the Sioux?" At this camp the men noted substantial rifle-pits and a message inscribed on a board, announcing that a large party of Montana prospectors had camped there on May 27th, preparing to head for the Black Hills in two groups. The names identify this as Captain Langston's party that had conferred with General Gibbon at the Crow Agency on April 8th. They had moved leisurely, prospecting every stream heading in the Big Horns. They had found neither "colors" nor Indians, revealing that the latter were still far to the east.

Still shivering in the fading snow-flurries, the column reached the site of old Fort Reno on June 2nd, 90 miles out from Fort Fetterman. There Captain van Vliet's waiting battalion greeted them with the ominous news that not a single Indian ally had kept the rendezvous. Crook's situation was now desperate. He *must* have Indian allies, or look the fool by blundering around blind-folded. His only hope of gaining allies was to send his few scouts out to secure them. This would utterly strip his command of guides, but during their temporary absence he could lead the column himself along the trail of the winter campaign. Without hesitation, he summoned Grouard, Pourier, and Richard and asked them to undertake the dangerous trip to the distant Crow Agency and there persuade, cajole, bribe, or shanghai as many braves as possible to join the expedition.

Since the mission might consume a week or more, the three scouts advised the General to proceed to the forks of Goose Creek (present Sheridan, Wyo.) and there await their return. He would find the place easily defended and well supplied with wood, water, and grass. Furthermore, it was on the safer edge of the Sioux country, yet gave easy access to all the Sioux-frequented valleys, from the Little Big Horn to Powder River. The forks were only one easy day's march beyond old Fort Phil Kearney, but along the Bozeman trail to the northwest, rather than due north on the trail the General had taken on the winter campaign. We can almost hear the trio saying, "You can't miss 'em, General."

As for themselves, the scouts expressed confidence in their ability to sneak through the enemy country in safety, and to induce the Crows to volunteer. Although Grouard was a stranger to the tribe, both Big Bat, known to them as "Left Hand," and Louis had traded among them out of Bozeman from 1865 to 1868. They probably also carried a plea from Captain Andrew S. Burt, 9th Infantry, who had made friends with the Crows while he had commanded old Fort C.F. Smith. After dark that night of June 2nd, the bold trio stole out of the Fort Reno camp on their crucial mission. Every officer and newsman bade them Godspeed, for they were now beginning to recognize the helplessness of their force without "eyes." They would be as nervous as Crook before the trio belatedly returned.

For the next three days the General guided the column for 63 miles over the Bozeman trail past Crazy Woman's Fork, then Clear Fork, and finally straight to the abandoned Fort Phil Kearney. But for lack of reassuring scouts, rumors of Indians suddenly began to circulate. The men debated every distant object, now more visible in the clear, spring-like air. Was it a spying redskin, or a buffalo? A dust-devil, or a smoke signal? Then two bearded prospectors strolled in from their large camp a day behind, saying that while prospecting from the Black Hills to the Big Horns, they had seen nothing of Indians, except a few fresh trails heading north. Lt. Foster ruled that honors were even, since the traffic of miners between Montana and the Hills was equal in the two directions.

On June 6th, Crook resumed the trail, expecting to reach the rendezvous at the forks of Goose Creek early that afternoon. But after passing the tragic Fetterman Hill, the trail faded out in a grassy valley. Turning north too soon, Crook crossed the divide to the head of Prairie Dog Creek and descended it, thereby resuming the trail of the winter campaign. After a taxing 18 mile march that ended in a cold and dispiriting downpour, the bewildered column bivouacked on the creek, roughly six miles east of their planned destination. None was more surprised than Captain Noyes, whose small party had hastened ahead that morning to exploit the trout waters of Goose Creek. When the main column failed to materialize at the expected time, they turned back in search of it. When they finally found it, fear of a night approach to trigger-happy pickets compelled them to remain out all night, to the concern of their friends.

The chroniclers were indeed confused that night. Captain Stanton officially located the camp on "Hay Creek," and reporter Finerty unofficially on "Beaver Creek." Lt. Bourke recorded that they were on a branch of Goose Creek, but the next day was surprised to find that it was Prairie Dog Creek. Others called it Peno Creek that night and Prairie Dog the next day. Lt. Foster said it best by writing that they were on "Prairie Dog Creek, or Peno Creek — nobody is absolutely certain which." Others were silent, but whether from confusion or discretion is not clear. That night the Adjutant announced that Crook was making for Tongue River!

Crook had clearly missed the trail. The Adjutant's announcement implies that he had belatedly discovered that he was on the trail of the winter campaign. But why did he elect to march north down this creek to Tongue River the next day? It was not the prearranged rendezvous, and he knew it was hard to defend, poorly supplied, and less strategically located. Worst of all, it was deep enough in enemy country to invite discovery, a dangerous eventuality when he planned merely to sit and wait for the Crows. Was he sensitive about his gaff as a guide and seeking to save face? Or, was he sparing his men the loss of confidence that an admission of an error might bring? Although unaware of it, his error was already bringing its penalty; a hunting party of Cheyennes, including Wooden Leg, had stumbled on his column that afternoon and watched it bivouac in the rain. They would follow it for a day, and then race for the camp of the winter-roamers to sound the tocsin.

The next day, June 7th, Crook sported after buffalo in the van, while the column trudged 17 miles down the sinuous Prairie Dog Creek to its junction with Tongue River at the Wyoming-Montana line, 188 miles from Fort Fetterman. In the narrow bottom, under commanding bluffs, the men set up what they presumed was a permanent base camp, "but nobody knows but Gen. Crook and he won't tell," wrote Lt. Foster. That midnight, the insomniacs heard a strange Indian voice from across the Tongue hail the camp. Ben Arnold, a frontiersman hired for courier service, was called upon to answer the mysterious voice. He later recalled that he understood little, for the language seemed to be Crow, and darkness prevented recourse to the sign language. Others stated that when Ben answered in Sioux, the voice fell abruptly silent. The next morning, however, the rumor mills were grinding out indignant stories about Ben's long-winded betrayal of every state secret to a cunning party of Sioux spies.

114

That day the troops idled in camp. A few Black Hillers, discouraged with luckless prospecting, ambled into camp and attached themselves to the expedition. A cavalry patrol found the fresh tracks of five Indians, thought to be the spies of the night before. Then two couriers rode in with mail from Fort Fetterman. Crook learned that Sheridan had ordered the 5th Cavalry up from Kansas to control the exodus of Sioux from their agencies. The best news was that 130 Shoshone allies were on their way and should join the command any day. The worst was that a down telegraph wire had prevented delivery of the call for Crow allies.

Bored with inactivity, the ranks speculated on Crook's secretive plans, the fate of the missing trio of scouts, and the whereabouts of the enemy. The concensus was that the redskins were far distant on the Yellowstone harassing Gibbon's force and that of the hopefully approaching Terry. But these debates turned academic in an instant, when at retreat on June 9th, a heavy fusillade of shots from the commanding bluffs across the river riddled the neat rows of soldier tents, fortunately nearly unoccupied. "A soldier was seriously shot through the tail of his blouse . . . Captain Luhn was seriously injured in the ridge-pole of his tent . . . and Colonel Mills was hurt in the stove-pipe," was Lt. Foster's comment. He added that the uncontrolled return fire of the packers and teamsters laid "a first-class foundation for a lead mine in the face of the cliff."

In more seemly and disciplined fashion, four companies of cavalry assembled their horses, saddled up, mounted, trotted a few feet across the Tongue, dismounted, and detached one-fourth of their number as horse-holders; the remainder then charged up the bluff on foot in skirmish order. They drove the raiders back beyond several successive ridges. They estimated the attackers at from 50 to 900, although they glimpsed no more than a handful at any one time, Lt. Capron specifying eight or ten. They were, in fact, but a few Cheyennes under Little Hawk, who had responded to the alarm Wooden Leg's hunters had brought in by launching a scouting and horse-stealing sortie. Their rapid fire was a cover for a bold attempt to stampede the horses, and might have succeeded, except that the animals had just been run in for grooming. The casualties totalled two soldiers slightly wounded and several animals hit.

The command idled away one more day in this ill-chosen camp before Crook finally decided to rectify his original mistake. On the morning of June 11th, the entire force retreated eleven miles back up Prairie Dog Creek and then broke a new trail for seven miles southwest to set up a new base camp at the forks of Goose Creek, once again in a rain. Everyone lavishly praised the advantages of the new location, some even fashioning the impression that they had advanced deeper into enemy country. The reasons the various chroniclers chose to give for the move are revealing.

Lt. Bourke, the General's aide and partisan, attributed the move to a need for fresh grazing. Finerty lamely wrote that Crook was "restive" and did not "like" the Tongue River location. Captain Stanton at least officially disclosed that the new camp had been "the place appointed to await" the Indian allies, and that it gave strategic access to all the valleys of the Indian country. Macmillan dared to call it a "retrograde movement," and ingeniously suggested that its purpose was "to throw the Northern Sioux, watching the course of the march, off their guard." It remained for Strahorn to call a spade a spade: "The expedition, having marched to Tongue River, has marched back again to Goose Creek, where it was originally Crook's intention to establish a depot of supplies after leaving Fort Phil Kearney. Through somebody's blundering, the trail was missed." This retreat failed to confuse the Sioux, but it did nearly cost Crook the services of the Crows.

The new base camp was as idle as the first. A few went out to fish or hunt, but most amused themselves with rumors and speculations. Where were the scouts and the promised Indian allies? Would Crook send the wagon train back to replenish steadily dwindling supplies? Now that two weeks had passed, would he strip down the cavalry and go after the Sioux? Officers and reporters tried to extract some clue from their sphynx-like commander, but even Lt. Bourke's devious queries met with snubs. Lt. Foster was moved to write that Crook "has a faculty for silence that is absolutely astonishing. There is one thing very certain: none of the General's plans will ever be discussed until after they are executed − a precious quality in a commanding officer. Grant is loquacious when compared to him."

But Crook's silence concealed, not plans, but acute anxiety. At dawn of June 13th, he dispatched a detail under Lt. Samuel M. Swigert, 2nd Cavalry, back to Fort Phil Kearney to find the expected Shoshones. When they returned that evening, empty-handed, Lt. Capron recorded that "the General is quite weary and nervous, and it is thought that he is feeling very anxious about the safety of the guides that were sent out from [Fort] Reno." He was nervous indeed at the waiting that ate supplies as fast as campaigning, and the growing horror of being forced to operate blindly with neither white nor Indians scouts.

The mounting tension finally broke on the afternoon of June 14th, when Frank Grouard and Louis Richard galloped into camp escorting a single tall Crow chief. Cheering soldiers led them to head-quarters, where they answered Crook's rapid-fire questions. Yes, more Crows were coming than the single chief here. No, Big Bat was not lost. He was holding 175 Crow volunteers ten miles out, where they awaited assurances that they were welcome. The elated General promptly ordered Captain Burt, the former friend of the Crows, to go back with Richard and escort the allies into camp, while he arranged a suitable military reception.

The revivified reporters gathered to pump Grouard for the story of the twelve-day mission. After leaving camp at dusk of June 2nd, the trio of scouts had traveled mostly by night to avoid hostile parties. Arriving at the Big Horn below old Fort C.F. Smith on June 7th, they prepared to raft across its flooded waters, only to be charged by a horde of feathered braves. Just in time Big Bat recognized them as Crows and identified himself to them as their old friend, Left Hand. Welcoming them effusively, the warriors escorted them to their village eight miles west on a branch of the Big Horn. In council that night, the scouts announced that they had come for volunteers to scout for Crook against their enemies, the Sioux.

At this first council the chiefs voiced the same objections to scouting for Crook as they had spelled out so uncomfortably to Gibbon two months earlier. But the scouts were not so easily put off. For the next four days they blandished the more responsive chiefs, taunted the young men, threatened to pull out and inform Crook that the Crows were women, and worked every Indian psychology on the wavering braves. Frank named Old Crow as their first convert among the chiefs, who then exerted his powerful influence on the young men. An item in the Bozeman *Times* of June 22nd fully confirms this story: "A council to obtain two hundred Crows for Crook was held, but the chiefs were averse to it. After lengthy discussion, chief Crow walked out from the circle and announced that he accepted Crook's proposition, when almost immediately about half of the warriors of the tribe volunteered, leaving the old men and boys to protect themselves at home."

Following this break, the entire village moved eastward to the Big Horn river. The scouts had learned that Crook had missed their rendezvous, for five Crows came in reporting that they had hailed a soldier camp at the mouth of Prairie Dog Creek under cover of darkness (June 7th), but had fled when answered in Sioux. On June 12th, the three scouts left the village with their volunteers to join Crook at the mouth of Prairie Dog Creek. They camped that night on the Little Big Horn, sending out scouts to look for signs of Sioux.

The next day they bagged some buffalo as they ascended Owl Creek, an eastern branch of the Little Big Horn that heads in the Wolf Mountains in the direction of their destination. The next morning from a peak Frank was surprised to spot Crook's white-tented camp, not east on the Tongue, but south at the forks of Goose Creek, as originally planned. To the Crows, the soldiers had obviously retreated from Sioux country, confirming their worst misgivings about the white man's clumsy and irresolute manner of campaigning. This triggered a near mutiny. Big Bat stayed behind to cool them down and hold them, while Frank and Louis hurried ahead with faithful Old Crow to see General Crook.

The return of Louis with their old friend, Capt. Burt, reassured the skittish Crows, and late that afternoon the colorful cavalcade mock-charged into Crook's camp where a formal line of troops received them and the General, outwardly solemn but inwardly rejoicing, welcomed them. The hubbub had scarcely subsided when it broke out again at the sight of 86 Shoshone warriors approaching in disciplined ranks under the command of Tom Cosgrove, a Confederate Cavalry veteran. They had left Camp Brown on their Wind River reservation on June 5th, 130 strong, but one-third had turned back, leaving the remainder to cross the Big Horns in search of Crook. That evening the enormously relieved General presided over a grand feast and council lighted by bonfires, after which the newcomers made the night ring with their singing, dancing, and visiting.

But even before holding this ceremonial council, Crook had held an officer's call, at which he ordered a strike force to make ready. They would cut loose not only from the wagon train but from the pack train as well. The men could take only a blanket a piece and no spare clothing. They would carry four day's rations and 100 rounds of ammunition in their saddle bags. Even the infantry and civilian volunteers would have to go mounted. They would have only the morrow to prepare, for they would start at daylight of June 16th. As Finerty put it, Crook was "spoiling for a fight."

Energy is laudable, but so is direction. Where was the General expecting to strike? The information gathered by the reporters, and even Lt. Bourke, reveals that enemy intelligence was not their forte. They learned from the Crows that Gibbon was camped opposite the Tongue, or Rosebud, where the assembled hostiles, "numerous as the grass," were harrassing him from south of the Yellowstone. The Sioux had stolen all the ponies of Gibbon's scouts (six weeks ago!). The hostile village was camped on Tongue River, somewhere between its mouth (135 miles distant) and Otter Creek (70 miles distant), or perhaps on the Yellowstone somewhere. From

118

this these experts concluded that the column would march 80 or 90 miles to the mouth of the Tongue or Rosebud. Since they would take only four day's rations, their 1300 would then forage off of Gibbon's 400!

This budget of intelligence not only failed to balance — it was woefully stale. But even Crook pretended to have no better knowledge when he officially reported on June 20th that "the Crow Indians were under the impression that the hostile village was located on Tongue River, or some of its small tributaries (O-39,1876)." That he wrote without truth is proved by his prompt movement directly to the head of Rosebud Creek, without so much as a pause at the crossing of Tongue River. We shall find that Crook's actions often belie his words.

Grouard recalled that he reported to the General that from the signs he had seen he supposed the Sioux were camped on the Rosebud. Since he could have seen signs only on his return from the Crow village, the reference was to the upper, not lower, Rosebud. He presumably also reported that the Little Big Horn was clear of hostiles. Reporter Davenport revealed that early on June 15th Crook sent five Crows out to scout for the enemy. On the same date the reliable Lt. Foster recorded that "a Sioux village of 700 lodges, which means 2500 warriors [sic!], is on the Rosebud, about 45 miles from here." Only this kind of information accounts for Crook's direct march to the upper Rosebud, rationed for a mere four days. Since his pack train could move as fast, and keep it up longer, than his cavalry, there was no need to leave it behind, if he had planned to march far.

With the benefit of hindsight and vastly more information than was available to Crook, we can state that on June 14th, the consolidated village of winter roamers, about 450 lodges strong, was camped on Rosebud Creek at present Busby, only 52 direct miles from Crook's camp at Sheridan. They were about to cross westward over the divide toward the valley of the Little Big Horn, fully aware of the proximity of the soldier force. In addition, a small party under the Cheyenne chief, Magpie Eagle, was approaching the same neighborhood as the van guard of the summer roamers.

On June 15th, Crook's camp sprang alive with preparations for action. Captain John V. Furey, the expedition quartermaster, corraled the wagon train and pack mules, where he would guard them with a force of teamsters and packers. Sheridan saw its first rodeo that day when 175 green infantrymen essayed to ride 175 unbroken wagon mules! The struggle was traumatic and exasperating for both, but the throng of cheering spectators found it wonderfully amusing. In fact, every man was either so shaken or so entertained that none thought to raise an obvious question. If Crook had planned to mount his infantry, why had he left them to idle away a solid week while postponing the training exercises until the last possible moment? But nightfall did find one thousand soldiers, 85 volunteer packers, teamsters, and miners, and 262 Indian allies ready for action.

At 6 a.m. on June 16th the confident troops left their dull camp with the Indian allies swarming in the van and on the flanks. Traveling north, they descended Goose Creek, crossed the Tongue, picked up a dry branch of the latter and followed it up northwest to the divide between the valleys of the Tongue and Rosebud. Here they halted for several hours in the afternoon, while the scouts investigated a buffalo herd that was acting as though disturbed by hunters. Plenty Coups, one of the Crows, recalled that he exchanged insults with a few scattered hostiles. So did Grouard, who noted that they fled in a direction that suggested that their village lay nearby on the Rosebud.

By this time the reporters had picked up the rumor that the hostile camp was not far down the Rosebud. The rumor was wrong, however, and would bring unfortunate consequences. Only Magpie Eagle's small party was camped on Trail Creek, a small eastern branch of the Rosebud not far above Busby. The main hostile village, however, was already moving into the valley of the Little Big Horn, having again sent Little Hawk to spy on Crook's force. It was their pause to hunt that had disturbed the buffalo herd, but they quickly spotted the approaching soldier column. They whipped their ponies back to the village to warn of this threat. That night, true warriors rather than boys and old men, streamed out to turn back the invaders before they could threaten the village of women and children. These braves were soon joined by others from Magpie Eagle's band. The combined total of 500 lodges could not muster a thousand warriors, and if no more than one-fourth stayed behind to defend the villages, the top limit on the attacking force becomes 750.

The hostile hunters having fled the scene, the Crows and Shoshones happily replenished their larders by making a rousing buffalo hunt that strewed the landscape with carcasses and filled the air with gunfire. Crook seethed at this careless broadcast of his presence, but dared to say nothing for fear of alienating the scouts on whom he so depended. In the meantime, the column resumed the trail to complete the day's rugged march of 33 miles. They bivouacked at 7:20 p.m. on the very source of the south fork of Rosebud

Creek. When Colonel Chambers, commanding the rear, reached the cavalry already in bivouac, he proudly turned to review his plucky infantry who had survived their first long day in the saddle. At that strategic moment, 175 mules relieved themselves by braying in one hideous chorus! The apoplectic Colonel stalked off in mortification, while the delighted cavalrymen slapped their thighs in uproarious mirth. That night the Indian allies, convinced of the proximity of a formidable body of hostiles, proved reluctant to undertake the nocturnal scouting missions that Crook requested.

Reveille sounded at 3 o'clock on the morning of the fateful 17th of June. A party of Crow scouts having been early sent ahead, the van of the long column began the march at 6 a.m. Moving down the south fork, they picked up the main Rosebud, which there runs due east for a bit before turning abruptly north. After an hour's ride of 3 miles, they noted the scouts signalling that they had found signs of the enemy. In the narrow valley, bordered north and south by rolling bluffs, Crook halted his command. The men unsaddled, picketed their animals in the lush bottom meadow, and with sticks and blankets erected impromptu shelters against the blazing sun. Eight companies of cavalry rested on the south of the trickle of water, the remainder of the force on the north bank. Time passed drowsily for an hour or more.

Faint at first, but growing steadily louder, came the sound of firing from the north beyond the bluffs. A few excited scouts then dashed in to warn that the Sioux, first seen far to the north, were now pressing closer. The alert Shoshones and the remaining Crows lost no time in rushing to the front, where they carried the battle alone for some time before the resting troops were aroused. The infantry and civilians on the north bank were the first to advance on foot in skirmish line to support the scouts. Once on high ground they sighted a furious number of Sioux and Cheyennes swarming from every direction against the Crows and Shoshones, driving them steadily back. Soon the cavalry joined the fray, principally on the right and left. One battalion, ordered to occupy the bluffs to the south, arrived just in time to deny this vantage point to a circling party of feathered warriors.

Almost before Crook could size up the situation, the resolute Sioux and Cheyennes, who proved wonderfully quick to exploit every opening, compelled him to throw nearly the whole of his 1300 effectives into action. The attackers shrewdly gave way before every charge of the troops, but as the advancing fingers splayed out, they attacked them separately from every quarter, making the most effective use of the broken ground. Their spirited war ponies whisked

121

them out of site at one point and returned them promptly at another, giving the troops a grossly exaggerated idea of their strength. Still, the weight of numbers could only have turned the battle against the hostiles, had Crook not tried to withdraw half of his cavalry for a separate attack on the village, which he believed to lie only six or eight miles down the Rosebud.

His battalion commanders, sensing victory, were mystified by the orders to withdraw, and when they obeyed, they took a severe beating. Nothing so fired up a warrior as the appearance of a retreat. They charged the moving units on the flanks, caught them in deadly cross-fire, and threatened to cut them off. The fighting was furious and incessant, and raged at a number of points not fully visible to one another. Skillful tactics and fierce execution marked the alert hostiles, and no less the Indian allies. Many soldiers, even companies, owed their survival to the brave Crows and Shoshones. The officers had not witnessed such brilliant and intense fighting since the Civil War.

Despite the difficulties, Crook succeeded, well before noon, in disengaging Captain Mills' battalion of 3rd Cavalry and Captain Noyes' battalion of 2nd Cavalry. He ordered Mills to lead them down the circling Rosebud to attack the village and hold it until Crook could bring the main command up. Grouard, assigned to guide Mill's column, protested the move, explaining that the canyon slopes were covered with brush and felled trees which the enemy could exploit as a ready-made ambuscade. Not until after Mills had left did Crook begin to realize that the hostiles made a desperate match for his depleted force. He tried to concentrate them, but every movement drew a furious attack. His troops proved powerless to do more than defend themselves.

Mills' column marched cautiously down the hill-girt valley, every eye alert. They reached the abrupt bend and followed the ominously narrowing canyon northward for a short distance. At that moment, Adjutant A.H. Nickerson galloped up with orders from Crook to return to the battlefield to support the hard-pressed main force. Mills promptly filed out of the canyon to the left and soon found himself on the flank and rear of the hostiles, still fighting furiously. At his approach, however, they broke off the action, fading into the hills and ravines to the north and west. The Battle of the Rosebud ended early that afternoon.

Crook made a final effort to push his now reunited command down the stream to find and destroy the village which he still believed was not far off. But when he saw the terrain for himself, and the refusal of his Indian allies to enter the narrows, he gave it up, and returned to bivouac in the valley where the fight had begun. Sober and chastened, the command buried its dead and treated its wounded. A survey of ten sources provides the names of nine soldiers killed and 23 wounded. The Indian allies suffered seven severely wounded and one Shoshone killed. There may have been as many as thirty more soldiers slightly wounded to make a grand total of about seventy casualties. The hostile losses were unknown, except for thirteen scalps garnered by the Indian allies.

On reviewing his plight that evening, Crook concluded that to resume pursuit of the enemy, dragging his wounded on travois, would be heartless. It would also be foolhardy in view of the hostile strength and determination, especially with his rations so low and ammunition nearly expended. He had no recourse save to retreat to his wagon train at the forks of Goose Creek.

The column started its slow march back early the next morning. That evening the Crows left in a body, partly to celebrate over their enemy scalps, partly to protect their families against the nearby Sioux, and partly in resentment of Crook's slowness in supporting them at the beginning of the battle. The next day the column reached the wagon train, safely corraled on Goose Creek. On June 20th, all but half dozen of the Shoshones also departed for their homes on the Wind River Reservation. On the 21st, the wagon train, bearing the wounded and escorted by two companies of infantry, started back to Fort Fetterman for supplies and reinforcements.

Under date of June 19th, Crook reported to Sheridan that the Indian attack "showed that they anticipated that they were strong enough to thoroughly defeat the command during the engagement. I tried to throw a strong force through the canyon, but I was obliged to use it elsewhere before it had gotten to the supposed location of the village. The command finally drove the Indians back in great confusion . . . We remained on the field that night, and having but what each man could carry himself, we were obliged to return to the train to properly care for the wounded . . . I expect to find those Indians in rough places all the time, and so have ordered five companies of infantry, and shall not probably make any extended movement until they arrive (M-67)."

Some of the correspondents, especially Davenport of the New York *Herald*, were not so fulsome in claiming a great victory. Crook came in for considerable criticism as the long summer campaign proved frustrating and futile. His annual report of September 25, 1876, is largely devoted to the "grand illusion," or official line regarding the causes of the war, but a few lines devoted to the Battle of the Rosebud reveal how resentful and defensive he had grown:

> The number of our troops was less than one thousand [by a dozen, but reinforced by over 300 Indian allies and civilian volunteers], and within eight days after that the same Indians [but in triple strength] met and defeated a column of troops nearly the same size as ours [actually only half as strong], including the gallant commander, General Custer himself. I invite attention to the fact that in this engagement my troops beat these Indians on a field of their own choosing, and drove them in utter route from it as far as the proper care of my wounded and prudence would justify. Subsequent events proved beyond dispute what would have been the fate of the command had the pursuit been continued beyond what judgement dictated. (O-39,1876)

Only the final sentence in this defense is acceptable. Crook's thirteen hundred effectives had certainly not "beaten" and "utterly routed" the attacking seven hundred and fifty. The latter disengaged by choice and in perfect order, as was their want after a good day's work. Crook's camping on the battlefield is a white man's empty symbol; the mobile hostiles celebrated in their comfortable lodges that night, while the chastened troops shivered on the bare ground under a single blanket. As Crook himself so insisted, his enemy was still full of fight and shortly proved it, while his force was compelled to retire and await reinforcements for seven solid weeks.

The essential facts are undeniable. The fight itself was a tactical draw, although Crook commanded superior numbers. But the fight was also a clear strategic defeat for Crook. The Indians fully achieved their objective — to halt Crook's punitive campaign far from their village. Crook utterly failed to achieve his objective — to whip the hostile force into submission.

Even the disappointed and partisan Sheridan could read it no other way: "The victory was barren of results, as . . . General Crook was unable to pursue the enemy . . . considering himself too weak to make any movement until additional troops reached him (O-39, 1876)."

Chapter 11
Terry Scraps his First Plan

At this point the great campaign stood at one check to General Reynolds on Powder River, one aborted effort by General Gibbon on the Yellowstone, one strike at a phantom by General Terry on the Little Missouri, and one check to General Crook on the Rosebud. It was now General Terry's turn again. But inexperienced as he was at Indian campaigning, his second effort turned into another fiasco.

Having extracted from General Gibbon his first reliable enemy intelligence, stale though it was, Terry realized that Major Moore's supply base at Glendive was altogether too far east. Even as the *Far West* sped him back from the conference with Gibbon on the afternoon of June 9th, he ordered Captain Powell and his company of 6th Infantry to lay out a new depot at the mouth of Powder River, and ordered the steamboat to start transporting the remainder of the Glendive garrison and supplies up to the same point.

Disembarking at Powder River that same afternoon, the General left for Custer's upstream camp with his cavalry escort and Mitch Boyer. The cavalcade had no more than started when the cold and heavy downpour that held Gibbon in camp came to drench the riders and swell the streams they had to ford. But anxious to set his plans in motion, Terry pressed on, splashing into camp at 9:50 that evening to complete a strenuous two days for a general who had spent so many years behind a desk.

The plan Terry was devising incorporated two stages. The first called for a reconnaissance by half of Custer's regiment up Powder River in search of stray hostiles in that direction. This was to be followed by a two-pronged offensive designed to trap the hostile village on the lower Rosebud between Gibbon's strong force ascending the Rosebud and Custer's weak force ascending the Tongue, crossing to the upper Rosebud, and descending the latter. Unfortunately, this plan also incorporated two fatal flaws. It assumed that a summer Indian village would remain essentially stationary for a month, and the pointless first stage could only endanger the second stage, either by delaying it or flushing the enemy from the trap.

On the morning of June 10th, Terry issued Special Field Order No. 11 to govern the reconnaissance of stage one:

> Major Marcus S. Reno, 7th Cavalry, with six companies (right wing) of his regiment and one gun from the Gatling battery, will proceed at the earliest practicable moment to make a reconnaissance of the Powder River from the present camp to the mouth of the Little Powder. From the last-named point he will cross to the headwaters of Mizpah Creek and descend that creek to its junction with the Powder River. Thence he will cross to Pumpkin Creek and Tongue River, and descend the Tongue to its junction with the Yellowstone, where he may expect to meet the remaining companies of the 7th Cavalry and supplies of subsistence and forage.

> Major Reno's command will be supplied with subsistence for twelve days and with forage for the same period at the rate of two pounds of grain that day for each animal.

> The guide, Mitch Boyer, and eight Indians to be detailed by Lt. Col. Custer will report to Major Reno for duty with this column.

> Acting Assistant Surgeon H.R. Porter is detailed for duty with Major Reno.

It is notable that these orders rigidly spell out Reno's route. Powder River forms the arc of a bow, bulging slightly to the east, while Mizpah Creek forms the string of the bow. The specified route, totalling about 175 miles, thus consisted of ascending the bow, descending the string, and terminally diverging to a rendezvous at the mouth of Tongue River. Terry verbally cautioned Reno to avoid the Rosebud at all cost, so as not to alarm the village on that stream.

It is notable, also, that these orders specify no target date for the rendezvous, save the deadline implied by twelve days' rations. But a march of 175 miles at a standard cavalry pace of 30 miles a day would bring Reno to the rendezvous on June 16th. This was probably the plan, for Terry ordered Custer's movements to bring him there on the 16th, and on that same day Gibbon instructed his command to be ready at any moment to take the offensive. If Reno was expected, but not ordered back in six days, why was he rationed for twelve, with its implied lattitude in timing?

Most revealing of all, these orders fail to identify the purpose of the mission, other than to call it a reconnaissance, which implies an intelligence more than a combat mission. All knew that a double offensive against the Rosebud village would follow this movement,

126

if Reno found nothing. But there is naught but a deafening silence regarding what Reno should do if he found something. Was he to light into any hostiles he might find and thereby alarm every Indian within a hundred miles? Or, was he to make himself invisible? In short, what *was* the purpose of this mission, when delay could be disastrous?

Custer took a dim view of this operation very early, for his June 12th dispatch to the New York *Herald* said "it is not believed that the latter [Reno] will find the Indians, as their presumed abiding place is not believed to be on Powder River, but on the Rosebud." His dispatch of June 22nd further exposed the pointlessness of the mission:

> Custer and most of his officers looked with little favor on the movement up Powder River, as, among other objections, it required the entire remaining portion of the expedition to lie in idleness within two marches of the locality where it was generally believed the hostile village would be discovered on the Rosebud, the danger being that the Indians, ever on the alert, would discover the presence of the troops as yet undiscovered, and take advantage of the opporturnity to make their escape.

It would indeed seem that a large, known village somewhere on the Rosebud should take precedence over possible strays on the Powder, but whatever the merits of the mission, Reno's command pulled out on the afternoon of June 10th, the left wing having turned over to them their rations and most of their pack mules.

As Reno's force faded into the river breaks, the remainder of the Dakota column prepared for a march down to the new supply depot. That evening Terry sent two separate companies of cavalry ahead to prospect and prepare the route for the wagon train, but one accomplished nothing and the other got lost. The next morning, June 11th, Charley Reynolds went hunting with Mark Kellogg, while Custer proved his competence as a guide. He told the story in a letter to his wife that evening:

> Terry came to my tent before daylight and asked me if I would try to find the road. He seems to think I have a gift in that way, and he hoped that we might get within ten miles of the river's mouth today. What rendered our condition more embarrassing was that the men had rations for only one day left. I started with one company and scouts, and in we "boldly plunged." One company had been sent out the previous day to look for a road and their failure to return the same day increased the anxiety. I thought likely they had lost their way and had slept in the badlands. Sure enough, we found them about 10 a.m. After passing through some perfectly terrible country, I finally struck a beautiful road along a high plateau and instead of guiding the command within ten miles of here, we have all arrived and the wagon train besides.

On reaching the Yellowstone the column found that the *Far West* had brought Major Moore with another company of infantry and some supplies from Glendive that same morning. The boat also brought a novelty, welcomed with unrestrained enthusiasm by the troops who had been traveling a dry trail for 294 miles and 26 days. Sutler John W. Smith had hastily erected a tent to dispense a few necessities, such as straw hats to ward off sunstroke, and a few luxuries of the John Barleycorn variety to a throng of men whose pockets had been burning with useless greenbacks ever since the paymaster's discrete visit. The casualties of this commerce were herded out on the prairie under guard, and when the crowd dwindled down, even the Ree scouts were permitted to invest their deer-sales money in one drink each.

The next morning, June 12th, the *Far West* left on its final run to bring up the last of the Glendive men and stores. Reporter Kellogg, invited along by Captain Marsh, declared the 86 mile down trip in three hours a welcome improvement over his customary mule. In anticipation of the boat's departure, the troops had madly scribbled letters home. On reaching Glendive, the bulging mail bags were transferred to a skiff to be taken to Fort Buford by a party under Sgt. Henry Fox of Company D, 6th Infantry. Just as the loaded skiff shoved off, it capsized. Sgt. Fox was drowned, but Captain Marsh quickly lowered a small boat that rescued the others and retrieved the sodden mail bags. All hands then turned to spreading the letters out to dry, Kellogg taking special pains with what he recognized as a Custer manuscript addressed to *Galaxy Magazine*.

Among the pieces of mail baptized in the river was a dispatch from Terry to his St. Paul headquarters, dated June 12th, which outlined stage two of his plan:

> Reached Powder River at a point 24 miles above here [mouth of the Powder] late on the 7th inst. No Indians east of Powder River. Reno with six companies of 7th Cavalry is now well up the river on his way to the Forks, whence he will cross to and down Mizpah Creek and thence by Pumpkin Creek to Tongue River, where I expect to meet him with the rest of the cavalry and fresh supplies. I intend then, if nothing new is developed, to send Custer with nine companies of his regiment upon the Tongue and thence across to and down the Rosebud, while the rest of the 7th will join Gibbon, who will move up the Rosebud. Have met Gibbon and concerted movements with him. Troops arrived in fine condition.

This dispatch reveals that Terry would transfer three companies of 7th Cavalry to make Gibbon's force stronger than Custer's, as confirmed by Kellogg's dispatch of June 21st. Custer, in his June 12th dispatch to the *Herald* paints a fuller picture:

> That portion of the expedition now here [at the new supply depot] will rest a few days, draw a sufficient amount of supplies, then march up the right bank of the Yellowstone to the mouth of Tongue River, there

128

to await the arrival of the Powder River scouting party . . .

After their return . . . Custer will select nine companies of his regiment and a detachment of Indian scouts, and with a large train of pack mules loaded with supplies for at least fifteen days, proceed up the valley of Tongue River some distance; then striking west, will move quickly to the Rosebud, upon which stream the Indians are reported to be in heavy force; then down the valley of the Rosebud. At the same time the remaining three companies of the 7th Cavalry, joined perhaps to the four companies of 2nd Cavalry now with Gibbon, will scout up . . . the valley of the latter [Rosebud] until Custer's column is met coming down, so that by these arrangements it will be seen that if Indians are anywhere in the vicinity where they are reported to be, the prospect of discovering them is excellent.

On June 14th the *Far West* returned with the last of the Glendive men and stores, and Terry and staff promptly established themselves on board, taking the headquarters company (Captain Baker's Company C, 6th Infantry) as boat guard. The wagon train and teamsters would remain at the depot, commanded by Major Moore, his force consisting of his own three companies of 6th Infantry and Captain Louis H. Sanger's two companies of 17th Infantry. Also detached here were a large number of 7th Cavalrymen, including nearly every one of the new, unmounted recruits, and the entire band. They totalled over 150, the equivalent of about three companies! Our best analysis places the total of enlisted 7th Cavalrymen for the coming offensive at 566, a decidedly depleted regiment.

In accordance with Special Field Order No. 12, dated June 14th, Custer's force of left wing cavalry, Gatling battery, and Indian scouts, left the depot on the morning of June 15th, for the first time supported only by pack train. When the greenhorn troopers encountered difficulty in managing their pack mules, the latter were all gathered in the rear in charge of Lt. Luther S. Hare. Early on the first day's march they passed several old Indian campsites (occupied the preceding winter by Sitting Bull's Hunkpapas?). The next morning a short march of ten miles brought the column to the rendezvous at the mouth of Tongue River, where camp was made among other old village sites (occupied by the Mineconjous?).

General Terry had remained behind on the *Far West* the morning of June 15th to pen another note to his St. Paul headquarters:.

Just at the last moment it occurs to me that I have not written you that henceforth letters for the expedition should be sent to Fort Buford. I have made arrangements for obtaining mail matter from there. Custer left this morning for the mouth of Tongue River and I am now on the boat which leaves in a few minutes with stores. After starting Custer up the Tongue, I shall go on to Gibbon and with three companies of the 7th, and nearly all of Gibbon's force, shall go up the Rosebud.

129

At 1:30 p.m. the *Far West* started up the river intending to join Custer's bivouac that night, but after making only 15 miles a machinery breakdown required a stop for repairs. At noon of the 16th she reached Custer, already in camp at the rendezvous point. Together they waited the rest of the day looking in vain for Reno's appearance. They waited all day of the 17th. Then the 18th. Then the 19th, growing more exasperated by the minute.

They had more reason to be impatient than they realized. Even had Reno returned on time, Custer could not start up the Tongue until June 17th. Since Terry would have to steam up to ferry Gibbon across the river, the latter could not start up the Rosebud before the 19th. Traveling 20 miles a day with infantry, Gibbon would be marching from mile 20 to mile 40 on the Rosebud on the 20th, at which time Custer, having made his circle, would be descending along the same stretch of that stream.

This would be *twenty-five* days after the village had last been sighted at mile 19 on the Rosebud! It was not reasonable to expect the village to remain so sessile, a fact which the scouts could have told the officers, if they did not know it perfectly well themselves. Terry's plan was utterly hopeless, even if Reno raised no alarm and returned on the sixth day. This conclusion uses only information available to Terry at the time. But today we know that on the 17th, the earliest Custer could get off, the village had already moved into the valley of the Little Big Horn.

*   *   *

Back on June 9th, Gibbon had been ordered to return to the Rosebud posthaste, but instead he sat comfortably in camp waiting out the rainstorm that Terry was splashing through. Not until 3 p.m. of June 10th did the cavalry move out, and the infantry did not follow until the next morning. Having consumed four days in plodding fifty muddy miles, they assembled at their assigned station on June 14th. The next day Captain Thompson left on a five-day cavalry scout upriver to Fort Pease, 64 miles distant, hoping not to find that the Sioux had escaped to the north.

On June 16th the Crows reported a heavy smoke in the southwest. It was probably only a prairie fire set by some hunters, as likely to have been friendly Crows as hostile Sioux, but the report provides the sole explanation for Terry's later insistence on scouting Tullock's Fork, an eastern branch of the Big Horn that joins the latter very near its mouth. We must therefore examine the matter.

Dr. Paulding's diary located both smoke and observers as

follows: "Scouts came in [June 16] reporting that from bluffs 25 miles up [opposite Armell's Creek], they had seen heavy smokes, like that from a fight, just this side of Pease and near the mouth of the Big Horn [forty miles from the observers over Tullock's Fork]." Lt. Bradley, his scouting ardor cooled by Gibbon's neglect, wrote: "Today [June 16] the Crows discovered a heavy smoke across and up the river, apparently on O'Fallon's Creek [an old name for Armell's and still older for Tullock's]. It suggested a world of speculation, one of the theories being that a Sioux village had been attacked and destroyed by Custer or Crook. It means more likely that the Sioux are moving in that direction and accidentally set the grass on fire. Toward evening it died out." Captain Freeman telescoped observers and fire into one location: "Crow scouts came in [June 16] and reported a big smoke on O'Fallon's Creek, a small stream about 15 miles [sic!] from here." Three days later he compounded his confusion by attributing the smoke to "Reno's command on the Rosebud."

Gibbon, in both his official and popular accounts, located this smoke "on the Little Big Horn," at least thirty miles further south. At the time of writing, however, he was trying to build the myth that Terry knew all along that the village was located there. But if it were there on the 25th, it certainly was not ten days earlier. And if the smoke were actually over the Little Big Horn, there is no explanation left for Terry's insistence on scouting Tullock's Fork. We see no alternative but to conclude that Gibbon, in fact, told Terry that the smoke had been seen on Tullock's Fork.

When Captain Thompson's scouting party returned from Fort Pease on June 18th, Bradley commented that "they had met no Sioux and saw no sign of them on this side and but little on the other. The Crow village, which was some weeks ago on the Big Horn, seems to have disappeared from that country — another indication that the Sioux are heading in that direction." But what Bradley did not know was that on June 12th, the departure of Crook's Crow allies had left the village so depleted of warriors that it prudently moved further west, Sioux or no Sioux.

*   *   *

Reno's reconnaissance had left Terry's camp at mile 24 on Powder River at 3:30 on the afternoon of June 10th to look for stray Indians to the south. His scouts included Mitch Boyer, four Dakota, and three Ree scouts, the fourth detailed by Custer having been left behind following an altercation with Reno. There is no evidence that Lt. Varnum, Chief of Scouts, or either of the interpreters accompanied the column. J.C. Wagoner and probably four civilian packers helped the troopers with the pack train.

That first afternoon they rode eight miles up the east bank of Powder River to bivouac for the night at mile 32. The details of the march come from Dr. DeWolf, the only diarist with the column. Though brief, the diary faithfully records geographical features and the hours and miles marched, the latter probably from an odometer attached to the Gatling gun. Its mileages nicely check modern topographical maps, and the miles and hours marched yield no aberrant speeds.

On June 11th Reno crossed to the west of the river at the Mizpah ford (mile 38), crossed Ash Creek (mile 48), and noted a smoke in the distance as they went into camp (mile 58). The next day he continued up the west bank, finding an abandoned pony at a deserted Indian campsite of about 30 lodges, probably representing a party of summer roamers. He bivouacked (mile 82) a few miles above present Powderville, and some nineteen miles short of the forks, i.e., the mouth of the Little Powder. But it was only 2 p.m., leaving ample time for the scouts to ride ahead and thoroughly examine the forks. Since they reported nothing, there was no point in marching the whole column to that point.

The twenty-five mile march of June 13th took the command southwest, up and over the divide to Mizpah Creek and then about ten miles north down this stream, in accordance with Terry's orders. Reno had gained a day by sending only the scouts to the forks, and was now half way down Mizpah Creek, with every prospect of a futile mission. That evening he probably talked with Mitch Boyer, who knew where Bradley had first sighted the hostile village on Tongue River. By moving west to that stream now, instead of lower down, they could glean some useful information by counting the lodgesites, without delaying their return. Reno decided to do this, though it violated the letter of his orders.

On June 14th Reno made a rough and winding march of twenty-three miles south of west over the next divide to camp on Little Pumpkin Creek a mile above its junction with Pumpkin Creek, an eastern affluent of Tongue River. The next day he circled westward up the little valley to the north slope of a high peak now called Liscom Butte; there he picked up the head of Lay Creek and followed it fifteen miles northwest to bivouac at its junction with Tongue River at mile 41 above the mouth of the latter. The Gatling gun upset on this rugged trail. Young Hawk, one of the Ree scouts, shot an elk up on the butte and was so delayed as not to rejoin the column until the next afternoon.

Reno had covered only eight miles down the Tongue (mile 33) on the morning of June 16th, when Mitch and the scouts galloped back reporting the old village site just ahead. A careful count had revealed about 400 lodges, even more than the Crows had estimated from the smoke a month earlier. And Mitch probably insisted that the villagers by now were far, far away, so that Terry's double attack on the Rosebud could close in on nothing at all. This placed Reno in a quandary. His first little step had now brought him to the brink of a big one. Should he return to obedience and speed down the Tongue to the rendezvous that night, as expected? But he could only report the size of a month-old village and leave Terry to revise his plan with no new intelligence to go on. Or, he could violate orders further and find out where the village was headed, so that an improved plan could be devised. He had been sent on a fool's mission. He could compound it and be safe, or rectify it at his own peril. Whether wise or foolish, Reno chose the risk.

Accordingly, Mitch led the command nineteen miles west toward the Rosebud. Since the village had moved on an arc to the north, they noted no Indian trail, but saw plenty of old buffalo sign. At 2 p.m. they reached a point 4½ miles from Rosebud Creek, opposite mile 23 on that stream. Here Reno halted for six and a half hours, while he sent the scouts ahead to make sure that the valley was now clear of Indians. They undoubtedly thoroughly examined the deserted campsite that Bradley had seen at mile 19.

Young Hawk rejoined the command here, where the troops were lighting fires to make coffee. He, too, went ahead to scout, but diverged slightly upstream to Teat Butte on the east bank at about mile 25, which the Cheyenne, Wooden Leg, gave as the next hostile camp above mile 19. From his vantage point Young Hawk spotted the camp site with birds flying over it and a lone pony grazing nearby. Riding down to examine it, he assured himself it was an old Sioux camp, where large pony herds had badly trampled the river bank at the watering place.

When the scouts returned reporting two old camps and a heavy trail leading up the empty valley, Reno ordered a resumption of the march at 8:30 that evening. He proceeded 4½ miles to the stream and then 3½ miles up to camp at 11:30 (mile 26½). Young Hawk said they bivouacked on the village site he had found. For the first time Dr. DeWolf mentions a heavy lodge-pole trail, but neither here nor any where else does he mention village sites. He does refer to poor grass here and the need to boil water. Pvt. Peter Thompson mentioned the lack of game and recalled that the "trail was so wide and so torn up by teepee-poles that we found it difficult to secure a good camping place at night. This was especially so around watering places that were so necessary to us."

On the morning of June 17th Reno took his command 6½ cautious miles farther upstream (mile 33), where he halted from 10 a.m. to 4 p.m. At this point the Rosebud, on ascent, makes a bend to the southwest and Greenleaf Creek joins it from the southeast. Wooden Leg names this as the next hostile camp beyond Teat Butte, and the scouts undoubtedly examined it also. Peter Thompson recalled that Reno ordered no bugles blown nor loud noises made, and double pickets posted, all betraying apprehension of discovery by the enemy. He adds that Mitch said they could overtake the village in a day's march, but at this time the village was actually on the divide beyond the Rosebud and its warriors were fighting Crook at mile 91 on the Rosebud. But Reno's men knew nothing of the battle raging there while they were peacefully drinking coffee.

During this six-hour halt, the scouts forged ahead along the heavy trail, already knowing that it did not turn up Greenleaf Creek to circle back to the upper Tongue. On reaching mile 45, they undoubtedly paused to examine the next village site, which Wooden Leg identified as the famous sun dance camp. They may even have loped on to mile 52, where Lame Deer Creek joins from the southeast. If so, they satisfied themselves that the trail still continued southwest up the main stream, and then headed back for Reno's command. This round trip of forty miles was as far as the scouts could have penetrated in the available six hours. We deem it impossible for them to have completed the seventy-five mile round trip to the Busby bend of the Rosebud, where it flows from due south. They could report no more than that the undiminished trail continued southwest up the Rosebud toward the Busby bend.

When the hard-riding scouts returned to the command, Young Hawk relates that Reno inquired of Forked Horn, the senior Ree scout, "What do you think of the trail?" Forked Horn replied, "If the Dakotas see us, the sun will not move very far before we are all killed. But you are leader and we will go on if you say so." Reno then remarked, "Custer told us to turn back if we found the trail, and we will return; those are our orders." At 4 p.m. Reno returned down the Rosebud, marching fourteen miles to camp on the deserted village site at mile 19. He had learned enough to justify the risk he had taken, and he would never be able to defend his action if he tarried long enough to be discovered. He now knew that the village had moved out of range of Terry's double attack. Unless radically revised, it would prove a humiliating futility.

134

After a 19 mile march on June 18th, Reno camped on the Yellowstone opposite and just above Gibbon's camp, and soon made contact across the river. Lt. Bradley, anxious for confirmation of his ignored findings, learned that "Reno's command had . . . scouted down the latter [Rosebud Creek] meeting with no Sioux, but finding recent traces of a large village at the place I discovered it on the 27th of May [at mile 19]. Mitch Boyer . . . counted 360 lodge fires, and estimated that there were enough besides to make the number of lodges about 400." An anonymous letter of July 4th to the Helena *Herald* further revealed that Mitch had also counted the lodges at the Tongue River site: "On Tongue River he came to the old Indian camp he had seen when out on a similar scout with Lt. Bradley . . . He counted the lodge fires that had been there; they numbered 800 lodges [he surely meant 400 lodges and· 800 warriors]. He followed their trail . . . to Rosebud River. He next saw their old camp only 20 miles from where the three men were shot [on the Little Porcupine, May 23]." This is all the information recorded as to the size of the village.

As to how far the trail was followed and where it was headed, Lt. Bradley recorded that "a well-defined trail led from the site of the village [mile 19 on the Rosebud] across the plains *toward* the Little Big Horn, and it is now *thought* that the Indians will be found upon that stream [italics added]." Lt. McClernand's official itinerary also reported the trail as "leading *toward* the Little Big Horn [italics added]." Gibbon's official report exhausts the matter in the single phrase that Reno "had seen no Indians," but his popular narrative adds the clause, "though signs of camps [note the plural] had been discovered on the Rosebud and a large trail leading up to it."

This evidence supports our conclusion, based on time and mileage, that Reno's scouts could not have reached the critical Busby bend of the Rosebud. They last saw the trail heading south-west up the Rosebud, which was indeed *toward* the Little Big Horn. That it might continue to the latter stream was an inferred possibility, but not an observation. This is further supported by a note Gibbon gave to Reno for delivery to Terry that very afternoon of June 18th:

> Col. Reno made his appearance at the mouth of the Rosebud today and I have communicated with him by signal and by scouts swimming the river. He had seen no Indians, but I gather from the conversations which the scouts had with Mitch Bouyer that they found signs of camps on Tongue River and Rosebud, and trails leading up Rosebud. I presume the only remaining chance of finding Indians now is in the direction of the headwaters of Rosebud or Little Big Horn. I have been anxiously

looking for the boat and shall be glad to meet you or to hear of your future plans. (O-9)

In this early note Gibbon *presumed* that the Indians might be found in the direction of the *headwaters* of the Rosebud, *or* the Little Big Horn, which is irreconcilable with his later claims, already quoted, that the smoke seen by his scouts on the preceding day showed that the village was all the time on the lower Little Big Horn! But this note contains another important signal. It reveals that Gibbon already saw that Terry's pincers attack was no longer tenable. This was why he asked to learn of Terry's *future* plans. He did not write to pass on intelligence, for he included little and Reno could convey it better at first hand; he was clearly seeking, not transmitting, information in this note.

Reno marched his weary men thirty-three miles down the Yellowstone on June 19th to camp at 4 p.m. about eight miles short of the rendezvous at the mouth of Tongue River. The mileage for the reconnaissance now summed to 238, about 63 miles in excess of what had been laid down in his orders. That afternoon he sent a courier to Terry, bearing Gibbon's note and his own ill-conceived report:

> I am in camp about eight miles above you. I started this a.m. to reach your camp, but the country from the Rosebud here is simply *awful* and I had given orders to cache the gun, but Kinzie is coming in all right. I am sure you cannot take wagons to Rosebud without going some distance up Tongue River.
>
> I enclose you a note from Gibbon, whom I saw yesterday. I can tell you where the Indians are *not*, and much more information when I see you in the morning. I take it the Tongue River is not fordable at the mouth and I will necessarily have to camp on this side. I have had no accident, except breaking the tongue of Kinzie's gun carriage. My command is well. I will be on Tongue River opposite your camp about 8 a.m. My animals are leg weary and need shoeing. We have marched near to 250 miles. (O-9)

The striking thing about this report is that it fully discloses the violation of orders without neutralizing it with the valuable information obtained. An officer who chooses to disobey positive orders should have the wit to recognize that the burden of justification rests on him, and should have the art to accompany the poison with an immediate antidote. Reno seems to have lacked both. And then when his provacative report released a tempest, he apparently compounded his errors by turning sulky and silent.

Terry's forseeable reaction was swift, and strong enough to leave its mark in his dispassionate diary. The entry for June 19th reads: "In afternoon received dispatches from Major Reno informing me that he had been to mouth of Rosebud. Also note from Gibbon.

136

Sent Hughes [Terry's aide] to meet Reno . . . Reno gave him no reason for his disobedience of orders." The indignant General was less restrained when he wrote a letter to his sisters on June 21st:

> Here we lay in idleness until Monday evening, when to my great surprise I received a note from Colonel Reno which informed me that he had flagrantly disobeyed my orders, and that instead of coming down the Tongue he had been to the Rosebud . . . It appears that he had done this in defiance of my positive orders not to go to the Rosebud, in the belief that there were Indians on that stream, and that he could make a successful attack on them, which would cover up his disobediance . . . He had not the supplies to enable him to go far [?] and he returned without justification for his conduct, unless wearied horses and broken-down mules would be justification. Of course, this performance made a change in my plans necessary. (M-60)

Custer, faintly echoed by Kellogg, also roundly condemned Reno for violating orders, but got so tangled in his pejorative rhetoric as to charge him with both rashness in alarming the village and cowardice in failing to destroy it. But all this heat merely obscured, perhaps intentionally, the real heart of the matter.

By disobeying orders, Reno did *increase* the risk of discovery already inherent in the scout *Terry* had ordered. But he moved cautiously and to the knowledge of his scouts was *not* discovered. We must reject Terry's accusations of "glory-seeking" in favor of the more rational motives already attributed to Reno. Terry's claim that Reno's defiance had sabotaged his plan was a gross misrepresentation. The fact is, Terry's plan was doomed from the start. Reno's violation of orders led to securing the proof of the plan's futility. Reno thereby saved Terry from an ignominious wild goose chase, and at the same time handed him some intelligence upon which to build a better plan. It was not Reno's disobedience, but the intelligence it uncovered, that made Terry *want* to discard his plan.

To be made the scapegoat for Terry's misplanning so traumatized the Major as to permanently addle his memory of the whole affair. In his account of 1886 he wrote that he had been sent on reconnaissance to search for Indians and to find General *Crook*! And that he successfully completed his mission by finding General *Gibbon* on the south bank of the *Little Powder*! The more placid Dr. DeWolf wrote his wife that the trails they found were "all old." But then added, "I think it is very clear that the Indians have scattered and gone back to their reservation."

Other members of the Dakota column, however, did glean some useful information from the returning reconnaissance. Lt. Godfrey recorded "a camp about three weeks old of about 350 lodges." Custer wrote his wife on June 21st that Reno had seen a week-old trail of 380 lodges, which the scouts thought they could overtake in a day and a half. In his *Herald* dispatch of the same date he added that Reno had struck the Rosebud about 25 miles above its mouth and ascended it for another 20 miles. Presumably this refers to the scouts, who penetrated, by this account, only to mile 45, the location of the sun dance camp. As to where the trail led, Custer said, "up the valley of the Rosebud." Even the intensely partisan Captain Hughes, who first debriefed Reno, admitted that the latter "did not pursue the trail he had found far enough to determine in which direction it finally turned."

Bradley had it right when he recorded the village as containing about 400 lodges. The reported ages vary, which is not surprising, since the village spent nearly a month in traveling from the Tongue to the sun dance camp. But the fact of momentous significance is that absolutely no one ever cited more than *one* figure for the size of the *five* successive camp sites examined. Either those five sites were progressively larger and no one, not even the scouts, had the wit to notice or report it, or, they were all essentially the same size. Only the latter alternative is reasonable, and it is confirmed by Godfrey's diary which later recorded the sun dance camp as containing 3-400 lodges.

Why is this so momentous? It reveals that the village was made up of winter roamers only, and that the summer roamers had not yet joined them by the time of the sun dance, held early in June. This is perfectly reasonable. The migration of summer roamers from the agencies peaked in mid-May, and it would take a month to join the main camp, stopping to hunt and renew lodgepoles. They would thus arrive after mid-June, a few in time to fight Crook on June 17th, as we have seen, but many more in time to fight Custer on June 25th. Reno's scout did not penetrate far enough to gather this crucial intelligence.

We have now identified one of the major keys to the disaster that was looming up. Terry's best and latest information was destined to be grossly out-dated before he could act on it. And it must be reiterated that no one on the expedition could know the destination of the village whose trail was last seen on June 18th no further up the Rosebud than the mouth of Lame Deer Creek.

Chapter 12
Terry Plans Again

The notes received from both Gibbon and Reno on the evening of June 19th carried sufficient clues to convince Terry that he must scrap his first plan and formulate a second. This he did on the instant, for when he sent his aide to Reno's bivouac that same evening, he armed him with orders for Reno not to march down the next morning, but to wait for Custer to march up.

Early on June 20th, Terry issued Special Field Order No. 15, directing Custer to proceed with the left wing to Reno's camp, there to take command of his re-united regiment and march to the mouth of the Rosebud to await further orders. By 8 a.m. Custer's column was in motion and at 11:30 reached Reno's camp. Terry, having reloaded stores aboard the *Far West*, steamed upriver to reach the same point an hour later. What Custer, and then Terry, had to say to Reno is not of record, but this was probably not one of Reno's happier days. Presumably both superiors extracted from him all they could about his scouts' findings. Then the Gatling battery, which had encountered hard going along the breaks of the Yellowstone, was transferred to the *Far West*, and Reno's men drew fresh supplies from her before Terry steamed upriver at 3:45 p.m. Fifteen minutes later, Custer's restored regiment resumed the march, making a total of 25 miles for the day.

The *Far West* tied up at Gibbon's camp, below and opposite the mouth of the Rosebud, at 8:35 the next morning, June 21st. There Terry was pleased to learn that Gibbon, in anticipation of an up river move, had already sent a battalion of infantry to prepare the road and re-bridge the creeks. Terry ordered the remainder of the Montana column to follow immediately, making for the mouth of the Big Horn. They got off at 10:00 a.m. under command of Captain Edward Ball, for General Gibbon and Major Brisbin had joined Terry on the boat.

The fact that Terry had so quickly ordered Custer to the Rosebud and Gibbon to the Big Horn reveals that his new plan resembled the first in its use of two columns, but differed by shifting them one river to the west. He first disclosed the new plan in a dispatch to Sheridan, written early on the morning of June 21st:

> No Indians have been met with as yet, but traces of a large and recent village have been discovered 20 or 30 miles up the Rosebud. Gibbon's column will move this morning on the north side of the Yellowstone for the mouth of the Big Horn, where it will be ferried across by the supply steamer, and whence it will proceed to the mouth of the Little Horn, and so on. Custer will go up the Rosebud tomorrow with his whole regiment and thence to the headwaters of the Little Horn, thence down the Little Horn.
>
> I only hope that one of the two columns will find the Indians. I go personally with Gibbon. (O-39)

This note contains as much as Terry ever disclosed about the intelligence he had extracted from Reno, meager and faulty though it is. But it reveals the outline of the plan, with its change in troop distribution, and uncertainty as to where the enemy might be. Custer is to take the *entire* 7th Cavalry up the Rosebud and across to the *headwaters* of the Little Big Horn. Terry is to take Gibbon's column up the Big Horn to the mouth of the Little Big Horn, with possible future movement covered by the phrase, "and so on."

At 9:30 a.m. of the 21st, the *Far West* steamed up to the mouth of the Rosebud to await the arrival of Custer's command. It was probably during this wait that Gibbon brought to Terry's attention the report of his Crows of having seen smoke near Tullock's Fork on June 16th. When Custer pulled in to camp two miles below the mouth of the Rosebud, Terry steamed down to ask him aboard for a briefing conference. Montana column diaries reveal that they halted their march some five miles out to await the results of this conference.

At this briefing, Terry must have summarized the intelligence situation, presented his general plan, and discussed tactical details with Custer, Gibbon, and Brisbin. Since the implementation of the new plan led to a shocking disaster, a full transcript of the discussion would be invaluable. But no conference notes of any kind, if made, have survived, so that the vacuum has usually been filled with partisan speculations. Yet some features of the meeting can be reasonably projected from events that preceded it. Others can be soundly inferred from actions taken as a result of it. And valuable confirmation emerges from what was said about it, as recorded

140

before the subsequent tragedy. We must be wary, however, of statements made after the tragedy, not merely because of the vagaries of human memory, but because of partisan interests and hindsight revisions.

We can easily project the intelligence summary that Terry presumably made, for we have already narrated all the known events which yielded such information. An important consideration of course, was the anticipated enemy strength. The latest and most accurate information, gathered by Reno's scouts, fixed the hostile village at about 400 lodges, representing some 800 warriors. Against Custer's force of 600 and Gibbon's 400, these odds were considered favorable for either alone. There was, of course, the possibility that the village might be reinforced by the arrival of summer roamers from the various agencies. But for reasons that remain obscure, the command fatally discounted the probability that these would make any material difference.

Another important consideration was the temper of the enemy, a matter the scouts understood well enough to fear, but which the military failed to appreciate. It is unlikely that the matter was even brought up at the conference, for the officers shared the stereotyped view that Indians invariably took to their heels when confronted by determined opposition, so that the soldier's only problem was to catch and corner the elusive redskins. They would pay dearly for these misjudgments. In this instance, the Indians knew that the whites were bent on stealing half their reservation and all their unceded lands. They had already suffered the proof that the army had declared open warfare upon them. They recognized the desperate crisis in tribal survival they faced. Though they had not taken the offensive against white settlements, they would defend themselves and their women and children with fatalistic resolution. The scouts could feel this by instinct, but scorn met their attempts to convey it to imperceptive officers.

The trickiest question was the location of the hostile village, even assuming it would remain together and not scatter. Its trail, then many days old, had last been seen on June 17th ascending the Rosebud toward its Busby bend, some seventy miles and three days' march distant. It was now June 21st, and the pursuit could not begin before another day, nor the Busby bend reached before the 24th. If the village had left the Busby bend no earlier than the 15th, and traveled slowly at ten miles every three days, it would have moved thirty or forty miles by the evening of the 24th; if it was in a hurry and moved fifteen miles every day, it would have traveled 150 miles — in any direction! If anything is certain, it is that no one with the command knew, or had the least means of knowing, *when* the village would be struck, or *where* it would be when struck. All post facto claims to the contrary are pure fabrication. Terry had been once burned by relying on stale intelligence and assuming a sessile village. He could hardly have wished to be burned again. He must, therefore, have carefully explored the possibilities with his subordinates.

Although the possibilities were many, they did not all carry equal probabilities. The Sioux, for example, rarely took their villages across the Big Horn for fear of the Crows beyond. But from the Busby bend they could move in one, or all, of three directions: south up the Rosebud, west to the Little Big Horn, or north down Tullock's Fork. Terry would insist that the latter stream be thoroughly scouted, proving that he recognized this possibility. If the village turned south up the Rosebud, it might turn left to the upper Tongue River. Terry would order Custer to watch for such an escape to the left, proving that he also recognized this possibility. Alternatively, the village might turn right from the upper Rosebud to the upper Little Big Horn, and continue to the mountains or to a higher branch of the Big Horn, such as Rotten Grass Creek, a name actually mentioned in this context. Finally, the enemy might move west from the Busby bend to strike the lower Little Big Horn; it was then more likely to ascend the latter stream in order to avoid Crow country. These possibilities fanned out over a hundred mile span, but the probabilities were apparently judged to favor the *upper* Little Big Horn.

In view of these unresolved uncertainties, a rigid plan calling for a simultaneous attack by two separate columns on a predetermined location and at a predetermined date, without regard to the enemy, is an absurdity, as Terry had so recently and so painfully learned. In the face of uncertainty, the only sensible plan must adopt flexibility as the means of accommodating multiple possibilities.

The objective was to strike the enemy wherever and whenever it might be found and, if possible, to use the entire available force to contribute to a successful outcome. The best guarantee of hitting the village was to send a strong, mobile strike-force to pursue its trail, wherever it might lead. Then if the strike could be made from the proper direction, the fleeing refugees might be driven toward a less mobile blocking force for final destruction. This would require the blocking force to occupy a preselected and strategic station, from which it would move only on advice sent from the strike-force.

There is ample and consistent evidence that this is precisely the plan Terry submitted to the conference and whose details were coordinated at that time. It was superior to his first plan because it recognized uncertainty and incorporated flexibility.

Terry's discarded plan had assigned only nine cavalry companies to Custer and had retained seven cavalry and five infantry companies to himself, presuming one infantry company would be left to guard Gibbon's base camp. The new plan, by contrast, gave Custer all twelve companies of his own regiment, and Terry only four of cavalry and five of infantry, supplemented by the Gatling battery. At one point in the conference Terry went so far as to offer Custer all sixteen companies of cavalry and the battery, leaving himself with but five infantry companies. There could be no more convincing evidence that Terry expected Custer to make the initial strike while unsupported, and his own force to do little more than block the escape of refugees. But the battery would impede Custer's mobility, and the entire lack of cavalry would impair Terry's agility in blocking; both agreed that there was neither need, nor advantage, in such a distribution. The all-cavalry composition of Custer's column was thus appropriate to pursuing and striking, while the predominant infantry and battery composition of Terry's column was appropriate to blocking.

The distribution of scouts favors the same conclusion. Gibbon had only twenty-four Crow scouts and four quartermaster scouts available, for Tom Leforge had sustained a broken collar-bone and John Williamson was absent on courier service. Custer had twenty-nine Ree scouts and four quartermaster scouts. Yet Terry transferred the pick of Gibbon's scouts to Custer's column — Mitch Boyer, George Herendeen, and six Crows. This prompted Lt. Bradley to lament:

> He [Custer] is provided with Indian scouts, but from the superior knowledge possessed by the Crows of the country he is to traverse, it was decided to furnish him with a part of ours, and I was directed to make a detail for that purpose. I selected my six best men, and they joined him at the mouth of the Rosebud. Our guide, Mitch Bouyer, accompanied him also. This leaves me wholly without a guide, while Custer has one of the very best that the country affords. Surely he is being offered every facility to make a successful pursuit.

If Terry expected to roam far from the mouth of the Little Big Horn, this transfer of guides would seem unreasonable. The transfer of Herendeen, hired only that day, was even more significant. He was not only familiar with the country, but had proved himself a daring and dependable courier. He told the story of his employment in 1878:

I was standing on the forward deck of the boat when I was called into the cabin where Terry, Gibbon, Custer, and Brisbin were around a table apparently holding a council of war. Terry showed me a map and asked for information about the country on Tullock's Fork and the Little Big Horn . . . I had been over the ground and told the General all I knew about it. Custer seemed pleased with the information I gave Terry, and said I was just the man he wanted and that he would like me to go with him.

I went out on deck again, and soon afterward Gibbon came out and spoke to me. He said I could consider myself employed to go with General Custer. I asked him what compensation I would receive and what I would be expected to do, and he replied I would act as scout and when Custer's command got to the head of Tullock's Creek, I would come down the Tullock with dispatches to Gibbon's command . . . General Brisbin came out of the cabin and I asked him where his cavalry would be in the next few days, so I could find him, and he replied about the mouth of the Little Big Horn.

This account makes it clear that Custer wanted Herendeen initially because of his familiarity with the country, but that the conferees soon decided that he was just the man to act as courier between the two commands. The conversation with Brisbin implied that Gibbon's force would keep its station at the mouth of the Little Big Horn, at least for a few days.

The rationing periods for the two columns are even more revealing. Both columns would be supported by pack train, but Custer's fifteen days' rations, starting on June 22nd, would last until July 6th. Traveling at a cavalry pace of thirty miles a day, he was supplied for a 450 mile march. It is no wonder that Custer considered himself prepared to chase the hostiles all the way to their agencies, if necessary, and that he could roam far from Terry's station. In striking contrast, Gibbon's column carried rations for only a few days; two sources specify six days, and others five, seven, and eight, the average being six. Since each infantry company had only four pack mules, even the sixth day's rations must have been carried in pockets. The period started June 24th at the mouth of the Big Horn; since it was a two day march to the Little Big Horn, Gibbon's column would be closely tied to that station, unless the *Far West* should succeed in getting that far with additional supplies.

After the battle, partisan efforts were made to build the myth that the campaign failed because Custer violated Terry's rigid plan for a simultaneous attack on June 26th by both columns on the village known all along to be precisely where it was found! Of course, no pre-battle records so much as hint at any accurate knowledge of the location of the village; it was presumed to be on the Little Big Horn, but this stream is a hundred miles long. Nor do the pre-battle records even hint at a simultaneous attack anywhere at any time. The oft-quoted date of June 26th was planned simply as the date of Terry's arrival at his blocking station. This was important for cooperation between striking and blocking columns, but it never was the planned date for an attack by anyone.

All of the pre-battle, and many of the post-battle records deny the myth and support reason. Terry himself, in his above-quoted report of June 21st, revealed that he knew not where and when the village would be found, and refers to Custer's march to the *headwaters* of the Little Big Horn. His aide, Captain Robert B. Hughes, in 1896, published a lawyer's brief in defense of the myth, but destroyed his own case by a slip of the truth by stating that the hostiles "were either on the Little Big Horn or on the Rotten Grass," which covered more territory than the infantry would traverse in a week! Terry's adjutant, Captain Edward W. Smith, wrote a dispatch on July 1st that clashes with the myth:

> At noon of the 22nd of June, General Custer, at the head of his fine regiment of twelve veteran companies, left camp at the mouth of the Rosebud to follow the trail of a very large band of hostile Sioux, leading up the river and westward in the direction of the Big Horn. The signs indicated that the Indians were making for . . . the Little Big Horn.
>
> At the same time, General Terry, with Colonel Gibbon's command of five companies of infantry and four of cavalry and the Gatling battery, started to ascend the Big Horn, aiming to assail the enemy in the rear. The march of the two columns was so planned as to bring Colonel Gibbon's force within cooperating distance of the anticipated scene of action by the evening of the 26th. In this way only could the infantry be made available, as it would not do to encumber General Custer's march with foot soldiers.

Another officer present at the conference, who later turned myth-builder, was Major Brisbin, who wrote a letter in 1892 to the then General Godfrey, claiming that "Terry intended, if he intended anything, that we should be in the battle with you." Reconcile this, if you can, with what Brisbin wrote on June 28th to the New York *Herald*:

> A consultation was held with Generals Gibbon and Custer and there General Terry definitely fixed upon the plan of action. It was believed that the Indians were on the head of the Rosebud, or over on the Little Big Horn, a divide of about fifteen miles separating the two streams. It was announced by General Terry that General Custer's column would strike the blow and General Gibbon and his men received the decision without a murmur . . .
>
> The Montana column felt disappointed when they learned that they were not to be present at the final capture of the great village, but General Terry's reasons for affording the honor of the attack to General Custer were good ones. First, Custer had all cavalry and could pursue if they attempted to escape, while Gibbon's column was half infantry, and in rapid marching in approaching the village, as well as pursuing the Indians

after the fight, General Gibbon's cavalry and infantry must become separated and the strenth of the column weakened. Second, General Custer's column was numerically stronger than Gibbon's, and General Terry desired the stronger column to strike the Indians; so it was decided that Custer's men, as usual, were to have the post of honor, and the officers and men of the Montana column cheered him and bade them God-speed.

Custer outlined the plan in a dispatch to the New York *Herald* written on the morning of June 22nd:

> Yesterday, Terry, Gibbon, and Custer got together, and with unanimity of opinion decided that Custer should start with his command up the Rosebud valley to the point where Reno had abandoned the trail, take up the latter and follow the Indians as long and as far as horse flesh and human endurance could carry his command. Custer takes no wagons or tents with his command, but proposes to live and travel like Indians; in this manner the command will be able to go wherever the Indians can.
>
> Gibbon's command has started for the mouth of the Big Horn. Terry, in the Far West, starts for the same point today, where, with Gibbon's force and the Far West loaded with thirty days' supplies, he will push up the Big Horn as far as navigation of that stream will permit, probably as far as old Fort C.F. Smith, at which point Custer will reform [rejoin?] the expedition after completing his present scout.
>
> Custer's command takes with it, on pack mules, rations for fifteen days. Custer advised his subordinate officers, however, in regard to rations, that it would be well to carry an extra supply of salt, because, if at the end of fifteen days the command should be pursuing a trail, he did not propose to turn back for lack of rations, but would subsist his men on fresh meat — game, if the country afforded it, pack mules if nothing better offered.

Reporter Kellogg's dispatch of June 21st not only confirms Custer's pursuit assignment, but describes the blocking function by saying that Gibbon's force will march "up the Big Horn valley in order to intercept the Indians, if they should attempt to escape from General Custer down that avenue."

Regarding the new plan, most of the diarists remained silent, while a few mentioned merely that Custer would ascend the Rosebud and Gibbon the Big Horn. Lt. Bradley, however, recorded under date of June 21st that "a conference took place on the boat . . . with reference to a combined movement between the two columns in the neighborhood of the Sioux village about the same time and assist each other in the attack." The next sentence reveals that Bradley meant "operations," not "attack," for he adds that "it is understood that if Custer arrives first he is at liberty to attack at once if he deems prudent. We have little hope of being in at the death, as Custer will undoubtedly exert himself to the utmost to get there first and win all the laurels for himself and his regiment." Of course, depending upon where the village was found, Custer might arrive first even if he moved like a tortoise!

It is now apparent that all our projections from available Indian intelligence, all our inferences from actions taken, and all the statements made at the time about the new plan converge on the same pattern. Custer's column, stronger, more mobile, better provided with scouts, and longer rationed, was expected to pursue and overtake the village wherever it might go, the probabilities being judged to favor the upper Little Big Horn. He was then to strike the village, probably while still unsupported, and from a direction that would drive it northward. Terry's column, weaker, less mobile, with fewer scouts, and shorter rationed, was expected to reach its blocking station at the mouth of the Little Big Horn by the evening of June 26th, hopefully supported by the supply boat. There it would intercept fleeing refugees, or, if advised of altered circumstances by Custer, would move to a more strategic point. It was a flexible plan that maximized the likelihood of making a strike wherever the village might be found, yet gave promise of bringing the entire force, slow as well as fast units, into the action.

When the conference aboard the *Far West* broke up before four o'clock, Custer hastened back to his camp to prepare his regiment to take the field the next day. Gibbon and Brisbin, however, remained with Terry on the boat, which would move up river the next day to overtake the Montana column already on the march. Late that afternoon the steamer ferried Lt. Low's battery, as well as thirteen mules injured on Reno's reconnaissance, across to the north bank on orders to overtake the marching column and report to Captain Ball.

On the morning of June 22, Terry delivered written instructions to guide Custer's operation, which we must quote in full:

> The Brigadier General commanding directs that, as soon as your regiment can be made ready for the march, you will proceed up the Rosebud in pursuit of the Indians whose trail was discovered by Major Reno a few days since. It is, of course, impossible to give you any definite instructions in regard to this movement, and were it not impossible to do so the Department Commander places too much confidence in your zeal, energy, and ability to wish to impose on you precise orders which might hamper your action when nearly in contact with the enemy. He will, however, indicate to you his own views of what your action should be, and he desires that you should conform to them unless you shall see sufficient reasons for departing from them. He thinks that you should proceed up the Rosebud until you ascertain definitely the direction in which the trail above spoken of leads. Should it be found (as it appears almost certain that it will be found) to turn toward the Little Horn, he thinks that you should still proceed southward, perhaps as far as the headwaters of the Tongue, and then turn toward the Little Horn, feeling constantly, however, for your left, so as to preclude the possibility of the escape of the Indians to the south or southeast by passing your left flank. The column of Colonel Gibbon is now in motion for the mouth of the Big

Horn. As soon as it reaches that point it will cross the Yellowstone and move up at least as far as the forks of the Big and Little Horns. Of course, its future movements must be controlled by circumstances as they arise, but it is hoped that the Indians, if upon the Little Horn, may be so nearly inclosed by the two columns that their escape will be impossible.

The Department Commander desires that on your way up the Rosebud you should thoroughly examine the upper part of Tullock's Creek, and that you should endeavor to send a scout through to Colonel Gibbon's column, with information of the results of your examination. The lower part of this creek will be examined by a detachment from Colonel Gibbon's command. The supply steamer will be pushed up the Big Horn as far as the forks of the river if found to be navigable for that distance, and the Department Commander, who will accompany the column of Colonel Gibbon, desires you to report to him there not later than the expiration of the time for which your troops are rationed, unless in the meantime you receive further orders. (O-39,1876)

Before proceeding futher we must pause to excavate these orders from an incredible overlay of the detritus of controversy. A century of partisan haggling over their disobeyance has concealed their useful signal in a furious noise, which is all the more deplorable since the issue belongs to the realm of military legalistics, not to the mechanics of battle. The dogma that any violation of orders automatically spells defeat is transparent nonsense. When perceptive disobedience snatches victory from defeat, who complains? It is thus not obedience or disobedience, *per se*, that determines the outcome of battle, but the appropriateness of the actions taken in the context of the conflict. To be sure, the violation had better be appropriate, or the violator will reap a justly bitter harvest.

In this particular case, the great debate has even lacked an arguable issue. Terry's instructions contain one tiny word, usually ignored, that made it impossible for Custer's actions to have constituted a violation. This key work is italicized in the following passage: "you should conform to them unless *you* shall see sufficient reason for departing from them." Terry thus explicitly authorized *Custer* to act as the sole judge — not Terry nor any other officer, not some barracks lawyer nor a court-martial, not even history. Only Custer. Period. One may quarrel with Custer's judgement, but not his authority to judge. Custer's obedience is therefore neither debatable, nor relevant.

If there is any message that comes through loud and clear in these instructions, it is the explicitly admitted uncertainty and the built-in flexibility. They admit the impossibility of giving definite instructions and refuse to hamper by attempting any. Only uncertainty demanded an examination of Tullock's Fork by both columns. Only uncertainty required Custer to feel constantly to his left to prevent escape to the south or southeast. Only uncertainty prompted the suggestion that Custer might have to proceed as far south as the head of the Tongue. The most definite statement of all is carefully hedged — it "appears almost" certain that the trail will turn toward the Little Big Horn. And only hindsight traps one into construing this as locating the turn at the Busby bend of the Rosebud. On the contrary, all the evidence implies an expected turn farther up the Rosebud.

Once again, these instructions specify no movement for Gibbon's force after reaching its station, but leave the possibility open as "controlled by circumstances." One of these circumstances was the uncertain navigability of the Big Horn by the *Far West*, to which the force was tied by its short rations. Another, not spelled out, was advice received from Custer's column by courier. Significantly, the instructions mention no attack, to say nothing of a simultaneous double attack. They merely venture to hope that the Indians will be nearly inclosed and their escape prevented. The only new feature is the order for Custer to report to Terry's station when his rations will have been consumed, namely, July 6th.

There is one feature of these instructions that betrays geographical confusion, or failure to be explicit about opportunities for exchanging intelligence between the two columns. Tullock's Fork heads so near the Busby bend that special courier Herendeen would not be able to scout its upper waters until Custer's column reached Busby bend. At that time Custer would have learned whether the hostile trail moved north, west, or south from the bend. Thus Herendeen could carry this valuable intelligence to Terry, but the instructions ask only that he report the results of the examination of Tullock's Fork.

Terry, Brisbin, and Hughes have all indicated that at the conference the proposed routes of the two columns were plotted on the map. Custer said he would march at the rate of 30 miles a day, while Gibbon would move slower at about 20 miles a day. Plotting the routes on modern maps reveals a flaw in the timing aspect of the plan. Gibbon's column would spend June 24th at the mouth of the Big Horn, ferrying the river and preparing to march; it should reach its station on the afternoon of the 26th. Custer's column would reach the Busby bend on the afternoon of the 24th. If Herendeen were sent through that night he would scout the full length of Tullock's Fork and meet Terry as he started his march. And if Custer were not to attack before Gibbon reached his station, he would have to march for two days beyond the Busby bend. It seems inescapable that either the village was expected to be found high up on the Little Big Horn and far from Terry's station, or,

149

Custer was expected to make a wide circle for no purpose save delay, hoping the village would stay put and that he would remain invisible.

These considerations deliver the final coup de grace to the myth that Terry knew the village was on the lower Little Big Horn and planned a simultaneous attack. If he had known this, his plan was fatally mis-conceived, for it arranged to deliver one column there two days ahead of the other! What actually happened, of course, was the very eventuality that the plan could least accommodate to, and precisely because of this timing flaw. On the evening of June 24th, Custer would find the trail leading west from the Busby bend, and at the next dawn he would sight the village on the *lower* Little Big Horn, at a time when Terry was only about to leave the Yellowstone. And Custer's attempts at invisibility would fail!

The Gods of War would smile that day — on the Indians.

Chapter 13
Custer Hits the Trail

At twelve noon of June 22nd, General Terry, Gibbon, and Custer reviewed the proud 7th Cavalry as it paraded smartly out of camp below the mouth of the Rosebud. For this departure there were no tears, nor spirited band music. Nor was there any encumbering wagon train or dejected detachment of dismounted recruits. A month in the field had transformed the troopers into bronzed veterans, their uniforms turning more ragged and individualistic as their maneuvers grew more efficient and precise. Their morale was up and their expectations high, for Terry had chosen them to pursue and strike the hostiles. They were proud of the assignment and confident that none could accomplish it better.

Even the morale of the Indian scouts was high, for they had found in Custer an officer who understood them – a rare and cherished experience for them. Of the preparation for departure, one of their number, Red Star, recalled: "Gerard told us he wanted us to sing our death songs. The Dakota trail had been seen and the fight would soon be on. Custer had a heart like an Indian; if we ever left out one thing in our ceremonies, he always suggested it to us. We got on our horses and rode around singing the songs. Then we fell in behind Custer and marched on."

The regiment now totaled only 31 officers and 566 enlisted men, with 25 Rees and four Sioux scouts from Dakota and six Crows loaned from Montana. The quartermaster employees included three scouts and two interpreters from Dakota, two scouts from Montana, and probably six mule packers. On adding reporter Mark Kellogg and vacationist Autie Reed, the grand total came to 647 persons. Lt. Maguire, in his official engineer's report of July 10th, gave the total of officers, men, and civilians as "nearly 650 men."

The eager column paraded two miles up the Yellowstone, forded the trickle of water in Rosebud Creek, and wheeled to march south up its west bank, the Indian scouts forging ahead and scattering in the hills on the flanks. The only discordant note was sounded by the pack train, the management of which had now become the regular duty of Lt. E.G. Mathey. Despite his efforts and those of the still green company packers, the mules began to throw their loads before they had cleared the bivouac area, and lagged farther behind in the dusty rear as the day advanced. Having marched to mile 10 on the creek by 4 p.m., the troopers went into camp.

No one mentioned seeing any Indian trails or campsites on this first afternoon, for they had remained on the west bank. Interpreter Gerard, who had stayed behind with General Terry to start four Ree couriers with the mail down to the Powder River depot, overtook the command as it was going into camp. Bloody Knife was also delayed, but by a clandestine overconsumption of sutler John W. Smith's wet goods in camp that morning.

At sundown Custer called a conference with his officers, who assembled to squat, al fresco around his tent. If we were limited to contemporary sources, the conference would appear to have been dull and routine. Lt. Wallace's official itinerary merely states that "Orders were given . . . that trumpet signals would be discontinued, that the stable guards would wake their respective companies at 3 a.m. and the command would march at 5 a.m. General Custer stated that short marches would be made for the first few days, after that they would be increased." Lt. Godfrey's diary merely adds that the short marches would be "from 25 to 30 miles a day."

Other evidence, however, indicates that Custer gave his officers a pep-talk to inspire responsible cooperation among them for the coming action. Lt. Gibson wrote his wife on July 4th that "we were cautioned to husband our mules and ammunition, and finally he asked all officers to make any suggestions to him at any time. This struck us all as the strangest part of the meeting, for you know how dominant and self-reliant he always was, and we left him with a queer sort of depression." Lt. Edgerly also wrote his wife at that same time:

> Custer talked to us for nearly half an hour, telling his general plan of campaign, etc. He said he had perfect confidence in the officers and men of the 7th, and didn't believe it was of any use for anybody or any other regiment to try what we could not, that his intention was to treat everybody as fairly as he could and make the trip as pleasant and successful as possible, and I want to say here that during the entire march from

Lincoln I did not hear one word of fault found with any of Custer's actions.

Lt. Edgerly reiterated this in a letter to Mrs. Custer, dated October 10, 1877:

> Custer said, 'I will be glad to listen to suggestions from any officer of the command, if made in the proper manner. But I want it understood that I shall allow no grumbling, and shall exact the strictest compliance with orders from everybody — not only with mine, but with any orders given by an officer to his subordinate . . .' Col. Benteen here asked who he meant by that remark about grumbling . . . and asked if the General ever knew of any criticism or grumbling from him. The General replied, 'No, I never have, or on any other [campaign] I have been on with you.'

The competent, but overly testy, Captain Benteen described this exchange in his narrative of 1890:

> It has come to his [Custer's] knowledge that his official actions have been criticized . . . and that while he was willing to accept recommendatons from the junior second lieutenant of the regiment, he wished the same to come in proper manner . . . and said he would take the necessary steps to punish, should there be a reoccurence of the offense. I said to General Custer, it seems to me you are lashing the shoulders of *all* to get at some; now, as we are all present, would it not do to specify the officers whom you accuse? He said, Col. Benteen, I am not here to be categorized by you, but for your own information, will state that none of my remarks have been directed towards you . . .

These accounts reveal Custer as acting responsibly in the interest of his mission, and unexpectedly tolerant in the interest of unity and cooperation among his officers. They do not paint him as arrogant and cocky, rash and irresponsible, or scheming and conniving. Yet the melodramatic school leaps to charge him with all these and more on the gratuitous assumption that he was so unsettled by a presidential snub, or by a secret ambition to become president himself, that he turned utterly irrational — and that explains the Custer "massacre!" However seductive melodrama may be, it is still a flight from reality.

Did Custer reveal his own estimates of enemy strength at this conference? Nothing recorded that day says so, but Lt. Gibson's July 4th letter gave a conference estimate of "at least 1000 warriors." Lt. Edgerly, in writing about the conference in his narrative of the 1890's, stated that "the general belief shared by Terry, Gibbon, and Custer was that the hostile Indians could not assemble more than 800 warriors, with the probabilities in favor of a lesser number." This was not offered as a quote from the conference, but it was written after, and in contradiction to, Godfrey's 1892 account. The latter has much to say on this topic, though his diary was silent:

> He [Custer] judged from the number of lodge fires reported by Reno

153

that we might meet at least 1000 warriors; there might be enough young men from the agencies visiting their hostile friends, to make a total of 1500. He had consulted the reports of the Commissioner of Indian Affairs and the officials while in Washington as to the probable number of hostiles (those who had persistently refused to enroll themselves at the Indian agencies) and he was confident, if any reliance was to be placed on these reports, that there would not be an opposing force of more than 1500.

All three of these statements place the winter roamers at 800 to 1000 warriors, more or less in agreement with Reno's report of 400 lodges and with the Indian Commissioner's estimate of 3000 persons (750 warriors) as winter roamers. Only Godfrey refers to an additional 500 summer roamers, and this may be spurious, for nothing of the kind was recorded in his diary. But even if Custer did mention such an estimate, he seriously undershot the mark.

Lt. Godfrey did preserve another recollection of a significant event that followed the conference when he came to the bivouac of the Indian scouts while making his duty rounds that evening:

Mitch Bouyer, the half-breed interpreter; Bloody Knife, the chief of the Ree scouts, and Half-Yellow-Face, chief of the Crow scouts, and others were having a "talk." I observed them for a few minutes, when Bouyer turned to me, apparently at the suggestion of Half-Yellow-Face, and said, "Have you ever fought against these Sioux?" "Yes," I replied, and then he asked, "Well, how many do you expect to find?" I answered, "It is said we may find between one thousand and fifteen hundred." "Well, do you think we can whip that many?" "Oh, yes, I guess so." After he had interpreted our conversation, he said to me with a good deal of emphasis, "Well, I can tell you we are going to have a damned big fight."

Numerous hindsight accounts emphasize the gloomy sobriety of the command after the conference as extra-sensory perception forewarned them of tragedy lurking in the near future. In refutation, we need only quote again from Lt. Edgerly's July 4th letter to his wife: "After Custer got through, Reno, Porter, Dr. Lord, Calhoun, Moylan, Smith, Weir, Gibson, and Crittenden came to my little shelter tent and sang for about an hour. Calhoun told us there that his wife had sent him a large cake and that the day after the fight he intended sending a piece around to each officer of the command." So much for premonitions!

On June 23rd the column resumed the trail at 5 a.m., fording the Rosebud, meandering in its narrow, hill-girt valley, five times in three miles to end up on its east bank, where they picked up the hostile trail. The column halted briefly at mile 19 to examine the village site that Lt. Bradley had spotted. Again they halted at about mile 25 to check the Teat Butte campsite and to allow the lagging pack train to come into view. They soon crossed back to the west bank and at mile 34 paused to note the third campsite on both banks

154

of the stream at the mouth of Greenleaf Creek. The day's march totaled 33 miles, but having lost a mile in frequent fordings, they bivouacked at 4:30 on the east bank at about mile 42. But not until sunset did the green pack train straggle in.

Regarding the campsites passed that day, Lt. Wallace officially recorded that "they were all old, but everything indicated a large body of Indians. Every bend of the stream bore some traces of an old camp, and their ponies had nipped almost every spear of grass." In his laconic diary, Charley Reynolds entered the age of the first village site as "about 20 days," and that of the third as "probably 12 days." He was almost exactly a week short on both estimates. George Herendeen judged the trail, presumably after passing the last village, at about ten days old, another underestimate.

That Lt. Godfrey's 1892 narrative sometimes falsely embroiders his more reliable diary is well illustrated by this day's march. The diary merely states that "after marching about 8 miles, we came across a very large village grounds and during the day we passed two more camps, all indicating a very large number of Indians." The later narrative, however, adds that these camps "included a great many wicki-ups . . . These we supposed at the time were for the dogs [!], but . . . they were temporary shelters of the transients from the agenices . . . Everybody was busy studying the age of the pony droppings and tracks, and lodge trails, and endeavoring to determine the number of lodges. These points were all-absorbing topics of conversation."

These insertions are almost certainly erroneous. Neither Godfrey, nor anyone else, recorded at the time the presence of wicki-ups. They were indeed temporary shelters, but not for summer roamers, who brought their families and used lodges like any other Indians. More important, we shall find that the diary provides the proof that the summer roamers had not yet reached these villages. Furthermore, the all-absorbing topic of conversation did not turn to Indian signs until the next day, judging from all the records of those two days. The reason is obvious. These three village sites had been camped on by Reno's half of the regiment and studied by his scouts. Being old hat, they provoked little excitement and less recorded comment.

This day's march in warm, sunny weather had been easy and routine. Custer had followed the precise schedule laid out at the conference — 45 miles for the first day and a half. They had retraced Reno's route along the old hostile trail just as Terry had ordered, and without finding anything new. In due time they expected to overtake the village, circle it, and strike it to add further laurels to the record of the 7th Cavalry. All were relaxed and confident. Benteen went fishing that evening in the trickle of the Rosebud, without success. Edgerly and Porter went there to bathe, presumably with better success. By nightfall the camp was in deep slumber, except for some tireless scouts who were out examining the trail ahead.

June 24th dawned clear and sunny and the column again pulled out of camp at 5 a.m. This was the day Custer expected to reach the Busby bend of the Rosebud and to send scouts to examine Tullock's Fork. Of this matter Herendeen wrote (1878):

> Soon after starting, Custer, who was in advance with Boyer, called me to him to get ready, saying he thought he would send me and Charley Reynolds to the head of Tullock's Fork to take a look. I told the General it was not time yet, as we were then traveling in the direction of the head of Tullock's, and I could only follow his trail. I called Boyer, who was a little ahead, and asked him if I was not correct in my statement to the General, and he said, "Yes, further up on the Rosebud we would come opposite a gap, and there we would cut across and strike Tullock in about 15 miles ride." Custer said, "All right, I could wait."

Soon after this some of the scouts came back on the run reporting another campsite just ahead, where the pole of a sun dance lodge still flaunted the scalp of a white man. Herendeen identified this scalp as having belonged to Pvt. Stoker, one of the three men killed outside of Gibbon's camp on May 23rd. On reaching the sun dance camp, located at about mile 45 on the Rosebud, Custer halted the command for half an hour to examine the grounds and to hold a brief officer's call.

Lt. Godfrey's diary reveals that this camp "was estimated as consisting of three or four hundred lodges," which, it should be noted, matches the size of the preceding camps. Nevertheless, his 1892 narrative claims that it was "much larger than the others. The grass for a considerable distance around it had been cropped close, indicating that large herds had been grazed there . . . It was whilst here that the Indians from the agencies had joined the hostile camp." We have seen that the narrative claimed the advent of agency Indians at the earlier camps, on the evidence of wicki-ups; it now repeats the claim for the sun dance camp, without evidence of wicki-ups, but because of cropped grass, which the official itinerary noted at all the preceding camps. We must conclude that the diary, which is Godrey's only genuine evidence, confirms all the rest; the sun dance camp was no larger than the others, thus proving that the summer roamers had not arrived at the main village when the sun dance was held on June 5-7.

However attentive the officers were to the artifacts of this camp, they were immune to the significant sacred mood that still

156

clung to the site. The sun dance, held almost annually in June or July, figured as the most profoundly religious ceremony of the Sioux. The bravest and purest among them suffered self-inflicted torture in the spiritual interest of the entire tribe. All shared in the renewal of faith and the reforging of unifying bonds. The dance was often the prelude to concerted and resolute tribal action, for it brought the scattered villages together for strength of numbers and fired their strength of purpose. In June of 1876 the tribe was facing extermination. If ever they sought a renewal of faith and common purpose it was then. The holy means to these ends was the sun dance.

It was the most influential of hostile chiefs, Sitting Bull, who had issued the call for the dance on this occasion. A courageous and admired warrior in his younger years, he was now followed as the living symbol of the old and true Indian ways and the champion of their defense; in short, The Great Patriot. It has become popular to disparage this chief in concert with his strongest personal enemy among the whites, Indian Agent James McLaughlin, and his bitterest rival among his own tribe, Gall. But in 1876 there was no question of his influential leadership of the hostiles, or winter roamers. Indians were not given to following the cowardly, the selfish, or the incompetent. Even the whites, ordinarily obtuse in Indian matters, universally recognized his eminence among the unsubjugated natives, although few, indeed, had ever laid eyes on him.

The ceremony and the leader fused at this moment of tribal desperation. Sitting Bull participated fully in the tortures of the flesh and the inspiration of the dance. They culminated in his prophetic vision of soldiers falling into the Indian camp up-side-down. This was powerful medicine, accepted by every Indian present. A resurgence of hope, spirit, and resolve flooded through the people. All the spiritual signs were gloriously favorable. They were destined to win a victory. Tribal culture would survive. The source of this confidence should not be disparaged, for magic works for those who believe, even as every true Christian must profess.

The soldiers may have been insensitive to all this, but not the Indian scouts. They had devoutly studied the camp signs the night before and come to an agreement as to their message. Red Star, one of the Ree scouts, later told the story:

> Here there was evidence of the Dakotas having made medicine, the sand had been arranged and smoothed, and pictures had been drawn. The Dakota scouts with Custer said this meant the enemy knew the army was coming. In one of the sweat lodges was a long heap or ridge of sand, on which Red Bear, Red Star, and Soldier saw figures drawn, indicating by hoof prints Custer's men on one side and the Dakotas on the other.

Between them dead men were drawn lying with their heads toward the Dakotas. The Arikara scouts understood this to mean that the Dakota medicine was too strong for them and that they would be defeated by the Dakotas. Young Hawk saw in one of the sweat lodges where they had camped, opposite the entrance three stones near the middle, all in a row and painted red. This meant in Dakota sign language that the Great Spirit had given them victory, and that if the whites did not come, they would seek them. Soldier saw offerings, four sticks standing upright with a buffalo calf-skin tied on with cloth and other articles of value, which was evidence of a great religious service. This was also seen by Strikes Two, Little Sioux, and Boy Chief. All the Arikara knew what this meant, namely, that the Dakotas were sure of winning.

In this over-awed mood the Rees proceeded three or four miles up the river, only to discover strange pictures of fighting buffalo carved in the rock face of some cliffs along the stream. After careful study, they concluded: "The message of the pictures to Custer's command was: Do not follow the Dakotas into the Big Horn country to which they have gone, for they will turn and destroy you." Being unfamiliar with this country, the Rees did not know that these "Medicine Rocks" had been inscribed in antiquity by long-forgotten red men. But it is a tribute to their loyalty and fortitude that in the face of such powerful contrary medicine, they continued to perform their duties faithfully, and when the ultimate confrontation came, many exceeded their duty by fighting hard beside the troops.

At the officers' call held during the half-hour halt, Custer announced a change in the order and pace of the march. Now that they were to advance beyond the farthest penetration of Reno's scouts, he was sending all of them out to scour the country for diverging trails, as Terry had ordered. Custer himself would take the lead with an escort of two companies, while the remainder of the column would trail a half mile behind. And in order to reduce the give-away dust cloud kicked up by the horses in such hot, dry weather, it would be well for the battalions to march in parallel columns.

The command then proceeded more slowly up the east bank of the stream, crossing two eastern affluents that carried running water. The first, at mile 53, was then called Muddy Creek, but is now known as Lame Deer Creek; the second, at mile 58, is now called Muddy Creek, whatever it may have been called earlier. All these names are used in various accounts, making for some confusion, but Lt. Wallace's itinerary makes it clear that they had crossed both, when Custer called the noon halt at 1 p.m., just beyond Muddy Creek, where the Rees remarked on the next deserted village site. Although Custer had been following the trail for eight hours, he had covered only 16 miles, a decidedly easy and cautious pace.

While the troopers lunched, Custer puzzled over the radical

change in the Indian sign that had started abruptly just above Lame Deer Creek. No longer was there one well-defined and heavy trail interrupted at appropriate intervals by a large campsite. Instead, the valley was now covered from one side to the other with innumerable lodge-pole trails, and campgrounds appeared in profusion. And many of the signs were suddenly much fresher. It was puzzling. Had the village broken up and scattered after the sun dance, with some continuing on, some doubling back, and others diverging right and left? Fearing this to be the case, Custer had called the halt, which he extended to four hours, while the scouts kept busy.

Furnishing the six Crow scouts with cavalry horses in order to rest their own tiring ponies, Custer ordered them to follow the trail ahead as far as they could get and still return to the advancing column by sundown. They should search carefully for diverging trails, especially to the left, and keep a special look-out toward Tullock's Fork. If they found anything crucial, they should send back a courier. Custer also sent Lt. Varnum with a party of Rees back to Lame Deer Creek to investigate a trail diverging to the left that Herendeen had discovered and just brought to his attention. Lt. Varnum referred to this back-scout in his letter of July 4th, but Herendeen described it more fully in 1878:

> As we passed Muddy Creek [Lame Deer Creek] I noticed that some lodges had left the main trail on the Rosebud and gone that way. I followed them a short distance, and then rode over to Custer and told him some of the lodges had gone up the Muddy. He halted the command at once and sent Lt. Varnum to find out where the trail on the Muddy went. Custer said he did not want to lose any of the lodges, and if any of them left the main trail he wanted to know about it. While Varnum was gone we halted and the men cooked dinner. He was absent about two hours and when he came back told Custer that the Muddy trail swung over [to?] the Rosebud and joined the main trail again, which freshened every moment.

It was undoubtedly at this prolonged halt that the command turned to discussing the size, age, and significance of these fresher trails. The records for the day are studded with references to numerous trails and camps, all characterized as new or fresh. But confusion reigned as to the significance of this sudden new pattern. Did it mean that the old village had been moving only short distances for new pasturage? Or had it broken up?

The Indian scouts must have soon realized that they were witnessing the evidence of an influx of summer roamers converging on Sitting Bull's village from many directions and in bands large and small, some very recently. These fresher signs overlaying the earlier trail of the main village made the pattern confusing. Even Custer was fooled, for he was worrying about diverging, not converging trails, and about a scattering, not an assembling village. Even with hindsight, only one member of the command put his finger on the key to the puzzle. This was lowly Pvt. Henry M. Brinkerhoff, who wrote years later: "About 2 p.m. we crossed a large Indian trail going directly north and coming from the south, and we then knew that the agency Indians were on their way to join the hostile Sioux camp. All signs pointed to the fact that there were a great many warriors in the bunch, as the trail in some places on the crossing of the Rosebud was a mile wide."

Brinkerhoff tells another incident of this halt that may be typical of the scouts' attitude, even though it is certainly apocryphal in other respects:

> General Custer was very much excited, and finally spotting Bloody Knife and me, he called us to him and told me to ask Bloody Knife how many warriors he thought there were on the trail. I did so, and Bloody Knife said that he did not understand. Custer demanded a positive answer and Bloody Knife told me to tell him to go count the spears of grass on the hills and he'd tell [learn?] how many Indians there were there. Custer said he was crazy . . .

A more authentic story of this halt comes from the Rees. Custer came to their circle and talked with them, Gerard interpreting. Stabbed jumped up and hopped about the fire pretending to dodge enemy bullets, while Custer watched. Stabbed then turned to Gerard, "I want you to tell Custer that I showed him how we fight, for when his soldiers go into the fight they stand still like targets while the Sioux are dodging about, so it is hard to hit them. But they shoot the soldiers down very easily." Custer handled this lesson in soldier skills very diplomatically by replying, "I know your people; you are truely like the coyote, you know how to hide, to creep up, and to take by surprise." Then Custer told the Rees that when the battle started, he did not want them to fight beside the troops, but to run off the Sioux ponies so as to leave them afoot. He thus recognized the problem of coordinating the maneuvers of Indians and troopers, and the danger of mistaking friend for foe among the redskins.

According to Lt. Wallace, it was about four o'clock when couriers returned from the Crow scouts in the advance, reporting "a fresh camp at the forks of the Rosebud." The main village had indeed camped next at the Busby bend of the Rosebud, about two miles below the forks where Davis Creek enters from the southwest, but the reported freshness was due to more recent overlay sign. The hard-riding couriers had completed a 24-mile round trip in about three hours. But they had not gotten beyond the Busby bend, or they would have brought the more important news as to where the trail led from that critical point.

Encouraged by this report, and that of Varnum that the Lame Deer Creek trail led back to the Rosebud, Custer ordered the column to resume the march. Lt. Wallaces' itinerary says: "At 5 p.m. the command moved out . . . passed several large camps. The trail was now fresh, and the whole valley scratched up by the trailing lodge poles. At 7:45 p.m. we encamped on the right bank of the Rosebud . . . Distance marched for today, about 28 miles." Since the main village had not camped between Muddy Creek and the Busby Bend, the intervening camps Wallace mentioned could only have been overlays made by converging summer roamers. This fact was all-important, but Custer was still pre-occupied with diverging trails, as revealed by Herendeen (1878): "Towards evening the trails became so fresh that Custer ordered flankers to the right and left and a sharp lookout had for lodges leaving to the right or left. He said he wanted to get the whole village and nothing must leave the main trail without his knowing it."

Custer had arrived at the Busby bend exactly on schedule as worked out at the steamboat conference. In two and a half days he had covered 73 miles. This last day's march had been exceptionally slow and easy, for it was interrupted by several short and one long, four-hour halt. It had taxed neither men nor horses of his command, although it had made hard work for the ever-moving scouts. Yet Captian Benteen, who knew the facts as well as anyone, later saw fit to tell Terry that Custer had driven his men 92 miles to this point! This laid the foundation for the conviction that Custer had deliberately violated Terry's plan by breaking down his men and animals to get there first, and thereby brought righteous disaster down upon himself!

On the contrary, the evidence proves that Custer faithfully observed his orders in both word and spirit. But he may have begun to wonder whether the situation contemplated by the plan was going to be realized.

Chapter 14
The Eve of Disaster

The 7th Cavalry pitched camp just below present Busby at 7:45 on the evening of June 24th. The troopers fell into the routine of preparing their evening meal and making themselves and their horses comfortable for the night. They did not know that they would get little sleep at this bivouac.

Dull camp routine may have occupied the troopers, but not their commander. Custer was waiting impatiently for the return of his Crow scouts, for he wanted badly to know two things. Was the village scattering, as he feared it might? If not, in what direction was it headed? He had probably been told already that only two or three miles up the river an oft-used Indian trail led ten miles southwest up Davis Creek to the divide and then thirteen miles north of west down what is now called Reno Creek to the Little Big Horn. Had the hostiles taken this trail? Or, continued south up the main Rosebud? Or, turned north toward Tullock's Fork? Or, split up to follow all three?

There was also a newer problem that required some thought. Every account makes clear reference to the freshness of the sign at this bivouac. As the most specific, Lt. Varnum wrote that they were only two days old, and Lt. Wallace recorded that the quarry was a mere thirty miles away. Should this prove true, the hostiles could not be high up on the Little Big Horn as the steamboat conferees had expected and planned for. It would be decidedly awkward if they were on the lower stream.

While Custer was fretting the Crows were learning just what he wanted to know. One of them, White-Man-Runs-Him, gave some details of this advance scout in an interview with General Hugh L.

Scott conducted on the very scene in 1919. The Crow stated that they had followed the hostile trail up Davis Creek to the divide, although he did not mention the next deserted campsite near that point. He said that "on June 24th, Hairy Moccasin, Goes Ahead, and I rode some soldiers' horses and came to that peak [not the Crow's Nest] and then rode back. The soldiers were just below Busby." When asked what they had seen from the peak, the scout replied, "We were not sure whether the Sioux were camping there [on the Little Big Horn?]. It was late and we could not see so well. We knew the trail and the way the Sioux were moving [on it?], but were not sure which way they went [after crossing the divide, or reaching the Little Big Horn?]." In a rather incoherent interview with Dr. Dixon in 1909, Curly, another Crow scout, indicated that he was with this group and that before returning to report to Custer they spent some time examining the head of Tullock's Fork.

According to Wallace's record, it was nine o'clock when these Crows returned to report that "the Indians had crossed the divide to the Little Big Horn." He had vaguely implied that Custer had sent them ahead from the Busby camp "to see which branch of the stream the Indians had followed." This proves that Custer did not have this information when he reached that bivouac, but the scouts could not have raced to the divide and back in the available hour and a quarter. They could, however, have made it from the Muddy Creek halt to the divide and back to Busby in the available eight hours. This is the basis of our earlier statement that Custer had sent all the Crows ahead from Muddy Creek and that only couriers had returned to tell him of the fresh campsite at Busby.

The returning scouts could at last assure Custer that the hostile trail did not scatter and break up, that it did not turn north toward Tullock's Fork, nor south up the main Rosebud. Instead, it turned up Davis Creek and crossed the divide, but having to look into the sun they could not spot the village in camp anywhere beyond. The implication was clear that the Sioux were on the Little Big Horn, and because the trail was so fresh, they could not be far from the mouth of Reno Creek, which joins the larger stream only twenty miles above its mouth.

Custer was undoubtedly pleased with this good scouting work that so reduced the spectrum of possibilities that he had to consider. He may have been even more pleased when the Crows told him that there was an observation point on the divide, called the Crow's Nest, from which they could see the country for miles around, including the valley of the Little Big Horn. A convenient pocket for concealing horses nestled at the base of the peak. Since it was only three or four miles south of the trail as it crossed the divide, they could easily reach it in time to spot the village by the tell-tale camp smoke at daylight the next morning.

The General promptly adopted this suggestion by ordering Lt. Varnum to take a detail of scouts to the Crow's Nest. The Chief of Scouts selected Mitch Boyer with four or five of the Crows, and Charley Reynolds with six of the Rees. Of this mission he later wrote: "Custer said he would move at 11 o'clock at night; I was to go at nine. He would go to the base of the mountains where I was to be, and I was to send him a note as early as possible of what I learned. I got to the Crow's Nest about 2:30 a.m. on the 25th, about 25 miles [closer to 16] from where I had left Custer." Having concealed their horses in the pocket, the scouts took up their vigil on the peak, while the exhausted officer stretched out for a nap until dawn.

The discovery that the hostile village was probably on the *lower* Little Big Horn had compelled Custer to make a swift and critical decision. He could hardly shirk the issue, for Terry had authorized him to make his own best decisions as guided by developing circumstances, unhampered by constraints based on conjecture. Custer had two major alternatives. One was Terry's recommendation that he make a two-day circle to pounce on the village from the south after Gibbon's blocking force had reached its station. The other was to march that night under cover of darkness to a point near the divide where he could lay concealed the next day while the scouts pinpointed the village; he could then make a night approach and launch a surprise attack at dawn of the 26th.

Terry's suggestion, of course, carried the weight of a superior's recommendation and gave Gibbon full time to reach his station. But this plan had been based on the assumption that the village would be found on the *upper* river. But under the new circumstances, a two-day delay while circling to the south would entail grave risks. He would have to lose contact with the enemy, and in two days the village could disperse or move far in any direction; it could double back on the Rosebud route he would necessarily leave open, or even approach and surprise Gibbon's weaker force on the march. Furthermore, there could be no assurance that his whole regiment could execute the circle without detection, and the latter would certainly trigger flight or dispersion.

The alternate plan, on the other hand, had certain advantages. With the village on the lower river, Gibbon's force on the morning of the 26th might even be closer to the action than contemplated by the original plan. Certainly the risk of detection would be less

164

if he spent the daylight hours well concealed than if he marched in a circle, and there would be no danger of losing contact with the enemy. Above all, there would be less delay to permit flight or dispersion. He now had the opportunity to press home a surprise attack on elusive Indians, and such opportunities were both rare and fleeting.

The bold and energetic Custer, who preferred the error of commission to the error of omission, chose the alternate plan. This is the fact. His reasoning, of course, is not of record. We have merely tried, as conscientiously as possible, to reconstruct the most probable reasoning, without drawing on melodramatic simplistics. The fatal flaw in the picture stemmed from Custer's, as well as Terry's, misevaluation of the strength and temper of the enemy, an error whose consequences would jeopardize any plan.

Custer had not sent Herendeen out to scout the head of Tullock's Fork, as Terry had requested. Since the Crows had been sent ahead that afternoon, undoubtedly with orders to keep a lookout in that direction, it was hardly necessary. But by now, Custer knew where the hostile trail led and that the village was probably on the lower river, an unexpected location that compelled a departure from Terry's recommendations. This important intelligence deserved prompt communication to the expedition commander, and Herendeen was ready and waiting. Yet Custer failed to send him. Was it a simple oversight? Or was it an omission of some sinister significance? We have no means of knowing. Hindsight, however, reveals that it could have had no influence on the course of events.

Having reached his decision even before sending the party to the Crow's Nest, Custer announced an officer's call for 9:30 that evening. After the officers had groped their way toward the feeble candle that marked headquarters, the General revealed his decision. According to Lt. Wallace's official record, "General Custer determined to cross the divide that night, to conceal the command, the next day find out the locality of the village, and attack the following morning [June 26th] at daylight. Orders were given to move at midnight . . ." Lt. Edgerly confirmed this in his July 4th letter: "Had officer's call about nine and were told that there were indications of a village within a day's march of us and that Custer intended making a night march and hiding in the hills the next day so as to strike the Indians at daylight of the 26th." Lt. Godfrey's diary is silent on this matter, but his narrative follows Wallace and Edgerly precisely, and adds that Custer detailed Lt. Luther S. Hare, Godfrey's subaltern, to assist the absent Lt. Varnum in commanding the scouts.

The officers picked their way back to their units to roust out their sleeping men. Cloaked in frustrating darkness, the troopers saddled up, packed the mules, and prepared for the cavalryman's bane – a night march. Lt. Wallace recorded that they marched eight miles from 1 a.m. to daylight. At the outset the column floundered across swampy bottoms, then stumbled up rocky ravines, climbing steadily toward the divide. In the blackness eyes were useless. Only the sound of jangling equipment and plodding hooves, and the choking dust kept the column in any sort of order. Far in the rear, Captain Keogh, commanding the escort for the hapless pack train, kept the air blue with less than merry oaths.

At the head of the column with Custer rode Fred Gerard, Bloody Knife, and Half-Yellow-Face, the chief of the Crow scouts. Gerard testified at the Reno Court of Inquiry that Custer ordered him "to be sure to have the Indians follow the left hand trail, no matter how small it might be; he didn't want any of the Sioux to escape him. He wanted to get them all together." When these orders were dutifully passed on to Bloody Knife, they evoked the remark, "He needn't be so particular about the small camps; we'll get enough when we strike the big camp." In response to Custer's inquiry, Gerard told him that they could expect to have to fight 1500 to 2000 Sioux warriors.

Custer apparently did not take Gerard's uncannily accurate estimate very seriously, but the interpreter's further testimony reveals that he was bent on concealing the command the next day and attacking on the 26th: "Custer asked these two Indians if he could cross the divide before daylight, and they replied no. He asked if he could cross after daylight without being discovered by the Indians in the bottom, and they said no. He then asked them if there was any timber where they could be concealed during the day where the Indians could not discover them." Gerard failed to reveal the answer to this last question.

Shortly before daylight Custer halted the command to wait for news from the Crow's Nest party. The troopers breakfasted and then laid down to nap during the ensuing five or six hour halt. It is often claimed that this "all night" march so exhausted the command that it was not fit for battle the next afternoon. But the record clearly refutes this charge. The men marched at night for two and a half hours only, and the resumption of the advance the next morning was delayed nearly four hours beyond the standard five o'clock departure. The distance left to be marched the next day did not exceed twenty miles and was spread over about fourteen hours.

A midnight interruption is, of course, no way to guarantee a good night's sleep, but if such an interruption rendered the 7th Cavalry unfit for duty, it should have been medically discharged to a man!

As the sun peeped above the horizon behind them, the scouts at the Crow's Nest began to scour the valley ahead with eager and practiced eye. Varnum had caught less than an hour's sleep when they called him up to see what they had discovered. He later wrote: "I saw the two [?] tepees, spoken of so often, on the branch [of Reno Creek] down which we went to the fight. The Indians tried to show me an immense pony herd in the valley of the Little Big Horn. I couldn't see it. They told me to 'look for worms' . . . I sat down and wrote a dispatch to Custer and sent it off at about 4:45. Before the Rees left with the message, however, the smoke of some of Custer's campfires were seen about ten miles off, possibly not so far [closer to eight miles]." In his July 4th letter, the Lieutenant also wrote that "we discovered the smoke of a village . . . The Crows said there were about two or three thousand ponies on the plains twelve miles off, but I could not see them, for their eyes were better than mine."

Since what one sees depends as much on trained perception as on visual acuity, the experienced scouts had no trouble locating the village, despite the fact that the tepees themselves were concealed in the valley. White-Man-Runs-Him recalled: "We could see some white horses on the other side of the Little Horn river. The horses were on the hills . . . I told Mitch Boyer it would be a good thing if they [the command] would hide here until night and then surprise the camp." Red Star also related that he "looked and saw a dark object and above it light smoke rising up from the Dakota tepees. It was at the upper end of the village; the tepees were hidden by the high ridge, but the smoke was drawing out and up. Beyond the smoke he saw some black specks he thought were horses. Charley Reynolds looked a long time, then took out his field glasses and looked a long time. Then he put them down and nodded his head."

Red Star and Bull had no more than left with Varnum's note, when the remaining scouts spotted two Sioux a mile and a half west of them. They watched the unsuspecting enemy ride along toward the head of Davis Creek. Alarmed that they might discover the smoke of Custer's camp, or even ambush the couriers, Lt. Varnum took Charley Reynolds, Mitch Boyer, and two Crows to liquidate the dangerous spies. Somehow they lost the trail and failed in their mission, but from the peak the others caught glimpses of the pair making their way down Davis Creek straight toward Custer's camp. The Crows said they saw six other Sioux hunting buffalo nearby on

Tullock's Fork, and the Rees mentioned four others prowling around the base of the peak. The scouts began to fear that the chances for a successful concealment of the command were fading fast.

Fortunately, Red Star, who carried Varnum's message, had a sufficient head start over the spies and drew ahead of Bull's poor horse. On reaching the camp at about eight o'clock, Bloody Knife greeted him and Custer and Gerard promptly joined them. According to Red Star: "Custer sat down on his left knee near Red Star, who was squatted down with a cup of coffee. Custer signed to Red Star, asking him if he had seen the Dakotas, and he answered by a sign that he had. Then Red Star handed the note to Custer . . . who read it at once and nodded his head . . . Custer said to Bloody Knife by signs, referring to Tom [Captain Tom Custer], 'Your brother there is frightened, his heart flutters with fear, his eyes are rolling from fright at the news of the Sioux. When we have beaten the Sioux, he will then be a man.' " Lt. Godfrey's diary refers to this by-play by saying that Bloody Knife told Custer that "we would find enough Sioux to keep us fighting for two or three days. Genl. remarked laughingly that he thought we would get through them in one day."

Since Lt. Varnum may have admitted in his note that he could not personally confirm the scout's sighting of the village, Custer decided that he had better go look for himself. Taking Red Star as guide and Gerard, Bloody Knife, and two Rees, the general immediately set out on the eight mile ride to the Crow's Nest. Since he could not have reached there before 9 o'clock, the camp smoke had undoubtedly diminished and visibility conditions had turned less favorable. Red Star related that with the aid of field glasses and careful instructions from Reynolds, Custer finally acknowledged that he saw the signs. But Herendeen, an exceptionally reliable source, wrote that when Custer returned from the Crow's Nest he said "he could not see the Indian village, but . . . [Boyer] said they could distinctly see it some fifteen miles off."

Gerard makes no specific reference to Custer, but related that "we . . . could see the large black mass moving in front and down the Little Big Horn and a dense cloud of dust over all and behind." He then added another item, which is significant for its possible reinforcement of the General's fear that the village might get away: "The camp we had found was the smaller camp, the larger camp being downstream further, and was on the way to the larger camp, and this led us all to believe that the Indians were stampeded." It is more likely that these signs indicated the arrival of another band of summer roamers.

It was Benteeen, writing in 1892, who claimed that Custer could not only see nothing but refused to believe his scouts. The tone of his claim, however, undermines all confidence in it: "He [Custer] could see nothing through the old telescopic glass they had and didn't believe there was anything to be seen; now, strange, perhaps, to say, I did believe it — another premonition. I knew it, because, why, I'd sooner trust the sharp eye of an Indian than to trust a pretty good binocular that I always carried; and I had got that from experience." The Captain did not bother to explain why the General soon decided to attack a non-existent village! Whether or not Custer saw the signs himself is immaterial, for he did accept the judgement of his scouts.

Having shown Custer the village and the lay of the land, the scouts broke their bad news — that Sioux spies had detected the command and must already be racing to alarm the village. White-Man-Runs-Him related that "if we hadn't seen the two Sioux, we would have suggested to him to stay here all day and make a night march." Red Star told of a hot argument between the Crow, Big Belly (Half-Yellow-Face?), and Custer:

Custer said: "This camp has not seen our army, none of their scouts have seen us." Big Belly replied: "You say we have not been seen. These Sioux we have seen at the foot of the hill, two going one way, and four the other, are good scouts, they have seen the smoke of our camp." Custer said, speaking angrily: "I say again we have not been seen. That camp has not seen us, I am going ahead to carry out what I think. I want to wait until it is dark and then we will march, we will place our army around the Sioux camp." Big Belly replied: "That plan is bad, it should not be carried out." Custer said: "I have said what I propose to do, I want to wait until it is dark and then go ahead with my plan."

The obvious conviction of the scouts was impressive. The General refused to commit himself, but he was angry and upset over the possibility of having been discovered.

Custer then led the entire observation party on a rapid ride back to the main command, which he found waiting on the trail only a mile short of the divide. It had advanced at 8:45, after Custer had left, and after proceeding four miles, had halted at 10:07. No one seemed to know who had ordered this march; Gerard testified that Custer had left orders for the command to remain in place until his return, and was angry on finding that it had moved without orders. But if this irritated Custer, still graver news soon came to disturb him more.

At this halt short of the divide, Herendeen had gone up a ravine a few hundred yards to find a secluded spot for a nap. On awakening, he had dimly seen something moving further up the ravine, but dismissed it as a deer. Mitch Boyer, on returning with Custer, told

Herendeen he had seen two Indians approach to within 150 yards of him before they took alarm and fled. He guessed they were heading back for their village "as fast as they can go." He had also seen two others driving loose horses.

No sooner had this been reported to Custer than his brother, Tom, came up to say that a squad of troopers had just had a run in with a party of hostiles on the back trail, where packers of Company F had lost a load of hardtack on the march. During the halt, Sergeant William A. Curtis had taken a few men to ride back and retrieve the load. As they approached the place, they came upon several Indians breaking open the lost boxes. They exchanged a few shots before the Indians scattered into the hills.

If Custer had been sceptical before, he was convinced now that his force had been thoroughly discovered. If he were now to conceal the command until darkness, as he had planned, the fully alarmed village might be nowhere in sight by dawn, and perhaps fully scattered — an ignominious end to an ambitious campaign. Reluctantly, he had to admit that the Crows had been right; his only hope now lay in attacking before the village could melt away. The new circumstances forced an immediate advance to the attack. In fact, they compelled Custer to abandon the very tactics he had employed at the Battle of the Washita eight years before. There, all under cover of darkness, he had been able to approach, divide his command into battalions, and place them all in position close to and surrounding the village; then, at a pre-arranged dawn signal, the several battalions had charged the surprised enemy in unison, completely routing them. Presumably, this was the plan he had been hoping to employ again, and it was only in the face of absolute necessity and with the greatest reluctance that he now abandoned it in favor of an exposed daylight approach over open country for an afternoon attack.

The General promptly held another officers' call, informing his men that from the Crow's Nest the scouts had pin-pointed a large Indian village in the valley of the Little Big Horn, only about fifteen miles distant. He then explained that since the command had certainly been discovered by enemy spies on the hills and even in their rear, there was no choice save to advance immediately to the attack. Not a single officer, then or later, registered the least demurral to the necessity of this action. Custer then instructed the company commanders to assign one non-commissioned officer and six privates to the company pack mules, to see that their men were properly supplied with ammunition on their persons, and otherwise readied for the expected fight. He would assign the companies

170

their positon in the march in the order in which they reported themselves ready. Captain Benteen promptly announced that his company was always ready, and was given the advance. Within a few minutes all were ready.

Custer also alerted the Ree scouts to what was coming and again reminded them that he was counting on them to run off the enemy pony herds. Stabbed, a forty-five year old leader of the Rees, then exhorted his tribesmen to fight well and bravely. "Today will be a hard battle. We have been told there is a big Sioux camp ahead," he told them. Lt. Godfrey observed that the Rees "seem to have become satisfied that we were going to find more Sioux than we could well take care of." But Stabbed produced the medicine to make the hearts of the Rees strong. All the way from their homeland, he had carried some clay, which he proceeded to rub ceremoniously on the chests of the braves. Then, having detailed Pretty Face to manage their pack mules, the keyed-up Rees also reported for action.

At 11:45 the column started the advance, but after marching only a mile Custer halted again at 12:07, just over the crest of the divide.

Chapter 15
Checkmate on the Little Big Horn

The sun beat down from a crystal sky at noon of the hot Sabbath of June 25th, 1876. The 7th Cavalry squinted against the glare and men and animals sweated freely into the dry breeze as they topped the divide between the Rosebud and Little Big Horn and halted a third of a mile beyond, at 12:07 by Lt. Wallace's official watch, set for Chicago time.

At this brief halt, Custer made battalion assignments of his force of 31 officers, 566 troopers, and 50 others. He retained for himself Companies C, E, F, I, and L, which totalled 13 officers, 200 men, and 8 others, after he directed Reno to take most of the scouts. To Major Reno he assigned Companies A, G, and M, which numbered 11 officers, 129 men, and 35 others. To Captain Benteen he assigned Companies D, H, and K, a mere 5 officers and 110 men. Beside these three combat battalions there was a support column, not the least in strength. This was the pack train in charge of Lt. Mathey and escorted by Captain McDougall's Company B. It numbered 2 officers, 127 men, and 7 others. These four units were destined to be widely scattered at the critical moment.

At this five-minute halt there was more on Custer's mind. He was now irrevocably committed to an approach to, and attack upon, the village in broad daylight. But there was no time to lose, for it was already past noon with the foe still fifteen miles away. A walking approach would keep the regiment nicely together, but expose it

*This chapter is based on extensive analyses that are presented in Part II. For information on the wounded, see Chapter 23, and on battle strengths, recruits, and casualties, see Chapter 24; for a chronology of events see Chapter 25, and for Indian strength see Chapter 29.

to detection all afternoon and delay the attack until five o'clock, leaving little daylight for the fight and pursuit of refugees. A maximum prudent speed would be in order, as every officer understood. He hoped the pack train, with one man detailed to each pair of mules, would not lag dangerously.

Another matter demanded immediate attention. Since the village lay a few miles below the mouth of Reno Creek, his approach should drive the refugees north as Terry planned. But suppose the village, warned of his approach, were moving upstream? The attack would then come from the wrong direction. Or, suppose there were satellite villages camped upstream? They might escape to the left, against Terry's caution. It was important to learn about these possibilities *now*, while there was still time to adjust the attack plan. Noting a line of bluffs only a mile to the west, Custer called Benteen over and ordered him to take his battalion to the left and send an officer to the bluffs to look for any sign of Indians in the upper valley of the river, and then hurry back to join the main command.

At 12:12 Benteen moved out on the left oblique while Custer headed for the right bank and Reno the left bank of the adjacent Middle Fork of Reno Creek. Not until twenty minutes later was the pack train able to follow in their wake. Scarcely a mile out, Custer began to suspect, or could see for himself, that the first line of bluffs might not afford Benteen a view of the valley. He dispatched Chief Trumpeter Henry Voss with permission for the Captain to proceed to the next divide, if necessary. After another mile he sent Sergeant-Major William H. Sharrow with permission to go even farther, but to observe the remainder of his original orders.

Custer and Reno trotted only part of the time so as not to outdistance Benteen, now hidden in rougher terrain. At 1:20 they passed a morass, 4.5 miles out, where they picked up the pace a trifle. In three more miles they sighted a lone tepee ahead where the Middle Fork joins the South Fork of Reno Creek. When still a half mile distant, Custer waved Reno's battalion over to join him on the right bank, at 2:00 according to Wallace's watch. A few minutes later they pulled up to the lone tepee to find that it stood on a deserted village site and contained the body of a dead warrior. The Indian scouts, previously ahead, had congregated around it to make excited preparations for action.

Interpreter Gerard, who had climbed a knoll a few yards north of the tepee, now caught a glimpse of pony herds and Indians milling in the distance. Waving his hat, he halooed to Custer, "Here are your Indians, running like devils!" Custer, anxiously eyeing his back trail, had been searching in vain for any sign of Benteen's outfit, but with

Gerard's confirmation of his worst fears, he could afford no longer to hold back for the missing battalion. He accordingly ordered Reno to take the advance with the scouts and step up the pace. The keyed-up Rees fell in with Reno, some in the advance, some on the flanks, and some in the rear, depending on the speed they could coax from their over-worked ponies.

The two columns trotted steadily for about three miles to approach the lower forks, where the North Fork joins the main stream. Custer asked the Crow scout, White-Man-Runs-Him, the meaning of the dust clouds visible ahead in the valley. The answer was, "The Sioux must be running away." Neither Benteen nor the pack train carrying all the spare ammunition was yet in sight, but with the enemy in flight, Custer had no choice save to pitch into them as quickly as possible. As reported by Reno, Adjutant Cooke came to him with Custer's orders: "The village was only two miles above and running away; to move forward at as rapid a gait as prudent and to charge afterwards, and that the whole outfit would support me."

Not knowing that Custer would soon turn to the right, Reno led out smartly, soon recrossing to the left bank to reach a natural ford across the Little Big Horn at 2:50. The advance scouts, having gotten beyond the obstructing bluffs on the east bank of the river, could see down the valley. Beyond the timber scattered along the west bank, they glimpsed some lodges of a standing village and incredible pony herds being driven in from the hills. The camp was unexpectedly large and obviously not in flight after all. Instead, the warriors were gathering to attack. On hearing this news, and being well aware of Custer's contrary conviction, Gerard passed it on to Adjutant Cooke, who was about to return to Custer, having seen Reno off. Reno forded the river and halted briefly to close up and form for a charge down the valley. During the five minute halt, he sent Pvts. McIlhargy and Mitchell, of Company L, to warn Custer that the village was not in flight, but gathering in his front in strong force.

Reno launched his two-mile accelerating run down the flat valley. As ordered, most of the Indian scouts diverged toward the river to run off the pony herds grazing on both banks, but others charged on the left flank of the flying column. With each minute they could see a little more of the endless village and the fast-gathering braves in their front. Reckoning on only 129 troopers as his disciplined force, Reno grew appalled at the horde of warriors and tepees he would have to charge through, with no support in sight. He could lead his men to a gallant, but futile death, or he could assume the defensive and await his promised support.

Reno chose the latter course. Halting the charge, he dismounted his men, deploying them in a skirmish line facing downstream toward the village with his right flank on the timber along the river. Every fourth trooper withdrew to hold horses, leaving ninety-five grim-faced men to hold off a swelling swarm of yelling savages. Long-range shots were ringing out, opening the Battle of the Little Big Horn at about 3:10. The Indians stormed out of a ravine ahead to drive in the Ree scouts and turn Reno's left flank. Recognizing that so open a position would not be long tenable, after ten minutes he ordered the troops to execute an orderly movement into the timber on the right flank, taking advantage of the cover provided by the brush and a former river bank.

The firing grew heavier as the warriors dashed their ponies ever closer to the new skirmish line. Gradually their fire extended until it was coming from every direction, even from the rear across the river. Then smoke began billowing through the timber as the hostiles set fires to drive the troops out. The ranks of the attackers grew to odds of at least five to one. The troopers proved too few to adequately man the extensive perimeter of the timber. The fifty rounds of ammunition each carried on his person began to give out, drawing men off the line to secure more from their saddle pockets. Reno looked in vain for any sign of his promised support. Without it, his position would ultimately become a death trap, especially when ammunition was exhausted. Before it was too late, he decided to charge out of the timber to seek a more defensible hill top on the bluffs across the river.

Many have criticized Reno for failing to drive his initial charge through the village of a thousand lodges stretching for miles down the valley. They have also criticized him for leaving his position in the timber. It is enough to point out that few of the men who were with him figure among such critics. But the same can not be said for the *manner* of his withdrawal. It started in confusion and de-generated to a panic.

Reno ordered the command to mount up in column formation in a clearing within the timber in preparation for the charge out. In the din of battle many of the scattered men, especially of Company G posted deepest in the woods, failed to hear the order. At least seventeen were left behind, some wounded. After the others had abandoned the skirmish line, the Indians penetrated the timber to deliver a devastating volley at the half-formed, stationary column. Though revolvers were still empty, Reno quickly pulled out.

Reno burst from the timber at the head of a ragged column and

175

a comet's tail of frantic troopers. Dashing a mile back upstream, he plunged across the river and spurred up a steep bluff to a hill top. The triumphant Indians instantly recognized this as a retreat without covering fire. They charged their ponies in close to engage in an easy buffalo hunt. They shot and knocked troopers from the saddle on the dead run. They poured fire into them when they jammed up at the crossing, where the banks were steep and the water deep. They found easy targets in the survivors churning up the exposed face of the bluff. No effort was made to organize a covering fire at the departure, on the run, at the crossing, or on the bluff-side. As Lt. Wallace splashed across the river his watch read 4 o'clock.

When the briefly demoralized remnants gathered on Reno Hill they numbered only seven officers and eighty-four men. Most of the Indian scouts were scattered over the valley and hills, still fighting or driving off captured pony herds. Although not yet fully known, the total casualties were enough to shock any commander out of his composure; forty killed and thirteen wounded, to say nothing of the missing. The number left behind attests to the disorganized start and the number of casualties along the route betrays a rout.

*   *   *

In the meantime, Custer had followed Reno for only a few paces when he abruptly turned right, undoubtedly intending to move downstream under cover of the bluffs before crossing to launch his promised supporting attack. Coming immediately to the North Fork, he halted to water his thirsty mounts. He then trotted about 1.5 miles along the eastern slope of the bluffs to the base of a high point that promised a view of the valley below. Here the command halted while Custer rode to the crest with his scouts, Mitch Boyer and four Crows.

This first view must have given Custer a shock. There lay the village, far larger than expected, and extending along the bottom for miles. It numbered nearly a thousand lodges, harboring some two thousand warriors. And it was doing anything *but* fleeing, although the squaws were knocking down some lodges. There came Reno's pathetically tiny battalion charging down the valley, headed for certain annihilation if it tried to storm through such a maze of tepees. The picture was scarcely what Custer had imagined when he ordered one battalion to make the initial attack. The 7th Cavalry would have its hands full this day!

We can hardly credit the claims that Custer, on beholding this ominous scene, exulted with cries of "Custer's Luck!" or "We've caught them napping!" It is more likely that, grimly sober, he began to regret that all the spare ammunition was with the pack train vulnerably far in the rear. In fact, on returning to his column, he instantly ordered Sergeant Kanipe of Company C to head back to find McDougall and ask him "to bring the pack train straight across to high ground — if packs get loose, don't stop to fix them, cut them off. Come quick. Big Indian camp." The lucky sergeant turned back on his critical mission.

Trotting down another mile to the base of a still higher bluff, now called Weir Point, Custer rode to its crest for another look. This time he was relieved to see that Reno had halted to form a skirmish line and was only lightly engaged. He should now be able to hold out until Custer's larger force could get into action. Turning to Mitch Boyer and the Crows, he told them they had completed their job by bringing him in contact with the enemy; they could now return to the pack train, for the troops would take over. The Crows, especially Curly, lingered for a while to watch before turning back, but Boyer, whose unheeded warnings had now come true, stubbornly rode on with Custer.

Convinced that he would need every man, Custer must have asked for the tenth time, "Where in hell is Benteen?" On returning to his command, he singled out Trumpeter John Martin of Benteen's own company, to follow on Kanipe's back trail and deliver a message to his Captain. Since Martin was an Italian with little fluency in English, Adjutant Cooke hastily scribbled a message for him to carry:

> Benteen. Come on. Big Village. Be quick, Bring packs.
> P.S. Bring packs.   W.W.Cooke.

The postscript was undoubtedly intended to read, "Bring *ammunition* packs," but the key word was omitted in haste.

The fact that Custer sent Martin on his own back trail shows that he expected Benteen to follow him, as ordered. That he addressed the note to Benteen, rather than McDougall, can only mean that he believed the Captain's otherwise inexplicable delay was due to helping the lagging train — contrary to orders. But whatever he may have thought had happened in the rear, Custer clearly wanted every man and every cartridge, and wanted them pronto.

Custer continued on downstream, presumably searching for a break in the bluffs that would enable him to get into the fight as soon as possible. He eventually found it in Medicine Tail Coulee, which led down to the river opposite the center of the village. In the past few miles the horses of seven troopers had given out, and their dismounted riders were plodding back to safety. He had sent

177

two couriers back, but had also received two from Reno. He would thus go into action with only 13 officers and 193 men, accompanied by Boyer, Boston Custer, Autie Reed, and Mark Kellogg. A total of 210.

It was probably 3:45 when a few Indians opened fire on Custer's column as it was filing down the coulee toward the river. The details of what followed will remain forever obscure. There are as many speculations as speculators. Custer did move back away from the river and then north along a ridge, where many bodies were later found distributed over a surprisingly large area. He and a few others ended up on Custer Hill, about four miles from Reno Hill. Most of the two thousand warriors had concentrated on this small force, those pouring from the village circling to the left, and those racing from Reno's treed command circling to the right, so as to surround the command completely — and at odds of ten to one. The rest of the regiment heard firing shortly after 4:20. It was probably all over by 4:45. Every man with Custer died. All 210.

*   *   *

While Custer and Reno were launching their puny attacks, separated in time and space, Benteen's battalion was poking along in the rear. Having left the divide at 12:12 with the others, he diverged to the left toward the first line of bluffs a mile distant. He detailed Lt. Frank Gibson to take a small party to the crest to examine the upper valley of the Little Big Horn. The report came back that a higher divide beyond an intervening narrow valley completely obstructed the view. Custer's couriers having arrived with permission to proceed farther, if necessary, Benteen veered to the right, soon finding an easier passage into the valley containing an insignificant stream. The crest of the higher divide afforded Gibson a clear view, with glasses, of the upper valley, although the lower was invisible because of a turn in the stream. He hurried down to report not an Indian visible anywhere.

Having so quickly determined precisely what Custer had sent him to find out, Benteen turned down the little stream to its junction with the Middle Fork and Custer's trail. At that moment he sighted the pack train approaching about half a mile above, and so trotted to get farther ahead. After half a mile he reached the morass and halted for fifteen minutes to water his thirsty horses. To this point, his circuit to the left totalled 5.5 miles, just one mile longer than Custer's route, and he reached it at 1:48, just twenty-eight minutes behind the faster-moving General.

178

As the head of the pack train reached the morass, Benteen pulled out at a leisurely walk, which he maintained for nearly five and a half miles. After passing a little over a mile beyond the lone tepee, Sergeant Kanipe passed with his call for the pack train, shouting of a big village ahead. A mile later Trumpeter Martin arrived with Adjutant Cooke's written message. This must have jolted Benteen awake, for we suspect that he had dawdled on the trail because he was convinced that there was no village and no battle to be fought that day. He was probably also embarrassed when he realized that in addressing the message to him, Custer must think he was lagging with the pack train. He pocketed the note and kept Martin with him, sending no one on to the pack train, only about two miles in his rear. But Benteen finally did take the trot and maintain it.

The column drew near the Little Big Horn ford at about 4:10, now a full hour and twenty minutes behind Reno! Here Benteen caught his first glimpse of the valley, where he saw some 900 Indians skirmishing with a dozen dismounted troopers — the tail of Reno's retreating comet. Some Indian scouts on a knoll motioned him to turn right down the east bank of the river, where they spotted soldiers on a hill top about a mile distant. The laggard battalion joined Reno's shattered remnants, who had assembled on Reno Hill ten minutes earlier, at 4:20 p.m. Benteen would spend the rest of his life concealing the dawdling on the trail that had kept him out of the initial attacks.

*   *   *

When Reno's battered battalion gathered on Reno Hill, the Indians remained below, looting the dead and firing only occasional long-range shots. A semblance of a picket line posted itself toward the river, and Dr. Porter, the sole surviving medical officer, tended the wounded. When Benteen arrived, he showed Reno his message from Custer, but they decided to wait for the pack train. While Reno went in search of the body of Lt. Hodgson, his adjutant and friend, Benteen, now contrite and all business, took temporary command, reinforcing the picket line with his troops, although the Indians were all mysteriously rushing pell-mell downstream.

Soon they were all hearing the firing from downstream, and as a belated response to Custer's request, Reno dispatched Lt. Hare on a fast twenty-minute gallop to the pack train and back, asking that some ammunition mules be rushed forward. Two such mules soon arrived, followed by the rest of the train at about 5:15. Scout

Herendeen, who had been left behind in the timber with thirteen troopers, led eleven of them in to Reno Hill, all afoot and three wounded. By then most of the Indian scouts were leaving, affected as much by the disorganization of the command as by the enemy strength. Varnum had lost contact with them, and lacking an interpreter, made no effort to resume control. Custer's four Crows left for home, and twenty-one Rees began driving a herd of captured ponies back to the Powder River depot, the appointed rendezvous should the command become scattered.

By this time the so-called Weir Advance, a thoroughly disorganized move to unite with Custer was under way, but it was too little too late. It occurred in three sections, spread over an hour, with no one in control of either the advance or the subsequent retreat. It began when Captain Weir took Company D downstream, entirely on his own hook, at about 4:55. Then at about 5:10 Benteen followed with Companies H, K, and M, also without orders, apparently. Finally, Reno ordered the remainder to follow at about 5:45, but hampered by the wounded and the pack train, they had not gotten far when the retreat began.

It was approximately 5:30 to 5:40 when Weir's and Benteen's units, having pushed about a mile and a half down the bluffs, posted themselves around Weir Point, the highest elevation. They observed formidable numbers of Indians about two miles further down milling around on what would prove to be the extensive Custer field. Godfrey recorded that "the firing had ceased except for an occasional shot." Edgerley testified that they "saw many Indians riding around and firing at objects on the ground." All were puzzled at what was going on and wondering what had become of Custer. That his force had already been wiped out never entered their minds.

The Indian horde soon began to swarm back in the direction of the troops, whose positions were not suitable for an effective defense. The retreat, which probably started at about 6:00, was not fully coordinated, and it seems that only Godfrey's independent covering maneuvers saved the others from a mauling. Although spirited firing developed, only one man of Company D was hit. To Edgerley's anguish, he was forbidden to rescue the wounded trooper, who was abandoned to the mercy of the Indians.

The command finally assembled again on Reno Hill by about 6:30. It was the cool Benteen who posted the companies on an elliptical defense perimeter. The pack train, the picketed horses, and the wounded clustered in the center under the slight protection of a shallow depression. Except toward the river, the slope was rather gentle, and just within long range were elevations, which the Indians soon occupied. They pushed so closely on the heels of the retreat that the troops were hardly in position when the onslaught began. It raged until darkness fell.

While some of the warriors joined the celebrators and mourners in the village, the others attacked in shifts, there being inadequate room for all on their skirmish line. The force of 367 defending on the hill consisted of 14 officers, 339 men, and 14 others, including thirteen wounded. But these were the best odds the regiment had yet faced, and some were digging in while others threw up cracker boxes and packs for breastworks. The fight was long and fierce, but the troops held their own, recovering a little confidence and morale. The toll this time was only five killed and six wounded.

When darkness brought a merciful cessation of firing, both officers and men began to speculate on Custer's whereabouts. Some thought that he, too, must be under seige somewhere like themselves. Others guessed that he had gone to bring help from Terry's column. But some expressed resentment at what they supposed was his desertion of the rest of his regiment. No one seems to have divined the truth. Most of the troops entrenched themselves with whatever they could find to dig with. It had been a grueling day, but they slept restlessly that night.

The crack of fatal shots from the cordon of Indians heralded the dawn of June 26th. It soon became evident that the hostiles were still out for blood. They poured in a heavier fire. They used every cover to approach within telling distance. Their best marksmen, posted on the surrounding elevations, made life miserable for those who had not entrenched well. They even launched mass charges in attempts to over-run the defense perimeter. One brave got close enough to strike a fallen trooper with his coup-stick, but a dozen bullets promptly tore through his body. Benteen's Company H, least well entrenched on the south perimeter, bore the brunt of the attacks. He retaliated by leading a yelling countercharge to throw the Indians back, and then induced Reno to do likewise on the opposite side. Casualties mounted rapidly and the wounded, poorly sheltered from the beating sun, began to moan piteously for water. Again, it was Benteen who organized relief parties. Under covering fire, Medal of Honor winners grabbed camp kettles and crawled down a ravine toward the river. Dashing to the open stream, they scooped up water and struggled back up the ravine with the precious fluid.

By noon the frustrated Indians began to withdraw from their lines. By afternoon the firing had dwindled to the point where water details could reach the river with little molestation. As the sun began to sink the troopers stood and cheered as they watched an enormous parade of Indian families with loaded travois file up the river on the west bank. For the first time in two days the company cooks fired up for a warm meal. That night the four persons still missing in the timber crawled safely into camp: Lt. DeRudio, Pvt. O'Neil of Company G, interpreter Gerard, and enlisted scout William Jackson.

On the morning of June 27th, not an Indian was to be seen. The Battle of the Little Big Horn was over. But the command was in no mood to celebrate. The casualties of the last day alone had reached seven killed and forty-one wounded, mostly of Benteen's company. With so many wounded and so many horses lost, the command was immobilized. That morning Reno prepared a message for delivery to General Terry:

> I have had a most terrific engagement with the hostile Indians. They left their camp last evening at sundown moving due south in the direction of Big Horn Mountains. I am very much crippled and cannot possibly pursue. Lieutenants McIntosh and Hodgson and Dr. DeWolf are among the killed. I have many wounded and many horses and mules shot. I have lost both my own horses. I have not seen or heard from Custer since he ordered me to charge with my battalion (three companies), promising to support me.
>
> I charged about 2 p.m., but meeting no support was forced back to the hills. At this point I was joined by Benteen with three companies and the pack train rear guard (one company.). I have fought thousands and can still hold my own, but cannot leave here on account of the wounded. Send me medical aid at once and rations.
>
> As near as I can say now I have over 100 men killed and wounded.

M	11K	10W	K	2K	3W
H	3K	19W	D	2K	8W
G	12K	6W	A	8K	8W

The hitherto unpublished casualty table appended to this letter appears on the National Archives copy; though incomplete, it is the earliest on record, having been prepared before Reno knew anything of Custer's fate, or of some of his own men. The appalling casualties of the entire battle totalled 263 killed, 59 wounded, and 25 missing in action (the four Crows and twenty-one Rees, all of whom survived). Only 359 persons remained on Reno Hill.

The 7th Cavalry had clearly suffered a disastrous defeat. As to *how* it happened there is no mystery whatever. The regiment of 31 officers and 566 men tackled two thousand warriors resolved to defend their women and children and their tribal existence. Man for man, the brave was a more experienced and skillful fighter than the soldier. The regiment was divided into four columns, only two of which attempted attacks, and then at separate times and places, each, therefore, against crushing odds. It was a classic *defeat in detail*.

But *why* had Custer attempted so much with so little? The ultimate reason was simply inadequate enemy intelligence. Custer, like Terry and Gibbon, underestimated both the strength and temper of the Indians. Up to the very last minute, the evidence Custer was so assiduously gathering seemed to conceal the true strength of the hostiles, and to indicate that they were in flight. Yet, Custer was keener on intelligence than his fellow-officers, a fact that will become more obvious as we follow this campaign.

But *why* did Custer not keep his regiment together? He tried to, but could not afford the delay necessary to achieve it. He detailed more men than he could spare to hurry the pack train along, but it was an amateur outfit. It was Benteen's dawdling, contrary to orders and common sense, that held his battalion out of action. And Custer attacked separately from Reno because he thought the village was in flight, and then terrain features delayed and displaced his attack. What the outcome might have been, *if* the regiment had been together, no one can say. But since fewer Indians had stopped Crook with more troops, only a week before, no one can defend anything better than a check instead of a checkmate.

Custer's decisions, judged in the light of what he knew at the time, instead of by our hindsight, were neither disobediant, rash, nor stupid. Granted his premises, all the rest follows rationally. It was what neither he, nor any other officer, knew that brought disaster.

Chapter 16
Rescue and Retreat

Having reviewed Custer's confident regiment as it paraded up Rosebud Creek, Terry, Gibbon, and Brisbin steamed upriver on the *Far West* to rendezvous at Fort Pease with the Montana column. The boat arrived early on the morning of June 24th to find the hard-marching troops had pulled in the evening before. Terry was eager to push on to the mouth of the Little Big Horn, so that by that afternoon of June 26th his force would be in position to block the flight of the hostiles when Custer struck them.

The blocking position, scarcely thirty miles distant, could be reached by an easy, level route up the west bank of the Big Horn, or by a rugged passage up Tullock's Fork suitable only for a pack train. The easy route would require the *Far West* to ferry the command to the east bank at their destination, but its timely arrival there could not be counted on. Furthermore, as a result of Gibbon's report of smoke having appeared over Tullock's Fork a week earlier, Terry harbored the conviction, or perhaps only a hunch, that a hostile village was encamped on that stream. He therefore chose the rugged trail up Tullock's Fork.

Under Terry's urgings the camp came alive that morning. Captain Kirtland, 7th Infantry, drew the assignment to remain behind with his Company B as guard for the wagon train and base hospital. Gibbon's two hired packers, John Bean and John Reisling, organized a hasty pack train to transport ammunition and rations, the latter probably limited to five days as we have already seen. Freighter Matt Carroll assisted the packers, since some of his team mules were converted to pack service. But inexperienced soldiers would have to provide the principal manpower for the pack train.

By mid-morning the *Far West* had delivered twelve Crow scouts to the south bank with orders to beat up Tullock's Fork until they spotted the anticipated hostile village. That afternoon she made five trips to ferry Major Brisbin's four companies of 2nd Cavalry, Captain Freeman's five companies of 7th Infantry, and Lieutenant Low's Gatling battery. Lieutenant Bradley commanded eleven mounted infantrymen and eighteen Crows, while Henry Bostwick scouted for the infantry and Muggins Taylor for the cavalry. Terry's use of these scouts would prove inefficient.

General Gibbon, having fallen ill, remained on the boat in the temporary care of Dr. Williams, while Major Brisbin led the column on a late four-mile march to a camp on Tullock's Fork. General Terry and staff joined the bivouac later with the lagging pack train. At dusk the advance party of twelve Crows galloped in as though bearing momentous news. They could only report, however, that six miles up the valley they had seen a buffalo wounded by arrows. In sheer disgust Bradley recorded that "after wasting eight hours in advancing ten miles, they return with this paltry bit of news." He recognized that one lone Indian, a hundred miles from any village, could have wounded that buffalo, but the greenhorns of the command exulted at this proof that a hostile village waited only a few miles distant for them to demolish in the morning.

June 25th dawned as clear and hot for Terry's command as it had for Custer's. Orders came to Bradley at four A.M. to dispatch six Crows up Tullock's Fork again, and half hour later he followed with the rest of his scouting party. Without overtaking the six in the lead, he pushed nine miles up the valley before a sixth sense warned him to halt and await news from the main column. Eventually a squad of cavalry rode up to announce that Terry had long since turned west toward the Big Horn and that he should cut across country to join him. The advance thus neatly became the rear as the disgusted Chief of Scouts climbed out of the valley, leaving the six Crows to fend for themselves.

Terry had broken camp at 5:30 that morning to head up Tullock's Fork on Bradley's trail, following his hunch that he would find a hostile camp. But when only three miles out, he had suddenly diverged to the right up a dry fork to reach the highlands. This abrupt change in direction, chosen in the absence of any scouts familiar with the country, courted disaster, for no worse route could have been selected. No member of the column ever offered an explanation for the change, but it carried one clear implication — Terry's hunch had vanished as mysteriously as it had appeared.

Having fully expected to follow a water course all day, the men had failed to fill their canteens, especially as the water tasted unpleasantly alkaline. On climbing out of the narrow valley they beheld, not an inviting plateau, but a forbidding labyrinth of sharp ridges, scored on all sides by steep ravines and eroded gullies. Terry's diary recorded nothing but a succession of starts and stops as the column wandered this way and that through the baffling maze, often obstructed and always uncertain. Horses and footmen alike labored on the rough climbs and descents. Unslakable thirst mounted as the sun burned hotter and hotter. Companies became separated and men straggled. The pack train fell far behind. Gun carriages broke down. Had an Indian force appeared, the exhausted and scattered column would have been trapped and helpless.

Bradley's party, guided by the Crows who knew every wrinkle in the terrain, overtook the wandering column about noon. Without retaining a single Crow to supplant his own helpless guides, Terry promptly sent the entire party to a high ridge some eight miles distant to examine the valley of the Little Big Horn. This sortie discovered nothing but further high ridges that cut off all view in the desired direction — as the Crows had probably known all along. Since their orders prevented them from going farther, the weary platoon turned back to hunt once more for the main column.

Terry's force continued to plod its tortuous way until it stumbled upon a dry stream leading west to the Big Horn. Down the rough breaks the men struggled, spurred on by the prospect of reviving water. Ultimately they reached a timbered oasis by the stream's edge. Terry's diary documents the scattering produced by the grueling march, far more punishing than any made by Custer's force. Terry reached the oasis at 1:30. The cavalry plodded in at 2:00. The infantry and battery limped in at 3:00. There is no reference to the pack train, but Bradley's party trailed in behind at 5:30, mistaking its guard for the infantry column.

Lieutenant McClernand clocked this much of the day's march at 23.5 miles, but it had covered scarcely ten miles toward the blocking position. The six Crows abandoned so early that morning brought the only success of the day. They trotted in ahead of Bradley, reporting that they had advanced far enough up Tullock's Fork to spot a heavy smoke over the lower valley of the Little Big Horn that afternoon. This was not the wisp of haze that betokened a peaceful village, but a cloud signifying something more portentous.

Deeply concerned at not meeting his own time-table, and disturbed by the report of heavy smoke, Terry ordered his played-out infantry and pack train to rest overnight at the oasis, while he drove on again with the cavalry, battery, and Bradley's tireless outfit.

Though this would divide his small force, he felt it imperative to reach his promised position on time. His leg-weary column set out at 5:30 in a steady, dark, and disagreeable rain that turned the river breaks to slippery mud. The several units found it increasingly difficult to maintain contact in the premature darkness. Soon a cavalry company wandered off into the breaks and had to be rescued. And then the battery lagged and became lost in the rear. This was a night march far more trying than Custer's.

Finally the advance halted, unable to move either forward or backward on a steep-sided finger of bluff. When Terry seemed irresolute in face of this impasse, Bradley at last summoned the courage to suggest the obvious — that perhaps one of his Crows could serve as guide! Little Face, one of the older Crows, rode forward and promptly led the column back by an easy and direct path for a mile or two to a suitable valley campsite. They bivouacked at midnight, having made twelve miles in six and a half hours, but still some distance from the Little Big Horn. As Lieutenant Maguire officially recorded it, they "passed the night in a slough of mud and disgust."

*   *   *

In the meantime, the *Far West* had been meeting troubles of her own. Terry's diary reveals that on the night of June 24th he had sent Gibbon's adjutant, Lieutenant Burnett, to Captain Marsh with orders to steam up to the mouth of the Little Big Horn by the 26th. These must have been reiterated orders, designed to overcome the Captain's reluctance, for the latter must have been earlier consulted regarding the feasibility of this pioneering feat of navigation. Early the next morning the adjutant returned to Terry, taking Dr. Williams but leaving General Gibbon aboard to continue his convalescence for another day.

Marsh devoted the morning of the 25th to loading his craft with firewood in preparation for his virgin navigation of the Big Horn. According to Engineering Sergeant James E. Wilson, the official itinerist of the voyage, the boat nosed into the shallow stream precisely at noon. The current proved surprisingly swift and the channel obstructed by shoals, rapids, and islands. The Captain resorted to the novel technique of hitching lines to trees on both banks at once. The powered capstans then wound in the lines, dragging the craft over the moist ground. When she tied up for the night at 8:30, she had covered only sixteen of the 53 river-miles to her destination.

On June 26th the crew resumed its labors at 3:30 A.M., but not until 9:30 did the boat pull abreast of the oasis, now deserted, where the infantry had slept off its fatigue. Adjutant Burnett then reappeared to admonish Captain Marsh to persevere in his efforts. He also informed Gibbon of Terry's advance with the cavalry after learning of the ominous smoke over the Little Big Horn. Suspecting that action might be imminent, Gibbon disembarked and rode briskly with his adjutant to overtake the infantry. Marsh continued his tedious navigation until 9 P.M., making a total day's run of 29 miles that still left him eight miles short of the station he was expected to reach that day.

By 10 A.M. of the 27th the boat reached an eastern affluent of the river, which Marsh pronounced to be the Little Big Horn. But he reckoned without Captain Baker of the boat guard, who contested the identification. After the infantry Captain had disembarked his company to reconnoiter three miles up the tributary, he returned with his conviction unshaken, and ordered the boat to continue the search upstream. The canny boatmaster finally took advantage of another rapids looming ahead to tie up for the night at 8:30. The day's run of 21 miles had carried them 66 miles from the Yellowstone and thirteen above their true destination.

A good night's sleep mellowed Captain Baker's stubbornness, and early the next morning, June 28th, he permitted Marsh to head back downstream. It turned into a merry-go-round trip, for Sgt. Wilson recorded that "the passage back to the mouth of the Little Big Horn was made in a very short time − the current forcing the boat right around so that the stern led the way on many occasions, and the downward run accomplished in a whirling, revolving fashion." Breathless, but safe, the crew tied up at an island opposite the mouth of what all now agreed was the Little Big Horn, there to await further developments. This interval of absence from her assigned station was destined to cause confusion.

*   *   *

Returning now to the muddy bivouac of Terry's advance cavalry, at the crack of dawn of June 26th, Major Brisbin routed Lieutenant Bradley from the slumber of exhaustion and ordered him to scout ahead toward the Little Big Horn without delaying for breakfast. Grumbling to himself, the Chief of Scouts sent out six Crows at 3:30 and followed with the others within a half hour. After advancing three miles he came upon the tracks of several Indian ponies and spotted a heavy smoke rising in the sky some twenty miles ahead. Pausing only to send back a note of these discoveries, he trailed the pony tracks westward two miles to the bank of the Big Horn. There his quarry had abandoned some personal effects in preparation for fording the stream. Inspection of these articles brought a surprise — they belonged, not to hostile Sioux, but to some of the six Crows that had been transferred to Custer!

At that moment Bradley sighted three Crows across the river, who came down to the bank to converse across the water with some of his own scouts. Interpreter Barney Bravo told him that the three were singing death songs. Then Little Face, streaming tears, rushed up to report that the trio were Goes Ahead, Hairy Moccasin, and White-Man-Runs-Him, who were mourning for White Swan and Half Yellow Face, both believed killed, and Curly, believed missing in action. They related that Custer had struck a big village the day before on the Little Big Horn, where the smoke could now be seen, but that the hostiles had swarmed out in such numbers as to destroy all the command except a few that remained surrounded and doomed on a hill top. Now all the Crows were weeping freely for Custer and his men as well as their own friends. Their complete acceptance of the story was unmistakable, and the shocked, Lieutenant could only hope that they were exaggerating the disaster.

Shaken to his boots, Bradley galloped back to deliver the appalling news in person. He found Terry with his staff and Gibbon, who had just ridden in. As they received his report, their initial reaction of shock began to give way to reassuring rationalizations which soon branded the story an invention of the Crows to excuse their cowardly desertion. Bradley, having already suffered scorn and scepticism too often, observed these reactions carefully, and wrote: "General Terry took no part in these criticisms, but sat on his horse, silent and thoughtful, biting his lower lip, and looking to me as though he by no means shared in the wholesale scepticism of the flippant members of his staff." When the General did respond, it was to give the order to march. Then, while still within sight of the night's bivouac, he called a halt.

Terry must have reasoned that it would be prudent to consolidate his meager and divided force. This should entail little delay, for Gibbon must have assured him that the infantry and pack train were following right behind him. At about 10:30 these troops did pull in, having made 12 or 13 miles that morning. They, too, heard the rumors of Custer's fate and like the others talked themselves into an uneasy rejection of the unacceptable possibility.

The united force resumed the southward march at about 11:00 A.M. On repassing the Big Horn ford, Bradley sent his Crows to bring in their trio of friends from Custer's command, but the following troops saw them break for the river and cross to their friends. Then the entire twenty-one, including Barney Bravo, faded into the hills en route to their distant village. Bradley's scouts, now reduced to eleven mounted infantrymen, rode in the advance into the valley of the Little Big Horn. At this point the credulous and sceptical alike could personally verify the presence of smoke further up the valley. After a total march of eleven miles, Terry called a noon halt at 2:20, on the west bank of the stream about four miles above its mouth.

Terry had now reached his planned position and at the appointed time, but his satisfaction was marred by a mounting anxiety. He had expected to wait here, prepared to pounce on any fleeing Indians, unless circumstances directed otherwise. But what were the circumstances? Did the upstream smoke signify a mere natural timber or prairie fire? Or, did it mean that Custer had already struck the Indians? If he had, and was successful, he was burning the village; but where were the fleeing refugees? Could it mean that the hostiles had vanquished Custer, as the demoralized Crows insisted? In either case the village must have been located on the lower Little Big Horn, instead of its headwaters, and this may have precipitated an early engagement.

And why hadn't he heard from Custer? He should have struck the head of Tullock's Fork two days ago, but there was still no sign of scout Herendeen, the appointed courier. Thoughts of this kind must have stormed through Terry's mind as he impatiently stretched out the halt to three hours. But in the face of the Crows' report and the evident smoke, he could remain idle no longer, courier or no courier.

Summoning scouts Taylor and Bostwick, Terry offered each a $200 bonus for delivering a dispatch to Custer's command. Both accepted the challenge, Taylor taking the bluff route up the east bank and Bostwick the valley route up the west bank. Although no copy of this dispatch has turned up, Godfrey recorded its gist the next morning when Taylor belatedly delivered his copy: "A scout came up with a note from General Terry to General Custer, saying some of our Crow scouts gave the information that we were whipped and nearly all killed; that he did not believe the story, but he was bringing medical assistance."

Terry resumed the advance up the west bank of the stream at 5:20, Bradley in the lead with his mounted infantrymen. He soon rounded up five stray Indian ponies, and further on spotted three or four mounted warriors watching the column from the hills.

Then at 6:40 courier Bostwick came charging back to report that he would search no further for Custer because the valley ahead was swarming with more than $200 worth of Indians. Disappointed, but warned, the General closed up his column with the pack train in the center and advanced cautiously in battle formation; he assigned Bradley's party to the left point along the stream and Lieutenant Roe's cavalry company to the right point along the hills.

Advancing warily, Bradley soon noted numerous parties of Indians scurrying over the hills ahead. So did Lieutenant Roe, who took them for some of Custer's Ree scouts and tried to approach under a flag of truce, only to draw sudden fire. A little later he observed far up the valley three groups of riders in formation, amounting to perhaps three hundred in all, which he insisted must be squadrons of Custer's cavalry. But Dr. Paulding, who claimed superior eyesight, reached the firm conviction that they "represented the exact appearance of an Indian camp on the march."

When the halt came and the points retired, Roe reported the scene as he interpreted it. But the Doctor insisted that he had seen "a lot of Indians, moving off leisurely not far from the smoke, and that it meant that even if our scouts had exaggerated matters, Custer had not succeeded in getting away with the camp and must have been repulsed." He said nothing to Gibbon, because he "wouldn't have believed me anyhow, he being an incredulous person." The militant physician thought the cavalry should have scooped up this band instead of camping to "lay on their arms all night."

Dr. Paulding, of course, had seen aright, but others beside Roe had been fooled by the twilight scene. Just before the halt came, Muggins Taylor came flying back, also thwarted in his efforts to find Custer. Captain Clifford recorded his story: "Taylor says he saw what he took to be a body of cavalry, and when they discovered him, fifteen men were selected and sent out to meet him. Upon nearing him, one of them concealed himself in a ravine and fired at him; he thinks the bullet went under his horse. He returned the fire and then jumped on his horse and escaped."

Having covered eight miles since the long noon halt, the command went into bivouac at 8:40 on the 26th on the west bank of the Little Big Horn, unaware that they were but eight miles from Reno's surrounded men and even fewer from the ghastly Custer Hill. It was a restless camp, especially for Terry. He could no longer doubt that the hostiles were nearby and in strong force. It was nearly certain that Custer had struck them, probably the day before, when the Crows first spotted the smoke. But it could scarcely have been a decisive victory, when instead of refugees there were warriors in strong force keeping a cool watch on his own movements. Was it a disaster, or dare he hope for a draw? As usual, the troubled General confided none of his hopes or fears to his diary.

Bradley was not so reticent, however. The final entry in his journal reads: "Before retiring, the officers assembled in groups and talked over the events of the day. I found that a majority of the infantry officers placed confidence in the report brought by the Crows of Custer's overthrow, and were prepared for unpleasant disclosures upon the morrow. Some of the cavalry officers shared in this conviction, but the majority of them, and about all the staff, were wholly sceptical . . . to argue with them was worse than useless."

The next morning, June 27th, it was not until 7:30 that the speculating column resumed its cautious advance. The scene was ghostly, for where Indians had swarmed the night before not one was now visible. About four miles out they came upon the eerie site of a vast Indian village, deserted of all life save a few skulking curs. The area, several miles in length and nearly a mile in width, was strewn with abandoned lodge poles, some neatly packed for moving, and with all manner of discarded utensils and gear. Every eye turned to two stately lodges left standing, with sacrificial ponies lying dead about them. On peering inside, the curious found the dead bodies of braves, laid out in style, three in one tepee and five in the other. But the resulting satisfaction soon evaporated at ominous signs of a cavalry saddle here and a uniform there. Dr. Paulding soon found a buckskin shirt bearing the label "Porter"; a sinister bullet hole pierced its right shoulder and blood covered the rest. He also picked up a pair of cavalry gloves marked, "Yates, 7th Cav." Captain Clifford came across some blood-stained underclothing belonging to Lieutenant Sturgis.

As the appalling implications were beginning to register on the command, a breathless and white-faced courier dashed in from Bradley's party, reporting that they had counted 197 bodies of dead cavalrymen, lying stripped and mutilated on a hill across the stream. 197! This was a shocking fraction of Custer's command. Thoroughly subdued, the column marched on, dreading what the next mile might uncover. Their worst fears became reality when they began to see decapitated and mutilated bodies bristling with arrows, and bloated cavalry horses with feet stiff in the air. A few of the objects could be identified as the remains of Lieutenant McIntosh, Charley Reynolds, and Isaiah Dorman. Finding a clear field ahead in the river bottom, Gibbon ordered the area policed for camping.

192

In the meantime, Muggins Taylor had forged ahead some time that morning, still carrying his undelivered dispatch to Custer. He was apparently the first to make contact with Reno's survivors on the Hill, and necessarily delivered his note to Major Reno. That officer, finally convinced that the approaching force was friendly, sent Lieutenants Wallace and Hare out to meet it. While the troops went into camp, Terry and his staff rode up Reno Hill. The time was 11:00 A.M.

Only then did the 7th Cavalry survivors learn of the gruesome fate of Custer's battalion, only about four miles away.

*   *   *

The meeting triggered an emotional binge for all concerned. The tensions that had been feeding on dread and uncertainty suddenly released themselves. The fear of doom lifted from Reno's survivors, and dread of the unknown fell from their rescuers. Only the profound shock of Custer's fate tempered the universal feeling of relief. Fortunately, there was work to be done and all hands turned gratefully to action as a means of easing their hearts and minds.

General Terry interrogated the surviving officers to learn the story of Custer's operations and Reno's desperate stand. He asked for a count of survivors and estimates of the killed and wounded. He dispatched Captain Benteen with his company to follow up Custer's trail to the tragic field, there to verify their identity and deduce what he could of the disaster enacted there. Reno's men turned to policing the hilltop area, dragging away offensive animal carcasses and burying the nearby dead. They rounded up stray horses and mules, and sadly put injured animals out of their misery.

The most pressing need was to care for the more than fifty wounded men lying in the hospital area. Drs. Williams and Paulding rushed to aid the over-burdened Dr. Porter. Crews were organized to carry the patients in blanket stretchers down the bluff and across the river to a cleaner area near Gibbon's bivouac. Terry offered a bonus of $100 to volunteers who would carry orders to the *Far West* to prepare to receive the casualties. Henry Bostwick and Pvt. James Goodwin, 7th Infantry, one of Gibbon's orderlies, volunteered for the mission and set out at nightfall in search of the boat. Unfortunately, this was the night she had moored far above her assigned station.

There was little soldierly camaraderie in either of the camps that night. Few of the 7th Cavalry complained of their improved lot, but Gibbon's men found their bivouac oppressive and intolerable with loathesome flies and a lingering stench. Captain Clifford penned a nauseatingly graphic description of the scene; he could not sleep until he moved his nose to the very water's edge. General Terry spent a sombre evening composing the first detailed report of Custer's disaster (O-39,1876). With painstaking care he couched it in objective terms, offering neither excuses nor recriminations — a rare example of innate nobility.

Early on June 28th, the 7th Cavalry death-marched to the Custer field to conduct a systematic search for bodies and to bury them as best they could. The beating sun and the squaws with their knives and hatchets had done their work too well. The bodies of three officers defied all attempts at recognition, and many a trooper became upset at failing to identify the remains of a buddy. In the afternoon the funeral column crossed the river to inter those who had fallen in the valley fight. Having buried a total of 259 of their comrades, they pitched camp just below Gibbon's force.

While most of Gibbon's men were constructing more litters for the wounded, Captain Ball led his Company E, 2nd Cavalry on a reconnaissance over the trail of the departing village. Terry reported that they found that the village "divided into two parties, one of which kept the valley of Long Fork [Lodge Grass Creek?], making, he thinks, for the Big Horn Mountains; the other turned more to the eastward. He also discovered a very heavy trail leading into the valley that is not more than five days old. This trail is entirely distinct from the one that Custer followed, and would seem to show that at least two large bands united here just before the battle (O-39,1876)."

The afternoon passed with no sign of couriers Bostwick and Goodwin bringing assurances that the *Far West* was ready to receive the wounded. Appalled at the thought of spending another night in so depressing and pestilential a spot, Terry ordered a move at 6:30 after the day's heat had moderated. He also promised Muggins Taylor a $50 bonus to leave at dusk for the distant Fort Ellis, carrying his official dispatch. The attempt to carry most of the wounded by hand-litters proved an absolute failure. Five and a half hours of struggling and cursing took them only four miles to just beyond the deserted village site.

Most of June 29th was devoted to constructing enough mule-litters and travois to carry all but the walking wounded. Gibbon seized this opportunity to make his first personal inspection of the Custer field. It was well he did, for he discovered and buried two more bodies. Although Bostwick and Goodwin were still ominously missing, Terry ordered the march resumed at 5:30 to try out the new litters. They had no more than proved an unqualified success when the belated couriers rode in to report the *Far West* ready and waiting. With this encouragement they kept marching, despite a miserable rain and pitch darkness that obscured the trail. They eventually found the steamboat, however, and tenderly loaded 43 wounded men aboard at about 2:30 on the morning of June 30th.

It was not hostile interference, but comic opera misadventures that had so delayed Bostwick and Goodwin. Having ridden out of Terry's camp on the evening of the 27th, they reached the mouth of the Little Big Horn early the next morning. But they searched in vain for the steamboat, due there two days earlier. Naturally concluding that she was stuck on a sandbar, they started down the rugged east bank, searching each meander of the stream. They had probably not gotten far out of sight and sound, when the boat came down like a whirling dervish to the station she had overshot the day before. But unaware of this, the couriers searched doggedly all day until they hauled up at the Yellowstone to hail Captain Kirtland's base camp across the big river. Earnestly assured that the boat had indeed forged upstream as ordered and must still be there, the baffled scouts turned in for the night. The next morning, June 29th, they retraced their steps up the river. About 3 P.M. they came upon the boat serenely moored at her assigned station! The worst blow was to find Captain Marsh already completing his preparations to receive the wounded, having been notified by Muggins Taylor early that morning.

The sheepish couriers reached Terry's marching column that evening, bearing the following dispatch from Captain Stephen Baker, dated June 29, 1876, 3:20 P.M.: ·

> General Terry's note just received. The couriers are now feeding their horses and will return to your command in half an hour.
>
> The boat reached this point at 10 A.M. on the 27th, and I took the company three miles upstream to ascertain if it was the Little Horn. But not being satisfied, we went up the Big Horn ten miles by water, at which point we found rapids which we could not ascend. We tied up there for the night, and next morning, June 28th, I concluded to return to this stream, where we have remained since.
>
> The landing is good, but is above the mouth of the stream which at present is fordable a short way from the Big Horn half a mile or so in a straight line. About 9 A.M. on the 27th [Sic! 28th] a Crow scout from General Custer's command reached the boat, but we could only make out from him that there had been a fight; this morning at 5 o'clock Taylor, the Ellis courier, came in and gave us the particulars. As his horse was used up completely, I gave him a fresh mount and started him on his way in less than an hour after his arrival. Captain Marsh has been busy all day arranging the boat for the reception of the wounded. We have not seen a hostile Indian up to this time. (O-9)

Drs. Williams and Porter took charge of the floating hospital, leaving Dr. Paulding to care for the remainder of the command all under General Gibbon. General Terry and staff, Major Brisbin, and Lieutenant Low's battery all boarded the *Far West* by 1:40 P.M. of June 30th, when Captain Marsh pushed off for a fast run down to the base camp at Fort Pease. That afternoon Gibbon's enlarged command held muster, then forded to the north bank of the Little Big Horn. On July 1st and 2nd the chastened column retraced its steps to the Yellowstone.

When Terry had reached this base on the afternoon of June 30th, he found an urgent dispatch awaiting him. One can better imagine than describe his reaction to reading the following telegram from General Sheridan, dated *June 6th*: "Couriers from the Red Cloud Agency reported at Laramie yesterday that Yellow Robe arrived at the agency, six days from the hostile camp. He said that 1800 lodges were on the Rosebud and about to leave for Powder River below the point of 'Crazy Horse's fight' and says they will fight and have about 3000 warriors. This is sent for your information (O-29)."

While waiting for the troops to march down, Terry and his staff had time to recover from the personal shock at the tragedy of Custer and his regiment. But this concern of the heart soon gave way to concern of the mind. The staff in particular began to worry when they realized that Custer's defeat spelled dismal failure for the campaign. What would be the fate of the expedition command when military superiors as well as public began the inevitable search for the cherished scape-goat? The apprehensive staff, perhaps subconsciously at first, began to devise a scheme to clear their chief, whether he needed clearing or not.

When matured, the scheme involved only the subtlest of falsifications. The first pretended that they had known the location of the hostile camp all along; the second, that June 26th had been specified from the beginning as the date for a simultaneous attack upon it by both columns; the third, that the rash and impetuous Custer had disobeyed orders, thereby sabotaging a perfect plan and snatching defeat from the jaws of victory. It mattered little that the facts denied these perversions, for they would be extraordinarily hard to correct when once firmly planted in the public mind. Its attraction lay in the fact that it shifted all of the onus, real or imaginary, from the vulnerable living to the invulnerable dead.

Some of Terry's staff fostered this scheme and pursued it for the remainder of their lives. They importuned Terry to advance this defense, immediately and forcefully. But whatever deficiencies the

196

General may have had as an Indian campaigner, he was a man of integrity and held Custer in esteem. His confidential report of July 2nd (O-33), which analyzed the disaster, completely failed to satisfy his staff.

On the morning of July 3rd, Terry placed his report in the hands of Adjutant Smith, briefed him as to his duties and powers on reaching the States, and saw him aboard the hospital ship. At noon, Captain Marsh nosed his craft into the current for her record-breaking voyage of mercy to the hospital at Fort Abraham Lincoln. The news she delivered to the Bismarck telegraph office at 11 P.M. of July 5th made newspaper headlines for weeks.

July Fourth was celebrated country-wide as the first centennial of the naton. But the solemn camp at the mouth of the Big Horn held no ceremonies. Sober and thankful letters to loved ones back home replaced rifle salutes and patriotic speeches. Enlisted survivors of the nerve-wracking experience on the Little Big Horn quietly signed a petition asking for the promotion of Reno to Lieutenant Colonel and Benteen to Major of the regiment.

On July 6th, the *Josephine* steamed up with a load of supplies and welcome mail. Mrs. Custer and the wives of other right wing officers had been planning to board her for a gala excursion and a wilderness picnic with their husbands. To the intense relief of the surviving officers of the regiment, the wives had missed the boat (C-61).

Chapter 17
Estivation in Tandem

Indian Inspector Watkins had been induced to prophesy back in November that a thousand troops could whip the few hundred savages who stubbornly defied the authority of the government. But in June, the Sioux and Cheyennes had halted Crook and annihilated Custer. Both Crook and Terry retreated posthaste to base camps, where they licked their wounds and awaited strong reinforcements before risking further confrontation. Crook's estivation endured for seven weeks and Terry's for six, during which their knowledge of the enemy decayed to zero.

The Wyoming column idled in "Camp Cloud Peak," moving slowly closer to and along the mountains, seeking relief from boredom by hunting and fishing. Captain Stanton had left the column permanently, leaving no one to keep an official itinerary. MacMillan of the Chicago *Inter-Ocean* also departed because of illness, but arranged with Lt. Frederick Schwatka, Company M, 3rd Cavalry, to supply his paper with even better dispatches. When the wagon train returned on July 13th, it would bring Dr. Valentine T. McGillicuddy, a contract surgeon and diary-keeper.

Crook's Crow and Shoshone allies had left, and so had Louis Richard, temporarily, leaving only Grouard and Pourier for scouting duty. When Captain Anson Mills, from a vantage point in the mountains, spotted a dark pall of smoke to the north on June 28th, Grouard ventured far enough to assure himself that it came from some point far down the valley of the Little Big Horn. Not till later would the command learn that Gibbon's clean-up details were burning the debris of the abandoned village.

On July 1st Crook led a gala party on a four-day hunting excursion into the summits of the Big Horns. That same morning Frank and Big Bat scouted as far as the head of the Little Big Horn, but hit the trail for home when they came upon a war party of Sioux. When Crook learned of this on returning from his sporting trip, he ordered Lt. Frederick W. Sibley, Company E, 2nd Cavalry, to hand-pick twenty-five troopers from his regiment to escort the two scouts on a determined mission to locate the hostile village and find out what it was doing. The General then left again on July 7th for another pleasure excursion.

Leaving camp at noon of July 6th, Lt. Sibley's cavalcade rode thirty-eight miles northwest along the base of the mountains before making a late bivouac. Early the next morning, the eventful 7th of July, the party pushed on to near the head of the Little Big Horn. The alert scouts soon sighted a number of strong war parties crossing the plains as though converging on Camp Cloud Peak. Frank hastily led the detail farther up into the concealing foothills, but the hostile outriders below soon picked up their trail and launched a pursuit. Before long a sudden fusillade of shots rang out, and Sibley dismounted his men for deployment in a skirmish line in the timber. They soon picked off two aggressive Cheyennes, one of whom flaunted a gorgeous warbonnet, but the growing number of attackers swelled the volume of fire and threatened to surround the handful of troopers.

Sibley's men feared they were doomed, until Frank proposed that they tether their mounts nearly in sight of the attackers, as bait, while the men faded into the brush and up the face of the mountain. The sensible Lieutenant accepted the suggestion. Soon they were clambering higher and higher among the rocks and ravines, carrying nothing but arms and ammunition. They paused in elation when they heard the firing below give way to whoops of triumph as the Indians closed in on the bait of horses. But on being reminded that fifty Indian-infested miles separated them from the safety of Crook's camp, they drove themselves to exhaustion for most of the night. Early the next morning they resumed their foot-sore hike along the shoulders of the range on painfully empty stomachs and in constant dread of discovery by war parties scouring the country below them.

Resting only briefly in the afternoon, the troopers continued their relentless, man-killing tramp for another night. But then they were compelled to risk a descent from the concealing mountain, ford the swift current of Big Goose Creek, and embark on a crippled hike across open plains. Sighing in relief, they came upon a pair of

199

hunting troopers, who raced back to camp to fetch an escort and led horses for the straggling party. Colonel Royall, who commanded the camp in the absence of General Crook, welcomed them safely at 10 A.M. of July 9th.

Cheated of their prey, the hostiles that night fired into camp and ran off three horses and a mule. The next day Louis Richard and courier Ben Arnold pulled in from Fort Fetterman, bringing the first shocking news of Custer's disaster. This evidence of Indian strength, as well as Sibley's experience, prompted Colonel Royall to order a battalion of cavalry to bring in Crook's overdue hunting party. To everyone's relief they all rode into camp that afternoon. Again that night the hostiles not only fired into camp, but set off a prairie fire that threatened to consume the infantry camp and the grazing range for miles around.

Richard had brought a dispatch from Sheridan which offered to reinforce Crook with Colonel Wesley Merritt's regiment of 5th Cavalry, and urged Crook "to hit them again and hit them hard" in retaliation for Terry's humiliating setback (C-7). The General's reaction to this advice may be easily imagined. He had found the hostiles too strong to handle and Custer had obviously found them stronger still. They had just driven Sibley's detail in like a flock of shorn sheep, and were now swarming around camp, threatening to burn him out. Until the wagon train returned with supplies, Crook could not move; without Indian allies, he would not move; and without strong reinforcements he dared not move.

Some delay was unavoidable, but the General delayed with eyes closed. Sibley's disaster iced his ardor for further scouting. Nor did it revive on July 11th, when Tom Cosgrove brought some 220 Shoshone allies back for service under their aged but impressive chief, Washakie. For weeks this chief functioned as Crook's entire intelligence department, as revealed by Lt. Bourke. Each dawn and dusk, the aged Indian rode to the summit of the nearest hill and scoured the horizon with a pair of fieldglasses. He spent the rest of the time convincing Crook of the awesome strength of the Sioux nation, cautioning him against any fool-hardy offensive, and urging him to wait until time, quarrels, and starvation would scatter the foe.

The chief proved mighty persuasive, for Crook wrote Sheridan on July 13th that "the best information I can get from my front is that the Sioux have three fighting men to my one, although I have no doubt of my ability to whip them with my present force, but the victory would likely be barren of results, and so I have thought it better to defer attack until I can get the 5th Cavalry here, and then

200

end the campaign with one crushing blow." He then added the week-old information from the Sibley scout that "the hostiles are, according to my advices, encamped on the Little Horn, near the base of the mountains, and will probably remain there until my reinforcements come up." (Chicago *Inter-Ocean*, July 18).

This final prophecy was already false. What Crook did not know, and could not find out because he had pulled in his scouts, was that the dedicated hostiles, the nucleus of winter roamers, had departed for the northeast right after the Sibley skirmish. A rear guard of loose summer roamers were all that remained to harass his camp and burn off the grass to deprive him of forage. He already outnumbered his foe.*

During these first three weeks of apprehensive idleness, Crook made no attempt to contact his sister force in the field, General Terry's column.

*   *   *

No less idle and blind-folded was Terry's force. Since Taylor and Williamson were absent on courier service, only Herendeen, interpreter Gerard, convalescing LeForge, and inconspicuous Bostwick remained. The Crows had deserted, but by July 1st Courier Wesley Brockmeyer had brought news from Powder River that all the missing Rees had reported there. Terry ordered two details of five Rees each to watch for hostile crossings at the mouths of the Rosebud and Tongue, but they are never mentioned again. On July 6th, Captain Ball launched a five-day reconnaissance upriver to Pompey's Pillar and back, but a moon-shot would have yielded as useful intelligence.

The most crippling blow to effective scouting was delivered on July 9th. Early that morning, Lt. Bradley, ordered to his post at Fort Shaw, left the expedition permanently. There are hints that he had become depressed by the scorn and scepticism that rewarded his brilliant and heroic service as Chief of Scouts. The intelligence-minded Lieutenant was ahead of his time.

Though dull on Indian intelligence, Terry was keen on military cooperation. As early as July 4th he had made his first attempt to contact Crook. None of the scouts appeared anxious for such perilous courier service, but a $500 bonus proved mighty tempting to one of Gibbon's teamsters, a red-headed frontiersman named Charles R. ("Sandy") Morris. That holiday night Sandy rode into the dark-

*Chapter 28 details the Indian movements after the Custer fight.

ness with Terry's dispatch to Crook. The next day Captain Clifford, in search of stray horses near the mouth of Tullock's Fork, flushed the sheepish courier from a hide-out in the brush. He confessed that after making fifteen miles the night before, Indians had fired on him, hitting his horse. He had turned back to hole up during daylight, but professed eagerness to resume his mission come nightfall.

At this point the story turns a bit hazy. Clifford says nothing of providing another horse, but does say that the next day Lt. Booth crossed the river after a stray white horse which proved to be Sandy's. He feared the missing rider had fallen prey to the Sioux. But on July 7th Terry ordered a pair of binoculars issued to C.R. Morris to aid his crossing of hostile country with dispatches. This implies a return to receive the glasses and an opportunity to secure a mount, though no one mentions this.

In any case Sandy did try again, but with no better success, for he returned on July 8th with a comic opera tale that proved his medicine bad indeed. He had reached the mouth of the Little Big Horn, but in rafting across, the swift current swept his unmanageable craft into the main stream and his horse escaped. The raft then ran under a low branch, sweeping him into the drink and sending his rifle to the bottom along with his hat and boots. He was morosely contemplating his few garments steaming in the sun, when a Sioux party trotted close. Retreating into the brush, Sandy buried himself for the night, only to have the hostiles bivouac a mere 200 yards away. The next day he limped back to camp, picking his painful way over cactus-strewn river breaks in his bare feet.

Still anxious to contact Crook, Terry posted a notice calling for volunteers, and then retired to compose a new dispatch dated July 9th. After describing the Custer disaster, he made a generous offer to cooperate with Crook:

> The great and to me wholly unexpected strength which the Indians have developed seems to me to make it important and indeed necessary that we should unite, or at least act in close cooperation. In my ignorance of your present position and of the position of the Indians, I am unable to propose a plan for this, but if you will devise one and communicate it to me, I will follow it . . . I hope that it is unnecessary for me to say that should our forces unite, even in my Department, I shall assume nothing by reason of my seniority, but shall be prepared to cooperate with you in the most cordial and hearty manner, leaving you entirely free to pursue your own course . . . (O-33)

The call for volunteers brought a response from three privates in Clifford's Company E, William Evans, Benjamin F. Stewart, and James Bell, the first two having similarly volunteered a month earlier. On the evening of July 9th, they started out with a temporary cavalry escort. That same day Herendeen started upriver to the Crow village to find braves willing to carry a duplicate and to induce the missing Crow scouts to return to duty. He may have been accompanied by LeForge, who was discharged as an enlisted scout that day and picked up as a quartermaster scout the next.

In the meantime the steamer *Josephine* had reached Terry's camp on July 6th with much-needed rations and forage. The next day a party of Crows, some having served with Crook, rode in bearing the first news of the Rosebud Battle, an action they painted in sombre colors. This disheartening news received confirmation on July 9th when courier George W. Morgan brought dispatches from Powder River, including reports of Crook's failure to vanquish the hostiles.

Camp boredom was relieved on July 14th when Herendeen returned, having found no couriers, but bringing back all the missing Crow scouts and twenty-three additional recruits, whom he left across the river in charge of LeForge. He intimated that a village of Crow allies might follow later. In the morning, after a night storm and flood, the *Josephine* ferried the scouts to camp and Adjutant Burnett mustered in the new recruits. Who took command of them in the absence of Bradley is not clear, for no one deemed it worthy of mention.

That evening Muggins Taylor returned from Fort Ellis by mackinaw bearing a dispatch from Sheridan that galvanized the bored and gloomy camp into sudden activity. Sheridan advised that the *Far West* would soon arrive with supplies to support a long campaign and that heavy reinforcements of infantry, recruits, and artillery were on the way. He had ordered Crook to cooperate with Terry and he wanted the defiant Sioux punished (O-29). Terry immediately ordered the *Josephine* unloaded in preparation to leave for the Powder River base, which he suddenly decided should be moved up and consolidated with the Big Horn base.

At noon of July 16th Terry took the *Josephine* down, expecting to meet the *Far West* and to use both boats to expedite the removal of the depot and its garrison. With him went Captain Moylan's company of 7th Cavalry to escort the regimental wagon train up to the Big Horn. The next day, Gibbon, left in charge of the camp, sent four Crows with a duplicate of Terry's dispatch to Crook.

*   *   *

It was July 12th when Terry's trio of soldier couriers, destined to win the Medal of Honor for their exploit, rode safely into Crook's

203

camp. Significantly, they had seen no Indians, though they had followed the old trail of Indians leaving the Custer field to where it divided at Lodge Grass Creek. They took the lefthand trail to the upper Rosebud, where they found it to divide again. A travois trail, thought to indicate wounded Indians, continued east toward the Tongue, but a pony trail turned up the Rosebud toward Crook's vicinity.

The day these couriers arrived heavy smoke was seen far to the north and east in the direction of Tongue and Powder Rivers. Since Indians would burn the grass behind them to cover a retreat and impede pursuit, but not ahead where they expected to graze their own herds and hunt buffalo, this was strong evidence of a departure of the hostiles, and confirmed the evidence of the three couriers. But it was ignored. The next day the long-awaited wagon train pulled in with fresh supplies, escorted by seven companies of reinforcing infantry, but Crook was still in no mood to move, or even to scout.

He revealed his views in his reply to Terry's dispatch, written on July 16th. When he "learned that the hostiles had received reinforcements," he decided to defer any movement until the arrival of the 5th Cavalry, which he expected "about the last of the month." On the basis of Sibley's stale findings he advised Terry that the hostile village was still located where the Little Big Horn debouched from the mountains, despite the later observation of "large smokes down Powder and Tongue Rivers." He assured Terry that he would "most sincerely serve under" him. When he moved, he planned to leave his wagon train on the head of the Tongue and go after the Indians in the mountains, and as a plan for cooperation he suggested that Terry join him (O-9).

To deliver this message, Crook selected a tall young Montana miner, named Kelly, who was judged sturdy and canny enough, but a wee bit daft. This was probably the Richard Kelly, whom Miles would later hire as a scout in October and November. Refusing both escort and mount, Kelly insisted his chances were best on foot, though the bee-line distance was nearly 120 miles. He started out July 16th, but returned that night to exchange his moccasins for cactus-proof boots. His second attempt took him as far as the Rosebud, but the sight of a hostile patrol turned him back.

Kelly had no more than reappeared on July 19th than the four Crows sent by Gibbon delivered their duplicate of Terry's dispatch. They had made a fast two-day trip up the Big Horn, Little Big Horn, and Owl Creek without encountering a Sioux. They, too, noted the two old trails. Thus encouraged, Kelly started out for the third time the next morning, planning to follow the Crow route in reverse, but changing from shank's mare to raft as soon as he found adequate water in the streams. By the time he reached Fort Pease, Terry's force had left, and he rafted on down the Yellowstone. When he delivered his dispatch on August 1st, his labors had become superfluous.

The evidence of the smokes and the two courier parties indicated that the hostiles no longer occupied one consolidated village, and that most had departed for the northeast. The signal was lost on Crook, however, for Washakie was now telling him that the hostiles, still in crushing numbers, had moved up into the Big Horns, intending to cross to the Big Horn Basin where buffalo were abundant. No one seems to have challenged this speculation, although the Sioux shunned this enemy-held valley.

On July 23rd, Crook composed another revealing note to Terry, to be delivered by all of Terry's couriers. He wrote that "it is now a pretty well settled fact that the Sioux are in the Big Horn mountains." Since there had been no scouting, what had been settled was Crook's mind, not the location of the enemy. He expressed doubt that the hostiles would dare attack their united force, and suggested, as a means of concealing their intention to cooperate, that whichever column struck them first should hold them until the other could get up. He proposed no means of holding slippery Indians, however, nor even hinted at target dates. He asked Terry on his approach to send a courier with the latest advices and plans. The final sentence read: "I am in constant dread of being attacked and burnt out, as the grass here is like tinder, and I may have to take the aggressive with my present force, which is under 1200 troops, in self-defense (O-9)."

Unaware that the enemy had already partially scattered and largely departed, Crook was paralyzed by his own phantoms. His apprehension and indecision are revealed in a report to Sheridan, also written July 23rd:

> I find myself immeasurably embarrassed by the delay of Merritt's column . . . On Powder, Tongue, and Rosebud rivers the whole country is on fire and filled with smoke. I am in constant dread of attack; in their last [of July 10] they set fire to the grass, but as much of it was still green, we extinguished it without difficulty; but should it be fired now, I don't see how we could stay in the country. I am at a loss what to do . . . All indications are that the Sioux are in the Big Horn mountains, from which they can see clear to the Yellowstone and discern the approach of Terry's column . . . I don't think they will fight us combined, but will scatter . . . Should the Indians scatter unhurt, they would have greatly the advantage over us, as we would be obliged to divide accordingly, while their thorough knowledge of the country and rapidity of movement would enable them to concentrate on and destroy our small parties . . . (O-7)

Crook finally sent out his first scouting party in weeks on July 25th. According to Bourke's diary, the Shoshones ventured out "as far as the south fork of Tongue River, four or five miles to the north-west" of the main camp. There an encounter with a few Sioux filled the air with insults but loosed no bullets. The Shoshones "returned to camp on a full run," prompting the alarmed command to rush to its defenses. But nothing happened. After dark Louis Richard and a few companions casually trotted into camp from a hunt, reporting neither Indians nor their sign in the foothills. The next morning Grouard and Cosgrove scouted the Sioux trail, satisfying them-selves that it represented a small spying patrol.

Beginning to suspect that all was not as described by Washakie, Crook moved camp five miles northwest on July 27th and found the area empty of Indians. He noted heavy smoke to the northeast, however, and its significance would soon dawn on him. The next day courier Fairbanks brought dispatches from Sheridan, dated July 25th, announcing that the 5th Cavalry should arrive about August 1st and urging Crook to assume the offensive immediately there-after (C-7). This prodded him into resuming scouting operations in earnest.

On July 31st Louis Richard led a party of Shoshones over the mountains into the Big Horn Basin to check on the claim that the Sioux Nation was assembled there. They returned to the camp now on the main Tongue on the evening of August 1st, reporting no hostiles in the mountains or in the valley, nor any sign of their having been there, save for small parties hunting lodge-poles in the foot-hills. They had not even seen any buffalo, and concluded the herds had all migrated eastward, tolling the Indians like Pied Piper.

That morning Crook had also sent Grouard and Cosgrove with other Shoshones to scout northwest along the base of the mountains. They returned the next afternoon without having seen a single live Indian. However, at the point where the Little Big Horn emerges from the mountains, they had found an immense, but old, village site with discarded cavalry relics proving the inhabitants had come from the Custer fight. The villagers had been reduced to eating dogs and ponies, and the grass had been completely cropped. This village had furnished the warriors for the Sibley skirmish, only three miles above in the mountans; the Shoshones discovered and scalped the corpses of the two Cheyennes killed in that affair.

Grouard had also traced the trail of the departing village as it led downstream, and at the mouth of Pass Creek (present Wyola, Montana) found another deserted campsite. From there the trails all led northeast toward the head of the Rosebud. Frank concluded

206

that the hostiles had long ago headed for the lower Tongue and Powder Rivers on their regular seasonal migration and would probably continue to the Little Missouri. Not one contemporaneous source dared to mention the vintage of these trails nor divulge the embarrassing implications.

Crook never had better use for his poker face. Could he have failed to realize that nearly all the time he had been paralyzed by visions of hordes of hostiles, they had been long gone? And if they had been half starving a fortnight ago, could they have remained together? It was appalling to contemplate how far they could have moved and scattered in that time. Under such humiliating circumstances, it is no wonder that everyone kept the secret.

That same August 2nd brought another dispatch from Sheridan, dated July 28th, in answer to Crook's "dread of attack" dispatch. "If you do not feel strong enough to attack and defeat the Indians," Sheridan wrote bluntly, "it is best for you to form a junction with Terry at once. I have sent to you and General Terry every available man that can be spared in the Division, and if it has not made the column strong enough, Terry and you should unite your forces." There was only ironic solace in the tag-line saying that "the conduct of yourself and command in the engagement of the 17th ult., and your actions afterwards have all been approved all the way through by myself and General Sherman, and he directs me to inform you that you need not mind the newspapers. (C-7)."

The same courier announced the approach of the 5th Cavalry, and the next morning, August 3rd, Crook marched eighteen miles southeast to join his reinforcements at the forks of Goose Creek. The next day he issued orders for the combined command to strip down to the most Spartan level yet in preparation for an offensive to begin the next morning. He then struggled over the following report to Sheridan:

> Three Crow Indians came through from General Terry on the 19th, and at that time all trails were leading up the Little Big Horn to the Big Horn mountains, not even a pony track going back. On the 25th or 26th, all the hostile Indians left the foot of the Big Horn mountains, so that it is now impracticable to communicate with General Terry by courier. I am fearful they will scatter, as there is not sufficient game in that country to support them in such large numbers.
>
> General Merritt joined me last evening with his command. Tomorrow morning we will cut loose from the wagons with about two thousand aggregate fighting men, including friendly Indians and a small party of citizen volunteers, move down Tongue River in direction we suppose hostiles have gone, carrying with us fifteen days' rations. If we meet the Indians in too strong force, I will swing around and unite with General Terry. (C-7)

This letter seems carefully designed to conceal what we have already revealed. The trails noted by the couriers on July 19th were of June 26-7 vintage, and some had turned east! The trail Grouard had reported heading for the Rosebud was associated with the Sibley scout of July 7th! Those who departed on the 25th or 26th were labeled *all* hostiles, when they were only the *last*! Could these have been honest errors? And why the illogical claim that since the enemy had left the country between the two commands, he could no longer send couriers to Terry? Was he trying to parry the forseeable charge that having misinformed Terry and invited him to join in a mountain offensive, he had failed to advise him of the drastically altered situation?

*   *   *

After Terry's departure on the *Josephine*, July 16th, Gibbon's camp paid no heed to bits and pieces of Indian intelligence that filtered in. On the 19th a courier from Powder River reported crossing an Indian trail heading north toward Fort Peck. That night the camp was alarmed by shots, signalling an attempted raid on the cavalry horses; the next morning the Crows picked up the trail of the raiders, thirty strong, also heading north. That afternoon other Crows returned from the mouth of the Little Big Horn, reporting that country barren of both Indians and buffalo. At dark of July 22nd, Clifford observed a red, fire-lit sky towards the Rosebud. Gibbon was as blind to such signals as Crook had been.

Terry floated in to Powder River on July 27th to greet the *Far West*. Since garrison, train, and supplies had to be ferried to the north bank for the march to the Big Horn, Terry put both boats to the work. Late on the 18th, however, he sent the *Josephine* back to Bismarck with his aide, Captain Robert P. Hughes, and a load of sick and wounded. Working alone, the *Far West* did not complete the ferry work until the 20th. To avoid overloads, tons of forage were left behind to be brought up later. Terry then steamed up for the Big Horn camp, leaving orders for the overland column to follow in the morning.

Terry's plans at this time were outlined by Lt. Byrne of Moore's command and by Captain Hughes (Bismark *Tribune*, July 26). It was expected to require some ten days to consolidate the forces at the Big Horn camp and to receive the expected infantry reinforcements. Terry would then take the combined column eighty miles up the Big Horn to the base of the mountains, where he would park his wagon train. He would then lead his own and Crook's armies

208

into the mountains to destroy the assembled hostiles.

Terry did not reach the Big Horn until July 26th, for the river had fallen so low that it took the *Far West* six days to cover the 164 river-miles. This gave the General plenty of time to register the effects of failing navigation on his plan. Reinforcements and supplies would be delayed at best and left stranded downstream at worst. He could no longer take the wagon route up the west bank of the Big Horn, for no boat could get up to ferry him across. The Tullock's Fork trail would require a pack train, with limited rations and no forage. He therefore decided to move his consolidated base down to the mouth of the Rosebud, since the trail from there would accommodate wagons.

On reaching camp Terry found Crook's dispatch of the 23rd awaiting him. He was pleased at the harmony of thought between Crook and himself. Crook had the hostiles corraled in the mountains and invited Terry to join him there in a cooperative action, which was precisely what Terry was planning to do. Without delay, he ordered Gibbon to move down to the new base opposite the mouth of the Rosebud.

Terry sped down on the boat the next morning, anxious to warn Moore's battalion of the change in location of the base. He found them that evening already in bivouac thirteen miles above the Rosebud, and had to order them to turn back. Both arrived at the chosen point the next day, and Gibbon's column marched in on the 30th. The infantry erected some earthworks, which prompted the GI's of 1876 to dub the place "Fort Beans," in harmony with Forts Pease and Rice. Here Quartermaster Nowlan hired three additional scouts: George W. Morgan (August 1 to September 31), a local frontiersman; Edward Begley (August 1 to September 23), known for years on the river as "Jimmy from Cork"; and Zed H. Daniels (August 7 to September 12, then transferred to Glendive), another veteran of Fort Pease, who had just returned by boat from his prospecting trip across to the Black Hills.

On August 1st the *Carroll* steamed in from Bismarck, bringing Lt. Col. Elwell S. Otis and six companies of 22nd Infantry, as the first contingent of the long-awaited reinforcements. Also aboard were two additional correspondents, James W. ("Phocion") Howard of the Chicago *Tribune*, and James J. O'Kelly of the New York *Herald*. A less welcome passenger was Lt. Col. James W. Forsyth, military secretary to Sheridan, bearing the following letter of July 20th from his superior:

> . . . I have made arrangements for the construction of the two new posts on the Yellowstone. They are to be similar to Fort Lincoln and

everything will be sent to the ground so that all now necessary is to know the points and to have the hostile Indians hit so that we can get a sufficient number of troops to guard the workmen. I therefore advise you to make arrangements to form a junction with General Crook . . . We cannot send any more troops . . . The military posts are to be for six companies of cavalry and five companies of infantry each . . . (R-26)

Anxious to lead his augmented command on a campaign to strike a retaliatory blow at the Indians who had humiliated the 7th Cavalry, Terry was dismayed at the request to divert his troops and transport to the construction of two substantial posts. But he soon convinced Forsyth that navigation of the river was deteriorating so rapidly as to make it impossible to carry out Sheridan's scheme until next spring.

The *Carroll* sailed back on August 2nd, taking the disappointed Forsyth and twenty soldiers sick with scurvy and typhoid fever. That afternoon Terry welcomed the *Durfee*, bringing General Nelson A. Miles and six companies of 5th Infantry; also aboard were the General's nephew, George M. Miles, quartermaster clerk and diarist, and chronicler Edwin M. Brown, Trumpeter of Company B. At the same time the *Josephine* arrived with recruits, remounts, artillery, and provisions. All of the expected reinforcements had now arrived, but since all had been landed at Fort Beans, four days were wasted in ferrying the entire command to the south bank. Terry then issued orders for the campaign to the mountains to begin on the morning of August 8th.

Although this distant movement was long planned, there had been no attempt to locate the enemy. Worse yet, few heeded the ample warnings that the hostiles, instead of being corraled in the Big Horns to the southwest, were already roaming the lower Tongue and Powder, *east* of Fort Beans. Witness the following evidence, known to all.

On July 29th, the *Carroll* had seen some two hundred warriors ransacking the forage left at Powder River by the departing garrison. They fired into the boat, wounding a soldier and prompting Colonel Otis to land a company to chastise them. The Indians promptly disappeared into the timber, free of casualties as far as the soldiers could tell. Then on July 31st the ascending *Durfee* and *Josephine* had likewise seen Indians lurking at the same point, although no shots were fired.

Major Moore, under orders to salvage the remaining forage, reached the scene on the *Far West*, August 2nd. When the swarm of Indians there refused to attack the strong force he landed, he shelled the timber in which they took refuge. While the forage was being loaded, scouts Wesley Brockmeyer and George Morgan, accompanied by the boat pilot, Dave Campbell, rode out to investigate, only to fall into an ambush. Brockmeyer met a fatal bullet, but Morgan quickly drilled the triumphant Indian. While Dr. Porter rushed to aid the wounded scout, Campbell lifted the hair of the slain warrior. The Doctor later sent the grisly trophy to Bismarck for display. Having salvaged 75 tons of oats and corn, the *Far West* arrived back at Fort Beans on August 4th (O-39, 1876 and C-54).

As related by Lt Byrne, an overland courier party from Fort Buford, including Pvt. John H. Cassidy, Company C, 6th Infantry, and "Jimmie from Cork," approached the mouth of Powder River on July 31st. They spotted Indians on both banks and hundreds crossing to the north side. This forced them to hole up for two nights and a day before finding a chance to continue to Fort Beans. Even at the latter post, Matt Carroll recorded on August 1st that "the entire country is seemingly on fire," and the next day Lt. Byrne wrote that "dense smoke in all directions shows that the Indians are busily employed in burning the grass."

Reporter O'Kelly wrote that a number of officers were urging Terry to strike these Indians at hand rather than to search for others in distant parts, but the General stoutly held to his resolve, formed many weeks earlier and reinforced by Crook's intelligence, to march to the Big Horns to join the latter in demolishing the Sioux Nation in one powerful blow!

The stage was set for a farce.

Chapter 18
A Punishing Stern Chase

The curtain rose on the August farce with Crook, convinced that the hostiles had moved to Terry's vicinity, poised to march there, and with Terry, convinced that the hostiles were still in Crook's vicinity, poised to march there. The joker was that both were wrong. The saving grace was that they would unexpectedly meet before either was left to wander alone in the other's empty theater. The tragedy was that in concert they would seriously punish their troops in a hopeless stern chase.

Crook's force had now swelled from twenty-five to thirty-five companies, making 1800 troops, 250 Indian allies, and 200 packers and volunteers for a total of nearly 2300. Merritt had also brought additional quartermaster scouts, including the competent Buffalo Bill Cody, his side-kick, Jonathan White, better known as "Buffalo Chips," Buckskin Jack Russell, and Jack Crawford, "The Poet Scout." The added press brigade boasted Cuthbert Mills of the New York *Times*, Barbour Lathrop of the San Francisco *Evening Bulletin*, and J.J. Talbot of the New York *Graphic*. New chroniclers of the campaign included Captain Charles King and Lt. Col. Eugene A. Carr, both of the 5th Infantry. Captain Andrew S. Burt, 9th Infantry, also began sending dispatches to his hometown paper, and Pvt. Richard Flynn, Company D, 4th Infantry, started keeping a diary.

Crook knew he could not pursue long-departed Indians with a slow wagon train, nor could he leave behind any of the reinforcements he insisted he dare not move without. Yet his pack train had not been increased by one mule. He suddenly found he could take no forage whatever, though he would have to cross burned-over country. In order to pack even fifteen days' rations, he had to strip down his men like never before. He might be reduced to mule meat, or if lucky, he might find Terry's depot, and if luckier still, the stores there might support a double drain. He had to bet long odds on weather, grass, and rations. He was fated to lose on all three. Ironically, the problem stemmed entirely from his insistence on heavy reinforcements, for which there was no longer any need.

On the morning of August 5th the formidable Wyoming column pulled out on a twenty-two mile march to bivouac on Tongue River four miles below the mouth of Prairie Dog Creek. Fire-blackened grass was the only sign that Indians had been around. Nothing was seen the next day as the troops forded the Tongue thirteen times, but scouts sent to the west reported encouraging indications in the Rosebud valley. On the 7th the column wound twenty-three miles over the divide to camp in the Rosebud valley below the site of the June 17th battle and just above a large deserted village site. Those who had figured in the battle decided that this site was just where they believed the hostile village stood seven weeks before. They noted the narrow valley they would have had to traverse to reach it, and agreed that only Crook's genius in recalling Mill's battalion had spared it Custer's fate.

Unfortunately, no Indian village had camped there on June 17th. But the hostiles had camped there about July 10th, when they were leaving Crook's front. Their heavy trail, now four weeks old, was overlaid by fresher sign left by a succession of rear-guard parties, which made it hard to read its age. This precipitated lengthy arguments among the scouts — a debate that would be renewed daily for weeks. Although admitting the debate, Bourke recorded the sign as ten to twelve days old, in miraculous agreement with Crook's claim that all had left on July 25-26! Captain King gave the age as two weeks, and Grouard as three. That the majority found them ancient is revealed by their conviction that they dated back to June 17th!

August 8th dawned in an opaque smog. After gasping for four or five miles to clear the old village site, Crook called a long halt and sent only the scouts ahead. Returning in the afternoon, they reported the heavy trail to continue for at least fifteen miles to the Busby bend of the Rosebud. They also noted other trails converging from the west and found pony tracks of an admitted rear-guard party made within the week. Late in the evening the column made a moonlight march to camp below Busby.

On the twenty mile march down the blackened valley on the 9th, several old camp sites, yielding evidence of near starvation, marked the Indian trail, and everyone noted the traces of Custer's column. The trail "was at first two weeks old, then ten days, then a week, and then four days," wrote reporter Davenport. It was probably all these and more because of the procession of rear-guards. As a foretaste of what was to come, the troops marched most of the day into the teeth of a cold driving rain. It stopped as camp was made below Lame Deer Creek, but then the mercury plummeted below freezing. Without an extra sock or blanket and no tents, the troopers turned blue.

A few miles out on the trail the next morning, a brief halt was called. Only Lt. Schwatka gave the reason: they had come upon a still-standing sun dance lodge, with the surrounding tepees ditched against rain. The column nooned at the mouth of Greenleaf Creek, where the scouts found the Indian trail turning east toward the Tongue. At that moment other scouts reported an enormous force approaching up the Rosebud valley. The enemy, at last! Fast preparations for battle were in the making, when someone spotted a long wagon train that betrayed the force as Terry's column.

*   *   *

Although Terry had received his reinforcements a day earlier than Crook, the ferrying work delayed his departure until three days after the rival force took the field. Terry left Captain Louis H. Sanger in command of Fort Beans with two companies of 17th Infantry, a battery of artillery, and some 120 dismounted recruits. Although he sent the *Josephine* to Bismarck for more supplies, he retained the *Far West* to patrol the river. His field force, though weaker than Crook's, was better supplied and equipped. The eleven cavalry companies (the 7th having been reorganized as seven companies) and twenty-one infantry companies totalled 83 officers and 1611 men. He also had about 75 scouts, including enlisted Crows and Rees. Muggins Taylor was back, but Williamson had failed to return with the Crow volunteers Terry had expected. A train of 240 wagons carried shelter tents, full rations for 35 days, and partial forage. The column was thus short on mobility, but long on endurance, as befitted his intention of moving to the distant Big Horns to establish a base for swifter operations with Crook's force.

On the sweltering morning of August 8th, the heavy column started up the Rosebud on the old Custer trail, which proved less suitable for wagons than expected, so that at day's end they had covered only 9½ miles. That night Barney Bravo and five Crows

214

left to notify Crook that Terry was on his way to join him. The second day turned cold and rainy with mud underfoot, holding the march to eleven miles. Already Terry was having trouble with his Indian scouts, whom he had ordered to report to him directly. Although Varnum still kept the rolls for the Rees and Burnett for the Crows, neither was apparently assigned any further scouting responsibility. Immediate supervision thus fell to Tom LeForge for the Crows and Fred Gerard for the Rees. Such tenuous control undermined the confidence of the Indians, who lost heart for their dangerous duties.

Early in the afternoon some Crows came back, having seen a few Sioux. Shortly after, Barney Bravo and his couriers rode back with the undelivered dispatch to Crook, insisting that twelve miles out they had spotted a party of Sioux moving westward from the Tongue to the Rosebud. At 6 p.m. the remaining scouts galloped in reporting "heap Sioux" ahead. Holding an unsatisfactory council with the Crows that evening, Terry decided that they had observed the warriors returning from the mouth of Powder River. He finally wrung a promise that a larger courier party would make another attempt to get through to Crook. But the next morning LeForge confessed that the courier party had refused to start out; he was even hard put to induce thirty Crows to scout the advance for the day.

Left uncertain as to what might lie ahead, Terry resumed the march on the 10th with the column better closed up and alerted for possible action. After making nine miles the Crows all stormed back, shouting that the whole Sioux Nation was approaching from upstream. This time, even the sceptics, squinting ahead, could plainly see an enormous column of dust, signifying a perfect horde of warriors.

While the Crows and Rees made excited preparations for battle, Terry cracked out orders to his troops. With bugles blaring, the 7th Cavalry, hot for revenge, deployed in a skirmish line in the lead. The 2nd Cavalry wheeled in behind them as support. The teamsters rushed their wagons up in tight formation, while the infantry moved on the double to protect its flanks and rear. When the command, "Forward!" rang out, the force moved out in battle array.

Minutes later every eye discerned a lone rider emerge from the dust ahead, running his horse like a warrior on a suicide charge. Slowly the image enlarged, and on closer approach, the daring warrior began waving — a large white hat! In another moment he pulled up before the lead officer to announce himself as Buffalo Bill and to extend the compliments of General Crook, who awaited General Terry in bivouac six miles ahead. With a mixture of chagrin, relief, and joy, Terry's force marched on to camp next to the Wyoming column at the mouth of Greenleaf Creek.

Members of the two commands mingled to eye one another with unrestrained curiosity. Crook's men reacted with envy and disdain to the luxury in which Terry's troops campaigned. Terry's men were appalled and impressed with the Spartan ways of Crook's troops. At noon, Crook served a pauper's lunch to Terry, and at evening Terry served a banquet to Crook. All agreed that the two generals epitomized the contrast in the two commands. Bourke confided his judgements to his diary:

> General Terry's manners are most charming and affable; he had the look of a scholar as well as a soldier; eyes, blue-gray and kindly; complexion, bronzed by wind and sun to the color of an old sheepskin-covered Bible. He won his way to our hearts by his unaffectedness and affability. He is the antithesis of Crook in his manner. Crook is simple and unaffected also, but is reticent and taciturn to the extreme of sadness, brusk to the point of severity. Of the two, Terry would be the more pleasing companion, Crook the stauncher friend. In Terry's face I thought I detected faint traces of indecision and weakness; but in Crook's countenance there is not the slightest trace of anything but stubborness, stolidity, rugged resolution, and bull-dog tenacity.

The two commanders pooled their information to decide on a future course of action. Perhaps Terry opened by asking pointedly why Crook had not warned him of the drastic change in plan. Perhaps Crook countered with the query why Terry remained unaware that the enemy had moved to his territory. If so, each having scored on the other, they proceeded to more fruitful discussion. Although the accommodating Terry was the senior officer, it is apparent that the views of the stubborn Crook prevailed.

Crook undoubtedly expressed the conviction that the hostiles had left his front some sixteen days earlier, and that he had been overhauling them on the trail to this point, where it turned east. Terry undoubtedly told of the hostiles that had arrived at the mouth of Powder River two weeks earlier. Somehow they failed to accept the implication that they were far behind the quarry. Crook must have insisted that the trail was now fresh enough to warrant a determined stern chase, for that is precisely what they decided to undertake with their combined forces.

Terry protected his interests, however, by ordering General Miles and the 5th Infantry to escort the wagon train back to Fort Beans, there to load his men on the *Far West*, to set up guard posts at the Yellowstone crossings and patrol the river; he was also to deliver supplies to the mouth of Powder River for the overland armies to draw upon. From his own provisions, Terry restored Crook's rations to fifteen days and arranged to carry the same for his own command by pack train. This forced him to forego forage, and whether by necessity or emulation, he stripped down his men to match Crook's. As a result both commands would now risk exposure of men and injury to animals. These conference decisions Terry reported to Sheridan that evening.

At this time an issue had first cropped up that was to generate friction between the two generals. Crook, being responsible for the Department of the Platte, was most concerned about Crazy Horse's following of southern Sioux who ranged south of the Yellowstone and threatened the settlements. But Terry, being responsible for the Department of Dakota, was most concerned about Sitting Bull's following of northern Sioux, who ranged all the way to Canada and threatened to escape in that direction. Neither was sympathetic to the other's worries.

At 11 o'clock of the 11th, the mammoth command of twenty-five companies of infantry and thirty-six of cavalry launched the stern chase of the distant hostiles. At this point the Rosebud runs closest to the Tongue, so that a nine mile march over the divide brought them to the valley of the latter, down which they moved four miles to bivouac at the mouth of Beaver Creek. Crook's army, with the most efficient pack train, had taken the lead and so had the experience of watching Terry's pack trains straggle in. They were appalled at the performance, but the green packers of Colonel Otis' 22nd Infantry won all laurels for ineptness.

On reaching the blacked-over valley of the Tongue, the command had noted a large camp site, occupied since the Custer fight, but still old. Here the trail divided, one branch heading upstream, another downstream, and others east toward the Powder River. Camp had scarcely been made when a cold deluge from the skies extinguished further concern about the break-up in the trail. Without shelter the men were instantly drenched from above; before long they found themselves lying in a rising flood of chilled water; without blankets or fires their teeth began chattering. Utter misery replaced sleep that night.

The downpour continued unabated the next day, the 12th. The commands could only stand all morning, dripping in the mire, while the scouts slopped out to determine which, if any, of the several trails was the main one. The grouchy troops complained of the luck that brought them to a heavy trail, only to have it split up, and grumbled that in the face of such a strong force the hostiles would scatter never to be seen again. Even the scouts argued hotly about the age of the trail, their estimates ranging from a hopeful three days to a hopeless three weeks. None knew that the break-

217

up here had occurred on July 14th, nearly a month before, but a few sharper minds were beginning to smell out the truth.

Irritated by discomfort, the two armies, championed by their respective correspondents, were already turning bitterly partisan. Terry's team accused Crook of being a liar or a dupe about the date of the hostile flight from his front. They branded him a fool for letting them escape from under his nose. They condemned him bitterly for not warning Terry so that he could move to trap them in flight. Crook's team concentrated on sneering at the military inefficiency of Terry's command, whose presence could only hamper their own winning of the war.

About noon, the scouts splashed back, having decided that the heaviest trail led downstream. In the unrelenting rain, the columns churned through the mud for thirteen miles before going into camp. The rain robbed everyone of a good sleep for the second night in a row.

The skies relented on the 13th, permitting a long march of twenty-four miles down the valley, interspersed with fordings. The prolonged tramping in wet shoes made the infantry painfully footsore; many accepted a lift on a horse or mule, while others straggled behind. The cavalry had it a little better, except that overwork without forage or adequate grazing was breaking down their mounts, especially in Crook's command; many horses were abandoned or shot. No sooner had the men dragged themselves into camp, than the exasperating rain returned to make the third miserable night.

A few deluded themselves into believing the trail was freshening, but Lt. Maguire called them still old, and Lt. King finally admitted that prospects of overtaking the enemy were now dead. Even Terry was not hopeful, for the scouts had examined the trail ahead this day. He prepared a note for Muggins Taylor to deliver to Miles at his new guard post at the mouth of the Tongue, advising that the trail turned toward Powder River, perhaps even beyond, and asking that another boat, if possible, be sent up from Fort Buford to patrol the lower Yellowstone.

Having wrung nine miles from their sore feet and failing horses by noon of the 14th, the columns reached Pumpkin Creek, which the troops dubbed "Squashy Creek," in the last flickering flame of humor. Those who had predicted that the hostiles would cross the Yellowstone at the mouth of the Tongue to find buffalo, fell silent when they saw the trail turn east up Pumpkin Creek toward Powder River. Six miles up Pumpkin Creek, with men straggling and horses collapsing, they camped. To everyone's sullen resentment it rained again for the fourth night.

Lt. McClernand recorded that the white scouts judged the trail to be freshening, while the Crows insisted it was still a defeating nine days or more old. That evening Muggins Taylor returned from the mouth of the Tongue where he had contacted Miles and the *Far West*. The new guard posts at the mouths of Tongue and Powder Rivers and the patrolling in the boat had uncovered no sign of river crossings, implying that the Indians were still headed east. Taylor also brought heartening news that would prove false — that 250 Crow volunteers were on their way to join the command.

As the tramp continued over the divide to Powder River on the 15th, the sun burst out but the temperature soared and the rough country made the hardest going yet. The breakdown of men and animals continued apace. They forded Mizpah Creek and Powder River a mile or so above their confluence and turned down river to camp on the east bank after a grueling twenty miles. Few had the heart to mention that the Indian trail also turned downstream, for evening brought more wrath from the heavens — the fifth night of misery.

With spirits hitting rock bottom, the commands managed to reach the old Terry-Custer camp near Locate Creek on the 16th. As evidence of frayed tempers, Godfrey recorded that none of the staff officers were speaking to one another, and Reno was making such an ass of himself as to exhaust even Terry's patience. The health of the men had deteriorated, with scurvy, dysentery, and rheumatism prevalent. Most shocking of all, Captain Archibald H. Goodloe, 22nd Infantry, suffered a severe paralytic stroke on the march, placing another call on Lt. Doane's talents at litter-making.

The sky turned mercifully clear on the 17th, but two unnecessary fordings of the river kept the troops suitably baptised. A number of chroniclers recorded that the Indian trail soon broke up and scattered eastward toward O'Fallon's Creek. This occurred over a range of 12 to 20 miles above the river mouth, with 18 miles as the single point most often mentioned. To the east the prairie was everywhere fire-blackened. Many hoped that the hostiles had headed for the Little Missouri en route to their agencies, so that they could go home, too. For the first time some one hit it on the nose; Lt. McClernanad officially recorded that it was "generally conceded that the Crows were right about the age of the trail, and that the Sioux are nearly two weeks ahead of us."

Crook had been making himself less and less obtrusive, but Terry retained the wit to send his Rees out as far as they would go on the scattering trail. The abused troops headed straight down Powder River, determined to abandon the wild goose chase in favor of a rest and re-outfitting they would no longer be denied. Nothing slowed them as they plowed twenty-four miles to the Yellowstone, Terry's division camping just below and Crook's just above the mouth of the Powder, all ragged, the infantry shoeless, the horses staggering, the sick-list appalling, and morale shattered.

Bad luck was still running, however, for neither the *Far West* nor a mountain of unloaded supplies was anywhere to be seen. After consulting with Lt. W. Philo Clark, whom Miles had left to man this guard post, Terry sent a note to Crook, offering what he could:

> The steamer left here last night, or rather yesterday afternoon, and was expected back before this. I hope that she will be here this evening. A part of the rations which I ordered are here; I presume that the rest are aboard the boat. I have here 60,000 lbs. of grain and will direct Captain Nowlan to issue to your quartermaster, whenever you send for it.
>
> P.S. Miles has a company on the river some 30 or 40 river miles below this point, but there is no news from it; the company went down night before last and took with it both scouts and Indians. I am sure that if anything is discovered, the intelligence will be sent up here. (C-7)

While the troops lunched on emetic hardtack, the gaunt horses banqueted on good grain. Grumbling, griping, and bickering became the order of the afternoon. Those most put out by the want of luxuries proved to be Crook's Spartans, now reduced by their own improvidence to sponging on Terry's stores.

This mis-guided stern chase of thirteen days for Crook's force and nine for Terry's had severely punished a major fraction of the frontier army, without coming within a hundred miles of an Indian. The sobering thought struck home that a few more campaigns of this kind and the Sioux would win the war *in absentia*!

Chapter 19
Reconnaissances, Rumors, and Recriminations

From the moment the energetic and out-spoken General Miles had added his six companies of 5th Infantry to Terry's force at Fort Beans back on August 2nd, he had become increasingly disgusted with the demoralized and time-wasting command. He wrote his wife that "the campaign thus far would not have been creditable to a militia organization." He chafed at the delays, expressed little faith in the proposed march to the southwest when the Indians seemed to be in the east. He grew impatient when the lumbering column moved at a snail's pace. The final exasperation came when the unexpected meeting with Crook resulted in the decision to launch a stern chase over an old trail with two armies combined.

Convinced that the hostiles would never allow such a legion to approach within leagues, and irritated at having been brigaded under the dispirited Gibbon, Miles seized the opportunity for an independent command. He suggested that his infantry could serve best by returning to guard the Yellowstone. Since this was Terry's own chronic worry, he consented. With complete satisfaction Miles accepted orders to establish guard posts on the river and patrol it on the *Far West*, dropping off supplies at Powder River for the overland armies.

Leaving Captain Simon Snyder with two companies to escort the train the next day, Miles hit the back trail with the other four that very afternoon, August 10th. His men had already tramped sixteen miles that morning, but he drove them another thirty-four in an overnight march to reach the river the next morning. He did not fail to emphasize that his footmen had accomplished more in one night than the whole command in three days. Just as they reached the river, Captain Marsh steamed up on the *Far West* from a patrol of his own, and ferried them across to Fort Beans.

The General learned that earlier that day Lt. W. Philo Clark, another diarist, recently relieved as adjutant of the 2nd Cavalry, had arrived with thirty-three recruits from Fort Ellis, along with Lts. William I. Reed and Francis Woodbridge, come to join the 7th Infantry. They had left Benson's landing on the 6th in several mackinaw boats, accompanied by free-lance sutler Matthew ("Cy") Mounts, a former Crow trader, in a boat of his own loaded with merchandise for the troops. They had brought news that John Williamson would arrive the next day with a village of 450 Crows, under Iron Bull and Good Heart, to join the expedition.

Within hours the refreshingly dynamic Miles arranged to have a flatboat ferry the wagon train across when it arrived; arranged for Clark to organize the Crow allies and his recruits for a scout down the north bank to Powder River; arranged for a small force under Reed and Woodbridge to descend to the same point in the mackinaws; and commandeered some scouts for his own use. The latter were probably George Mulligan, who had come out with Major Moore, and George Morgan, whom Miles would hire as a scout in September. He probably also took Billy Cross, an able half-breed Sioux, who remained to serve with him in September; he and White Cloud, a Sioux, had been "Ree" scouts detached to Fort Beans on August 8th.

That evening Miles embarked his four leg-weary companies on the *Far West* to steam thirty-four river-miles down to the Tongue, where he landed Captain Andrew S. Bennett's Company B to man a guard post on the north bank. The next morning he sped another thirty-seven river-miles to the Powder, where he set up another guard post. He unloaded only a few supplies, for he had left orders for the wagon train and escort to continue down to this point. Because of limited ferrying capacity, however, the train would not leave Fort Beans until the 17th, nor reach its destination until the 22nd.

Miles was eager to locate another post still farther down the river, but Captain Marsh warned him that if the boat shot Wolf Rapids, only six river-miles below the Powder, they might not be able to get back because of falling water. That evening, the 12th, Miles sent George Mulligan and companion to Fort Buford to deliver Terry's report and his request of General Hazen, now commanding that post, to send an additional boat to patrol the lower river. The two couriers reached the fort safely on the 15th. By then Miles was patrolling back upriver, but the negotiation of Buffalo Rapids,

222

twenty-four river-miles above the Powder, delayed his arrival at the Tongue River post until after dark of the 14th.

In the meantime, reporter O'Kelly and a hired courier named Burke had left the overland armies to reach Fort Beans early on the 12th, hoping to join the more active Miles. Although disappointed to find that he had already left, O'Kelly was in time to see Williamson ride in at the head of a colorful cavalcade of 450 Crows. Lt. Clark served them all a feast of one day's rations, and then asked for volunteers to scout with him down the north bank. This aroused singularly little enthusiasm and the council broke up with the the promise of an answer in the morning.

The attitude of the Crows had provoked Captain Sanger to contemptuous anger. Unfortunately, he outranked Lt. Clark, who would soon demonstrate an exceptional knack for dealing with Indians. The testy Captain either did not know, or did not care, that the Crows had received no rations all summer and that the arms embargo had hampered their hunting. Their Agent, Dexter E. Clapp, had been pleading with Washington to stop starving a friendly tribe that was furnishing such faithful scouts to the army. Sheridan would soon relax the arms embargo, but the resumption of rations would be longer delayed. At the moment, however, the hungry Crows were compelled to sell their services for food or the means to hunt it.

The next morning the chiefs first offered to provide a party of scouts in exchange for five days' rations for the entire assemblage. Captain Sanger indignantly vetoed this proposition as outrageous. The chiefs then asked for ammunition for all, but the Captain bluntly refused it to any who did not volunteer as scouts. Clark then tried to purchase thirty ponies to mount his recruits, but the Crows could not eat money. The upshot was that Captain Sanger summarily threw the Crows out of his post and ordered them all back to their agency.

O'Kelly railed at the ungrateful Crows for refusing to aid a government that pampered them in every way! But the Bozeman *Times* railed at the "pusilanimous Captain" for refusing to compensate the Crows with a few rations, and then denying them the privilege of answering Terry's call on their own. Yet thirty or forty defiant braves did ride out to find the expedition. The insulted Crows asked interpreters Williamson and Mounts "why such an ass had been left in command." Their agent also reported that the Crows "were much disgusted by the treatment they had received from an officer named Sanger in command at the mouth of the Rosebud."

Having failed to make allies of the Crows, Clark and his recruits joined Reed and Woodbridge and reporter O'Kelly in the journey

223

down in the small boats on the afternoon of the 13th. They engaged Benjamin Thompson to pilot the flotilla, which included Cy Mount's craft. The next afternoon they tied up at Captain Bennett's post at Tongue River. Soon Muggins Taylor rode in with his dispatch from General Terry, then marching on the lower Tongue. After dark Miles steamed up on the *Far West* to learn from the dispatch that Terry feared the hostiles might have moved even below Powder River.

Since the Tongue River post was no longer useful, Miles loaded its garrison on the boat the next morning and sailed for Powder River, followed by the boat flotilla. Arriving that evening of the 15th, he sent scouts down to O'Fallon's Creek, thirty-one river-miles below, but only fifteen bee-line miles. They returned reporting no evidence of Indian crossings. Not content with this effort, Miles then sent Lt. Edmund Rice's Company H down in the small boats, still piloted by Ben Thompson, to set up a post opposite the mouth of O'Fallon's Creek.

Other scouts having reported signs of a crossing up near Buffalo Rapids, Miles steamed up to investigate on the 16th, leaving only the three Lieutenants, the recruits, and Cy Mounts to man the tiny Powder River outpost. Finding the crossing trail inconsequential, Miles arrived back at Powder River at 6 p.m. the next day to find the demoralized army had straggled in to bicker over inadequate stores.

*　　　　　*　　　　　*

For the next week the accommodating Terry and the uncooperative Crook carried on a tug-of-war, while the soldiers grumbled and others began to desert the depressing scene. Resting and re-outfitting the troops from short supplies available only at Fort Beans entailed delay, which was especially exasperating after two months of no accomplishment. The future looked even gloomier, for there was no alternative to resuming the stern chase.

Just how unpromising that was became apparent when the Rees returned from scouting the hostile trail seen on the day's march scattering east from Powder River. Terry quickly informed Crook of their findings by note: "My Rees have come in; they say that they have been as far as the next creek, I suppose O'Fallon's, and that all the trails tend directly east, as if making for the Little Missouri, and that they have burned the entire country behind them." This meant that they had crossed O'Fallon's at some unknown time *before* August 11th, when the beginning of heavy rains would have prevented firing the prairie in their wake.

The body of this same note proposed a reconnaissance that

224

annoyed Crook and triggered the tug-of-war between the two Generals:

> The Far West has just arrived. I have just given orders to take her stores off, and then I propose to send her down to Wolf Rapids to make an examination and determine the question whether she can get back again, if she goes below there. If she can, I shall send her down as far as Glendive Creek to ascertain if the Indians have crossed. Starting early tomorrow morning she can be back by tomorrow night. I should like if you would send on her some of the people in whose judgement you have the most confidence to look out for trails coming down to the bank and going up the other side. (C-7)

Feeling no concern about Terry's Indians crossing to the north, Crook wanted no part of this reconnaissance by steamboat. Instead, he wanted the *Far West* sent instantly to the Rosebud for supplies. But since the rank, the boat, and the supplies were all Terry's, he could only submit. Grudgingly, he sent Buffalo Bill and Louis Richard to participate in the boat scout that meant nothing to him. The trial of Wolf Rapids proved successful, and early the next morning, the 18th, the voyage down to Glendive began, with Miles in command and O'Kelly as supercargo.

While the boat was gone, Terry and Crook had some curious exchanges, as Bourke recorded. The stores unloaded from the boat consisted of two days' forage and insufficient rations for two armies, but Terry was so eager to get on with the chase that he consulted with Crook that morning, offering to share what he had. He was puzzled to find his subordinate less geared to action than his reputation promised. Crook complained that the rations would not load his pack train to its fifteen-day capactiy. Terry proposed that they live on horse-meat, if necessary. Crook then demanded more forage to recruit his broken-down horses, which could only come from Fort Beans. That evening Terry wrote another note to Crook:

> Since I saw you, I have found that our supplies of subsistence are larger than I supposed. The whole force here is rationed to include September 1st, except that your commissary still needs 200 boxes of hard bread. Of these, I can furnish 100 boxes and still have a little bread, a little coffee, and a little sugar left. The difference between this amount and the 15 days' rations, of which you spoke, is so slight that I think it ought not to detain us. But perhaps your animals are in such a state that a further supply of forage and a longer rest would be desirable for them. If such be your wish, I am certainly willing to wait until the forage can be obtained.
> P.S. Col. Chambers [Crook's infantry commander] mentioned to me today that his men need shoes badly. If the steamer goes to the Rosebud, I can give him the shoes which he needs. (C-7)

We here see the cautious Terry so impatient to push on that he offers to overshare his own limited supplies, while the bull-dog

225

Crook maneuvers for delay. To be sure, Crook's men and animals were in the poorest shape, and his infantry was desperate for shoes, although Terry learned the latter only from Crook's underling. But Crook was concealing another motive. Chafing in his role as subordinate, he was planning to break away as soon as he could wangle enough stores.

In the meantime, Miles was scouting down the river on the *Far West*. Knowing the hostiles had moved eastward, he picked up Lt. Rice's company at O'Fallon's Creek in order to re-station it at Glendive Creek. Cody and Richard enjoyed the novel experience of scouting for Indian trails from the pilot-house of a steamboat, but they covered the seventy-eight river-miles without discovering a sign. Lt. Rice's company landed to set up its lonely guard post at Glendive and the boat tied up there for the dark hours as usual. Early on the 19th she turned back and by late afternoon Miles reported to Terry that no trace of crossings had been seen on either leg of the journey.

Cody's original autobiography is as truthful as a normal memory permits, but it states that when Bill reached Glendive on this trip he found Rice's guard post had been under seige for days; Miles therefore sent him to sound the alarm to Terry. He says he rode seventy-five miles in pitch darkness over unfamiliar badlands to report to Terry the next morning far ahead of the boat. Cody forgot that Rice had gone down on the boat with him and that no Indians were seen. Unless he ran his horse up the river channel, his ride covered only forty-five miles, though at night and over strange river breaks this was superhuman enough. But not one chronicler referred to the alarm he claimed to have delivered. Yet Cody did, in fact, make this ride.

Reporter Mills on August 23rd directly confirmed the ride and clinched the lack of any alarm, but said the purpose was to look once more for Indian crossings. No trails, however, had been seen in daylight going down and a daylight return would be made in a few hours; an intervening search by a break-neck rider in the black of night seems absurd. Nevertheless, there was an obvious reason for Cody's ride. Terry had hoped to resume the chase before the boat got back and wanted information, whether positive or negative, as soon as possible so as to guide his movements. But Crook's reluctance had vetoed any prompt action.

Soon after receiving Cody's negative report, Terry went to consult Crook, whom he finally found washing his only suit of underwear in the muddy river. In another afternoon conference, Terry agreed to delay operations until the *Far West* could haul down

226

forage, shoes, and rations for Crook. Once that was accomplished, they would move out, resigned to resuming the stern chase.

When the boat returned that afternoon Miles disembarked all but Bennett's Company B and established his own camp on the north bank. Terry ordered the boat to steam up to the Rosebud to procure supplies for Crook. He also belatedly ordered the evacuation of Fort Beans and removal of its stores and garrison to the mouth of Powder River. Unaware that Sanger had ordered the Crow village home, Crook sent Captain Burt and scouts Grouard and Pourier on the boat to bring down these additional allies. Various loose officers, scouts, and correspondents went along to enjoy a moonlight excursion.

On the morning of the 20th the Indian scouts made it painfully clear that they had lost faith in the campaign. Chief Washakie bade farewell to Crook and led all the Shoshone allies out on the homeward trail. The Crows, equally disgusted, immediately followed suit. On their trek up the river they encountered the party of volunteer Crows who had defied Sanger's orders. They, too, turned back with the others. This stripped Crook of all Indian allies and left Terry with only the faithful Rees.

That day Miles readied Sergeant Mitchell and seven men to take mail to Fort Buford by skiff, while Terry composed a report to Sheridan, which summarized the futile stern chase and Miles' steamboat scout, and then continued:

> . . . We shall therefore move up the Powder until we strike the trail again and then pursue it. It will lead, as I think, to the Little Missouri. Hitherto we have carried no forage and have depended entirely upon grass for our animals, but the country from here eastward appears to have been systematically burned by the retreating Indians. Our scouts report that the burning is complete for the distance of 20 miles — for how much further we do not know. I think, therefore, that it would be unsafe to attempt to follow the trail without forage, and I have sent the steamer to my old depot at the mouth of the Rosebud to bring down grain. This involves a delay of three days, but I think that in the end time will be saved by waiting. (O-28)

The heavy demands of Crook's army were draining the available stores so rapidly that Terry was beginning to pray for the arrival of supply boats from below. To his relief, Miles reported to him that the *Carroll* was approaching and should arrive on the morrow. As predicted, at 5 p.m. on the 21st she reached the foot of Wolf Rapids, but finding them impassable for so large a vessel, tied up there.

This boat, under Captain Burleigh, had sailed from Bismarck to reach Fort Buford on the 16th, where she learned that the *Key West*, ahead of her with sixty-five infantry recruits, had been fired upon by Indians on the 14th only four or five miles below the fort.

227

The unarmed recruits had been unable to retaliate, but no one was injured. General Hazen provided a boat guard and sent the *Carroll* up the Yellowstone on the 17th with orders to remain and patrol the lower river, as Terry had requested. Her passengers saw no Indians, not even at the Glendive post, but they brought the story of the firing on the *Key West*. A few chroniclers ballooned this to a rumor that Sitting Bull's entire army was moving toward Canada.

Supplies were now arriving in reassuring abundance, for on the morning of the 22nd, the large wagon train from Fort Beans pulled in to Miles' camp. Terry ordered forty of the wagons to prepare to serve his force on the coming movement. But Crook was more annoyed than ever when Muggins Taylor rode in from the *Far West* reporting that she had run aground at Buffalo Rapids, where she was partially unloading. Crook did receive his shoes, however, when she floated in the next morning.

Just as the supply problem seemed to be easing, the hostile heavens poured a chilling rain on the long-suffering troops. Their morale, which had recovered a little, promptly submarined. Recriminations broke out between the two armies with redoubled vehemence. Bourke wrote: "We have two Brigadiers; consequently we have two rival organizations in all the signification of acrimonious and splenetic jealousy. The two commanders agree well together and are both noble-minded men; human nature crops out among the subalterns to a fearful extent." The Aide was too discrete about the commanders; their differences were sharp indeed, but Terry's diplomacy and Crook's silence kept them concealed.

Again expressing his lack of confidence in the campaign, Miles wrote his wife that "there is too much demoralization in these commands, and everyone is anxious to go home." There was even dissension within commands, for Colonel Carr, probably Crook's most accomplished Indian campaigner, wrote his wife that "it has reached beyond a joke that we should be kept out and exposed because two fools do not know their business. I would leave the expedition today, if I could. There is no liklihood of our doing anything under present auspices." The reporters all turned uniformly gloomy and openly disparaging. Davenport, already half ostracized for failing to praise Crook at every opportunity, now intemperately attacked the General's personal integrity and Micawber-like military strategy.

As a prominent feature of the August 23rd preparations for the renewal of the offensive, the medical officers began weeding out all the officers and men disabled by the preceding weeks of exposure and hardship. The total grew to eighty enlisted men and four officers.

Drs. C.C. Byrne and J.A. McKinney, both sent up from Fort Buford, loaded them all on the *Carroll* for evacuation to Forts Buford, Lincoln, or Omaha (O-16). But other demands on the vessel would delay their hospitalization.

Reporters Lathrop and Talbot, thoroughly disillusioned, seized the opportunity to escape from such a self-punishing operation. Bourke admitted that he could not blame them. Even Buffalo Bill resolved to join the exodus, having resigned his appointment as scout for Crook's column on the 22nd. The euphemists attributed his resignation to "pressing theatrical engagements," but Cody himself, actually otherwise unemployed, openly pronounced the campaign hopeless.

Sometime on the 23rd a courier rode in from Glendive with dispatches from Rice. Bourke recorded that Indians in strong force had attacked Rice's post, but had been driven off. Other diarists, however, wrote only that Indians had been seen there crossing to the north bank. Miles wrote on the 24th that Rice had "reported Indians in his vicinity two days ago," which dates the event as the 22nd. The dispatches must have been innocuous indeed, for the hypersensitive Terry dismissed them with the remark, "I do not attach great importance to them."

Another all-night tempest drenched the irritable command and blew down their shelters on the night of the 23rd. The next day, in a sea of mud and disgust, preparations were completed for the planned departure of both armies on the morrow. This time Terry would not strip down his troops, but would take twenty days' rations and forage by wagon. The *Far West* ferried them and four of Miles' infantry companies to the south bank, leaving Bennett's company and Sanger's battalion in charge of the base camp. Terry directed the *Far West* to remain above Wolf Rapids, while the *Carroll* would be released to deliver the evacuees to Fort Buford and then return to her patrol duties.

That dismal morning of the 23rd Terry came to advise Crook that he could now make up the full quota of supplies, if he would send his pack train to the landing to receive them. But neither Crook nor his army was visible anywhere in the misty rain. Presuming they had moved to some nearby drier ground, Terry penned a note to Crook and asked Lt. Charles B. Schofield, Brisbin's staff officer, to deliver it:

> I came up on the boat to see you, but found you had gone. The boat brought up your additional rations, but of course will not land them. I can send your supplies, forage, and subsistence to the mouth of Powder River, if you wish it; but if you could send your pack train to the landing, it would be better, for the boat is very busy.

I propose to start in the morning. My cavalry will move up on your trail until it can find a crossing, the infantry on the east bank.

Please inform me to what point you will send your train.

I enclose notes from the Commanding Officer at Glendive Creek. What do you think of them? I do not attach great importance to them. At any rate, I see nothing in them to change our plans. Please preserve these notes. (C-7)

Baffled in his attempts to locate Crook, Lt. Schofield gave Terry's note to Muggins Taylor, who eventually overtook the Wyoming column on the march far up Powder River! Clearly, Crook had not notified his superior of his departure. He had refused to move earlier for lack of forage and rations. But now he had left without waiting for his full allowance. There can be but one explanation for this — a desire to give the trusting Terry the slip. His troops would pay for this unprepared departure. But this day they floundered through eleven miles of gumbo up Powder River. Only then did Crook send notice of his absence.

Terry's reaction is carefully restrained in his reply that same day:

Your note crossed one from me to you. I sent Lt. Schofield out to find you, supposing you were within four or five miles, and intended to go out and meet you if you were near. My note has explained fully all that I wished to say.

I still intend to leave at six in the morning. I hope your march will not be so long as to prevent my overtaking you. (C-7)

As we have seen, Terry had little trouble in controlling Custer's peccadilloes, but Crook's sly insubordination was another matter.

Chapter 20
Terry's Campaign Fizzles Out

A week of rest in camp, with tolerable weather in its initial days, had accomplished something for the battered bodies of the troops, but nothing for their spoiled spirits. One punishing stern chase had failed, and now, with an additional week's handicap, they were facing another. This time, however, the armies would separate, each to pursue its own will-o-the-wisp.

Anxious to restore some semblance of authority over his command, Terry marched seventeen miles up Powder River on August 25th to bivouac at the point where the hostile trail scattered to the east. If he expected to find Crook waiting for him there, he was disappointed, for the latter had marched that day to Locate Creek, 23 miles out and therefore well beyond the range of scattering trails. Terry still hoped to overhaul his subordinate the next day, but just as he was going into camp, Buffalo Bill galloped in with news that brought a change in plans.

We must turn the clock back to outline the events that prompted this change. The steamer *Yellowstone*, laden with supplies had left Bismarck on the 14th, to be followed the next day by the *Josephine*, carrying construction materials for a post on Tongue River, as well as Lt. Col. J.N.G. Whistler with two more companies of 5th Infantry. Also aboard was Texas Jack Omohundro, Buffalo Bill's associate in the theater as well as on the plains. At Fort Buford she picked up Charles S. Diehl, a young reporter for the Chicago *Times*, who had been waiting there since August 5th, sending back a stream of dispatches with false date-lines.

The two boats nosed up the Yellowstone together on the 21st, and the next morning met Sgt. Mitchell's skiff couriers floating down from Miles' headquarters. They told Texas Jack of "Indians scattered along the banks of the river for thirty miles on either side." On the forenoon of the 23rd, while still some miles below Glendive, Indians fired on the *Yellowstone,* killing Pvt. Dennis Shields of the boat guard. Texas Jack, who had earlier landed to bag some deer, found hostiles swarming on both banks. Return fire from the boat guard so quickly scattered the Indians that no troops were landed.

The next morning the boats paused briefly at Glendive, where Lt. Rice told Diehl that "the Indians had been very troublesome, appearing in large bodies in the adjoining woods and on the bluffs, and had made several attempts to steal the stock . . . [Having] a 3-inch Rodman he could shell the woods, which alone prevented the savages from making an attack." As proof that the Indians had not fired a shot, the Record of Engagements lists no action at Glendive, although it notes the trivial attacks on the steamboats.

Later that day, just as the passengers on the *Josephine* spotted a skiff tied up on the south bank, a shot rang out and a white man crashed out of the brush, racing for the steamer. When picked up, badly wounded in the arm, he gave his name as Charles Pickens, a deserter. He said he had left Powder River a few days before with Pvt. Charles Piquet, another deserter, but last evening Indians had attacked them, killing and mutilating his companion. Further passage of the boats upriver proved uneventful, although a few Indian signs were noted.

Near the mouth of O'Fallon's Creek on the morning of the 25th, the two vessels encountered the *Carroll,* which had left Wolf Rapids with her evacuees and escapees. After exchanging news, the *Carroll* turned back upriver with the other two, to the dismay of her passengers. Learning that the armies were marching up Powder River, Col. Whistler sought a courier to advise Terry of his arrival with construction materials. Cody accepted this job, apparently preferring a return to action over cooling his heels on a boat that was going nowhere. He galloped straight across country to overtake Terry as he went into camp that afternoon. He was mistaken, however, in remembering he carried dispatches from Sheridan.

Numerous chroniclers recorded the budget of news that Cody brought. Most referred to Indians swarming on the lower river; some mentioned their crossing and firing on the boat; a few gave exaggerated rumors of attacks on the Glendive post. This news was the kind most calculated to reawaken Terry's chronic fear of Indians escaping to the north. It also seemed to localize a target for his favorite kind of pincers movement. Without delay, he took Cody and a cavalry escort on a fast ride up the Powder to consult with Crook.

232

The two commanders held another conference, undoubtedly gentlemanly, but certainly strained. Terry suggested that the hostiles had all moved to the lower river intending to cross to the north. They could catch them in a pincers movement, if he took his army down by boat to hit from the north, while Crook followed on their trail to strike from the south. But Crook, although committed to the stern chase, maintained that the southern Sioux would not turn to the river, much less cross it to the north. If his Indians turned south, as he expected, he must follow them to protect the settlements in his own Department.

The two generals thrashed out a compromise that promised to please each according to his success in predicting the movements of the quarry. Crook would follow his Indian trail wherever it might lead, promising to advise Terry of his findings and any change in plan they might dictate. Terry promised to order supplies to Glendive for Crook's use, should the trail lead him there. He would return to the river to patrol by boat down to Glendive, alert to attack hostiles found on either bank.

Riding back to camp that evening, Terry sent Cody to ask Whistler to retain all the boats for his use, and to obtain clarification of the reports of Indian activities downstream. Cody managed to find Whistler and the three boats tied up at Wolf Rapids, which they had reached that noon. In the meantime, Terry composed an after-thought note to Crook:

> There is one thing which I forgot to say and that is that it appears to me that the band which has gone north, if any have gone there, is the heart and soul of the Indian mutiny. It is the nucleus around which the whole body of disaffected Indians gathers. If it were destroyed, this thing would be over, and it is for that reason that I so strongly feel that even if a larger trail is found leading south, we should make a united effort to settle these particular people. (C-7)

Circumstances would prove Terry mistaken in believing that it was Sitting Bull's hard-case followers who had crossed near Glendive; it was actually a small band under Long Dog. But even if Terry had been right, Crook wanted no part of chasing Terry's Sioux to the neglect of his own. He sent a cool parting note the next morning:

> My understanding has always been that Crazy Horse, who is an Oglala and represents the disaffected people belonging to the Southern Agencies, is about equal in strength to Sitting Bull, who similarly represents the Northern Sioux; besides, it is known that at least 1500 additional warriors left Red Cloud Agency and joined Crazy Horse this spring and summer and are supposed to be with him here.
>
> Should any considerable part of the main trail lead in the direction of the Southern Agencies, I take it for granted that it must be his, which will not only increase the embarrassment of protecting the settlements

in my department, but will make me apprehensive for the safety of my wagon train.

Should I not find any decided trail going southward, but on the contrary find it scattering in this country, or crossing to the north of the Yellowstone, you can calculate on my remaining with you until the unpleasantness ends, or we are ordered to the contrary.

We march this morning. Good bye. (C-7)

Terry's command had not proceeded far on the back trail to the Powder River depot on the morning of the 26th, when another courier rode in with a dispatch from Sheridan, dated August 17th, which compelled further changes in Terry's plans. General Hazen had forwarded it on August 23rd by Sgt. Mitchell's mail party and sent an abstract by another courier. These reached Whistler on the *Josephine* after he had dispatched Cody on the 25th. Reporter Howard wrote that Whistler brought the dispatch to Wolf Rapids on the 25th and forwarded it the next morning.

The final courier was probably Robert Jackson, a quarter-blood Blackfoot Indian, whose enlistment as an Indian scout expired at Fort Lincoln on June 25th. His younger brother, Billy Jackson, had fought as a "Ree" scout with Reno on the Little Big Horn. From where Bob brought the dispatch is uncertain, but reporter Diehl identified the courier who delivered it to Terry as an Indian. A quartermaster report made out by Captain O.E. Michaelis, Terry's Ordnance Officer, reveals that he had hired Robert Jackson "to carry dispatches from Powder River to General Terry in August; to be paid $25."

General Hazen had abstracted this dispatch as follows:

That 1500 men would winter in, at, or near the mouth of Tongue River, with General Miles in command, consisting of the 5th and part of the 22nd Infantry now in the field, also a regiment of cavalry, to be designated.

That at the close of the season's operation, General Gibbon's command would retire to Montana, the 7th Cavalry to Lincoln, and the detachment of the 17th and 6th Infantry to be stationed at the most convenient posts.

That the General commanding the Department will return to St. Paul not later than the 15th of October. (O-14)

Sheridan sent this unexpected directive because he had won authority to take full control of the Sioux agencies, to which he was sending strong garrisons to demand unconditional surrender of the hostiles and to disarm and dismount the friendlies. In order to prevent a grand exodus to unceded territory, he had to occupy it by a post at the mouth of Tongue River — a temporary cantonment, since low water prevented construction of a permanent post. Terry thus suddenly found himself saddled with the very burden he thought he had escaped when Major Forsyth had come out a few

234

weeks earlier.

Since the transport of winter supplies for 1500 men would usurp all the steamboats, Terry was now reduced to marching overland toward Glendive. This, however, would enable him to make a swing to the north, following his hunch that Sitting Bull had crossed the river and was heading for Fort Peck via the Dry Fork. Accordingly, he ordered Gibbon to take the main column to the mouth of O'Fallon's Creek and there await him. He ordered Major Moore's battalion to escort the wagon train back to the depot, while he hastened ahead to supervise operations there. But first he dashed off another note to Crook, which a party of eight Rees delivered and then remained to serve the nearly scoutless Wyoming column:

> I have had a reply to my dispatch to Whistler. Rice was not attacked, but the steamer Yellowstone was. I shall return, cross over, march far enough north to determine, if possible, whether the Indians have made for Dry Fork, and if they have not, or if I believe there is still a considerable body of them on the river, I shall turn to the right. I shall cover the country west of Glendive Creek and be at the Creek in five days [i.e., August 31st], unless I go north.
>
> I shall send a steamer to Buford with orders to take on supplies and come up to Glendive and await orders. She will supply you. (C-7)

The morning of August 27th was a busy one at the mouth of Powder River. On Terry's orders, Whistler took the *Josephine* with her construction materials and the 5th Infantry over Wolf Rapids and up to the mouth of Tongue River, which he reached in time to occupy the site of Post No. 1, or Cantonment Tongue River, on August 28th. In the meantime, the *Far West* ferried all the wagons to the north bank, where some formed a train to be escorted to Glendive by Moore's battalion. The others began hauling cargo, unloaded from the deep-draft boats, around the rapids, where the *Far West* could reload them for Tongue River. Unfortunately, the river was falling fast, so that on the 31st, Captain Marsh unloaded her supplies and Bennett's Company B at the foot of Buffalo Rapids and abandoned the upper river.

On the afternoon of the 27th, Terry, having prevailed upon Cody to remain in his service as scout, sped down to O'Fallon's Creek with the *Yellowstone* and *Carroll* to ferry Gibbon's men to the north bank. When this was completed he sent both boats down to Fort Buford, where on the 29th they finally disembarked their impatient load of evacuees. Many of the latter would enter the hospital there, while the others would await the next downriver vessel. Two days later, the two boats started back to Glendive with more supplies.

About 6 p.m. of the 27th, Terry started his swing march to the north with pack train support. The principal chroniclers of this sortie are officers Freeman, Godfrey and English, reporters O'Kelly, Diehl and Howard, and scouts Texas Jack and Zed Daniels. By the evening of the 28th the force encamped about twenty-five miles northwest, near the head of Bad Route Creek. After dark Terry sent Cody and Herendeen to Glendive, about thirty-five miles distant, to pick up the latest news. Contrary to Cody's recollections, they made a short and uneventful trip.

On the forenoon of the 29th, as the column approached the Missouri-Yellowstone divide, they happily sighted vast herds of buffalo. Ravenous for fresh meat, they halted to conduct a grand buffalo hunt. Texas Jack, spotting two Indians spying on the hunters, said nothing, but both he and Zed Daniels realized that Indians had been interested in the same herd. A week later they would learn that the column had badly frightened Long Dog's small Hunkpapa village, which abandoned its tepees in headlong flight. In the afternoon the main column continued along the south slope of the divide, while Captian Ball's battalion made an overnight reconnaissance along the north slope, searching for what Grouard had described as the regular Indian trail to the Dry Fork and Fort Peck.

The march of the 30th took the column to a camp on Deer Creek about thirteen miles north of the Glendive post. Neither Indians nor trails had been found. Then Captain Ball's battalion returned to report that they had found Grouard's trail unused this season. The final discouragement came that evening, when Cody and Herendeen returned from Glendive reporting no Indians seen there for days and no dispatch from Crook. The frustrated Terry faced another failure of one of his hunches. After dark he sent a Ree with a note for Crook, presumably admitting his failure and offering his cooperation if Crook had enjoyed better luck.

Just as they were about to march the next morning, another courier brought news that a fresh trail of 150 warriors had just been found near Glendive, and that a report had been received there that Sitting Bull's band had tried to cross the Missouri down at Fort Berthold, but was driven back by the friendly tribes there. The latter information referred to an event of August 21st. A dozen Sioux warriors had appeared on the west bank of the Missouri to trade with the Berthold village across the river. The Rees, rejecting the trade offer, fired across the stream to drive off the Sioux. The latter yelled back threats to bring the village that had licked Custer to destroy the Rees, saying it was camped only sixty miles west on the Little Missouri near the Turtle, or Killdeer Mountains (O-13).

236

In response to this news, Terry detached Major Reno and the 7th Cavalry to exhaust the search for river crossings by making a four-day scout to Fort Buford and back. He then led the rest down Deer Creek to establish a camp adjacent to the Glendive post. There he found the *Silver Lake* had brought supplies, and learned that the *Benton*, bringing the final two companies of 5th Infantry, had burst a steam chest some twenty miles below and was unable to move. He sent the *Silver Lake* down to rescue the marooned troops and cargo, but she ran fast aground herself.

Reporter Howard, apparently so disgusted with the campaign that he lacked the heart to report it, went down on the rescue mission to find the *Benton* preparing to send a small boat to Bismarck for repair parts. Risky though it was, he leaped at the chance to escape to the States. The crew of the broken-down boat contrived jury-rigged repairs that enabled her to float down to Fort Buford, where she loaded thirty-two sick soldiers and reporters that the *Carroll* had earlier stranded there. She then limped down on one engine to drop off twelve patients at Fort Lincoln on September 6th (O-12).

Moore's battalion escorted the wagon train in to Glendive, and the two companies of marooned infantry tramped in on September 2nd. A reconnaissance Terry had sent out the day before also returned, reporting that they had failed to find a ford by which Terry's force could reach the south bank for cooperation with Crook or a move toward Sitting Bull at Killdeer Mountains. This was another disappointment, for heavy smokes had been seen on the breaks on the south bank.

The *Carroll* and *Yellowstone* steamed up with more supplies for Tongue River on the 3rd. Happy to sever connections with Terry's demoralized command, Miles loaded a wagon train and headed with his infantry for his new cantonment, of which he took command on September 10th. Reno also returned from his scout, his two days of lazy marching having taken him less than thirty miles below Glendive, but he had reported by courier that the lower valley was burned over and clear of crossings all the way to Fort Buford. In the evening the *Far West* passed down, declaring the upper river closed to navigation. This was another blow, for winter supplies would now have to go overland to Miles' post, demanding every wagon and diverting troops to escort duty. Terry could not long hold a fighting force in the field that would compete for supplies. The days remaining to the campaign were strictly numbered.

The outlook for Terry was bleak indeed. His every effort to redeem his military fortunes after the terrible blow to Custer had met with frustration. Supplies and reinforcements had been delayed. The stern chase with Crook had turned into a fiasco. His own swing to the north had proved futile. His was the most disastrous campaign in the annals of the northern plains, with precious little time left to alter the verdict. He could discern but two faint escape hatches, both closing fast. If Crook had found the hostiles nearby, there was a fleeting chance to strike a cooperative blow. Or, if he could march home by way of the Killdeer Mountains, he might have the luck to surprise Sitting Bull.

But to make any choice, Terry must first hear from Crook. He had fulfilled his own promise to reach Glendive August 31st, and to make supplies available to Crook there. But it was now the 3rd, with Crook nearing the end of his short rations. But where was he? Why had he sent no word? Racked by worry and despair, the haggard Terry prayed for a courier.

*   *   *

Having bid a cold goodbye to Terry and freed himself to follow his own military genius, Crook marched eastward on the morning of August 26th from his camp twenty-three miles above the mouth of Powder River. He, as well as some others, wrote as usual of following the "trail," leaving the unwary reader to assume this was the heavy Indian trail they had abandoned nine days before. But that trail had scattered lower down, leaving little to follow. What Crook actually pursued was the heavy wagon trail that Terry's engineers had smoothed and bridged on their outbound march in the spring!

Reporter Davenport wrote of this first day's march of twenty miles that they followed "on the wagon trail made by Terry in June, anticipating that it would soon be intersected by the Great Sioux Trail." Clearly, this was not even a stern chase but a blind fishing expedition, *hoping* to find a trail! The troops were stripped to the bone, with two days of their less than fifteen days' rations already consumed; there was no forage for the gaunt animals, although they were crossing burned-over country. Crook would stick to this soldier road for 160 miles, destined never to find a large trail. He would travel it slower with his mobile pack train than Terry had with loaded wagons. He moved hesitantly, uncertainly, making long halts that wasted his dwindling provisions, while his indecision undermined the confidence of his officers and men.

Of the next day's tramp over fire-blackened prairie, Pvt. Flynn's diary, confirmed by Lt. Capron's, said they "continued on Custer's trail — no Indian sign discovered." To remind the men of former

238

delights, it began to rain again as they made camp. Lts. King and Capron noted that they continued the next day on the Terry trail, and at sundown a furious hail storm stampeded some horses and flooded the bivouac. Still no Indian signs had been found and Colonel Carr wrote that "speculation is rife as to where we are going, but I do not believe that Crook knows. It struck me today that he may be en route to Red Cloud Agency with the view that he had driven the Indians in."

The column made but a short march on the morning of the 29th and camped at noon on the impressive divide between Cabin and Beaver Creeks. Bourke's diary (reconstructed because he had lost the original), apparently based on a dispatch from reporter Finerty, claimed that here the Indian trail became fresher, as from converging paths. Unfortunately, they had not been following a trail, and certainly a fresh, heavy one would scarcely prompt a two-day halt!

Crook halted early in order to send out all of his few scouts to scour the country to find any kind of a trail. This proved no easy search, for the scouts remained out for thirty hours! "Where are the Indians, and where are they going?" Reporter Mills asked. He confessed that "now we are, so to speak, feeling out for the enemy and looking for a trail." The idle troops waited for the answers all the rest of the 29th and all day of the 30th, trying to warm skimpy strips of bacon over sagebrush fires and to brew coffee with brackish water. Many turned up at sick call with fever, diarrhea, neuralgia, and rheumatism, betraying the deterioration of morale. Crook relaxed the strictures against hunting, but the black prairie proved barren of everything but elusive jack-rabbits. Then on the night of the 30th a bone-chilling "norther" whistled through the camp on the exposed divide.

The recorded details of the results of the thirty-hour scout are so thin as to speak volumes. Some thought the scouts were looking for Terry's column. According to Finerty, Crook thought the village might lie on the head of either Glendive or Beaver Creeks — located in opposite directions — but the scouts reported "no Indians at the point designated." Both King and Bourke said the scouts had gone east toward the Little Missouri, but studiously avoided any mention of their findings. Reporter Mills wrote that while the main body of scouts were still east, another party came in from the south reporting a fresh trail of thirteen lodges fleeing south, but "trails of thirteen lodges only we are not looking for." Davenport stated that Grouard, Richard, and Crawford reported nothing but "many scattering trails in the neighborhood of Beaver Creek," thereby proving that "the large trail we had followed . . . to the Powder was undoubtedly dissipated." There is no escape; Crook had not been following a trail and in five days had not found one.

On the 31st the shivering troops fled from the norther into a sheltering valley near the head of Beaver Creek, a distance of only ten miles. Once again, discontent spread as the troops lay in camp all that afternoon and the next day, while the scouts made another twenty-four hour search for the missing quarry. As the only consolation, they had at last passed beyond the burnt area, but some perceived that the hostiles must have left the area prior to the fire-quenching rains that had started three weeks earlier.

The weary scouts dragged in on the afternoon of September 1st with a little encouraging news, but few could muster enough interest to get their story straight. Bourke heard that Grouard had found a fresh trail and brought in four abandoned ponies. Lt. Capron described the trail as large with many smaller ones turning off toward the agencies. Strahorn learned that they had found a heavy trail, a week or more old but overlaid by fresh pony tracks, leading north down Beaver Creek. It may have been this trail that Colonel Carr said contained a campsite of over 350 lodges.

Before resuming the march next morning, Crook wrote a letter to Terry:

> . . . We have been delayed two days scouting for the trail, it being very dim [!], but we have at last found it going down this stream [Beaver Creek] apparently about the same size as when it left the Powder, which would rather indicate that no number of them have crossed the Yellow-stone. Two small trails have already chipped off and lead off in the direction of Red Cloud. I shall push on the main trail and should they separate will endeavor to follow the largest, and in case of their being no large one, I shall go toward the agencies.
>
> Should I get near Beauford [Fort Buford] when my rations are exhausted, I shall endeavor to replenish there. We have had one severe storm since we separated, which with the cold nights we are having has developed much sickness and some cases that ought to be sent in.
>
> I have taken the liberty to retain some of your Ree scouts, as I have no one who knows the country the trail seems to lead in. I am in hopes this will find you on their trail so that in case of [their] separation, we can follow different parts of their trail. (O-9)

The column marched twenty miles north down Beaver Creek on the 2nd to camp opposite Sentinel Buttes. Lt. Capron dubbed the trail "quite old — ten days at least," and Strahorn mentioned passing an abandoned camp of a thousand warriors. Some of the Rees who had been out for two days reported a fresh trail leading down from the Yellowstone and marked by a wounded pony and a Sioux corpse. The trail may have been heavy that morning, but it soon dwindled to twelve lodges, according to Davenport, and others said it broke up and scattered to the east. Colonel Carr wrote that "if Crook chooses to follow, he will be turning east tomorrow . . . He still thinks that the Indians may stand and fight us, and will probably never see where his mistake lies."

Crook's high hopes of the morning crumbled during the march. Not having sent off his morning's letter, he wrote another that evening, assigning all but three of his Rees to deliver both to Terry:

> Frank [Grouard] failed to send my note of [off?] this morning, which now I am glad of, as this day's march shows that the Indian trail has been scattering . . . the larger part going in the direction of the Little Missouri, while about 150 lodges still continued down this creek about seven miles below this point (as far down as our scouts have been). About fifty pony tracks, with lodges, crossed here about two days since, going in the direction of Sentinel Buttes. It is my intention to follow this fresh trail in the morning. It is impossible to tell whether this separation is to be final, or whether they intend coming together again. I shall do my best to solve this question within the next few days, letting the ration question take care of itself.
>
> I would like to retain such of your scouts as remain here with me as long as I am in their country with guides who know it not. We are having as fine grass for our animals as I ever saw and they are in better condition than when I left the Powder. Should I learn of anything of importance, I will try and communicate it to you. (O-9)

That night the pickets fired on a handful of hostile spies who approached the bivouac from the east and fled back again. The incident drew little attention from the troops curled tight under flimsy blankets, for it had turned cold enough to cover the ground with frost.

*   *   *

Terry received Crook's belated dispatches on the evening of August 3rd. If he held out hopes for a reprieve, he was quickly disappointed. Crook had found no Indians and only a brief trail that promptly scattered. He had not gotten beyond Beaver Creek and would probably soon start for home. All hope of a redeeming stroke died then and there. In resignation he wrote Crook that "it is doubtful whether I can do anything more, except guard the river," and then reiterated that supplies for Crook were waiting at Glendive, not Fort Buford (C-7).

Deeply depressed, Terry officially announced the termination of his campaign on September 5th. Colonel Otis and the 22nd Infantry were ordered to remain at Glendive, and Captain Sanger and the 17th Infantry at Powder River, both as forwarding stations for the Tongue River supplies. General Gibbon, who had been im-

241

patient for leave all summer, was ordered back to Montana with his column. Major Reno with the 7th Cavalry and Major Moore with the 6th Infantry were to march overland to Fort Buford, but at a leisurely pace in order to throw back any hostiles that Crook might drive north. Some officers were granted leave and boarded the *Yellowstone* that afternoon with Buffalo Bill.

That evening the officers gathered at Terry's headquarters for an emotional farewell sing. They were sentimental over breaking up the long comradeship, happy to be returning to homes and families, secretly relieved to end the hardships, but openly dejected by the dismal failure of the campaign, and deeply sorry for their well-liked but luckless, commander. The General was withdrawn and melancholy.

The sad departures began the next day, with Terry and his staff leaving on the *Josephine* for Fort Buford, where the next day they began supervising the heavy supply operation. With them went reporter Diehl, leaving only O'Kelly and Texas Jack to remain with the overland marchers.

Terry was destined to make one more futile gesture. At Fort Buford on the 9th he received word that Long Dog, a notorious Hunkpapa with twenty-three lodges, and Inkpaduta, an infamous Santee with five lodges, had crossed the Missouri at Wolf Point, a sub-agency about forty miles below Fort Peck, on the 6th (O-18). The General sent orders to Reno to speed to that point and hit these hostiles. Reno pushed his force across country to arrive on the 13th. There he met a double disappointment. Long Dog had long since fled to the Canadian border, far out of reach. He also learned that Terry's column had nearly stepped on the little village on the swing north — but had missed the chance for a victory, puny though it would have been.

Two days later Terry steamed up to Wolf Point on the *Chambers*, only to learn of this new failure. He ferried the command to the north bank and ordered it home, Moore's battalion to take post at Fort Buford and Reno's to return overland to Fort Abraham Lincoln. O'Kelly and Texas Jack joined Terry on the *Chambers*, which delivered them to Bismarck on the 20th. That evening the dejected General left by train for his St. Paul headquarters. By September 26th the dispirited remnants of the once crack 7th Cavalry trudged into Fort Lincoln.

The long drawn out effort to whip the hostiles into subjection was all over for General Terry and the Dakota column.

Chapter 21
Crook's Consolation Prize

Crook's neglect of scouting had brought one disaster. His neglect of logistics would bring another. But what he lacked in brilliance and foresight he made up in tenacity. He dared not relinquish the hope that if he just kept going, something would turn up. Blind luck would eventually favor him, but he would fail to capitalize on the opportunity beyond a hollow newspaper triumph.

On the raw and drizzly morning of September 3rd, the Wyoming column pushed east from Beaver Creek on the old Terry trail to camp on the head of Andrew's Creek, having passed small Indian trails criss-crossing in all directions. The troops fretted at marching away from supply sources with rations so short, but would have fretted more had they known that Crook had started out with less than fifteen days' provisions without having made any effort to have supplies delivered at some future rendezvous. That evening a party of scouts were eating supper in the advance, when a dozen hostiles hailed them, asking if they were Sioux. An answering flurry of harmless shots abruptly dispersed them.

The next day's march wound down the badlands of the Little Missouri on the route Terry's engineers had earlier prepared. Again they crossed scattered trails, all headed south. Another norther pelted them with ice-water to begin ten days of incredibly bad weather. The only cheering note was the discovery of a flourishing stand of ripe corn where Terry's animals had been grained in May; some wild fruit proved especially welcome to the scurvy-ridden men.

Shrinking provisions occupied eveyone's mind. Pvt. Flynn learned that only two days' rations remained. Probably to conceal the original deficiency, word was circulated that drenching rains had spoiled some hardtack and the burning sun some of the bacon. Even the faith of the officers began to crumble. Captain Munson, 9th Infantry, came to Bourke to complain that "there was much solicitude among officers and men to know what General Crook's purposes were for the future." Even the loyal aide confessed that he "shared to a considerable extent Captain Munson's apprehensions; as it was certainly a gloomy prospect to have an expedition of two thousand men left without rations in the midst of the desert."

To the bewilderment of his command, Crook ignored the south-bound trails to drive due east again on the 5th, taking advantage of Terry's road work out of the badlands. They climbed out of the canyon and over the divide to the head of Heart River. In the afternoon a platoon of scouts, miles off the south flank, stumbled on a south-bound party of Sioux. Big Bat tumbled one brave from his pony, but the rest scampered off in the dense fog. Reporter Mills learned that Crook had finally conceded that the hostile camp had broken up and headed for the Black Hills.

All chroniclers lamented that the commissary issued only half-rations that evening. In an interview with Crook, Finerty learned to his horror that only slightly more than one day's rations remained. The troops, huddling in the cold rain, grumbled, worried, and questioned. If Crook had intended to march hundreds of extra miles, why had he moved so slowly with such long halts? Why was he marching away from both supplies and Indians? Did he really know what he was doing, or was he floundering? That evening the word came out that they would turn south and head for Deadwood, 175 miles distant! Dismay, fear, and resentment filled the camp.

Not having reported for a full month, Crook wrote to Sheridan, first summarizing his operations to date. Exemplifying his habit of using his pen to bend events to his purposes, he built the impression that the hostiles had remained in one large village and that he had marched hot on its trail for four hundred miles to where it first split up on Beaver Creek:

> . . . My Column followed the trail down Beaver Creek . . . where the Indians scattered, . . . the separation taking place apparently about twelve days ago.
>
> I have every reason to believe that all the hostile Indians left the Big Horn, Tongue, and Powder River country in the village, the trail of which we followed. This village was very compact and arranged in regular order of seven circles of lodges covering an area of at least two thousand acres. With the exception of a few lodges that had stolen off toward the agencies, there was no change in the size or arrangement of the village until it disintegrated . . . (O-39,1876)

Although Crook had let his disastrous ration problem "take care of itself" ever since August 5th, he procrastinated until his men faced

244

actual starvation. In this same report he asked Sheridan to speed rations to Custer City, which he intended to make his winter base of operations.

The last of the Ree scouts sped away with this dispatch to deliver it to Fort Abraham Lincoln forty-eight hours later. The Wyoming column, however, was neither so fleet nor so joyful. The next morning it turned south in a cold, rainy, fog, so dense as to imperil navigation on the ocean of prairie. Gumbo mud, clinging to the feet of men and animals, brought straggling and break-downs. Surreptitiously, the laggards snatched skinny steaks from the foundered animals. At a miserable camp on an alkali lake a few miles beyond Rainy Buttes, the troops had to gulp their mite of bacon raw and take the chill from thin coffee with wisps of smouldering grass. Bacon-free rations issued for the next day were euphemistically recorded as quarter-rations. Bourke said it all in four words — "wet, cross, hungry, and disgusted."

The 7th proved an aggravated repetition. The march was longer, the weather worse, the mud heavier, and stomachs emptier. The number of straggling soldiers and collapsing animals soared. The scare-crow men pounced on foundered animals before their hearts stopped pulsing to devour the flesh raw. Few cared about the many little Indian trails all winding south, or even the heavy trail that ran parallel on their right flank. Again they camped where there was no fuel, but then neither was there bacon to be warmed.

"I am a hippophagist!" wrote Colonel Carr that evening, and added that he had overheard a headquarters orderly remark that "General Crook ought to be hung." It was not hardship that burned both men and officers; they expected that and could take it. What riled them was the growing conviction that Crook's tight-lipped silence covered a vacuum, that he was blundering at their expense, that their sacrifices would prove futile. Even Crook perceived that matters had slipped from serious to desperate. He ordered Lt. Bubb, his Chief of Commissary, to speed ahead to Deadwood to purchase provisions on the open market and send them back to the command. As escort, Captain Anson Mills handpicked the fifteen best-mounted men from each of the ten companies of his 3rd Cavalry. Tom Moore took charge of a pack train, and Grouard and Jack Crawford served as guides. Dr. Stevens and reporters Strahorn and Davenport joined the rescue column, as it pulled out that evening.

The main column struggled and straggled on the 8th to a camp where they at last found some timber. Since no rations remained, the commissary worked late selecting animals to be shot and butchered for issue to the haggard men. They spent much of the night warming themselves before wood fires, cooking horse meat and trying to dry their muddy and tattered clothes and blankets for the first time in a week.

In the meantime, Grouard had been leading the rescue column on a hard night march, navigating through rain and fog by sheer instinct. Halting only for a brief nap, by dawn of the 8th they were again in the saddle, bucking the never-ending rain, fog, and mud. In the afternoon, ahead and to their right, they glimpsed Slim Buttes, a long craggy ridge running north and south. At 4 p.m. Frank galloped back to announce that beyond the next rise he had spotted a herd of Indian ponies and the lodges of a small village in an amphitheater indenting the eastern edge of Slim Buttes.

Hastily waving the troops behind a concealing ridge, the officers canvassed the situation. Although their mission was to speed for supplies, they were also at liberty to pitch into any hostiles they thought they could handle. Some officers clamoured for an immediate attack, while others urged caution, for other villages might be near. After a long debate, it was decided to retire to a safe distance for the night and make a surprise attack at dawn. No effort was made to alert the main column, should their small force run into a hornet's nest.

When aroused at 1 a.m., the congealed troops fumbled long in the dark saddling up. At 2:30 they started cautiously forward in the black, rainy fog to within a mile of the village, and there organized for the attack. Lts. Emmet Crawford and Adolphus H. von Luettwitz, each with fifty dismounted troopers, were to steal quietly forward and extend skirmish lines on the right and left sides of the sleeping village. When they were securely in position, Lt. Frederick Schwatka, with twenty-five mounted troopers, was to charge straight through the village and form on the opposite side. Lt. Bubb, with the final twenty-five men, dismounted as horse-holders, was to remain behind with the pack train, ready to dash up at the first sound of fire and close the circle.

The three assault units groped forward in the darkness, but they had reckoned without the alert pony herd. On their near approach the herd stampeded straight for the village, sounding a thunderous alarm. Compelled to abandon the plan on the instant, Schwatka's mounted detail charged with pistols blazing, driving the ponies ahead of them. Instead of splitting, the two foot details raced to a position on the east side of the village. The startled Indians frantically slashed their way out of their tepees, tightly secured against the rain, seizing their weapons and scattering the women and

246

children westward into the bluffs. Schwatka's men retained possession of nearly two hundred ponies as they stormed through the lodges, and in their wake the footmen loosed volley after volley into the fleeing villagers.

The plan to surround the enemy had failed and Bubb's rear guard, shielded from the sound of firing, had not appeared on schedule. Fearing that escaping Indians would soon bring reinforcements to overwhelm his small force, Captain Mills belatedly sent word to Bubb to dispatch couriers to bring help from the main column and then hurry his own men forward. The Lieutenant sent two packers to find Crook and then rushed up with the led horses and pack train. Assigned the duty of holding the captured pony herd, he entrenched on the east side, where his men found their hands full fending off Indian dashes to recapture the animals.

Although Schwatka's charge had driven the Indians from their village, they rallied to return a heavy fire from surrounding bluffs and ravines. One of their first bullets shattered the knee of von Luettwitz. Crawford led a series of foot charges that drove the angry braves to the bluffs on the southwest, but then had to dig in because of commanding heights beyond. In less than half an hour the action was over, with the troops safely entrenched, but on the defensive against a circling ring of well-placed Indians.

Not all the braves had taken position in the surrounding bluffs, however. When an unsuspecting trooper walked near the village a single bullet tore through his brains. The shot had come from a brush-filled ravine at the edge of the village, but an attempt to smoke out the sharp-shooter quickly yielded three more casualties. Mills ordered the area guarded from a safe distance, and settled down for the long anxious wait. Since it was as dangerous for soldiers as for Indians to roam the deserted tepees, he postponed their looting until Crook's arrival.

Keeping an apprehensive eye out for hostile reinforcements, the command took stock of the situation. In the growing light they counted the lodges, strung along Rabbit Creek, a header of the Moreau, or Owl, River. They were disappointed to find only thirty-seven lodges, but after months of frustration, routing a small village was better than none at all. Despite the utter surprise of the attack, the seventy-five warriors had made a good showing against twice their number. No one could prove an Indian casualty, but one trooper lay dead and Dr. Stevens was busy tending one officer and seven men wounded.

Lt. Bubb's inspired couriers raced seventeen miles on the back trail to meet Crook's infantry already marching and the cavalry just leaving camp. At the alarm the men shed their fatigue as they had the rain. Crook organized a relief column of medical personnel and the best-mounted men of the cavalry, all under command of Colonel Carr. They rushed ahead to reach Mills' force before noon, followed soon by Crook and the remaining cavalry. Even the rear pulled in by 2 o'clock. Crook was displeased with Mills' failure to send for help the afternoon before, but even he gladly settled for a weak blow.

The new-comers camped beside the village, taking over a large tepee for a hospital, where the surgeons set about amputating the shattered leg of Lt. von Luettwitz. Crook posted strong pickets to guard against expected hostile reinforcements, and ordered details to scour the lodges for usable provisions before readying the village for destruction. He then called for volunteers to help Lt. W. Philo Clark flush out the sniper concealed in the ravine. All the loose soldiers headed for the lodges to forage for Indian delicacies to assuage their fierce appetites. They found plenty to munch on while the cooks fired up for a feast.

Clark's detail found that more than one sniper was hidden in the ravine. When a flurry of bullets answered his call to surrender, the detail poured volley after volley into the stronghold. The return fire was as spare as it was deadly. One bullet shattered both legs of a trooper, who died that night after an amputation. Scout "Buffalo Chips" White rose up to spot the source of the shot and fell dead with a bullet through the heart. At least one other received a ball through the ankle. Big Bat Pourier boldly jumped into the ravine and quickly danced back out again, flourishing the bloody scalp of a warrior. After a furious bombardment, a few terrified women scrambled out, covered with mud and gore. When they were well treated, they helped induce the others to surrender.

The desperate party that had inflicted three deaths and at least four wounds proved to consist of four braves, hampered by fifteen women and seven children. The riddled bodies of one brave, three women, and one infant were found, but left unburied and before long, scalpless. The others walked out, many wounded. Their leader was recognized as American Horse, the Elder, or Iron Shield, an Oglala chief, who stalked out holding his entrails in with bloody hands; despite the doctors' best efforts, he, too, died that night. The two other men, Charging Bear and Black Fox, emerged unscathed.

By this time searchers in the village were turning up horses, saddles, clothing, and even a guidon, all with 7th Cavalry markings. The captive women said that they were en route to the agencies to surrender. They named the village chiefs as the mortally wounded

248

American Horse, and Roman Nose, a Mineconjou. There is doubt of the latter's presence, but Red Horse, another Mineconjou chief, was there by his own account.

The captives also warned that runners were bringing reinforcements from Crazy Horse's camp near the Little Missouri. He was said to have three hundred lodges, but the directions ranged from west to north and the distance from six to twenty miles. Since Carr's cavalry would arrive five hours sooner, a longer distance was probable. It may have been forty miles west on the Little Missouri, or thirty miles northwest in the Cave Hills, as the Indians later told sutler John W. Smith. The captives further revealed that Sitting Bull's group had split up. About half, or sixty to one hundred lodges (Long Dog and Inkapaduta?) had crossed the Yellowstone (August 22nd?), while the rest under Sitting Bull had turned down the Little Missouri to the Antelope Hills (Killdeer Mountains?) to fatten up their horses and to trade with the Rees (unsuccessfully on August 21st?).

The troopers had turned to feasting and napping, when at 4 p.m. a sudden flurry of shots rang out, heralding the promised retaliation by warriors from Crazy Horse's village. Here, at last, came the very opportunity that Crook had been driving his men so hard and so long to bring about — a pitched battle with a large force of dedicated hostiles, whom he could whip with his two thousand troops. Yet, in the preceding four hours he had made no preparations, set no traps, sent no scouts out to give early warning of the time, direction, or strength of the anticipated attack. On the contrary, the horses were all on herd with the men eating or napping in an amphitheater commanded by bluffs. Were they too demoralized to give any more?

The Sioux swarmed on the hills, skipping from one vantage point to another, to pour in a heavy fire. Others succeeded in stampeding a cavalry herd, but Corporal J.S. Clanton, Company B, 5th Cavalry, managed to turn them back to safety. The two to three hundred attackers were grossly outnumbered, but with the advantage of position, they fought furiously and stubbornly. They forced Crook to throw every man into action on foot and to unleash the full firepower of two thousand carbines and "Long Toms." When charges drove the braves back, they circled to attack from another point. Such charges and countercharges continued for several hours until numbers, firepower, and darkness prompted the Sioux to make an orderly withdrawal.

As Colonel Carr summed it up, "There were about 200 Indians, but they succeeded in making us display all our force and drawing all our fire." No soldiers were killed, but five cavalrymen were seriously

249

wounded. This second engagement was far more massive and prolonged than Mills' slim charge through a small village. Yet only the latter is famed as the Battle of Slim Buttes, because of newspaper reports. Crook made no effort to exploit his long-sought opportunity, either before or during the battle. He fought a masterly defense of two thousand against two hundred! It is hard to escape the conclusion that it was an opportunity missed.

What the command failed to achieve counted less at the moment than the triumph of capturing a village stocked with food and robes. They had full bellies at last. Perhaps, too full, for the tons of captured provisions, judged adequate for three days, shrank so rapidly that the remainder had to be reserved for the sick and wounded. And they were still far from the Black Hills with no relief detail speeding ahead for supplies.

September 10th again dawned cold and rainy, but gave ample proof that Crook had failed to cool the Sioux. Creeping up in the first misty light, they threatened to drive the pickets in. It took four companies of infantry, sent up the bluffs on the south and west, to hold them out of camp while the column formed for march. Crook assigned the 5th Cavalry to the rear guard with orders to destroy the village and liberate the captives. Under heavy fire, half the cavalry relieved the infantry on the bluffs and the other half burned the village.

About 8 a.m. Crook pulled out with the main column, the travois train of wounded in the advance closely guarded by the infantry. While he receded into the distance, the Indians hotly engaged the rear guard as it withdrew to take the trail. Inspired by this retreat, the warriors charged furiously from all directions. The withdrawal might have turned into disaster, save for Colonel Carr's skillful handling of the troops. Even so, they were hard pressed and added one severely and several lightly wounded troopers to the full toll of the three engagements at Slim Buttes. The enthusiasm of the Sioux waned after a moving fight of two miles, finally freeing the rear guard to step out after the main column, long out of sight.

Crazy Horse proved that morning that he was still full of fight. So did the weary 5th Cavalry. But Crook marched in the distant van, showing no interest in converting the retreat to a victory. Still traveling south with Slim Buttes on his right, he soon found that the high ridge made a right angle to the east, cutting across his path. Probably to spare the travois-born wounded, he camped at noon after only ten miles. The rear guard joined as the camp was being made. The troops supped in the rain on slaughtered Indian ponies, a rude come-down from buffalo and berries, but an improvement over expired mules.

That evening Crook composed a lengthy dispatch to Sheridan relating events of the past week (O-39,1876). If there is virtue in brevity, Crook's references to the three battles of Slim Buttes are saintly indeed. Of the first he reported merely that Mills, having found a village of thirty-odd lodges, "attacked them by surprise yesterday morning, capturing the village, some prisoners and a number of ponies, and killing some of the Indians." Of the second, he wrote that "our main command got up about noon that day and was shortly after attacked by a considerable body of Indians." Of the third, he wrote not a word. The General seemed reluctant to discuss his contributions to affairs at Slim Buttes.

The fighting had keyed up the men, but a severe let-down followed on the 11th. They awakened to another day of cold rain and fog, facing starvation. Crook again chose Mills to forge ahead to Deadwood with Lt. Bubb to secure provisions. This time he took Lt. George F. Chase as subaltern and only fifty picked cavalrymen mounted on captured ponies. Grouard went as guide and bearer of Crook's report, while Jack Crawford carried reporters' dispatches. Davenport and Strahorn again joined the relief party as it took the lead in leaving camp that morning.

The slow main column was soon winding up and over the rugged Slim Buttes, the terrain resembling a moon-scape, except for the rain and slippery mud. Late on the long march they crossed a lodge-pole trail heading southeast toward the river agencies, but not even Crook had the energy to worry about it. They finally made another miserable horse-meat camp, but the train of twelve travois and mule-litters did not pull in until long after dark.

The command was now on the edge of disintegration. Yet the next morning Crook ordered Major J.J. Upham to pick 150 sullen 5th Cavalrymen and embark on a stern chase along the trail ignored the day before. The disgusted force plodded off, armed with two ounces of buffalo meat, a few coffee beans, and what horse meat the famished men had chanced to save from the night before. They would not return for three days.

Why Crook ordered this new stern chase is incomprehensible. When he had found Indians attacking his command, he had marched away. Now, on finding an old trail, he ordered it chased. It is precisely this inconsistency that robs him of any defense for either action. He could have justified piling into or after the hostiles at every opportunity, regardless of the condition of his men. He could have justified withdrawing from action because of the bad condition of his men. But not both at the same time! In this campaign bull-dog

Crook's tenacity varied inversely with the proximity of the enemy.

All chroniclers unite in branding September 12th as a day of horror — a calamity unmatched in their memories. What strength and will remained to men and beasts drained away in the interminable struggle against rain and mud. Fully half the infantry fell out on the march. Hundreds of mounts collapsed and expired. Those dismounted, unable to lug their saddles, abandoned them in heaps on the prairie. Ammunition grew so burdensome that it was cached. Frequent halts became necessary, but as Schwatka moaned, they amounted only to "suffering at a standstill." The officers, helpless to maintain control, watched the column string out over ten miles. After seventeen agonizing hours on the road the advance collapsed on reaching camp about four miles west of present Newell, S.D.

They had reckoned that twenty miles should have brought them to the Belle Fourche River, which circles closely along the north edge of the Black Hills. But after thirty-five killing miles they were still five short. Where the advance halted was a camp by euphemism. Most simply dropped in their tracks in the mud and lay all night in the rain. Some heroes managed to stay on their feet, slaughtering ponies for the few who could eat. Stragglers stumbled in all night and the next forenoon. The fate of the wounded went unrecorded, for Dr. McGillicuddy, who was in charge of the travois train, never found the moment required for his usual brief diary entry.

In the meantime, Mills' relief party had traveled all day and most of the night of the 11th. Davenport confirms Grouard's story that the Captain's attempt to navigate by compass introduced "eccentricities" in their course — until Frank seized the lead. Riding all day of the 12th, they forded the Belle Fourche and ascended Whitewood Creek, one of its southern tributaries, to reach Crook City after dark. This mining settlement, adjacent to present Whitewood, was only ten miles from Deadwood. Bubb purchased thirteen wagon-loads of provisions and fifty beeves on the hoof, which he started the next morning on the trail back to the Belle Fourche.

Crook's scarecrows came to life slowly on the still rainy morning of the 13th. Not until noon had the thin cavalry details carried the last stragglers into camp. The command might never have moved, but a courier from Bubb announcing that provisions would meet them at the Belle Fourche brought them to their feet. The move began with a difficult fording of one rain-swollen creek and ended with another of the Belle Fourche. Camp was made on the south bank and every eye glued itself on the trail up Whitewood Creek.

252

Finally in the afternoon a wagon train and beef herd materialized on the mountain slope approaching the camp, turning it into a cheering bedlam. The voracious men mobbed the wagons, but bacon, coffee and flour were soon distributed and cook fires stoked up. Issues of fresh beef quickly followed. Two thousand happy minds had a single thought. They huddled around the cook fires far into the night, eating, cooking, and eating again. They could not get their fill of Bubb's manna.

The next morning an epidemic of diarrhea hit the gorged men — but no one cared, especially when the sun burst out in all its glory for the first time in ten days! Major Upham's disgusted Indian-chasers plodded in, "the worst tired men I ever saw," wrote Colonel Carr. Their last-gasp effort had proved futile. The trail was too old to hope of overtaking its makers. They had not seen an Indian — but a few hostiles had seen them. That very morning they had come upon the scalped body of one of their own men who had been hunting in the advance. Their spirits soared, however, when they, too, joined the general feasting.

That afternoon there came an inundation of wagons and carriages from every mining community within striking distance. Some came to welcome the troops, whose presence spelled relief from Indian harrassment. But most came to market, at Shylock prices, every edible they could scrape from their larders. Then a courier rode in with a bundle of six dispatches dated from August 1st to September 11th. In the last, Sheridan demanded that Crook establish a fighting cantonment on Powder River in Indian country, instead of hiding from the hostiles in the center of the Black Hills at Custer City. He ordered Crook to meet him at Fort Laramie on September 17th for a strategy conference (C-7).

On the 15th the command moved five miles to a nice camp up Whitewood Creek, where Crook turned over his command to Colonel Merritt and prepared to leave for Fort Laramie. Early the next morning he and his staff, accompanied by the remaining reporters, rode to stay the night at Deadwood, where cheering miners feted them. Not until the 24th did his cavalcade pull in to Fort Laramie to see Sheridan. The battered troops, waiting for supply trains and resting at Custer City, took a month to reach their winter quarters, when Crook officially announced the termination of his campaign.

The Big Horn and Yellowstone Expedition had been in the field for four and a half months. The hostiles had checked them on the Rosebud and then eluded them all summer. They had finally burned thirty-seven empty tepees and retreated from a few reinforcing braves. But the troops had taken such severe punishment that they

253

would remain out of action for months. For the moment the whippers were whipped.

Chapter 22
Victory at the Agencies

The President had planned to escape his dilemma by allowing the citizenry to occupy the Black Hills while the army whipped the hostiles into subjection, thus forcing a cession of the unceded Indian lands as well as the gold-bearing portion of their "permanent" reservation. All this was to be cloaked in the palatable guise of defending the nation against Indian aggression and intransigence.

The plan had been set in motion back in November of 1875. Within a year it had succeeded to perfection in every feature, save one. Instead of whipping the hostiles into subjection, the hostiles, still roaming free, had nearly whipped the army. But fate operates in devious ways; it was precisely the series of stinging military disasters that propelled the plan to success. From the beginning, only the conscience of Congress had prevented the direct seizure of the coveted Indian lands. But the specter of losing a war quickly swept this obstruction away.

Even the force of conscience had swayed less than the full Congress. Two of its western members had early tried to steal the Sioux lands by brazen acts of legislation. As early as January 18, 1876, Representative William R. Steele of Wyoming introduced a bill "to open to exploration and settlement" all the unceded lands within the Territory of Wyoming. One clause in the bill declared that "the true meaning" of the treaty of 1868 was the exact opposite of the wording that forbade exploration and settlement! The Committee on Indian Affairs reported the bill back *favorably*, but an embarassing debate on July 8th so clearly exposed the sneaky contradictions of the treaty that a shamed House voted the bill back to the Committee for a decent burial (O-6).

Emboldened by this attempted skullduggery, Representative Jefferson P. Kidder of Dakota, on February 28th, introduced an even rawer bill to open the Black Hills portion of the Sioux reservation to settlement! But not even the Committee on Indian Affairs could find any way around the inalienable rights of the Sioux to their own reservation, and so failed to report it back in any form (O-6).

In the meantime, the public, as well as Congress, were happy to ignore what the armies were doing in the Sioux country — until July 7th, when every newspaper in the land scare-headed the terrible disaster the Sioux had inflicted on the gallant Custer and the crack 7th Cavalry. The public reaction was instantaneous, universal, and instinctive. The Indians had launched a bloody war. They were massacring the army. The honor and security of the nation were in jeopardy. Exterminate the red devils! It was a Pearl Harbor in miniature.

Congress responded that very day, albeit with a touch of suspicion. It called on the Secretary of War to report on the origins of the conflict and the objectives of the military operations, with all relevant correspondence. So thoroughly had the propaganda line been prepared that within twenty-four hours Secretary J.D. Cameron was able to submit a summary report backed up by fifty-nine pages of documents! The timing was perfect. The public, already hallucinating, would never be more receptive to the grand illusion.

The Secretary solemnly proclaimed that the terms of the Sioux treaty had been "literally performed on the part of the United States." (By sending thousands to invade the reservation?) Even most of the Sioux had likewise honored the treaty, but some "have always treated it with contempt," by continuing "to rove at pleasure." (A practice legalized by the treaty!) They had even gone so far as to "attack settlements, steal horses, and murder peaceful inhabitants." (These victims were white violators of the treaty who dealt the Indians worse than they received!) As proof of Indian guilt, the Secretary for the first time publicly unveiled the infamous Watkins report. Too gamey to broadcast when written, it now went down like smooth whiskey.

The Secretary directly denied that gold-seeking was the cause of the war, and avowed that its object was to serve the best interests of the peaceful portion of the Sioux! We cannot refrain from quoting one paragraph of this nimble double-talk:

> The present military operations are not against the Sioux Nation at all, but against certain portions of it, which defy the Government, and are undertaken at the special request of that bureau of the Government

charged with their supervision, and wholly to make the civilization of the remainder possible. No part of these operations is on or near the Sioux reservation. The accidental discovery of gold on the western border of the Sioux reservation, and the intrusion of our people thereon, have not caused this war, and have only complicated it by the uncertainty of numbers to be encountered. The young warriors love war and frequently escape their agents to go on the hunt or warpath, their only idea of the object of life. The object of these military expeditions was in the interest of the peaceful parts of the Sioux Nation, supposed to embrace nine-tenths of the whole, and not one of these peaceful or treaty Indians has been molested by the military authorities.

Within weeks, events would expose every word of this brazen snow-job as false. But at the moment it enabled the public to see with crystal clarity that the defiant savages had started the whole thing and that simple justice demanded punishment, if not ex-termination — and confiscation of their lands. It could not have fooled Congress, but as dutiful representatives of the people's wishes, that body jumped to answer the call of the public. Although it would take over a month to forge a sure-fire means of confiscating the Sioux lands, Congress betrayed its change of heart by starting to churn out a few lesser, but revealing, bills.

On July 31st the Senate passed a House joint resolution author-izing and directing the President to take all necessary steps to prevent any metallic cartridges from reaching the Sioux country (O-6). On August 12th, the President happily signed a bill which restored the authorized strength of Enlisted Indian Scouts to one thousand, thereby repealing a reduction to three hundred passed only months before. On August 15th, he signed another bill increasing the strength of cavalry companies engaged in the war to one hundred men each (O-46). By that date Congress had already solved the problem of land confiscation.

But the very first action Congress took was one that played directly into the hands of General Sheridan. Though relatively in-nocent in appearance, it provided the essential key to the all-out war that the angry General now determined to prosecute. The moment he had learned of the fates of Crook's army and Custer's regiment, Sheridan had turned vindictive. For him, the war ceased to serve as a military means to a civil end; it became a war of revenge to destroy an enemy that had humiliated the U.S. Army. No longer would he bar any holds — least of all, spare the innocent, despite the Secretary of War's pious claims that friendly Indians were not being molested.

To prosecute his war of vengeance, Sheridan needed to gather the absolute control of the war into his own hands. He could coun-tenance no peace overtures, no negotiations, no intervention whatever from weak-hearted civilians, until he had brought all the Sioux and Cheyennes to their knees. But to move against the agency Indians would inevitably drive them out to their unceded lands, where they could continue to make fools of his troops — unless he first established strong bases there, from which he could launch relentless attacks, winter as well as summer. Without this key, the door to subjugation would remain closed to him.

On July 7th, the very day he became certain that the enemy had destroyed Custer's force, Sheridan telegraphed Sherman to press his demand for new posts in the unceded country. Again, on July 12th, he wired imperiously; "Do not neglect to urge the appropriation for the two posts on the Yellowstone . . . Our summer's work, with all its hardships and losses, may be of no avail if those posts are not established." The very next day Congress debated Sherman's request for the funds (O-6). It met with no obstacle, for the presence of war, regardless of its causes, effectively nullified the treaty prohibiting such posts. Having already ordered the mobilization of artisans and supplies, Sheridan sent Colonel Forsyth to consult with Terry on July 20th. Two days later the President signed the $200,000 appropriation bill, officially giving Sheridan his coveted key (O-46).

Although Colonel Forsyth returned with word that failing navigation would delay construction until the next June rise, Sheridan could brook no such disastrous delay. He decided that if artisans could not construct permanent posts, the troops could build themselves winter huts. Accordingly, on August 17th he dispatched orders to Terry to build winter quarters at Tongue River and for Crook to do the same at some suitable point in the Powder River country. The letter to Crook summarized his plans and progress to that date:

> The bill for increasing the company strength of [regiments of] cavalry in the field passed Congress and I have designated Fort D.A. Russell as the rendezvous for equipping and mounting the recruits for your cavalry . . .
>
> I will give orders to General Terry today to establish a cantonment for the winter at Tongue River and will send supplies there for 1500 men, cavalry and infantry. I think also of establishing a cantonment for the winter at Goose Creek, or some other point on your line, for a force of 1000 men. I will send you 100 of the best Pawnee scouts under Major [Frank] North, regularly enlisted, as Congress has increased the number to one thousand.
>
> We must hold the country you and Terry have been operating in this winter, or else every Indian at the agencies will go out as soon as we commence dismounting and disarming them . . . (C-7)

This letter did not catch up with Crook until September 14th, by which time Sheridan had himself decided on the proper location for Crook's winter post. Construction of the Tongue River Cantonment, as we have seen, began on August 28th, and that of Cantonment Reno, on the upper Powder River adjacent to old Fort Reno, began on October 12th. Sheridan thus neatly slipped the key into the lock.

Sheridan had not delayed, either, in imposing his second demand — military control of all the Sioux agencies. It was on July 18th when he wired Sherman to press this matter within the executive branch. On July 22nd, the day the President signed the bill for the new posts, Sherman held a conference with the Secretaries of War and the Interior. Before the day was over he telegraphed Sheridan:

> Mr. Chandler says that you may at once assume control over all the agencies in the Sioux country. He wants for a good reason both of the agents at Red Cloud and Spotted Tail removed and their duties performed by the commanding officers of the garrisons; also that no issues of rations be made at any of the agencies unless the Indians be actually present; that all who are now or may hereafter go outside of the reservation be treated as you propose, as enemies, disarmed and their ponies taken away ... (M-58)

This gave Sheridan not only the key — it gave him the lock, nay the whole door! Of course, army officers could not legally serve as Indian agents, but after a flurry of consternation this was evaded by calling them "temporary" agents to serve only until subservient civil agents could be rounded up. It is significant that when Sheridan quoted Sherman's wire to Terry (Chicago *Tribune*, July 31, 1876), he inserted the word, "absolute," so as to give himself *absolute control* over the agencies, meaning that neither President, Congress, nor consititution could stay his hand!

In the same letter Sheridan ordered a complete military takeover of the Red Cloud, Spotted Tail, Standing Rock, Cheyenne River, and Lower Brule Agencies; the army officers there must demand "unconditional surrender" of every Indian that returned to the agencies, whether from an innocent hunt or a hostile camp, and must confiscate all their arms and ponies and hold them as prisoners of war. These harsh measures, not wholly restricted to combatants, were as nothing, however, compared to the plans the General had in store for the non-combatant, friendly agency Indians.

Sheridan began rushing troops from other departments of his military division to garrison, at regimental strength, each seized agency. As revealed in the Chicago *Inter-Ocean* of August 7th, he also planned a total embargo on arms and ammunition — not limited to metallic cartridges — in order to reduce the friendlies to bows and arrows, even for staving off the starvation threatened by the disruption of rationing procedures when army novices replaced experienced Indian agents. A further intention, most revealing because least justified, was to confiscate the arms, ammunition, and ponies of the agency Indians, no matter how friendly or loyal. As future events would prove, he scheduled these terroristic measures for the day when he had all his agency garrisons in position, his new posts established in unceded Indian territory, and his campaigning armies home from the field.

The ostensible reason for these dark measures was to cut off aid and support to the hostiles, but the effect was to reduce hostile surrenders to a trickle and impel alienated friendlies to swell the ranks of the combatants. Since this was forseeable, even to Sheridan, his real motives were not so simple. A letter he wrote to Crook on August 23rd hints at more vindictive motives:

> The misfortune that came to Custer virtually destroyed all hopes of making the campaign successful by getting a fight out of the Indians. Since that time I have been bending everything to the only plan which will ultimately be successful, namely, to get military control over the Indians at the agencies, and the permanent occupation of the Yellowstone country — by this I mean all the country west of the Black Hills. Good progress has been made . . .
>
> The 7th Cavalry had to go in, as the Indians at the Missouri river agencies will not permit the dismounting and unconditional surrender without sufficient force to compel them.
>
> I ordered the 11th Infantry from Texas and will soon have at Standing Rock nine companies and at Cheyenne Agency nine companies. Col. Mackenzie has at Red Cloud nine companies of cavalry and nine of infantry and artillery, and as soon as it gets a little nearer winter, the work of the disarming and dismounting will commence. (C-7)

While Sheridan was maneuvering for vengeance, Congress was forging a weapon to compel a cession of the Black Hills and unceded lands — the original civil objectives of the war. This weapon would meet with quick success, while the army was still reaping humiliation. The generals would howl in anguish when they discovered that their "absolute" control was a chimera. Nevertheless, it was the war, and especially its reverses, that put Congress in the mood to implement what the executive branch had as yet only threatened.

The weapon that Congress forged, and President Grant signed on August 15th, was tragically simple. It merely attached a proviso to the annual appropriation bill for the Sioux tribes. This bill included one million dollars for rations alone, since the agency Indians could no longer feed themselves by the chase nor raise their own provisions. The proviso prohibited the payment of a single sou of the appropriation to any *band* engaged in hostilities, and further prohibited any *future* appropriations until the Sioux first: a) relinquished all claim to their unceded lands and to that portion of their reservation lying west of the 103rd meridian (the western 40-mile strip of present South Dakota, a fraction of which the Black Hills occupied), b) granted right-of-way for three roads across the remaining reservation to the Hills, c) agreed to receive their supplies at the Missouri River (to reduce freight charges!), and d) agreed to a plan that would make them fully self-supporting (O-46).

Although the specifics of the self-support plan were left open, the remaining provisos constituted a blunt and non-negotiable ultimatum to the men, women, and children of the Sioux Nation:

CEDE, OR STARVE!

The demands of this ultimatum utterly explode every claim that the objectives of the war were anything else than to wrest from the Indians their Black Hills and unceded lands. In any resort to war, the demands the victor imposes on the vanquished conclusively expose his true objectives, no matter how dense the verbal camouflage of deliberate propaganda or sincere self-deception.

The President lost no time in selecting a seven-man Commission to carry the ultimatum to the agencies. Since Congress had left no room for negotiation, he could afford to garner a little good will by including some "Indian sympathizers" on the Commission. He chose one for its President, George W. Manypenny, the outspoken former Indian Commissioner, and added Bishop Henry B. Whipple, long a missionary to the Minnesota Sioux. Other appointees were Newton Edmunds, ex-Governor of Dakota Territory and an experienced treaty "negotiator"; Albert G. Boone and Jared W. Daniels, both former Indian agents; and Henry C. Bulis of Decorah, Iowa. An Assistant Attorney-General, A.S. Gaylord, provided the legal starch the Commission would need.

On August 24th, Commissioner J.Q. Smith drafted a directive to guide the Commission. He reminded them that the proviso left no lattitude in regard to the cession of lands, nor the right-of-way for roads. This applied as well to receiving supplies on the Missouri, but on this point President Grant had intervened. Convinced that the Sioux could never support themselves by tilling the barren soil of their reservation, he suggested that they be removed to Indian Territory, i.e., present Oklahoma. Smith accordingly directed the Commission to offer removal to the south as the preferred alternative to receiving goods at the river. When it came to the self-support plan, the Commissioner had almost nothing to suggest. He implied that farming offered the sole path to such a goal, and hinted that existing treaties might afford the Commission some ideas (O-5, 1876).

The Commission dutifully assembled at Omaha on August 28th to formulate its strategy. The members were thoroughly conversant with the long history of double-dealing with the Sioux, for they spelled out the whole tragic story in embarrassing detail in their final report. But they failed to disclose therein the gratuitous chapter they added to this shameful history by transforming the four demands of the Congress into an even harsher ten-point program (O-3).

The first three points were identical with the first three demands of Congress, except that the Commission exacted its own pound of flesh by demanding the cession of an *additional* triangle of reservation land lying between the forks of Cheyenne River, *east* of the 103rd meridian. Since this victimized only Indians it drew no comment from any white man, then or since. The fourth point offered the President's alternative of moving south to Indian Territory.

In exchange for compliance with these demands, the fifth and sixth points proposed that the government should assist the Indians in the work of civilization, furnish schools, allot land and erect houses for those who farm, and provide subsistence. All but the last of course were merely repromises to honor the unfulfilled promises of the 1868 treaty; the last was a resumption of an expired obligation, but with foul-blow restrictions. Rations would be provided until the Indians became self-supporting, *except* that they would be denied to any families whose men did not labor, or whose children did not attend school! But the benevolent government would aid them in finding employment (!), and marketing their surplus (!) production.

The seventh point made a transparent bid for moral Brownie points: all agency employees must be married according to Holy Writ, and squaw-men and half-breeds deemed undesirable would be banished from the reservation. The heart-break of banishing husbands and children was easy to ignore, since the motives were more profane than sacred; the greatest thorns in the side of a dishonest or tyrannical Indian agent were the squaw-men and their children who could recognize, publicize, and counteract chicanery and tyranny.

The eighth point promised that Congress would provide the Indians with an orderly government, subject them to the laws of the United States, and protect them in their rights of property and person. Within weeks the Sioux would learn how empty such high-

262

sounding words can be. The ninth point required an Indian force, under Presidential direction, to police the agreement and enforce the peace. The tenth demanded an accurate annual census; although there were sound reasons for this, the principal effect was to reserve to the agent the spoils of cheating on rations.

It should now become clear why the red man needed no enemies when he had "Indian-sympathizers." In order to speed the blessings of honest, Christian toil, the Commission had escalated the original ultimatum to:

CEDE AND LABOR, OR STARVE

Under military escort, the well-briefed Commission proceeded to the Red Cloud Agency, where it presented its proposal to a gathering of chiefs on September 7th. They opened this, as well as succeeding councils, with a pious prayer from the Bishop – then made it brutally clear that they had come for signatures, not negotiations. In bewilderment, fear, and dismay, the chiefs retired to counsel long among themselves. Several times they returned to reason and plead with the Commission, but found them utterly flint-hearted. They asked why the whites were allowed to live and mine on their reservation? Why soldiers were swarming over their agency and holding friendly Indians as prisoners of war? Why the army had invaded their unceded lands to attack their legally roving relatives? They vowed they would never move to the south, but agreed to send a delegation to see that detested country. They would even cede their lands, but they pleaded for *something* meaningful in return. The Commission ignored the questions and the pleas. The spiritual Bishop reminded them of the material advantages of submission over starvation. The attorney rudely told them to sign – he was in a hurry.

Finally, the specter of emaciated wives and bloat-bellied children drove the despairing chiefs to "touch the pen." On September 20th, twenty-nine Oglalas, five Cheyennes, and six Arapahoes (who had never joined the conflict) signed the Aritcles of Agreement, exactly as originally proposed. Only by a slip of the tongue did the whites ever refer to it as a treaty. And no one ever mentioned that it was the Government of the United States that had solemnly pledged its word to accept no land cessions without the express consent of three-fourths of the adult male Indians.

An irresistible domino effect prevailed as the Commission hastened from one agency to the next. With no more than a day's deliberation at each, the chiefs at Spotted Tail signed on September 23rd, at Standing Rock on October 11th, at Cheyenne River on October 16th, at Crow Creek on October 21st, at Lower Brule on October 24th, and even the innocent Santees on October 27th.

The President's plan had triumphed. The white man now held clear title to the vast unceded Sioux lands and to much more of the "permanent" reservation than contained hills or gold. An enlightened, industrious, and Christian civilization could once again march on without hindrance from savage, indigent, infidels. Praise the Lord!

*   *   *

And pass the ammunition. The war was not yet won. The savages were now trespassing on the white man's land! To fully realize the civil objectives the roamers must be herded on to the shrunken reservation. To realize the military objectives, the whole Nation must be whipped into subjection.

General Sheridan, waiting impatiently at Fort Laramie to confer with Crook, was already seething at the way the Commission at Red Cloud was interferring with his "absolute" control of affairs. General Crook, hurrying to meet his superior, reached that agency on September 20th. His blood pressure sky-rocketed when he saw the Commissioners fraternizing with his enemies. Most irate of all was Colonel R.S. Mackenzie, who, as commander of the heavily-garrisoned agency, considered it subject to his exclusive control under martial law.

The three officers held a council of war at Fort Laramie on September 22nd. They shared the conviction that the presence of the Commission made a dangerous breach in military control and jeopardized their own freedom to subjugate friendlies as well as hostiles. They were especially incensed by the promise of personal and property rights for Indians, and the attempt to whisk them away to the distant south. They spurned the fact that the Commission was carrying out the will of Congress to achieve the civil objectives of the war. The officers laid plans to humble the home-body and roaming Indians both. They also arranged for Colonel Mackenzie to draft an indignant letter protesting civilian interference to be sent up through channels so that each could add his licks by way of endorsement.

Mackenzie's verbose letter, dated at Camp Robinson, September 30th (M-53), is a revelation. It displays emotion so disproportionate to the professed provocation as to seem irrational. He reveals his angry reaction when Red Cloud and Spotted Tail defied his orders to deliver up every Indian that had sneaked back to their agencies,

264

whether hostile or friendly. Then the Commission came to counsel with these defiant chiefs, and were even now arranging to send them on a pleasure-junket to Indian Territory! Thus provoked, he *demanded* of his superiors, including the President, to suspend "any action resulting from the agreement of the commission," and to proscribe "any further communication with the Sioux" by civilians of whatever rank, "except through the military authorities." The message could have been no clearer had the Colonel asked, "Since when has the civil government had any authority over the military?"

General Crook endorsed this letter with the initial statement, "I heartily concur." He then added a typical Crookism: "These agencies are and have been the head and front of all the trouble and hostilities which have been in progress." But in truth, it was Crook who was "behind" the current hostilities. He had previously tried to camouflage his hand by pointing the accusing finger at the roving bands. But now he focuses on the agency Indians. Guess what's coming!

Sheridan's endorsement was typically blood-thirsty: ". . . there is scarcely an instance . . . where the Indians have left their places of [roaming] abode, until after the conclusion of a fierce strife which disabled and broke them down." Having protested the presence and actions of the Commission, he claimed it "can have no other result than crippling, as it has already done, the action of the military." What had Sheridan planned, if what he did do was only its crippled residue?

General Sherman's endorsement revealed how far out of touch with his command he had fallen. Unaware of what had been cooked up at Fort Laramie, he wrote that "it is rare we have in such close connection the frank opinion of three such able men and officers." Then, missing the whole point, he opined that moving the Platte Sioux to the Missouri "would end this last work of Indian subjugation."

Of course, this impertinent letter had no influence whatever on the course of events. Immune to the protest, even had they known of it, the Commission proceeded with their civil mission. And Sheridan, rejecting all the Commission's promises, proceeded with his plan to humble the agency Indians. He chose a date late in October for his "Operation Friendly." All the Sioux agencies would feel his harsh hand, but the Oglalas most of all.

Red Cloud, chief of the Oglalas, and Red Leaf, chief of the Loafer band, so-called because it was the most devoted to agency life, had moved their villages a little away from the officious troop headquarters at Camp Robinson. At dawn of October 23rd, the two chiefs awakened to find their camps surrounded by Colonel Mackenzie's guns. The soldiers ransacked the tepees and scoured the hills, seizing every fire-arm, bit of ammunition, and pony they could find. Then they herded the dismayed, but angry, Indians back near their post, where General Crook deposed Red Cloud from his chieftaincy and proclaimed Spotted Tail chief of all the Platte River tribes.

The eyes of the Sioux were thus nicely opened to what the Commission had meant when it promised to impose an orderly govenment and protect their rights of property!

At Standing Rock Agency, on the afternoon of October 22nd, the Sioux watched in apprehension as the heavy garrison formed on parade to welcome General Terry's army marching down both banks of the Missouri River. That day and the next the troops confiscated all their arms, ammunition and ponies. A few days later some of the troops proceeded down river to assist the garrison at Cheyenne River agency to serve the Indians there in similar fashion (Bismarck *Tribune*, Nov. 1). The Missouri Sioux thus became as enlightened as their brothers on the Platte.

These bloodless triumphs over docile Indians thoroughly humbled those that remained on the reservation. Others recovered some pride by sneaking off to join forces with their roving relatives. The confiscations were not designed to grease the axles of land cession, for the land had already been ceded. But they did punish and humiliate just those who had bent most to the white man's will. Sheridan was greatly pleased with his coups, and never acknowledged the rebuke inherent in the reparations the federal courts later compelled the government to grant his victims.

Having vanquished the friendlies, the army turned once again to the hostiles, still roaming freely over the lands their agency relatives had been forced to cede. Crook started out with a fresh army under Colonel Mackenzie and some four hundred Enlisted Indian Scouts. At dawn of November 25th, they surprised a snow-blanketed village in the Big Horn Mountains, consisting of 183 lodges of Cheyennes — nearly all the roaming Indians of that tribe. Though Mackenzie's Indian allies alone exceeded the number of warriors in the village, the fight was a hard one. But the troops eventually succeeded in burning down the lodges and driving the inhabitants out into the ice and snow (R-5). The destitute refugees fled north to the Oglala camp on Tongue River, losing more women and children to exposure than they had lost warriors to bullets. Crook did not follow the refugee trail, but wandered around for a few weeks in other directions, and then retired from the field to sit out the remainder of the war.

From his Tongue River Cantonment, the aggressive and tireless General Miles campaigned all winter long, harrassing the Indians more effectively with his ten companies of "walk-a-heaps" than Crook, Terry, and Gibbon had been able to do with their summer armies. Early in October, Sitting Bull's village left the Little Missouri and headed north and west for the annual fall hunt. On crossing the Yellowstone a little above Glendive, the chief found the new road already worn by the army supply trains. On October 10th, and again on the 14th and 15th, his angry warriors descended on wagon trains. But the small infantry escorts were able to hold their own with their deadly "long tom" rifles (M-32).

Hearing of these attacks, Miles' command stormed out of its winter huts and pursued the Indian trail northward, overtaking Sitting Bull on the head of Cedar Creek. On October 21st, a stormy, two-day council with the chief broke up in a battle, and Miles slogged after the largest contingent that fled back to the Yellowstone. Many of these were Missouri Sioux, only recently driven out by the military take-over. A considerable number surrendered at the mouth of Cabin Creek on October 27th, yielding up hostages to assure their unsupervised return to their agencies (R-37). But since conditions were still intolerable there, only a fraction turned themselves in.

But the wiley Sitting Bull had doubled back north toward Fort Peck with his Hunkpapa followers. Returning briefly to re-outfit his infantry, Miles launched a month-long winter campaign into the Fort Peck area. He soon split his force into three battalions in order to pursue every trail and rumor. Lt. Frank Baldwin's detachment succeeded in striking and scattering Sitting Bull's own village on Red Water Creek on December 8th (R-37). With scarcely a rest, Miles then led his command up Tongue River in search of the Oglala camp to which the Cheyenne refugees had fled. On January 8th, in a snow-storm, he attacked and dispersed the village near the mouth of Hanging Woman's Fork (M-18).

By this time, friendly Indians sent out from the various agencies as "peace-talkers," began to convince the roamers that the troops would prove relentless in keeping up the harrassment (M-3 and M-30). The only hope for the women and children was to submit themselves to the mercy of the white men at the agencies. The incessant blows, and these talks, began to tell, and the majority began preparing for surrender. This was too much for Sitting Bull and his Northern followers; they began moving toward the Canadian border. By early May, even Sitting Bull himself sought sanctuary in Canada, thus effectively withdrawing his followers from the conflict.

One small band of Northern Sioux, led by the Mineconjou chief, Lame Deer, refused to listen. They separated and moved west to the Rosebud, near the mouth of what was then known as Muddy Creek. There, on May 7th, Miles' troops caught them, killing the chief and scattering the rest. From that day Muddy Creek became Lame Deer Creek (M-27).

Before the month of May closed, nearly all the despairing hostiles had surrendered. A few hundred were lucky enough to submit at Tongue River where General Miles treated them exceptionally well for five years at his unofficial agency. The others threw themselves on the untender mercies of the military who retained control of the regular agencies. The Cheyennes and Oglalas, under the proud Crazy Horse, death-marched into the Red Cloud Agency. Most of the Northern Sioux surrendered at the Spotted Tail Agency, instead of their Missouri agencies.

The army promptly banished the Northern Cheyennes to the hated agency of their southern relatives in Indian Territory, which led a year later to another outbreak and tribal tragedy. Ere this, Crazy Horse, the Oglala war-leader, had succumbed to a soldier's bayonet. Then all the Platte Indians trekked to the despised Missouri River to save a few dollars in freight charges, prompting a sizeable group to break away and join Sitting Bull in Canada.

The army had at last whipped the hostiles into subjection.

*   *   *

Sitting Bull, the acknowledged champion of the Sioux, deserves a final salute.

Refusing to grovel, the proud chief had banished himself to Canada. The Queen did not accept these political refugees as her permanent wards, but they met their first small measure of justice at the hands of the fearless and fair-minded Royal Canadian Mounted Police. It proved no idyll, however, for the disappearance of the buffalo soon brought them face to face with starvation.

On assurances of a pardon and dignified treatment for his people, Sitting Bull finally surrendered to the officers at Fort Buford on July 19, 1881. Not yet having found an American who would tell the truth, he was promptly confined at Fort Randall as a prisoner of war. May 10, 1883 arrived before the military freed him to join his Hunkpapa tribesmen on the Standing Rock Reservation.

268

There he fought his last bitter campaign — a war of nerves. Still the dedicated champion of his children, the Sioux, he fought stubbornly for their just and dignified treatment. But for six years the Indian bureau had been successfully destroying tribal cohesion by "breaking" all chiefs and headmen and reducing the proud nation to a spiritless, rudderless rabble.

The strong-minded and forceful Indian Agent, Dr. James McLoughlin, met his superior in the stronger-minded, proud and perceptive Sitting Bull. No trick in the bureau's bag proved powerful enough to humble the indomitable chief. Even he could forsee the inevitable result.

On December 15, 1890, a detail of brain-washed Indian police came like a gestapo squad to the chief's hovel to arrest him on charges trumped up by the agent.

Probably the greatest leader and strongest character the tribe had ever produced stoically bared his breast to a flurry of bullets.

PART II. FACETS

Chapter 23
The Medical Service and the Wounded

The Medical Service of the United States Army, headed by the Surgeon General, carried the responsibility for providing medical service to the Indian-fighting army of the 1870's. Although a primitive organization by modern standards, its dedicated personnel struggled mightily against unsanitary conditions at isolated military posts, tended army wives and families as well as stray frontiersmen and settlers, and shared in all the hazards of Indian campaigns. The novel surroundings of these doctors, the most broadly educated of army officers, prompted many of them to engage in scientific pursuits ranging from medicine to botany, zoology, geology, anthropology, ethnology, and even linguistics.

The Medical Department of that era was anything but a self-sufficient corps. Its meager personnel consisted of surgeons, civilian as well as military, and a few non-commissioned officers. The duties of nursing and feeding the sick and wounded fell upon enlisted men drawn from the regular company ranks. And Medical Officers found themselves subject to orders from the Secretary of War and line officers, as well as the medical chain of command.

The Secretary of War appointed, with officer rank, Surgeons and Assistant Surgeons, USA, to the Medical Department on the basis of rigorous and exacting examinations that admitted only the most highly qualified men of the profession. Commanding officers were also empowered to employ civilian doctors, as needed; these were the "contract"surgeons, officially designated Acting Assistant Surgeons. The Secretary of War also selected by examination a number of non-commissioned officers for appointment to the Medical Department as Hospital Stewards, USA. Since the quota could not exceed the total number of posts and stations, commanding officers were likewise empowered to appoint, when necessary, Acting Hospital Stewards from the regular enlisted ranks. These Stewards were responsible to Medical Officers, but in turn had full authority over the regular company privates whom Commanding Officers detailed as hospital attendants, i.e., nurses and cooks. These were prized extra duty assignments that carried extra pay and brought relief from all other company duties save standing inspections and musters.

The continental United States was divided into military Divisions, Departments, and Districts. The commanding officer of each Division and Department appointed to his staff as Medical Director a military surgeon who controlled the duty assignments of all medical officers within his command. In the field, a commanding officer customarily appointed a Chief Medical Officer to his expedition staff. A Hospital Steward, assisted by hospital attendants on detached service from their companies, usually served him. Hospital attendants, not so detached, usually served regimental and battalion surgeons. In the field, the allowance of hospital attendants amounted to one nurse per company and two cooks per regiment, although this quota was apparently seldom filled unless unusual circumstances demanded it. Regulations also dictated that each medical officer in the field be habitually attended by an orderly bearing an emergency medical knapsack. Such orderlies were appointed from time to time by the Adjutant (O-37).

Such was the organization of the army medical service in the spring of 1876, when the Dakota column began to assemble at Fort Abraham Lincoln. As fast as medical personnel arrived, Assistant Surgeon J.V.D. Middleton assigned them to temporary duty at his post hospital to await the departure of the expedition. The first to report were two Hospital Stewards, Alfred W. Dale and Joseph H. Rhinehart, both from Fort Ripley, near Brainerd, Minnesota. Having been snow-bound on the train with the Gatling battery, they did not reach the post until March 20th. Nearly a month later, a trio of contract surgeons began arriving. Dr. Elbert J. Clark, from the Cheyenne River Indian Agency, appeared on April 15th. Dr. James M. DeWolf arrived by train on April 18th with Companies E and L, 7th Cavalry, from Fort Totten on the shores of Devil's Lake, Dakota Territory. Dr. Isaiah H. Ashton, the least experienced of the trio, arrived on April 20th to take his first army contract (O-12).

General Terry reached Fort A. Lincoln on May 10th, bringing the Medical Director of his Department, Surgeon William J. Sloan, to organize the medical service, and Assistant Surgeon John W.

Williams to serve on the campaign. Two days later the three contract surgeons and the two stewards were relieved from temporary duty at the post hospital to join the expeditionary force camped outside the post. When General Terry assumed formal command on May 14th, he appointed Dr. Williams to his staff as Chief Medical Officer and assigned him temporarily to serve the Gatling battery and head-quarters company. The same orders assigned Dr. Ashton to the infantry battalion, and Drs. DeWolf and Clark to the 7th Cavalry and Enlisted Indian Scouts. Dr. Williams also received orders to engage on a contract basis Dr. Henry R. Porter, a physician of nearby Bismarck, who had been serving Camp Hancock of that city (O-8).

Dr. DeWolf, who left a brief diary and lengthy letters, recorded that Custer rejected all efforts to have Dr. Ashton assigned to his cavalry, because of inadequate military experience. He also mentioned that when Dr. Porter eagerly accepted the proffered contract, he exchanged places with Dr. Clark, but only fleetingly, for when the command pulled out on May 17th, Dr. Clark rode with the 7th Cavalry.

When the column was a week out on the march, Dr. DeWolf summarized the assignments of medical officers, and from special orders (O-8,O-40) and muster rolls (O-33,O-41,O-42) we can identify the enlisted personnel. Dr. Williams, as Chief Medical Officer, was now relieved of company duty, and the two stewards, Dale and Rhinehart, assisted him. He also had two attendants, Corp. John J. Callahan, Company K, and Pvt. Christopher Pandtle, Company E, 7th Cavalry, both so detailed by departmental special order No. 5, dated May 14th. Dr. Porter, assigned to the headquarters Company B, 6th Infantry, and the Gatling Battery, had Pvt. Charles Palmer, of the headquarters company, as his attendant, detailed by the same order. Dr. Ashton served the infantry battalion with Pvt. Andrew Johnson, Company C, 17th Infantry, as his attendant, as shown by the company muster roll. Dr. DeWolf served the 7th Cavalry right wing and the scouts, with Pvt. Harry Abbotts, Company E, as his attendant, so detailed by regimental special order No. 34, dated May 6th. Dr. Clark attended the left wing, with Pvt. William Robinson, Company M, as his attendant, so detailed by regimental special order No. 44, dated May 16th.

By June 7th, the expedition had covered 294 miles to camp 24 miles above the mouth of Powder River. Although the column had found no Indians, it had met with sickness and accident, as detailed by Dr. DeWolf and reporter Kellogg. Both recorded that an unnamed trooper had accidentally shot himself through the heel on May 21st. This was Trumpeter John Connell, Company B, 7th Cavalry, who

272

was detached to the Powder River base hospital on June 15th, and did not return to duty until after the Custer battle (O-41).

The Doctor also noted that on May 26th Dr. Williams successfully treated a trooper for a rattlesnake bite. Pvt. Francis Johnson (Kennedy) left an account mentioning his snake bite and his return to duty shortly after May 31st, but omits reference to the story, told with such relish by Kellogg, that Drs. Williams and Porter had plied him with twenty-six ounces of whiskey:

> Twenty-four ounces had been guzzled without effect on the man or the poison, but the last two ounces weakened both. The man lay in a drunken stupor for several hours, but the snake poison was killed and the man is slowly recovering. Many amusing remarks were passed among the lookers-on. Some would like a bite themselves, others wished for a preventative, while all expressed admiration for the curative powers of whiskey straight.

Dr. DeWolf wrote his wife on June 2nd that "Leeper, the painter of Co. E," had developed an abscess of the hand. This was actually Pvt. Frederick Lepper, Company L, 7th Cavalry. He, too, was detached to the base hospital on June 15th and did not return to duty until after the Custer battle. In the same letter the doctor mentioned that another unnamed soldier had partial consolidation of the lung. This was Pvt. Kane, Company C, 7th Cavalry, who was detached to the hospital and diagnosed on June 16th as having valvular heart disease. He was evacuated on July 19th aboard the *Josephine*.

The last of the marching casualties occurred on June 6th, when Pvt. David McWilliams, Company H, accidentally shot himself with his revolver while mounting his horse. Dr. DeWolf described the ball as passing down through the right calf to emerge from the foot. Kellogg's prognosis was that the unlucky trooper would be laid up for a month. He was, in fact, the fourth and last man sent to the Powder River hospital, where he remained until July 4th, when the *Far West* added him to her load of battle casualties.

A piece of scrap paper bearing an undated and unsigned medical memorandum throws some light on these and other casualties (O-9):

LIST OF SICK TRANSFERRED FROM SUPPLY CAMP TO HOSPITAL
Farley, Wm., Pvt. Co. H, 7 Cav. Gunshot wound, June 25 [Sic! 26]
Kain, Wm., Pvt. Co. C, 7 Cav. Valv. Dis. of Heart, June 16
DeLaney, Michael, Pvt. Co. K, 7 Cav. Gunshot wound, July 7
Hoyt, Walter, Pvt. Co. K, 7 Cav. Disloc. finger, rt. hand, July 14.

This memo lists those transferred on July 19th from the Powder River hospital to the *Josephine* and received at Fort A. Lincoln on July 21st. Company records show several of these men as absent, sick, at Ft. Lincoln since July 19, the date the *Josephine* left Powder

River. On the 21st, Dr. Middleton recorded the delivery to his post hospital by this boat of "three wounded men and one sick man." His month-end summary of patients received from Terry's command mentions "one hand dislocation." (O-12).

When Major Reno's reconnaissance started up Powder River on June 10th, Dr. DeWolf rode out with it as the regular right wing surgeon; so did Dr. Porter, presaging his eventual replacement of Dr. Clark as a 7th Cavlary surgeon. Dr. DeWolf implied that for lack of a horse he could take no steward on this mission, but he probably did take Attendant Abbotts.

On June 11th the remainder of the Dakota column marched down to the mouth of Powder River, where a supply depot was being established. Major Orlando H. Moore's battalion of the 6th Infantry from Fort Buford had earlier manned a supply depot at the mouth of Glendive Creek, but was now in the process of moving to this new location. Assistant Surgeon George E. Lord, from Fort Buford, had been serving this command. Company C records name Pvt. Leslie Haven as his Acting Hospital Steward, but no attendant has been identified.

Terry planned to leave Major Moore's and Captain Sanger's infantry battalions, and the numerous troopers detached from the 7th Cavalry to garrison the new supply depot. Custer would lead the left wing of his cavalry and the Gatling battery overland on June 15th to the mouth of Tongue River to meet Reno's returning reconnaissance. Terry would establish his headquarters on the *Far West* with headquarters Company B, 6th Infantry as boat guard, and steam upriver to join Custer. These plans entailed some changes in medical assignments.

Dr. Williams chose Drs. Clark and Ashton to remain at the supply depot, where they promptly set up a hospital to care for the four sick men and serve the large garrison. As assistants they kept Acting Steward Haven and Attendant Palmer, as well as Pvt. William Finnegan, Company B, 6th Infantry, newly appointed as an additional acting steward. Dr. Lord, now relieved of duty with Moore's battalion, became the Regimental Surgeon for the entire 7th Cavalry. By an order of June 14th, Terry promoted Attendant Callahan to Acting Hospital Steward to serve with Dr. Lord. When the regiment was re-united, Dr. DeWolf, served by Attendant Abbotts, retained the right wing, while Dr. Porter, presumably inheriting Attendant Robinson, took over the left wing. Dr. Williams went with Terry aboard the *Far West*, taking Stewards Dale and Rhinehart, as well as Attendant Pandtle.

Reno's scouts rejoined the regiment on June 20th and all

marched up to the mouth of the Rosebud the next day. Although Dr. DeWolf named no casualties of the reconnaissance, two had become sick enough to be transferred to the *Far West*, the only facility there that could take them. The June muster roll for Company I identifies Pvt. Mark E. Lee as absent sick on the boat since June 22nd; he apparently recovered in time to be appointed hospital attendant on July 1st to serve the battle casualties then already aboard. Very probably, Pvt. David Ackison, Company E, who would be evacuated with the battle casualties under a diagnosis of "constipation," was similarly transferred on June 22nd. If others were also detached to the boat at this time, they returned to duty by June 30th and were therefore not recorded as absent.

General Gibbon's Montana column of 7th Infantry and 2nd Cavalry was not so lavishly supplied with medical personnel. The infantry had left Fort Shaw in March with only one contract surgeon, Dr. Hart, but snowblindness promptly incapacitated him for further field duty. At Fort Ellis, Assistant Surgeon Holmes O. Paulding, of that post, joined the command. He had formerly served the 7th Cavalry at Fort Lincoln, and like Dr. DeWolf left letters and a diary. The latter names Steve Tracy as his hospital steward, and muster rolls identify three attendants: Pvt. Robert F. Williams, Company E, 7th Infantry, and Pvts. James Bovard, Company F, and Matthew Canning, Company H, both of the 2nd Cavlary.

When Gibbon's column left for the Yellowstone on April 1st, Dr. Paulding recorded that he was "the only medical officer in the outfit — Gibbon refusing to employ a contract surgeon tho' he has the authority." The General instead appointed a line officer, Lt. Charles A. Coolidge, Company A, 7th Infantry, as "Acting Surgeon!" Lt. Bradley says that Coolidge "had amused himself for some years past by employing his leisure in the study of medicine and is well qualified for the post." These were not Dr. Paulding's sentiments, however. He conscientiously assisted the Lieutenant and supplied him with a medical knapsack, but he never again displayed any respect for General Gibbon.

After Custer launched his fateful march up the Rosebud on June 22nd, Terry steamed up to join the Montana column at the mouth of the Big Horn, where Captain Kirtland and his Company B, 7th Infantry, received the assignment to guard a base camp and hospital. Apparently Steward Tracy and Attendants Williams and Canning remained there in charge of nine sick men. One of these was Sergeant Michael Rigney, Company I, 7th Infantry, so sick with consumption that he would be evacuated to the Fort Buford hospital aboard the *Far West* with the battle casualties; another was scout

Tom Leforge, nursing a broken collar-bone.

On the morning of June 25th, the Terry-Gibbon column began its march up the Big Horn. Dr. Williams accompanied Terry's headquarters, apparently assisted by Steward Rhinehart and Attendant Pandtle. Dr. Paulding served all the troops, taking only Attendant Bovard, as far as can be told from his diary. The *Far West* also started up the Big Horn the same day, with Sergeant James E. Wilson, Corps of Engineers, to keep the official boat itinerary. He recorded that "a few sick men in charge of Hospital Steward Dale occupied the rear portion of the cabin deck." (O-50) Besides the two sick men from Reno's scout, mentioned above, Dale's patients included General Gibbon, who would remain aboard for two days.

On the afternoon of June 25th, Major Reno's battalion opened the Battle of the Little Big Horn by launching the initial attack on the hostile village, while Custer diverged to the right for a supporting attack from farther downstream. Dr. Lord and Steward Callahan rode to their deaths with Custer's battalion. Drs. DeWolf and Porter entered the fight in the valley with Reno's battalion. During the subsequent retreat to the bluffs, Dr. DeWolf was killed while scaling the bluffs a little downstream from the others. This left Dr. Porter as the sole surviving medical officer, but Attendants Abbotts and Robinson also survived.

Dr. Porter apparently saw but one wounded man during the fight in the timber. This was probably Pvt. George Lorentz, Company M, whom he described as receiving a fatal chest wound when the force was about to flee the timber. He delayed to give the doomed trooper a dose of laudanum and then scrambled to follow the departing column. Barely managing to clamber into the saddle of his terrified horse, he stuck there as it bolted through flying Sioux to overtake the troops. Fortunately for the command, he arrived atop Reno Hill miraculously unscathed.

In order to determine the severity of the various battle actions and to gauge the flow of casualties that came to the busy Dr. Porter, we must identify the event in which each man was wounded. Of course, there were no wounded from the Custer engagement, so that the events of interest are Reno's fight in the timber, the running retreat to the river, scaling the bluffs, the hill top fight that same evening, and the skirmish line, charges, and water parties of the second day.

The company records name every wounded man and date the injury. In order to identify the event, however, we had to call on every battle account, the testimony given at the Reno inquiry, and every other resource. These proved adequate for the first day of fighting, but not for the second. The results of this extensive analysis are summarized in Table 1 (names, companies, wounds, and mode of evacuation are further detailed in M-28).

The analysis pinpoints all the men of Companies A, G, and M that were wounded in Reno's initial fight. Six were hit while still in the timber, of whom four managed to join the retreat, leaving three behind to be brought out later by scout Herendeen. Four others were struck during the run back to the river and one more fell while scaling the bluff. Those who reached prompt sanctuary on Reno Hill numbered eight wounded troopers, although Reno, in his official report, apparently excluded a lightly wounded G Company man from his total of seven.

The assortment of arm, leg, and body wounds, some serious and some not, occupied Dr. Porter for about an hour, when Herendeen led in the three left behind. Later, the Indian scouts brought in their two wounded, Goose, a Ree, and White Swan, a Crow. The total for Reno's engagement thus came to thirteen.

The difficulty in transporting some of these wounded men contributed its part to the disorganization of the strung-out Weir advance. Four of the five wounded in Company A had to be placed on blankets and each carried by four to six men on foot, while other troopers managed the led horses. Since this monopolized nearly the whole company strength, Captain McDougall turned back with a platoon of his Company B to render aid. Fortunately, the other casualties were able to ride.

The lagging wounded had scarcely gotten into motion under Dr. Porter's watchful eye, when the Weir advance turned into a disorganized retreat. Lt. Mathey picketed the pack mules and the arriving horses in a shallow, central depression on Reno Hill. He also cleared an adjacent hospital area protected by a hasty breasworks improvised from ration boxes and dead animals. In the meantime a horde of hostiles, inspired by their triumph over Custer, laid seige to the command. In the ensuing evening fight on the hill top, Dr. Porter received five more wounded troopers, as well as John S. Wagoner, chief packer. Major Reno, an exceedingly careless man with figures, officially reported that the evening's toll mounted to the absurd figure of forty-six wounded!

At first light of June 26th the Indians re-opened the fight with numbers swelled and enthusiasm renewed. Company H bore the brunt of this day's fight, and having failed to entrench during the night, they sustained nearly half the casualties. Many were light wounds, however, from spent, long-range bullets. Most of the troopers were hit on the skirmish line, but we can pinpoint only nine

TABLE 1. WOUNDED MEN BY EVENTS

ENGAGEMENT	OFF.	EM	OTHER	TOTAL
RENO'S VALLEY FIGHT, June 25				
In timber	0	6	2	8
Retreat to river	0	4	0	4
Scaling bluffs	0	1	0	1
Subtotal	0	11	2	13
HILL TOP FIGHT, June 25	0	5	1	6
HILL TOP FIGHT, June 26				
On skirmish line	1	8	0	9
Benteen's charge	0	1	0	1
Reno's charge	1	0	0	1
Water parties	0	6	0	6
Unidentified (mostly skirmish line)	0	24	0	24
Subtotal	2	39	0	41
GRAND TOTAL	2	54*	3	59*

*Counting the twice-wounded Pvt. Hetler only once.

278

of these, including Benteen's negligible finger wound. The Indians charged so close that the Captain gathered reinforcements from the unofficered pack details from Custer's companies and a platoon of Company M, who then began to share in the casualties.

The flood of wounded men kept Dr. Porter and his attendants frantically busy. Nevertheless, during the height of the action, the Doctor is said to have grabbed a carbine and headed for the skirmish line, but a chorus of protests from his patients turned him back.

To repel the enemy, Benteen led a yelling charge that must have yielded casualties, though we can identify only one of his sergeants wounded. Reno led another charge, in which Lt. Varnum sustained a light leg wound. By this time agonizing cries for water from the hospital area prompted Benteen to organize water parties. Several accounts agree that these sorties brought one death and six wounds, but of the latter we can identify only Pvt. Madden, Company K, who suffered a shattered leg, and a private of Company G.

By the time the battle subsided that afternoon, Dr. Porter's flow of patients for the day reached forty-one, making fifty-nine for the two days. Early the next morning he amputated the shattered leg of Pvt. Madden, using "sanitary whiskey" for anesthetic. Although there are references to two amputations, the second is unidentified, unless it was Pvt. Tanner, Company M, who was severely wounded in Benteen's charge; since he died on the 27th, we have listed him among the killed. The Doctor's surgical assistant was the Ree interpreter, Fred F. Gerard, who had been left behind in the timber and had rejoined the command only the night before. He had often been called upon to play the role of doctor in his twenty-five years as an Indian trader.

At 11 a.m. of June 27th, the Terry-Gibbon column reached Reno Hill to rescue the spent remnants of the 7th Cavalry and bring them the first news of Custer's annihilation. Drs. Williams and Paulding hastened to aid Dr. Porter in looking after his load of patients, usually described as 50 to 52. The afternoon was spent in moving them on blanket stretchers from the offensive hill top to Gibbon's somewhat cleaner camp in the valley.

The medical officers devoted the 28th to the vexing problem of providing transportation to evacuate the wounded. This became a matter of improvization, for there was not a wheeled vehicle in the entire command. The idea of rafting down the Little Big Horn was quickly discarded. General Gibbon suggested hand-stretchers, Dr. Williams Indian travois, and Lt. Gustavus C. Doane, 2nd Cavalry, two-mule litters, with which he had had experience (O-32). By late afternoon, details had readied six two-mule litters and four travois, presumably including the two whipped up by the Indian scouts to carry their own wounded. Crude hand-litters had to be used for the twenty-five others unable to ride.

At 6:30, in the declining heat of the day, the march down the Little Big Horn began. It broke down about midnight, having struggled only 4.64 miles, just the distance to traverse the deserted Indian campsite. It had taken four men to carry one hand-litter and another four to spell them every ten minutes. The wounded groaned and gritted their teeth as the bearers stumbled in the dark over rocks and sage-brush. Dr. Williams summed it up: "The hand-litters proved useless, for the men employed as bearers broke down and sufficient relays could not be had. The travois worked well. The double-mule litters were ineffective, except for luggage, for the animals were so restive that the wounded feared to be placed in the litter. (O-32).

The next day the hand-stretchers were discarded and Dr. Williams supervised the fashioning of six more travois. Lt. Doane, still confident in his mule-litters, set details to making thirteen more, while he combed the mule herd for the most docile animals. As soon as a litter was finished, he formed a crew of four soldiers and two mules and coached them in their jobs. The men had to gentle the mules in their strange rigs, train them to walk in step, and compel them to turn in sequence instead of the simultaneous mode that brought disaster. They soon learned to damp the oscillations of the springy poles when the mules learned to stride in unison.

By 5:30 p.m. the column formed once more to make a short trial of the new rigs in the cool of the evening. Lt. Doane's insistence on hard drill paid off, for the cortege proceeded with gratifying ease compared with the previous day's misery. The latter had been enough to induce six patients to choose the saddle, for only twenty-nine were now being carried. General Terry was so pleased with the results that when couriers arrived with assurance that the *Far West* was ready to accommodate the injured, he ordered the march continued.

Of this successful march, Dr. Williams reported that "19 of the more severely wounded were placed on two-mule litters, 10 on the travois, and 30 of the less severely wounded on horseback. Each mule-litter was attended by four men, one leading the forward mule, one the rear mule, while one walked on either side of the litter to steady the swaying movement of the side poles. Among the gravely wounded on the mule-litters was one amputated at the place of election in the leg [Madden of K], another with a shot perforation of the knee-joint [probably Heyn of A], and four with penetrating wounds of the chest or abdomen [probably King and Reeves of A,

280

Bennett of C, and George of H]. On nearing the bank of the Big Horn, the leading mule of the litter bearing the amputated man knelt down and the patient rolled off, but was, fortunately, uninjured (O-32)."

Extravagant praise for Lieutenant Doane's ingenious litters came from everyone except the medical officers, who preferred the Indian travois constructed with a deep bed placed transversely to the drag poles. So many reports of experiences in transporting wounded during the Sioux War poured in to the Surgeon General's Office that he issued a special review of the reports the next year (O-32). Although there were two schools of thought, the majority of medical officers favored the travois, because it required but one animal, was easier to construct, far easier to manage, and just as comfortable. Surprisingly, it was medical, not line, officers who emphasized the advantage of one versus four attendants in avoiding drastic depletion of the combat force!

As darkness fell on the marching cortege, the sky clouded over and rain began to fall. The trail turned slippery and uncertain, and even Half-Yellow-Face could not find an easy way down the bluff in the pitch darkness. The column halted while dismounted men slid down a ravine to the river. By good fortune they were hailed by pickets from the *Far West*. Captain Freeman set the infantry to building bonfires at intervals along the path to illuminate the descent for the litters. The fifteen-mile march of mercy ended at about 2 P.M. of June 30th, and by dawn the long-suffering wounded were snugly bedded down on the hay-strewn deck of the boat. Walter ("Bub") Burleigh, the steamboat clerk, entered in his log that forty wounded men were stowed aboard (C-12). Our analysis shows forty wounded soldiers evacuated at this time, but also two wounded Indian scouts.

The spent troops went into camp on the river bank and all the walking wounded were left in the sole charge of Dr. Paulding, assisted by 7th Cavalry Attendants Abbotts and Palmer. The next day when the hospital ship left for the Yellowstone at 1:40 P.M., Drs. Williams and Porter were aboard, and presumably Stewards Dale and Rhinehart and Attendant Pandtle. Two additional attendants were assigned, as revealed by Terry's special order of August 2nd: "The verbal orders of July 1, 1876, detaching the following enlisted men for duty with the hospital, is hereby confirmed, to take effect from that date: Pvt. Hobart Ryder, Co. M, 7th Cavalry, Pvt. Mark E. Lee, Co. I, 7th Cavalry." The date of July 1st is significant, for at that time the *Far West* was anchored at Fort Pease, while the 7th Cavalry was still marching down the Big Horn. These two men,

281

therefore, must have accompanied the wounded on the boat.

In a few hours of breakneck navigation Captain Marsh took his hospital ship down to the base camp at Fort Pease. But there it had to wait several days for the troops to march down overland. On July 1st, Corp. George H. King died of his wounds, as recorded in Terry's diary and in clerk Burleigh's log. The next day all the wounded were painfully carried ashore in order to enable the boat to ferry the overland column when it arrived that afternoon. The walking wounded were assigned to a separate 7th Cavalry hospital area, but on July 4th Terry ordered the two hospitals consolidated under Dr. Willaims.

Forty-two patients were reloaded aboard the steamboat on the morning of July 3rd. The injured White Swan was left ashore in the care of his Crow tribesmen, but the consumptive Sgt. Rigney of the 7th Infantry took his place. For the first leg of the coming voyage, Dr. Porter would be the sole medical officer on the boat. Although the records are silent, probably Stewards Dale and Rhinehart and Attendants Pandtle and Lee sailed with him. Others may have been drawn from the headquarters company which continued to serve as boat guard.

It was not until noon of July 3rd that Captain Marsh received orders to cast off for his memorable voyage of mercy to the hospital at Fort Abraham Lincoln. His craft had churned the waters under a full head of steam for only a few hours, when Pvt. William George of Company H died of his wounds. As usual, the boat tied up for the brief black hours of the summer night. The next morning, having made 164 river-miles, the boat nosed in to the Powder River depot. Its unexpected arrival transformed a centennial 4th of July celebration into a funeral service for Pvt. George.

Pvt. William Farley of Company H went ashore to the depot hospital, while the convalescent Pvt. David McWilliams of the same company, whose enlistment was about to expire, took his vacated berth on the boat. The 7th Cavalrymen detached to the depot gathered up the personal effects of their officers killed in action and placed them aboard for delivery to bereaved families. To the considerable relief of the over-burdened Dr. Porter, Dr. Ashton boarded to help serve the floating hospital for the remainder of the voyage.

Captain Marsh swung the *Far West* out into the current again, heading for Fort Buford, 235 river-miles distant. Reaching there early on July 5th, he paused only long enough to drop off the consumptive Sgt. Rigney. Pushing on into the broader waters of the Missouri, the boat made full steam for Bismarck, now but 310 river-miles distant. On passing Fort Berthold, Goose was given over to the care of his tribesmen. At 3 P.M. that afternoon another patient succumbed to his wounds, Pvt. James C. Bennett of Company C, but his body was retained on board. At 11 P.M. of July 5th the *Far West*, hastily draped in improvised mourning, tied up at the Bismarck wharf. The good Captain had driven his craft, crew, and precious cargo 709 miles in 59 hours, including tie-ups at night, calls at posts, and stops for wood. His record-smashing trip had maintained an average of 12 miles an hours.

The burden of tragic news carried so swiftly by the steamboat abruptly roused the sleeping frontier town and then spread across the river to the fort. The local presses were soon turning out "extras" and the telegraph office was flashing the news to a shocked nation. The next morning the two doctors delivered their thirty-seven wounded men, one sick man, and one lifeless body to the alerted post hospital at Fort Abraham Lincoln.

The shaken Dr. Middleton, with the simple eloquence imposed by the limited space in the ledger containing his Medical History of the post, captured the whole tragic story in five brief sentences:

> July 6. The Str. Far West arrived this morning, bringing terrible news from the expedition and 38 wounded men for treatment in the hospital. Genl. Custer with his command met an overwhelming force of Indians on the Little Big Horn about 20 miles above its mouth and five companies, or all belonging to them who were in action, were completely cut to pieces, not one man being left. Drs. Porter and Ashton accompanied the wounded.
>
> This has been a very gloomy day at the post. There are 24 women here who have been made widows by the disaster.

Chapter 24
The Quick and the Dead

The more basic and elementary the question asked about the Battle of the Little Big Horn, the less likely it is to have received a satisfactory answer. What was the strength of Custer's full command on that fateful day? How many were raw recruits? How many fought in the separate engagements that made up the over-all battle? How many were killed in the several fights? How many were missing and rumored to have been captured and tortured? These relevant questions have never been answered except in speculative fashion.

Battle statistics of this kind are usually assembled from troop returns and muster rolls. The monthly returns name only those soldiers absent on the last day of the month, specifying when, where, and why; they also list by name all alterations (gains and losses) during the month, giving dates and reasons; they add a tabular summary of the number present and absent by company, rank, and reason. By contrast, the bi-monthly muster rolls provide a full roster of names, with enlistment dates and notations of duty status of those present and absent; they name alterations for the preceding two months and add a tabular summary. Every second month the returns and rolls coincide in time (June 30th, for example) and should agree in information.

Custer's command included the 7th Cavalry (officers and enlisted men) and others (enlisted Indian scouts, quartermaster employees, and citizens). The monthly quartermaster reports of persons hired, the returns and rolls for the enlisted scouts, and those for all but Custer's battalion of five companies of 7th Cavalry are adequate for the compilation of battle statistics. A frustrating problem arises, however, in the case of Custer's five companies; since the responsible officers and non-commissioned officers were killed, these records are incomplete. An official reconstruction was limited to the essential identification of total battle losses, without identification of men detached in the field before the battle. This deficiency in the records has left the battle statistics in limbo.

The standard procedure for compiling battle statistics subtracts detached persons from regimental strength to yield battle strength; subtracts battle survivors from battle strength to yield battle losses; subtracts body counts (not given on returns and rolls) from battle losses to yield the missing. This whole sequence is stymied when detached persons are unidentified. Fortunately, there is a reverse procedure that adds battle losses to battle survivors to yield battle strength and then subtracts battle strength from regimental strength to yield detached persons. Surprisingly enough, in the present instance a combing of all available sources provides sufficient information to apply this reverse procedure successfully.

Aggregate Battle Statistics

The returns, rolls, and supplementary information on the non-cavalry components of Custer's command are adequate to provide full battle statistics by the standard procedure. These are presented in the right half of Table 2. Campaign strength and detachments are omitted, since there were transfers between Fort Lincoln and between Gibbon's command. Their battle strength totalled fifty, but only fifteen were still present on Reno Hill on June 27th. Ten were killed and buried, leaving twenty-five missing. These, of course, were twenty-one Rees (officially listed as missing) and four Crows (officially listed as deserted). The Rees promptly reported for duty at the Powder River depot, and the Crows later resumed duty at the Big Horn base camp.

The other half of Table 2 presents the figures for the 7th Cavalry, using the reverse procedure for Custer's five companies. The returns and rolls agree that the regimental strength was 46 officers and 790 men, but that 13 officers and 72 men did not serve on the campaign for a variety of reasons. Our interest is in the resulting campaign strength of 33 officers and 718 men. Beside a substantial officer shortage, the men thus averaged only 58 per company, instead of the 70 authorized at that time.

The partially reconstructed records identified total battle losses as those whose names had appeared on the rosters before the battle, but not after, corrected for those whose loss was not battle-connected. Labeled as killed in action, they came to 16 officers and 237 men (line 9 in the table); to this we have also added five troopers who died of wounds from July to October, to yield an ultimate total of 258 (line 10).

To complete the table we must now provide figures for battle surivivors and burials (body counts). When the former was reported to General Terry, probably on June 27th, he recorded it in the back of his diary; following the names of the fifteen surviving officers appears the notation, "Remaining men wounded and unwounded, 329". This is confirmed by Adjutant Smith, whose newspaper dispatch of July 1st mentioned that "the number saved with Reno was 329, including fifty-one wounded." This crucial figure is entered in line 4.

On June 28th, the surviving 7th Cavalry conducted a systematic search for bodies and buried them. The next day, General Gibbon, while touring the Custer field, found and buried two more bodies, those of reporter Kellogg and a nameless trooper. When Adjutant Smith reached Bismarck on the *Far West*, he wired headquarters in St. Paul on July 6th (Chicago *Tribune* for July 7th) that "261 dead have been buried." His newspaper dispatch of July 1st also mentioned that "two hundred and sixty-one bodies have been buried from General Custer's and Major Reno's commands. The last found was that of Mr. Kellogg." This crucial figure is entered in line 6. These entries permit the remainder of the table to be completed by calculation.

It is now evident that two officers (Quartermaster Nowlan and Veterinary Surgeon Stein) and 152 troopers were detached in the field to leave a battle strength of only 31 officers and 566 men, the latter averaging a mere 47 per company. Even with fifty auxiliaries, Custer approached the hostile village with a total of only 647 persons. This was hardly a formidable force to throw against two thousand desperate warriors defending their women and children, to say nothing of their way of life. It is ironic that in the preceding February, General Terry had telegraphed for reinforcements on the grounds that the 550 available 7th Cavalrymen were "not sufficient for the end in view." Neither were 566!

It is now evident, also, that the burial details missed no more than two bodies of dead troopers on the several fields of action. This scotches once and for all the claims that 20 to 42 troopers were missing from the Custer field, and the blood-chilling inference that they had been captured and burned at the stake by the red fiends! These claims of many missing men either referred to the temporarily

286

Table 2
Aggregate Battle Statistics

	7th CAV.			OTHER*				GRAND
	OFF.	EM	TOT.	EIS	QME	CIT.	TOT.	TOTAL
1. Campaign strength, May 17	33	718	751					
2. Field detachments, June 10-22	2	152	154					
3. Battle strength, June 25	31	566	597	35	13	2	50	647
4. Present, June 27	15	329	344	8	7	0	15	359
5. Apparent losses, June 27	16	237	253	27	6	2	35	288
6. Burials, June 28-9	-	251	251	2	6	2	10	261
7. Apparent missing, June 29	-	-	2	25	0	0	25	27
8. Battle survivors, June 27	15	329	344	33	7	0	40	384
9. Killed in action, June 25-6	16	237	253	2	6	2	10	263
10. Killed and died of wounds, Nov.	16	242	258	2	6	2	10	268

* EIS = enlisted Indian scouts
  QME = quartermaster employees
  CIT = citizens

missing, but healthy and free, Indian scouts, or merely reflected ignorance as to the large number of men detached in the field before the battle.

Breakdown by Companies

By resorting to the reverse procedure it has proved possible to break down the aggregate statistics by company and by names. Table 3 summarizes the figures by companies for field detachments, battle strength, and killed in action.

First, we must outline the measures used to identify by name the survivors of Custer's five companies. Wounds and Medal of Honor awards identified one group. An exhaustive search of battle accounts and Reno Court of Inquiry testimony identified another group. A few could be spotted by their assignments to special duty (departmental and regimental order books), such as fatigue details, all other members of which were present, as would be expected. The largest number, however, consisted of men whose names appear on the Reno petition.

The Reno petition of July 4th opens with the clause, "We, the enlisted men, the survivors of the Battle of the Heights of the Little Big Horn on the 25th and 26th of June, 1876, of the 7th Regiment of Cavalry, who subscribe our names . . ." This is an unmistakable declaration that the 235 appended names were intended to include only battle survivors. If padding had been the intent, hundreds of both legitimate and illegitimate names could have been added. But only 81% of the names of legitimate survivors, still present on July 4th, appear, and not a single name of the legitimate survivors who had been evacuated on the *Far West*. No names of men absent at Powder River are included. Of 207 names from the non-Custer companies that can be easily checked, only three were illegitimate, although the trio were present at the signing. All this is powerful evidence that a conscientious effort was made to meet the qualifications of the opening clause (M-31). We infer, therefore, that the 28 names from the Custer companies were all legitimate survivors.

Since the petition asked that Reno be promoted to Lieutenant Colonel (and Benteen to Major), there have been attempts to discredit the document. It was even submitted to the FBI for a comparison of petition and payroll signatures, some of which were reported different. This is a finding of no significance, since it can not possibly reveal the true sentiments of the man whose name appears

Table 3
7th Cavalry Statistics by Company

	DETACHED			BATTLE STRENGTH					SURVIVED			KILLED		
	OFF.	EM	TOT.	OFF.	EM	TOT.	Ro*	Ra*	OFF.	EM	TOT.	OFF.	EM	TOT.
HQ & STAFF	2	17	19	6	2	8	0	0	2	0	2	4	2	6
Right Wing														
Co. A	0	4	4	3	47	50	11	0	3	39	42	0	8	8
Co. D	0	11	11	2	50	52	12	0	2	47	49	0	3	3
Co. G	0	16	16	2	43	45	0	9	1	30	31	1	13	14
Co. H	0	2	2	2	45	47	8	0	2	42	44	0	3	3
Co. K	0	21	21	2	41	43	0	2	2	36	38	0	5	5
Co. M	0	6	6	2	55	57	25	0	2	43	45	0	12	12
Total	0	60	60	13	281	294	56	11	12	237	249	1	44	45
Left Wing														
Co. B	0	21	21	2	45	47	1	10	1	43	44	1	2	3
Co. C	0	11	11	2	49	51	23	1	0	13	13	2	36	38
Co. E	0	9	9	2	45	47	6	0	0	8	8	2	37	39
Co. F	0	15	15	2	46	48	11	0	0	10	10	2	36	38
Co. I	0	9	9	2	45	47	7	0	0	9	9	2	36	38
Co. L	0	10	10	2	53	55	13	0	0	9	9	2	44	46
Total	0	75	75	12	283	295	61	11	1	92	93	11	191	202
Grand Total	2	152	154	31	566	597	117	22	15	329	344	16	237	253

* Ro = October recruits
  Ra = April recruits

289

on the document. Even if all were forged, and all were averse to the petition sentiment, it would not affect their status as battle survivors.

These several means, which often overlapped but never contradicted, served to identify forty-nine battle survivors from Custer's five companies. This is precisely the number required to reach the aggregate total of 329. The minimum number for any company is eight, including one non-commissioned officer, which more than meets the pack train details. In the case of Company C, every man not identified as survivor can be directly identified as detached, and this applies to many men in the other companies. Having thus established battle survivors, it becomes possible to identify field detachments and battle strengths, as summarized in Table 2.

A total of 152 troopers, including the band, were detached in the field between June 10th and 22nd. The records, supplemented by inferences from duty status, identify 131 men detached to the Powder River depot on June 15th, including an inadequate few from Custer's five companies left behind on June 10th, when Reno's reconnaissance departed. Three more can be identified as detached at the mouth of the Rosebud on June 22nd. This leaves eighteen men, all from companies E, F, I, and L, of Custer's battalion, who were detached but without certainty as to when or where. Many were certainly left at Powder River on June 10th, and a few must have been detached to the *Far West* on the 22nd, for Sgt. Wilson officially recorded that aboard were "some soldiers left in charge of property belonging to the absent portion of the command." These could only have come from Reno's reconnaissance, for the left wing left its property at Powder River, and Gibbon's column left its at Fort Pease. It is not improbable that Terry commandeered such men as a headquarters squad, since he had assigned his headquarters company to guard the *Far West*. Significantly, the need for this squad would have terminated when the entire command returned to the boat on June 30th, in time to be reported present for the muster taken that afternoon.

It has been widely believed, in accordance with testimony given at the Reno Inquiry, that on June 25th the 7th Cavalry was loaded with raw recruits. The usually judicious Col. William A. Graham wrote, on the authority of Godfrey and Edgerly, that "the companies contained from 30 to 40% recruits without prior service (M-22)." Such statements are misleading at best and false at worst. In order to clarify the issue, we must define terms as we shall use them.

In 1876 military training was rudimentary by modern standards. Reliance was placed on organization and discipline, rather

290

than on individual combat skills. Incidentally, the Indian practiced the reverse policy; warriors were less organized and disciplined, but far more proficient in fighting skills. At frontier posts the heavy burden of house-keeping chores left little time for even disciplinary drills. For years a general order limited the ammunition allowance to ten rounds per man! In 1876 even this extravagance was firmly squelched. Furthermore, battle experience was a rarity. Over the preceding five years the 7th Cavalry had been engaged but twice, and only portions at that.

In such a context, we shall call a soldier with less than six months service a "raw" recruit, and one with more a "trained" recruit. After five years of service we shall call him a "veteran," whether battle-tried or not. We shall use these terms in quotes, so as not to mislead anyone who might prefer other definitions.

During the eight months preceding the campaign, the 7th Cavalry received two consignments of recruits. The 160 men delivered from October through December of 1975 (all but five in October), we shall label October recruits. Col. Edward Luce found from service records that 48% of this consignment had either five years of prior service or Civil War experience (M-49). By our definitions, then, half of these were "veterans" and half "trained" recruits by June 25th. The 69 recruits delivered from January through April of 1876 (all but four in April), we shall label April recruits. Since their service records remain unchecked, we arbitrarily *assume*, to be on the safe side, that one-fourth were "veterans" and the rest "raw" recruits.

Among the 718 troopers who constituted the campaign strength of the regiment, there were 19% October and 10% April recruits, which translate to 9% "trained" and 7% "raw." Since many of these were detached in the field, especially the unmounted April recruits assigned almost entirely to Companies B, G, and K, the battle strength of 566 troopers included 20% October and 4% April recruits (Table 3). These figures translate to 11% "trained" and 3% "raw," pehaps still too high, since the "rawest" were undoubtedly chosen for detachment.

These figures certainly deflate the claim that the 7th Cavalry had been singularly saddled with raw recruits.

Fatalities by Events

The available evidence is sufficient to pinpoint by name the events in which every officer and "other" died. Problems arise only in the case of enlisted troopers, some of whom were detached from their companies at the time of the battle as pack train details, orderlies, couriers, stragglers, etc.

The first problem is to determine whether any of the 191 dead troopers from Custer's five companies and headquarters staff were detached to fall elsewhere than in the Custer engagement. The company records date every one of these fatalities June 25th, suggesting, though not proving, that all fell with Custer. At this stage of the analysis, the supporting evidence is merely negative; not a single hint to the contrary could be uncovered.

The second problem is to determine whether any of the 46 dead troopers from the seven non-Custer companies were detached to die with Custer. There is positive evidence that two Company K troopers did so; Lt. Godfrey named Sgt. Hughes as Custer's flag-bearer, and stated that a Corporal was detached as hospital steward, clearly Corp. Callahan, assigned to Dr. Lord. Battle accounts, testimony and recorded dates establish that few of the remaining 44 could have fallen with Custer, but we can go even further on the following evidence.

Reno appended the first casualty table to his note to Terry written on the morning of June 27th (quoted in Chapter 15). Although he excluded the entire right wing, even though its pack details and escort Company B were with him, the table is invaluable, for knowing nothing of Custer's command at the time, none of the 38 left wing fatalities he tabulated could have occurred with Custer. This leaves only six to be accounted for individually.

Reno omitted one fatality and added an extra wounded man for Company M; this was clearly Pvt. Tanner, recorded as wounded on the 26th and dying on the 27th. He also omitted one fatality for Company D; this was clearly Farrier Vincent Charley, wounded and abandoned on the Weir advance, whose fate was not yet known. Reno also omitted a third fatality from Company K besides the two detached to Custer; Lt. Godfrey mentioned a third man detached as Dr. DeWolf's orderly, undoubtedly Pvt. Helmer, killed in isolation with the Doctor thus leaving his fate as yet unknown. Reno omitted one fatality from Company G, whom we have identified as Pvt. Rapp because he was similarly omitted from another roster of the dead compiled before July 1st but not published until July 26th in the New York *Herald*. We believe Rapp was one of thirteen troopers left behind in the timber with Herendeen, who led only eleven back to Reno Hill, since two had become separated. One of these was Pvt. Goldin, who returned alone ahead of the others to be found by Sgt. Culbertson in the brush beside the river; the second must have been Rapp, ultimately killed in the timber and his fate as yet unknown. Finally, Reno failed to list two fatalities in right wing Company B, but Pvt. Dorn was killed on the 26th and Pvt. Mack on the 25th, probably though not certainly in the hill-top fight that evening.

If we now add the known fatalities among officers and "others," our analysis yields 263 total killed, 210 with Custer and 53 elsewhere. Since the total is fixed, a confirmation of either subgroup confirms both subgroups. Such confirmation is found in the burial counts. Lt. Godfrey's narrative gives a total burial count of 265 and 212 for the Custer field; though both are slightly excessive, the difference of 53 for the non-Custer burials confirms our analysis exactly. We have also found nine burial counts for the Custer field alone; when corrected for the omission of the two late finds of June 27th and for omission of "others" when indicated, they range from 208 to 214, with a definite mode at 208. Since the official total burial count was 261, the difference of 53 for the non-Custer burials again confirms our analysis precisely. There is the further implication that if two bodies were missed, they fell with Custer.

Table 4, which summarizes fatalities by events, thus presents our first conclusion, that 210 were killed in the Custer engagement and 53 in other events, with reassuringly little error.

The table further presents the breakdown by events for non-Custer fatalities. The available evidence proved sufficient for this purpose, except in the case of Company G. For this company we had to settle for the uncertain but perfectly reasonable results yielded by assuming that every mention referred to a *different* trooper. Burial counts provide only rough confirmation. For example, Pvt. William White learned that eighteen bodies had been buried on the night of the 26th and the next morning; this would cover our twelve on the hill top and six of the thirteen on the east bank. Matt Carroll and Lt. Johnson recorded finding twenty-five bodies on Reno's valley field when the Montana column camped there; this approximates our twenty-seven on the west bank. Edgerly's 1881 narrative and Freeman's diary mention forty bodies of Reno's men buried after the Custer field had been policed; this checks our total for Reno's valley fight.

Strengths and Casualties by Engagements

Our ultimate goal is to identify the battle strengths and casualties for each of the several engagements. We have already made these breakdowns for killed and wounded. We must now attempt the same for battle assignments of every trooper. Although there

Table 4
Fatalities by Events

	OFF.	EM	OTHER	TOTAL
Custer's engagement, June 25	13	193	4	210
Reno's engagement, June 25				
Open skirmish line	0	2	0	2
In the timber	0	7	2	9
Run to the river	1	14	1	16
Scaling bluff, east bank	2	9	2	13
Subtotal	3	32	5	40
The Weir advance, June 25	0	1	0	1
Hill top fight, June 25	0	4	1	5
Hill top fight, June 26				
On skirmish line	0	5	0	5
In Benteen's charge	0	1	0	1
On Water parties	0	1	0	1
Subtotal	0	7	0	7
Non-Custer Total	3	44	6	53
Grand Total	16	237	10	263

can never be a guarantee of completeness, we have taken into account the following categories of men separated from their companies at the time of the battle: a) Seven men per company assigned to company pack mules, b) Four men assigned to headquarters pack mules (two from L and one each from F and I), c) Seven stragglers from Custer's battalion who reached Reno Hill (five from C and one each from F and I), d) Fourteen men displaced as couriers and/or by special duty (five from K, two from I, and one each from A, C, E, F, H, and L). The results of this final analysis are assembled in Table 5 for the sequence of separate engagements.

It is apparent that Reno's valley fight was a far costlier affair then the Major was willing to admit. Although he testified that his battle strength was only 139 persons (121 military and 27 scouts), we find that it was 175 (140 military and 35 scouts). The fight took a toll of forty killed and thirteen wounded, to say nothing of the missing. The number left in the timber reveals the disorganized start of the retreat; the heavy casualties on the run back to the hill top, and the high ratio of killed to wounded, reveal that it degenerated into a panic, even though a temporary one. In his official report, Reno claimed that "he succeeded in reaching the top of the bluff with a loss of three officers and twenty-nine enlisted men, and seven men wounded." He not only understated his killed and wounded, but ignored the missing and the non-military personnel.

The hill top fight on the evening of the 25th was a different story, though Reno chose to misrepresent it. The arrival of the other battalions swelled the battle strength to 367 (353 military and 14 others), and the casualties were limited to five killed and six wounded. Yet Reno officially reported that "we held our ground with a loss of 18 enlisted men killed and forty-six wounded, until the attack ceased at about 9 p.m." Why Reno made this absurd claim is moot, but how he obtained his figures is clear; he subtracted his false claim of casualties in the valley fight from his total of 47 killed and 53 wounded among the non-Custer companies, thus compressing two days' casualties into one evening and throwing in four deaths of detached men from Company K!

Since all but Benteen's Company H were well dug in for the hill top fight of the second day, there were only seven killed, two beyond the skirmish line in charges and water parties. But there were six wounds for each death, mostly among Benteen's company and the reinforcements he drew from Company M and Custer's pack details. The high proportion of light wounds apparently came from spent bullets fired from distant high points.

The foregoing analysis deflates a whole series of excuses fab-

295

Table 5
Battle Strength and Casualties by Engagements

	OFF.	EM	OTHER	TOTAL
A. Reno's valley fight, June 25				
1. Battle strength	11	129	35	175
2. Killed	3	32	5	40
3. Survived	8	97	30	135
a. Wounded	0	11	2	13
b. Left in timber one hour	0	12	1	13
c. Left in timber till June 27	1	1	2	4
d. Missing for days	0	0	20	20
B. Custer's Fight, June 25				
1. Initial strength	13	200	8	221
a. Straggled back to Reno Hill	0	7	0	7
b. Sent back, missing for days	0	0	4	4
2. Battle strength and killed	13	193	4	210
C. Weir advance, June 25				
1. Battle strength (including wounded)	14	340	14	368
a. Reno's battalion	7	96	8	111
b. Custer stragglers	0	7	0	7
c. Benteen's battalion	5	110	0	115
d. McDougall's battalion (one Ree missing)	2	127	6	135
2. Killed	0	1	0	1
D. Hill top fight, June 25				
1. Battle strength (including wounded)	14	339	14	367
2. Killed	0	4	1	5
3. Wounded	0	5	1	6
E. Hill top seige, June 26				
1. Battle strength (including wounded)	14	335	13	362
2. Killed	0	7	0	7
3. Survived	14	328	13	355
a. Wounded	2	39	0	41

ricated to explain how a horde of "savages" so decisively defeated a "whole" regiment of crack U.S. Cavalry. On June 25th, the regiment was only at two-thirds strength, and divided into four separate commands. Reno's initial mounted charge was launched by 129 troopers. Custer's later and distant attack was made with 193 mounted troopers. The remaining 244 men, being far in the rear, never participated in an attack. There is no longer any point in exaggerating the proportion of recruits in the regiment. It is no longer necessary to inflate the number of warriors beyond the total population of the tribes involved, nor to pretend that every brave carried an inexhaustible supply of ammunition for his new repeating rifle and brace of six-shooters, all supplied by traitorous Indian agents.

When the Indians outnumbered the mounted cavalry ten to one, as on Custer Hill, they clobbered the troopers. When they outnumbered dismounted and entrenched troopers four to one, as on Reno Hill, the honors were more even.

Chapter 25
A Little Big Horn Chronology

Custer's four independent columns, in making their fourteen-mile approaches to the hostile village, pursued several paths at different speeds to weave an intricate pattern of motion in time and space. These intricacies have been thoroughly blurred by the exasperating discrepancies in clock-times, speeds, and routes that characterize the accounts of battle participants. Although the Reno Court of Inquiry strove to clarify these very features, the testimony proved so contradictory as to compound the confusion.

The discrepancies stemmed from a variety of sources. Fading memory played an important role in confusing landmarks and mileages, although there are instances of deliberate misrepresentation. The wide discrepancies in clock-times largely arose from the fact that standardized time-zones were not then in vogue. The available watches were not all set alike, and those lacking watches, or too busy to glance at them, relied on sun-time. The watch of the official itinerist, Lt. Wallace, was apparently set to Chicago time, an hour fast by present time-zones, and an hour and twenty minutes fast in sun-time because of the twenty degree difference in longitude. Fortunately, estimates of time-intervals are less disparate than clock-times.

In constructing the chronology here offered, the clock-times have all been adjusted to Wallace's official watch. For directions, mileages, and geographical landmarks we have relied on modern topographical maps. For ephemeral landmarks we have had to depend on participant accounts. We have utilized all known contacts between columns, both visual and by courier, as checks on relative positions. But in a kinematic analysis of this sort, the most powerful tool is the inexorable constraint imposed by the simple rule that distance, divided by time, yields speed. In applying this constraint, it is useful to know that the standard cavalry walk covered three miles in an hour, the trot six, and the gallop nine.

It is convenient to begin with the relevant geography, starting at the halt, about one-third of a mile beyond the divide, where Custer made battalion assignments. The point of this halt can be located on the map as very close to the head of a principal branch of Reno Creek, which we shall call the Middle Fork. At this point the stream flows nearly north, but soon arcs to the west to join the Little Big Horn about 12.5 miles from the halt. The hostile *village*, extending for several miles along the west bank of the river, began just over two miles below the mouth of Reno Creek. *Reno Hill* was about one mile below the creek mouth on the east bank, and *Custer Hill* was four miles farther downstream on the same side.

At four and at seven miles below the halt, minor tributaries, flowing in narrow valleys separated by high divides, enter the Middle Fork from the southeast, more or less parallel with the head of Middle Fork. At eight miles below the halt, the Middle Fork joins the South Fork, making what we shall call the *upper forks*. After three more miles, the North Fork joins to form what we shall call the *lower forks*. After a final one and a half miles, Reno Creek enters the Little Big Horn just below a natural *ford* of the latter.

The first key ephemeral landmark encountered on descending the Middle Fork was a *morass*. Lt. Mathey, in charge of the pack train, located it four or five miles below the halt; Captain McDougall, commanding the pack train escort, located it four miles above the upper forks, which also places it four miles below the halt. This point is clearly just below the mouth of the first minor tributary mentioned above, and we shall fix the morass at 4.5 miles below the halt.

The next key ephemeral landmark mentioned by many participants was a deserted village site at a forks, marked by a *lone tepee* containing the body of a brave killed in Crook's Rosebud fight. In establishing which fork this was, we must avoid testimony from those who accompanied the Reno-Custer battalions, for special events confused them, as we shall see. Lt. Mathey located the tepee 7 to 8, and 7.5 miles below the halt, and Captain McDougall 8 miles below the halt. Benteen located it 4.5 miles above the ford, and therefore 9 miles from the halt. The tepee thus stood at the upper forks, a location confirmed by White-Man-Runs-Him, the Crow scout whom General Hugh L. Scott interviewed on the very scene in 1919. The Crow clearly distinguished the two forks and specifically located

299

the tepee at the upper one.

Having established these key landmarks, we now turn to the few clock-times that Wallace read from his watch. The last time notation in his official itinerary is the crossing of the divide at 12 noon. He also testified from official memoranda, that the halt was called at 12:05 p.m. This five-minute march at a walk locates the halt about one-third of a mile beyond the divide. He similarly testified that the march was resumed at 12:12 p.m., except for the pack train, which McDougall testified left twenty minutes later, at 12:32 p.m. Finally, Wallace testified that he looked at his watch at two later times. The first was at 2:00 p.m., when Custer waved Reno across to join him on the right bank about half a mile above the lone tepee; this implied that they had covered 7.5 miles in an hour and forty-eight minutes at an average pace of 4.26 m.p.h., which is reasonable enough. The second was at 4:00 p.m., when Wallace recrossed the river on Reno's retreat to the bluffs. All the remainder of Wallace's times are guesses that are contradictory and incompatible with distances and speeds. But Lt. Godfrey recorded a watch reading of 4:20 p.m., which he finally decided referred to the arrival of Benteen's battalion at Reno Hill. This checks so nicely with Wallace's clock-times, that their watches must have been set alike.

Working within the foregoing framework of geography, landmarks, and clock-times, we have applied the distance-time-speed constraint to information from participants as a means of constructing chronologies for all four columns that are consistent both within and between columns. These are presented in Table 6 in full detail, displaying clock-times, time-intervals, mileages, and speeds. Such reconstructions can never be definitive, and the principal merit of these is the full exposure of detail and methodology that should facilitate refinements on the basis of better ideas or additional information. We shall not trace through these chronologies, but allow an interested reader to study them at his leisure. We shall, however, discuss three major revelations that emerge from them.

The first discovery was that at the lone tepee on the upper forks Custer merely ordered Reno to take the lead with the scouts and step up the pace, and that it was not until a half hour later, when both battalions reached the lower forks, that Adjutant Cooke brought Reno orders from Custer to attack the village two miles ahead.

The evidence for this is very strong. The lone tepee was 6.5 miles from the village by the dog-leg route followed and 5 miles in a bee-line, and no one had yet sighted the village tepees. Hence these particular orders could not have been given at the lone tepee, and

300

would have been premature in any case. By contrast, the lower forks were only 3.5 dog-leg and 2.5 bee-line miles from the village, which by that time had been sighted from a knoll. White-Man-Runs-Him, who so clearly distinguished the two forks for General Scott, also specifically identified the lower forks as the ones where Reno received his attack order. This is confirmed by Reno himself in his official report of July 5th: "As we approached . . . one standing tepee about 11 a.m., Custer motioned me to cross to him, which I did, and moved nearer to his column until 12:30 a.m. [Sic!], when Lt. Cooke, adjutant, came to me and said the village was only two miles above . . . and to charge . . ." Reno's slip of the pen has usually been corrected to 12:30 p.m., instead of to the now obvious 11:30 a.m. In this half hour, the two columns would have trotted the three miles from the upper to the lower forks.

By the time of the Reno Inquiry, faded memories had confused the witnesses, but a careful reading of Reno's and Wallace's testimonies reveal an interval of ambiguous duration and mileage between the order to take the lead and the order to attack. Other witnesses failed to distinguish these separate but similar events that transpired at separate but similar locations, collapsed everything to one fork or the other. This effect of a dimming memory is nicely illustrated in the successive accounts of scout Herendeen. In his early dispatch of July 7th he located the lone tepee 3-5 miles above the ford (i.e., at the upper forks), where he said Custer merely ordered Reno to push ahead with the scouts. But later at the Reno Inquiry he testified that he was standing by the tepee, about a mile from the ford (i.e., at the lower forks), when he heard Custer order Reno "to charge the Indians and he would support him,"

The resolution of this confusion delays Reno's charge, engagement, and retreat beyond Wallace's garbled estimates, so that it now nicely fits the evidence of cross-sightings with both Custer's and Benteen's battalions.

The route of Benteen's approach has always been shrouded in mystery, partly because most of his officers gave jumbled accounts (including Godfrey), but mostly because of Benteen's deliberate misrepresentations. He testified under oath that Custer's "senseless orders" had sent him "valley hunting ad infinitum," and that if he had not possessed the genius to "violate his orders" after wandering "ten miles" into the boondocks, he might have ended up "at Fort Benton." The resort to such persiflage to account for his prolonged absence raises the strong suspicion that he alone was responsible for the delay. In fact, it proved a simple matter to penetrate the conscience-stricken captain's verbal smoke-screen.

Table 6. Four Column Chronology

	clock	miles	min.	mph	cum. miles
A. RENO-CUSTER APPROACH					
Leave halt near divide	12:12	-	-	-	0
Pass morass	1:20	4.5	68	4.0	4.5
Reno joins Custer on right bank	2:00	3.0	40	4.5	7.5
Pass lone tepee; Reno takes advance	2:07	0.5	7	4.3	8.0
Pass lower forks; Reno ordered to attack	2:37	3.0	30	6.0	11.0
B. RENO'S ATTACK					
Trots and gallops to ford	2:50	1.5	13	7.0	12.5
Fords river and reforms	2:55	-	5	-	-
Charges and halts (saw Custer on bluff)	3:10	2.0	15	8.0	14.5
Moves into timber	3:20	-	10	-	-
Starts retreat from timber	3:55	-	45	-	-
Lt. Wallace re-crosses river	4:00	-	-	-	-
Advance reaches Reno Hill	4:05	1.5	10	10.0	16.0
Rear reaches Reno Hill (seen by Benteen)	4:10	-	5	-	-
C. CUSTER'S ATTACK					
Waters in North Fork	2:45	-	8	-	-
Reaches first lookout; sees Reno charge	3:00	1.5	15	6.0	12.5
Returns to column; sends Kanipe back	3:05	-	5	-	-
Reaches Weir Point; sees Reno engaged	3:15	1.0	10	6.0	13.5
Returns to column; sends Martin back	3:20	-	5	-	-
In Medicine Tail Coulee; first shots?	3:45	2.5	25	6.0	16.0

D. BENTEEN'S APPROACH

Event	Time				
Leaves halt at divide on left oblique	12:12	-	-	-	0
Joins Custer trail; sees train ½ mi. above	1:42	5.0	90	3.3	5.0
Trots to morass	1:48	0.5	5	6.0	5.5
Leaves morass as train arrives	2:03	-	15	-	-
Walks to lone tepee	3:13	3.5	70	3.0	9.0
Meets Kanipe (3.25 mi. in 33 min.@5.9mph)	3:38	1.25	25	3.0	10.25
Meets Martin (3.25 mi. in 33 min.@5.9mph)	3:53	1.00	15	4.0	11.25
Trots to near ford; sees rear of Reno retreat	4:10	1.75	17	6.2	13.0
Reaches Reno Hill	4:20	1.0	10	6.0	14.0

E. PACK TRAIN APPROACH

Event	Time				
Leaves halt near divide	12:32	-	-	-	0
Advances 3.5 mi.; seen by Benteen	1:42	3.5	70	3.0	3.5
Reaches morass as Benteen leaves	2:02	1.0	20	3.0	4.5
Leaves morass	2:22	-	20	-	-
Passes lone tepee	3:32	3.5	70	3.0	8.0
Kanipe arrives (¾ mi. in 10 min.@4.5mph)	3:42	0.5	10	3.0	8.5
Halts to close up	3:57	-	15	-	-
Lt. Hare arrives (1.5 mi. in 10 min@9mph)	4:50	3.0	53	3.4	11.5
Ammo. mules reach Reno Hill	(5:10	1.5	20	4.5	(13.0)
Pack train reached Reno Hill	5:15	1.5	25	3.6	13.0

Lt. Frank Gibson, Benteen's own subaltern, was the only officer to tell the simple truth about the battalion's scout to the left. He wrote his wife on July 4th that "Benteen's battalion was sent to the left about five miles to see if the Indians were trying to escape up the valley of the Little Big Horn, after which we were to hurry and rejoin the command as quickly as possible." What could be clearer or more sensible? Even Benteen's own official report of July 4th confirms the spying nature of his mission and his orders to rejoin the main column, by saying that Custer gave directions "to move . . . to the left, to send well-mounted officers with about six men, who should ride rapidly to a line of bluffs . . . to our left and front, with instructions to report at once to me if anything of Indians could be seen from the point. I was to follow the movements of this detachment as rapidly as possible . . . If in my judgement there was nothing to be seen of Indians, valleys, etc . . . to return with my battalion to the trail the command was following."

It was not until later that Benteen began to supplement these orders with the phrase, "I was to pitch into anything I came across," as though his mission were part of a pincers attack. His truculent testimony revealed that after he had gone about a mile, first came Chief Trumpeter Henry Voss and then First Sergeant William H. Sharrow with permission from Custer to go beyond the first or second line of bluffs, if necessary, but to observe the remainder of his original orders. He made much of this permission, but suppressed the fact that his original orders required him to rejoin the main command as quickly as possible.

Benteen first said the first line of bluffs was five miles distant, but by 1890 he had shrunk this to two miles. They were, in fact, only a mile distant, although an oblique approach might have covered two miles to reach them. They formed the divide between the Middle Fork and its first minor tributary which joined just above the morass. Benteen detailed Lt. Gibson to ride to the crest and examine the country with glasses, but when he reported he could see nothing but a higher ridge beyond an intervening valley, Benteen bore to the right hunting for an easier passage over the first divide. In a letter of August 8, 1908 to Godfrey, Gibson told of this second ascent:

> I crossed an insignificant stream running through a narrow valley, which I knew was not the Little Big Horn, and so I kept on to the high divide on the other side of it, and from the top of it I could see plainly up the Little Big Horn Valley for a long distance with the aid of the glasses; but in the direction of the village I could not see far on account of the sharp turns in it, or at any rate a turn which obstructed the view. I saw not a living thing, and I hurried back and reported to Benteen, who then altered his course so as to pick up the trail [of Custer].

304

So much for Benteen's genius in disobeying senseless orders that took him ten miles from Custer's trail! Having so quickly determined precisely what Custer had sent him to find out, he did not take his battalion to, much less beyond, the second divide, but turned down the first minor tributary to rejoin Custer's trail as ordered. By his own admission he reached it about half a mile above the morass, and therefore at the mouth of the first tributary. He could not have traveled more than five miles to reach this point, which Custer had reached in four! Benteen also admitted that he left the halt at 12:12 and on reaching the main trail he saw the pack train about half a mile above. By the pack train chronology the time was thus 1:48 p.m. Benteen's full scouting circuit of five miles consumed one hour and a half, an estimate he also offered. His pace averaged 3.3 m.p.h., signifying a slow walk in the rugged climb and a little trotting in smooth places. This is confirmed by Godfrey, who testified that having the rear position, he had to trot occasionally to keep up.

Benteen then trotted his column to pull ahead of the pack train and reached the morass at 1:48 p.m., only twenty-eight minutes behind the faster-moving Custer-Reno column. But he did not reach the Little Big Horn until 4:10, a full hour and twenty minutes behind Reno! There is no escape from the conclusion that Benteen was delayed, not so much by his brief scouting circuit, as by dawdling after he reached the main trail. This was the secret he was concealing in his testimony and continued to conceal for the rest of his life. He first testified that he had not trotted until approaching the Little Big Horn, but on realizing how damaging this admission was, he suddenly insisted he had trotted the entire way! But Godfrey flatly denied this and Lt. Edgerly testified that they had walked at a leisurely pace down Custer's trail. All admitted they had watered so long at the morass that the pack train pulled in as they were leaving. All of this is supported by the chronology.

Benteen poked along until he had passed a couple of miles beyond the lone tepee, when he was suddenly aroused by meeting Trumpeter Martin bearing Cooke's written order to hurry the packs because of the large village. Although he then took the trot, he pocketed the message and retained the courier. For this, too, he had to contrive tortuous excuses. In his official report he claimed the train was safe and could be defended from Reno Hill, of which he knew nothing at the time. Unfortunately, the message had ordered him to hurry the train, not protect it. He testified that the train was seven miles behind him, still stuck in the morass, although he could have known nothing of the kind. Judging from the way a rebellious conscience could goad the Captain into irresponsible statements, it is even possible that he knew the train was only two miles behind him, as our chronology suggests.

Why had Benteen loitered, contrary to orders, when he knew that delay could only jeopardize the success of an attack and his own participation in it? We suspect that he was convinced from the start that there was no hostile village near and that they were on a wild goose chase, a conviction reinforced by Gibson's failure to spot an Indian in any direction. Of all the witnesses, Benteen was the only one who insisted, adamantly and absurdly, that Custer did not believe there was a village. To shift his own scepticism to another to suit his deception was not out of character. Had he followed his orders to hurry and rejoin the command, he would not have been absent at the critical moment. This carries no implication, however, that his presence would have saved the day. It was probably this realization that put enough elastic in Benteen's balky conscience to enable him to distort the facts forever after.

Table 7 presents a simple chronology of events on Reno Hill for the afternoon of June 25th. The principal feature it brings out is the temporal dispersion of the Weir advance. It was during Lt. Hare's fast twenty-minute ride to fetch the ammunition mules that Captain Weir, without orders, started downstream in the direction Custer had gone, taking only his Company D. This move initiated the advance at about 4:50 p.m. Then fifteen minutes later, just after the ammunition mules arrived, Benteen apparently took Co.'s H, K, and M down on Weir's trail, also without orders. When McDougall arrived with the rear of the pack train, he posted his Company B on the picket line vacated by Benteen. It was not until a half hour later, at about 5:50, that Reno ordered Companies A, G, and B and the pack train to move out on Benteen's trail. The advance, therefore, took place in three sections, spread over a full hour of time. When Weir's company reached its farthest advance near Weir Point at about 5:20, the Custer engagement, probably initiated an hour and a half earlier, was undoubtedly concluded.

Table 7
Events on Reno Hill, June 25

	Clock
Reno's battalion assembles on Reno Hill	4:10
Benteen's battalion reaches Reno Hill (downstream firing from now on)	4:20
Reno goes in search of Hodgson's body	4:25
Reno returns to Reno Hill	4:35
Reno sends Hare after ammo. mules	4:40
Weir takes Co. D downstream	4:50
Hare returns from pack train (3 mi. in 20 min.@9mph)	5:00
Reno sends Hare to Weir to contact Custer	5:05
Ammo. mules reach Reno Hill	5:10
Benteen takes Co.'s H, K, and M downstream	5:12
Pack train reaches Reno Hill	5:15
Varnum takes pack spades to bury Hodgson	5:17
Varnum meets Herendeen's party arriving from timber	5:20
McDougall mans vacated picket line (for half an hour)	5:20
Weir's Co. D reaches Weir Point	5:20
Benteen's column reaches Weir Point	5:42
Reno takes Co.'s A, B, and G downstream	5:50
Retreat from Weir Point begins	6:00
Command reassembles on Reno Hill	6:30

307

Chapter 26
The Indian Population

The army that so confidently took the field to whip the hostiles into subjection suffered humiliating reverses before ultimately achieving its goal. Failure to "know thine enemy" played no small part in the early disasters. Yet the military later exploited the prevailing ignorance of matters Indian as a cover-up for its failures. A century's accumulation of literature on the campaign has shed little light on Indian aspects of the war, despite its clear importance. But contrary to accepted dogma, the obscurity surrounding Indian affairs is not impenetrable.

Although a number of innocent tribes have from time to time been named as participants in the war, the "hostile" force consisted primarily of Sioux and secondarily of Cheyennes. The latter, more powerful in spirit than in numbers, stemmed mainly from the Northern division of their tribe. The numerous Sioux Nation comprised three principal divisions, but the major force came from the Teton division. All seven of its bands contributed warriors: Oglala, Brule, Hunkpapa, Miniconjou, Sans Arc, Two Kettle, and Blackfeet Sioux. The middle division of Yanktons and Yanktonnais contributed a few Yanktonnais, but a mere handful of the Eastern, or Santee, division joined the conflict.

Whites invariably label free Indians "hostiles," although in 1876 the hostility was purely of the defensive variety. They were the attacked, not the attackers, the defenders, not the aggressors. But even among their own people they were a minority in thus defending the traditional tribal ways, for they were simply the last to realize that they were resisting the irresistable. Only a portion of the Teton bands engaged in the fighting, for the attitudes of individual Indians toward their common plight covered the full spectrum from suicidal resistance to resigned capitulation. It is convenient to mark off this spectrum of attitudes into three ranges, each representing a sizeable fraction.

We have called one group *agency Indians*; having already forsaken roaming and hunting, they remained at the agencies struggling to learn how to support themselves, an effort so often futile as to leave them wholly dependent upon government rations. We have called the contrasting group *winter roamers*; dedicated to traditional ways, they spurned the agencies in favor of roaming their rightful unceded territory even in winter, subsisting by the chase and trade. The middle, or transitional, group we have called *summer roamers*; they were agency-dependent during the forbidding winter season, but roamers and hunters during the inviting summer months.

It was the strategy of the military command to direct its punitive columns against the winter roamers and such summer roamers as might desert their reservations. The subjugation of these groups, with the resulting intimidation of the agency group, was expected to "settle the Indian problem once and for all." Effective planning, however, would seem to have called for reliable information on the total Indian population, the number of winter roamers they must certainly locate and strike, and the possible number of summer roamers who might be out at the moment of striking. They did have good estimates of the winter roamers, but the available total population figures were grossly exaggerated. Still, the military erred seriously by showing more neglect than concern about the summer roamers. With the advantage of hindsight, vastly more information, and the time to analyze it, we can reconstruct with reasonable accuracy what the army actually had to face.

It was the duty of the agent to count his Indians to the best of his ability and to base thereon his estimates for regular rations and "annuities" of blankets, clothing, trinkets, etc. These counts, or estimates, he submitted to the Indian office, where they usually appeared in his own and the Commissioner's Annual Report. The figures submitted by the Teton Sioux agents for the fall of 1875 were egregiously exaggerated, and reliable censuses did not become uniformly available until 1890. The reasons for inflating the counts were numerous and compelling. It was the "party line" of the army to attribute everything to graft in the rival Indian Department, and this self-serving propaganda has solidified as accepted dogma. The most elementary analysis, however, relegates graft to a petty cause.

The counts were exaggerated primarily because the very life of the agency Indian and his family depended upon it, for their rations were based on these counts. The official ration could scarcely satisfy, in either degree or kind, the needs of a sedentary white. For an active, meat-loving Indian, it was starvation fare, and unpalatable to boot. At times, short rations were deliberate policy, stemming from the smug and pious conviction that starvation would sooner transform the lazy heathen into a virtuous farmer. But even when the intentions were more liberal, the ponderous bureaucratic machinery delivered the provisions late with exasperating frequency, and too often not at all. The Indian's only recourse was to inflate his numbers, and he went about it with ingenious enthusiasm.

Another reason was that the agent's job, and sometimes his life, depended upon inflating his counts. He knew as well as the Indian that his rations were inadequate and uncertain and that only by inflation could he avoid the starvation that provoked unmanageable turmoil. Even consideration of humanity toward his wards prompted such action. The most notorious example was Dr. Valentine T. McGillicuddy, the domineering but honest agent at Pine Ridge; he got away with inflating his estimates for this reason until he was relieved in 1886. He added a sour note to the maneuver, however, by bragging annually of the funds he saved by his unique success in reducing the ration per Indian!

The third reason stemmed from the fact that the number of Indians frequenting a given agency was subject to wild and unpredictable fluctuations. If a conscientious agent succeeded in tolling in a band of winter roamers, he was compelled to plan for a continued drain on his supplies, even if the stay might prove temporary. The alternative was to risk running disastrously short at the most critical moment. The Indian nature contributed further to this problem. Even the agency variety loved dearly to visit with friends and relatives at other agencies. They did not confine their visits to an hour or a day, and so were sometimes enrolled at several agencies at once. The apparent agency population soared to fantastic levels in 1875, when the Great Council for ceding their lands drew hordes of winter roamers, who pretended to come in to several agencies in succession.

These were all compelling and unavoidable reasons for inflated counts. It is true that they provided ample opportunity for graft, if the agent were so inclined, as they sometimes were. But they just as surely swelled the counts when the agent was a paragon of honesty.

All these problems were especially acute at the Fort Peck Agency (O-18) in the remote plains of eastern Montana, near the mouth of Milk River and not far from the Canadian border, a line invisible to Indians. The northern winter roamers gradually migrated into Montana as the buffalo herds receded westward. In 1871, Agent

A.J. Simmons, of the then Milk River Agency, made a valiant effort to bring in these obstreperous bands. Since they were enemies of his regular tribes, he made Fort Peck his Sioux agency. For a year or two he managed to control a band of semi-civilized Santees, still roaming from the Minnesota uprising of 1862. But they soon returned to Canada, where they settled on a reservation far north of the border. It was years after their departure, however, before they were stricken from the rolls at Fort Peck.

Agent Simmons enjoyed a more turbulent, but lasting success with a band of Yanktonnais, whom he gradually brought under control in the following years. Their habits were still more roaming than sedentary, and official policy left them to subsist themselves by semi-annual hunts, with rations furnished for only a few months of the year. Since the reservation extended to the border, they roamed as often in Canada as in the States, and the poor agent was never able to corral them for even a half-respectable count. They participated minimally in the war, however, and in the 1880's many transferred to join their relatives at Standing Rock Agency.

Simmons also had a go at taming the wildest of the wild — Sitting Bull's Hunkpapa band. He succeeded in holding councils and distributing presents; at times he enticed a few within rifle-shot of Fort Peck, and never gave up hope. But his successor, W.W. Alderson, washed his hands of these fractious bands in the winter of 1874-5, refusing to have anything more to do with them. As a result, they flocked briefly and tumultuously to other agencies, swelling their counts while still leaving their mark on the Fort Peck rolls.

Counting Indians was the bane of the Indian agent, and the more so as the Indian Office demanded ever more accurate censuses. The earliest counts were simply of lodges, often as declared by the chiefs. Later procedures identified chiefs and headmen by name and took their word for the number of men, women, and children in their villages. This was eminently satisfactory to the Indians, for they could control such counts to their complete satisfaction.

The next refinement was to make each lodge-head identify himself by name and display in person all dwellers in his tepee. This was resisted, often violently and to the peril of the agent, until the Indians devised the technique of spiriting lodges and small fry around faster than the agent's eye could follow. The latter could not be everywhere at once, and tepees were amazingly mobile, to say nothing of the kids, who had a ball sneaking through the tall grass and along gullies to materialize in the maximum number of tepees.

311

And every cradle-board in camp blossomed out with a reasonable facsimile of an infant. This procedure had a marvelous way of increasing the percentage of children. But even such counts as these were too troublesome to be routine; for years after such an effort, the agent merely adjusted his rolls for known gains and losses. The next true count might then show a striking change.

It was not until the army took over the Teton agencies a month after the Custer defeat that the threat and application of force frightened the Indians into standing still for a genuine census. Unlike the powerless and single-handed agent, the army could muster the force and personnel to conduct a head-count; it felt no obligation toward those who refused to report and stand still — they could starve over the hill if they. chose. Even with their real and fancied superiority the officers suffered some embarrassing experiences.

Lt. Col. William P. Carlin, taking command of the military post at Standing Rock in August of 1876, promptly ordered a count of lodges on the reservation. The result of 300 represented about 2100 Indians, but the Colonel, figuring only five to a lodge, reported a mere 1500 present (O-44). Appalled to learn that the agent had been issuing to 4500, the righteous Colonel smelled fraud. To prove it, he ordered Captain Edward Collins to take a precise census. On September 15th the Captain reported that he had compiled a list of names of all lodge-heads, each "residence being visited and the number reported being then examined and verified with all the care possible, and it is believed to be tolerably correct." His total? 4558 (O-44)!

Hark to the snickering of the deposed civilian agent in the background! He had knowingly accepted an inflated count in order to feed his wards adequately, but he could see that the wiley savages had made fools of his self-righteous accusers by slight-of-hand tricks that upped the count another notch! If the Colonel was chagrined the records say not, but reinforcing troops soon arrived to cow the natives. In this more ominous climate, Captain R.E. Johnston, newly appointed Acting Indian Agent, completed an accurate October census that showed 2344 Indians present (O-44).

It is illuminating to peruse the counts reported for the four main Teton agencies during the period in question. In January of 1875 the Spotted Tail agent triumphantly reported the first successfull count of his Brule Sioux. The total of 9,610 included 69.1% children! This represents about five children per couple, which is hardly compatible with the fact that the American Indian was a relatively infertile race with a nearly static population. The chiefs must have been satisfied, indeed, with the antics of the children that day. In September of 1876 the occupying troops took another count that gave a total of 4614 with 62.2% children. Lt. Jesse M. Lee did a little better in July of 1877 when he counted 7005 with 50.5% youngsters. But he even allowed 48.2% among the 1364 hostiles who surrendered that spring. By 1885 a better count showed a proper 39.2% children, though an 1890 census revealed a large drop in total (O-43).

The record at Red Cloud Agency was a little better. Although an army count of November, 1876, totalling 2484, included an excessive 50.5% children, there were only 41.2% among the 1168 hostile Sioux who surrendered there in 1877, and only 40.8% among the 869 surrendering Cheyennes (O-36). For the next ten years inflation ran rampant under Dr. McGillicuddy, who neglected to conjure up figures for men, women, and children. But when he was relieved in 1886, a highly accurate military count showed a fall to 5,159 with 41.0% children (O-5).

After the officers had conquered the technique of making accurate censuses at Standing Rock and Cheyenne River Agencies, the agents kept the faith, with only minor lapses. For years these counts consistently ran between 39 and 41% children. So did the excellent counts of the Southern Cheyennes at the Upper Arkansas Agency. The first respectable count at Fort Peck came in 1887 and showed 945 Yanktonnais with 39.6% children.

Over a long span of years, among both Sioux and Cheyennes, whether agency or surrendering Indians, reliable counts ran 25% men, 35% women, and 40% children, with a range no greater than ±1 percentage point. A supplementary examination of fewer counts that enumerated lodges as well as persons, established that the Sioux ran seven persons to the lodge and the Cheyennes eight. These particular figures were in wide use at the time among knowledgeable persons, who also commented specifically on the tribal difference. We thus conclude that the seven persons per Sioux lodge averaged 1.75 men, 2.45 women, and 2.80 children, while the eight persons per Cheyenne lodge averaged 2.0 men, 2.8 women, and 3.2 children.

These conversion factors are judged to be quite reliable as *averages*, although they obviously cannot apply with precision to every sample. They are useful in converting between lodges, persons, and warriors, the three most common ways of expressing Indian numbers. It is certain that the true warrior class, i.e., the young men on whom the tribes depended for their aggressive fighters, ran appreciably less than the 25% men; but for defending their village in an emergency the total number of males capable of the effective use of arms may have exceeded this fraction. With full admission of this uncertainty, we can only estimate fighting strength at 1.75 and 2.0 per lodge for the Sioux and Cheyennes, respectively. These conversion factors have another valuable use; they not only betray padded counts, but furnish the means to correct them.

Despite these defects in reported populations, the raw figures for the period 1872 through 1890 graphically illustrate the significant events before, during, and after the war. Not until 1890 can the absolute numbers be trusted, but throughout the entire period, abrupt *changes* are instructive. Figure 1 presents these raw data for the relevant Sioux agencies. The Cheyennes are excluded, for they require special treatment. The Fort Peck Sioux are also excluded, since their figures are so nearly hopeless; fortunately, they participated minimally in the war.

In order to bring out significant features, the ten Sioux agencies have been divided into three groups. One consists of the five agencies (Sisseton, Santee, Devil's Lake, Yankton, and Crow Creek), which served only Santee, Yankton, and Yanktonnais bands that did not participate in the war, and were therefore not occupied by the army after Custer's defeat. They were populated by "good" agency Indians with no stake in the about-to-be-raped Black Hills. The curve for these unoccupied agencies starts in 1872 with a total count of 6330 and rises by slight inflation to a maximum of 6970 in 1877. The absence of any dip in 1876 proves that these bands took no part in the war. Over the next two years the figures decline slightly, coincident with the replacement of round number estimates by precise censuses in the last of these agencies. The ensuing plateau holds at 6,150 for the next eleven years to 1890. The significant conclusion is that the true population of these Indians remained remarkably static over the full eighteen year period.

The picture is strikingly different for the five agencies serving the wilder Tetons. As protagonists in the war, all five of their agencies were occupied by the army in the summer of 1876. Again, separate curves are shown for the three Missouri agencies (Standing Rock, Cheyenne River, and Lower Brule) and the two former Platte River agencies (Red Cloud and Spotted Tail, destined to become Pine Ridge and Rosebud, respectively). Both exhibit an accelerating upturn from 1872 to 1875, reflecting all the inflationary pressures we have described. The incredible peaks then give way to precipitous and profound falls in 1876, reflecting the great war exodus as well as accurate military counts. It should be noted that these are fall counts, made after the arrival of troops had driven out still more Indians.

In the case of the Missouri agencies, reliable counting largely

314

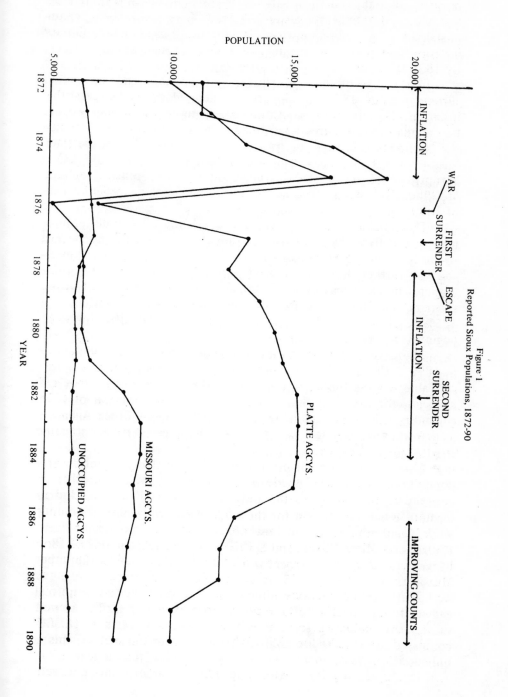

Figure 1
Reported Sioux Populations, 1872-90

315

persists, so that even the relatively few surrenders in 1877 are detectable, and the heavy surrenders from Canada in 1881 are unmistakable. The subsequent rise is the result partly of temporary inflation and partly of transfers from Fort Peck to Standing Rock. By 1889 the counts are fully trustworthy.

In the case of the Platte River agencies, thousands of hostiles surrendered in 1877, an effect exaggerated by some persisting inflation. Despite this, a second notch reveals a second exodus to Canada of once-surrendered Indians in November of 1877, when the authorities insisted on moving the agencies to the detested Missouri River for a season. Steady inflation follows this dip, but is abruptly broken in 1886, when a military census replaced McGillicuddy's whims, and again in 1889, when the excellent census of 1890 was extrapolated back a year.

The reliable censuses of 1890 establish the total Sioux population at the five Teton agencies at only 18,200, in striking contrast to the peak of 35,800 reported in 1875. Since the population, as we shall further show, was indeed static, the actual number at these agencies in 1875 was only 15,200, for some 3000 were still winter roamers. The false peak in 1875 therefore reflects an inflation of 125%! Claims of 40,000 Sioux at the Battle of the Little Big Horn begin to look rather ludicrous.

There is even more to learn by comparing tribal populations in 1890 with knowledgable estimates of early years. The upper half of Table 8 gives the 1890 populations, broken down by tribes and agencies, for the eight Sioux bands that fought in the war of 1876 (including all the Yanktonnais and therefore Crow Creek Agency). The lower half of the table presents a number of tribal estimates for the pre-agency years from 1850 to 1869, which emanated ultimately from old fur company traders. These include a careful 1850 compilation made by Thaddeus A. Culbertson (M-13), brother of Alexander, the eminent fur trader; one of 1861 by the Indian Commissioner (O-5); one of 1866 by Governor Newton Edmunds while negotiating treaties (O-5,1866); one of 1867 provided by Jim Bridger and Mitch Boyer at Fort C.F. Smith (O-47); and one of 1869 by General David S. Stanley (O-5), long in command on the upper Missouri.

The total populations for the eight Sioux bands show no real growth trend over the forty years covered by the table. The average of the five estimates for the twenty pre-agency years is 18,300, compared to 19,270 for 1890. Whether real or an artifact, this is only a 5% increase in twenty-seven years, more than a generation. This evidence, together with that derived earlier from the well-

Table 8
Sioux Population, 1850-1890

	Brule	Oglala	Hunkpapa	Miniconjou	Two Kettle	Blackfoot	Sans Arc	Yanktonnais	TOTAL
1890									
Standing Rock			1990[1]			560		1810	4360
Cheyenne River				1230	740	210	660		2840
Lower Brule	1040								1040
Crow Creek								1080	1080
Fort Peck								1120	1120
Red Cloud		4180[2]							4180
Spotted Tail	4220			100	230		100		4650
Total	5260	4180	1990	1330	970	770	760	4010	19270
1850-1869									
Culbertson, 1850	3500	2800	2240	1890	420	3150	1750	2450	18200
Commissioner, 1861	3420	2200	2680	1280	960	1248	1600	3840	17228
Gov. Edmunds, 1866	3500	2450	2100	2590	1400	1540	1960	5250	20790
Bridger-Boyer, 1867	2210	3340	2100	3850	840	1050	980	4000[3]	18370
Gen. Stanley, 1869	3000	2000	2000	2000	1500	900	1500	4000	16900
Average	3126	2558	2224	2322	1024	1578	1558	3908	18298

1 Including 250 who remained in Canada.
2 Average for 1889-90 is 4500, but best counts in 1886-7 are used.
3 Omitted from original and replaced by an estimate.

counted and non-involved bands, implies a static population, with numbers far less than often assumed.

The distribution of this population between bands, however, exhibits less stability. The Yanktonnais band of the middle division appears to have held its own, but the Brules and Oglalas seem to have grown at the expense of the Miniconjous, Sans Arcs, and Blackfeet. Such shifts between bands, and also between agencies, continued actively after 1876, making for complications in our next step.

Our ultimate goal (to be achieved in a later chapter) is to arrive at reasonable figures for the numbers and bands of Indians in the village on the Little Big Horn. We can carry the present analysis one important step closer to this goal by establishing the number who were absent from their agencies in 1876 and the number who later surrendered. The *absentees* can be calculated as the difference between our population figures and the military censuses taken in the fall of 1876 (corrected, as needed, for excess children, and for early returnees). The net *returnees* can be calculated as the army-counted number who surrendered in 1877 and 1881, adjusted for those who escaped late in 1877 and surrendered again in 1881. If we are successful in identifying the minimum number present at the agencies in 1876, and in finding counts of all who surrendered, the absentees and net returnees should be equal.

The data necessary for this absentee-returnee analysis were assembled by extensive and repeated searches of the Indian agency records, army records, and contemporary newspapers. They were laboriously checked against one another and for internal consistency. The analysis was first made by agencies, for which the data are essentially complete. This was then broken down by bands, for which the data were less complete, especially for the Cheyenne River Agency. Here resort was made to "educated guesses," but within a framework of reliable totals. This still left discrepancies by bands arising from shifts in tribal affiliations.

The final results are assembled in Table 9, which for the first time includes the Cheyenne tribe. A detailed analysis of the Cheyenne figures, which will play a key role in attaining our ultimate goal, will be postponed to a later chapter. The fact that the tabulated total of absentees, 7944, and of net returnees, 7788, so nearly agree, provides assurance that the conditions necessary for validity were reasonably met. The lack of equal agreement within bands reflects the shifts in tribal affiliations.

The first significant finding revealed in this table is that the total population of the Sioux and Cheyenne tribes that participated in the war was only 21,870 persons. The second is that only some

Table 9

Absentee-Returnee Analysis of Hostiles in 1876

Band	Pop. 1876	Pst. 1876	Abst. 1876	Sur. 1877	Esc. 1881	Sur. 1881	Net Ret.	Max. Lodges out
Brule	5260	4387	873	865	191	191	865	125
Oglala	4180	2336	1844	1320	556	556	1320	264
Hunkpapa	1990*	333	1657	213	0	1158*	1371	237
Miniconjou	1330	346	984	945	399	753	1299	186
Sans Arc	760	170	590	643	254	524	913	131
Blackfoot	770	645	125	130	0	107	237	34
Yanktonnais	2930	2755	175	175	0	0	175	25
Cheyenne	3680	2114	1566	1478	0	0	1478	196
Total	21870	13926	**7944**	5899	1400	3289	**7778**	1216

*Includes 250 who remained in Canada.

8,000, or 37% of these persons were absent from their agencies during the war. Another finding, of which we shall make later use, is presented in the last column of the table, headed "Maximum Lodges Out." It converts to lodges (using a divisor of 7 for the Sioux and 8 for the Cheyennes) the numbers of tribal absentees or net returnees; the larger of these two was used in order to err on the side of too many rather than too few. This yields a total of 1216 absentee lodges, corresponding to 8,600 persons and 2150 warriors.

It must be emphasized that not all of these absentees actually fought in the war. A minority never lifted bow or gun. Some who left the agencies did not leave the reservations. Some did not flee until the army took over the agencies in July-August, or until the confiscation of arms and ponies in October. These absentee figures, therefore, merely impose a constraint, or *ceiling*, on the number who could actually have fought. The village on the Little Big Horn could not have contained even this number of Indians. This conclusion may come as a severe shock to many students of the Custer battle, but it must be admitted that the evidence which now compels this conclusion has been almost entirely neglected.

The Indian Office in late 1875 estimated the number of winter-roaming Sioux at 3000 (430 lodges), a figure we shall find quite accurate. To this number, however, we must add about 400 Cheyennes (50 lodges) to make a total of 3400, representing 480 lodges and 850 fighting men. It was this force only that the army felt it necessary to seek out and destroy. It was their failure to judge the number of reinforcing summer roamers that brought disaster.

Chapter 27
The Gathering of the Winter Roamers

Accurate assessment of the strength and temper of the Indian foe was not the only problem in military intelligence that baffled the military command. To strike, one must first find. One simple fact reveals how poorly it solved this problem: four months of campaigning harvested four days of contact with the Indians. After a summer of hard marching the futile search was abandoned.

The evidence available today again enables us to reconstruct what the army would like to have known at the time — the movements of the winter roamers after the initial blow that General Reynolds struck on March 17th. We are privileged to gather all the evidence, official and unofficial, contemporary and reminiscent, and check it against the constraints imposed by time, distance, geography (topographical maps), and even the weather to achieve this reconstruction.

According to Wooden Leg, the most reliable and detailed of Cheyenne chroniclers, the winter roamers of his tribe had spent the winter of 1875-76 with a few Oglala friends in the middle reaches of Tongue River, before moving almost due east to the west bank of Powder River early in March. According to White Bull, the Miniconjou nephew of Sitting Bull, the roamers of his tribe spent the winter on the lower Tongue, harassing the wolfers at Fort Pease and raiding and being raided by the Crows. Before March, however, they, too, moved eastward, as confirmed by Dr. Eastman. A few joined the Cheyennes, but the majority joined the Hunkpapas, who had wintered near the mouth of Powder River.

The Indian informants of George E. Hyde told him that Crazy Horse's Oglalas left Bear Butte, at the northeast edge of the Black

Hills, in January to camp in small villages along the eastern edge of Powder River valley in its middle reaches. Both Black Elk, an Oglala, and Dr. Eastman confirm this general location of the Oglalas, who usually kept a few Cheyennes with them. By March, therefore, nearly all the winter roamers had distributed themselves along the valley of Powder River, leaving the Tongue, Rosebud, and Big Horn valleys deserted, as both Crook's winter expedition and Gibbon's Montana column would discover.

Runners from the agencies had delivered the government ultimatum to surrender by January 31st, or be driven in by troops. The chiefs received the news with contemptuous indignation; the Indian was just as offended by unilateral violation of an agreement as the white man. Convinced that troops were as little disposed to winter hostilities as the Indians, they shrugged off the ultimatum as an empty threat and burrowed deeper into their winter robes.

March 17th brought a rude awakening for the camp that General Reynolds attacked, burning the tepees, running off the pony herd, and driving the dismayed villagers out into a severe cold wave. The survivors got the message: war had been declared and they were marked for extermination. From that moment the scattered winter roamers began to consolidate. Their chiefs harangued them to resist injustice. They sent out parties to secure arms and ammunition, and scouts to watch the agencies and army forts. They vetoed suggestions, however, for attacks on white settlements and outposts. Instead, they led the retreat into the heart of their unceded territory to defend themselves.

Our reconstruction begins on this March 17th. The place was the west bank of Powder River, some 140 miles above its mouth, at the mouth of Thompson Creek about four miles below (north) present Moorehead, Montana. The village was one of Cheyennes, Miniconjous, and Oglalas, officially reported to contain 105 lodges, a figure supported by a number of participants. Indian estimates, however, consistently run lower, perhaps because they did not include all three tribes.

A wounded squaw found in the village told Lt. Bourke that they "had with them a force of Miniconjou Sioux, but the forty new canvas lodges . . . belong to some Cheyennes." The brother of Bull Eagle, a Miniconjou, assigned the Cheyennes fifty-five and the Oglalas ten. Those who surrendered the next spring told Lt. W. Philo Clark that there were sixty Cheyenne and fourteen Oglala lodges. He Dog, an Oglala, told Mari Sandoz that he had joined the village with eight lodges just before the attack and implied the presence of forty-two Cheyenne lodges. Because of the uncertainty,

322

we arbitrarily assign forty lodges to both the Oglala and Cheyennes and twenty-five to the Miniconjous to make the official total of 105. These figures are entered in Table 10, which summarizes the growth of the village of winter roamers.

Wooden Leg says that on the night of the battle he rode twenty miles south to help recapture the stolen pony herd from the soldiers, returning the next day. The refugees must have huddled in the bitter cold for three nights near the smoking village, salvaging what they could and distributing the recovered ponies, while awaiting a thaw that all white sources agree did not come until the 20th. On this day the refugees must have left, for Wooden Leg says they "waded" Powder River and traveled northeast for four days through "mud and water," "fording" the Little Powder and finding Crazy Horse's camp, apparently on the 23rd, "far up a creek east of Powder River." This must have been the East Fork of the Little Powder, the only lengthy eastern affluent in this area. A crippled, but determined journey of forty miles in four days locates Crazy Horse's camp just west of present Boyes, Montana, on the eastern rim of Powder River valley. These, and all subsequent moves are summarized in Table 11.

Crazy Horse's village was a small one, for it could not fully supply the needs of the refugees. We give it twenty Oglala and ten Cheyenne lodges, for Wooden Leg now says the Cheyennes totalled fifty. A Cheyenne woman, Kate Bighead, says they remained here "for several days," and because of the wounded, frost-bitten, and weary, we leave it here through the night of March 27th.

The refugees next moved to seek Sitting Bull's camp, which the wounded squaw had told Frank Grouard was situated "about sixty miles" down Powder River. This distance corresponds to a point opposite Chalk Butte, a high point on the divide some fifteen miles east of the river. This large Hunkpapa and Miniconjou camp had wintered near the mouth of the river, but on March 16th the Fort Peck Agent reported that it had moved upstream. A part of the village turned east to trade with the friendly tribes at Fort Berthold, which they reached April 1st, significantly still unaware of Reynold's attack. The remainder under Sitting Bull ascended the eastern edge of the valley toward Chalk Butte. With this group was the brother of Bull Eagle, who left them on April 9th and came in to the Cheyenne River Agency on April 18th, reporting that "a few days" before he had left, the refugees had joined them after their flight of "eighty miles" from their destroyed village.

This not only roughly dates the arrival of the refugees at Sitting Bull's camp, but locates the latter about forty miles below

Table 10
Growth of the Village of Winter Roamers

	Mar. 17	Mar. 23	Apr. 1	Apr. 18	Apr. 27	May 16	June 7
Cheyenne	40	50	50	50	60	80	100
Oglala	40	60	60	60	60	60	70
Miniconjou	25	25	55	55	55	55	55
Hunkpapa			70	140	140	154	154
Sans Arc				55	55	55	55
Santee					15	15	15
Blackfoot						12	12
Brule					?	?	?
Total Lodges	105	135	235	360	385	431	461

Crazy Horse's camp. This implies a point not five miles north of Chalk Butte on the head of present Spring Creek, a short eastern affluent of Powder River, about eleven miles southwest of present Ekalaka, Montana. Wooden Leg made the distance fifty miles, instead of forty, but indicated they traveled northeast along the eastern rim of the valley, passing Chalk Butte en route. The Cheyenne, Two Moon, remembered that they made a large camp near Charcoal Butte, which seems to be the Cheyenne name for Chalk Butte.

Sioux sources locate Sitting Bull's camp on Blue Earth Creek in the Blue Earth Hills. In October of 1876 Lt. Col. Carlin, at Standing Rock, learned that the Blue Earth Hills lay at the very head of O'Fallon's Creek, whose source is just north of Chalk Butte. Old Montana maps label this same area the Blue Mud Hills, and we believe Spring Creek was called Blue Earth Creek by the Sioux. Iron Hawk, an Oglala present in the destroyed village, told Judge Ricker that "they fled on foot north to the Blue Earth river, a stream at the head of it . . . and found a vast number of other Indians camped on the Blue Earth, a small stream — many different tribes." Stanley Vestal also locates the camp "in the Blue Mountains, on Beaver Creek, some sixty miles down the Powder," which must refer to the Blue Earth Hills, not the present Blue Mountains on Beaver Creek, a hundred miles farther north.

Wooden Leg says that the move to this village was made in four days of travel, but there were heavy snows on March 30 and 31, which may well have held them in camp. We thus date the start March 28th and the arrival April 2nd, which corresponds more closely to "a few days" before April 9th. He also says that they remained in this camp for five or six nights, but he left and returned to it from a 250-mile scout beyond Tongue River, suggesting a longer period. Two Moon remembered a long, happy stay with plenty of game. We therefore leave it here until the morning of April 9th, the day the brother of Bull Eagle left it, presumably because it was moving farther away from his own destination, the Cheyenne River Agency.

Wooden Leg describes the size of this triple village by saying that the Cheyenne circle was the smallest and the Hunkpapa the largest; the Oglala was next largest and the Miniconjou not quite so large. Using the fifty Cheyenne lodges as the reference base, reasonable estimates of the others become seventy Hunkpapa, sixty Oglala, and fifty-five Miniconjou, for a total of 235. By difference, this makes Sitting Bull's original camp one of seventy Hunkpapa and thirty Miniconjou lodges.

325

Table 11
Movements of the Winter Roamers

Date	Events
March 17	Reynolds attacks in bitter cold on Powder R., mouth of Thompson Cr.
18-19	Huddle near village in bitter cold, salvaging and distributing.
20-23	Move in thaw 40 mi. NE to Crazy Horse camp on E. Fk of L. Powder R.
24-27	In camp with Crazy Horse.
28-29	Move 20 mi. NE along east side of Powder Valley.
30-31	In camp for two days of snow.
April 1-2	Move 20 mi. NE to Sitting Bull camp near Chalk Butte.
3-8	In camp with Sitting Bull; snow on 3rd and 8th.
9-10	Move 15 mi. N; Bull Eagle's brother leaves for agency on 9th.
11-14	In camp.
15-16	Move 16 mi. N to head of Sheep Cr.
17-20	In camp; Sans Arcs arrive.
21	Move 9 mi. NW down Sheep Cr.
22-24	In camp; first sign of new grass.
25	Move 10 mi. NW to camp on Powder at Mizpah Cr.
26-28	In camp; Santees and Cheyennes arrive; new grass everywhere.
29-30	Move 23 mi. W to Tongue R., mouth of Pumpkin Cr. (mile 13)
May 1-5	In camp; Kill Eagle arrives; first raid on Gibbon, May 3.
6	Move 8 mi. up Tongue to Ash Cr. (mile 21)
7-11	In camp; Cheyennes arrive.
12	Move 8 mi. up Tongue to Garland (mile 29)
13-16	In camp; last Gibbon raid, May 13; sighted by Bradley, May 16.

Table 11 (Cont'd)

17	Move 13 mi. NW, close to Yellowstone
18-20	In camp, hunting buffalo; Gibbon hears firing on 19th.
21	Move 16 mi. W to Rosebud Cr. (mile 7)
22-24	In camp; Cheyennes arrive; attacks on Gibbon, May 22-24.
25	Move 12 mi. up Rosebud (mile 19).
26-28	In camp; sighted by Bradley May 27.
29	Move 7 mi. up Rosebud to Teat Butte (mile 25).
30	Move 8 mi. up Rosebud to Greenleaf Cr. (mile 34).
31	In camp.
June 1-2	In camp; snow on June 1; Wooden Leg leaves June 2.
4	Move 11 mi. up Rosebud to sun dance camp (mile 45).
5-7	In camp, sundancing; rain, June 6; Wooden Leg spots Crook, in rain.
8	Move 12 mi. up Rosebud to Muddy Cr. (mile 57); Wooden Leg leaves Crook on Tongue R.
9-11	In camp; Wooden Leg returns and Little Hawk leaves to attack Crook on May 9; latter returns May 10; rain on June 9, 10, 11.
12	Move 12 mi. up Rosebud to Busby (mile 69).
13-14	In camp.
15	Move 12 mi. W. up Davis Cr. to divide; Little Hawk goes to scout Crook.
16	Move 9 mi. down Reno Cr.; L . Hawk sees Crook and returns.
17	In camp. warriors fight Crook on Rosebud.
18	Move 7 mi. to and up L. Big Horn.
19-23	In camp, celebrating; influx of summer roamers.
24	Move 8 mi. down L. Big Horn; Cheyennes arrive.
25	In camp. Battle with Custer; Cheyennes arrive.
26	In camp; beseige Reno Hill; move upstream in evening.

327

Wooden Leg now relates that twice the triple village moved slowly, because of winter-poor ponies, northeast for two days, camping for several nights between moves. This should have taken them some thirty-one miles down the east rim of the valley to the head of present Sheep Creek, where we leave them for the nights of April 16th to 20th. At this camp a band of Sans Arcs joined to make a fifth circle. Wooden Leg now allots the Cheyennes fifty lodges, the Oglalas, Miniconjous, and Sans Arcs "perhaps sixty or seventy," and the Hunkpapas "as many as 150." To be conservative, we allow the Sans Arcs fifty-five, and the Hunkpapas 140 to make a total of 360. The increment of seventy Hunkpapas signals the return of those who had been trading at Fort Berthold.

After three or four sleeps, Wooden Leg says the enlarged camp swerved northwest to camp lower down on the next branch of Powder River. We suggest, instead, that they moved ten miles northwest down Sheep Creek to camp the nights of April 22-24. Here he mentions that "new grass is beginning to peep up." This checks with "J.W.O." with Gibbon's column at Fort Pease, who wrote on April 23rd that "the ground will be soon covered with a carpet of living grass," and with Dr. DeWolf who wrote on April 25th at Fort Lincoln that "the grass begins to start."

Kate Bighead and Iron Hawk now join Wooden Leg in speaking of a camp on Powder River itself, the latter implying the west bank. We therefore move the village another ten miles down Sheep Creek to the oft-used Mizpah ford to camp near the mouth of Mizpah Creek (a western affluent at mile 35 on Powder River) for the nights of April 25-28. At this camp Wooden Leg says the Cheyenne chief, Lame White Man joined with his band. This party of ten lodges had left Red Cloud Agency some time earlier, but had only now found the hostile camp. He also mentions a few scattered Brules, and a small band of Blackfoot, although the latter did not arrive until a few camps later. He refers also to a few Santees, under the notorious Inkpaduta, still wandering after the Minnesota outbreak of 1862. Dr. Eastman, whose uncle was with this party, gives their total as fifteen lodges. These arrivals enlarged the camp to 385 lodges.

When the village left Powder River for the Tongue, Wooden Leg says the grass was coming up everywhere and the ponies were growing stronger. Two Moon also remembered that about May, when the grass was tall and the ponies strong, they started for Tongue River. Although Wooden Leg says they camped at two or three places on the divide, the distance is so short that we believe some of these were on the Tongue. Accordingly, on April 29th and 30th we move the village twenty-three miles west over the divide to camp

328

at the mouth of Pumpkin Creek (at mile 13 on the Tongue), where we leave them through the night of May 5th.

That the village had reached the Tongue by May 1st is supported by the fact that Gibbon's Crow scouts at Fort Pease lost all their ponies to hostile raiders on the morning of May 3rd. For the next ten days they hovered around the camp and Lt. Bradley trailed some down and across the Yellowstone toward Tongue River. At this camp Kill Eagle, a Blackfoot Sioux, with twelve lodges of Blackfoot and fourteen of Hunkpapas from Standing Rock, joined the village at the mouth of Four Horn River, the Sioux name for Pumpkin Creek. This was the party Wooden Leg had thought joined earlier.

The Terry-Crook column in August noted enough campsites on the lower Tongue to cover out-bound spring sites as well as returning July sites. We therefore move the village eight miles up the river to Ash Creek to camp the nights of May 6-11, and then eight miles farther to present Garland (at mile 29) for the nights of May 12-16. Here on May 16th Lt. Bradley first located the village. It was here also that the Cheyenne chief, Dirty Moccasins, arrived with the largest band so far; Wooden Leg says they had come from Otter Creek (at mile 65), moving thirty or forty miles down to join them (at mile 29, or 34 miles from Otter Creek). After this arrival, he gives the Cheyenne circle eighty lodges, thus allowing twenty to this party. Including Kill Eagle's party, the total now reaches 431 lodges. Bradley's Crows, judging solely from the village smoke, estimated it at "no less than two or three hundred lodges," but Mitch Boyer counted some four hundred on June 16th.

Wooden Leg says they next moved west to the Rosebud, camping twice en route on short affluents of the Yellowstone, while conducting successful buffalo hunts. Kill Eagle mentions only one camp on the divide, which is more reasonable in view of Bradley's scouting excursions in this area. We therefore move the village on May 17th about thirteen miles northwest to the head of present Gravey Creek and leave it there for the nights of May 17-20, hunting buffalo. It was the pre-occupation with hunting that gave Gibbon's camp a peaceful interlude. On May 19th Bradley's scouts heard firing in the direction of this hunting, and were nearly detected by an advance party of hunters.

On May 21st we move the village sixteen miles west to the first camp on the east bank of the Rosebud, which Wooden Leg located at mile 7. This site was not noted by Reno on June 18, by Custer on June 22, or Terry on August 9, presumably because all followed the west bank of the stream in this region. But it is significant that on May 20th Gibbon camped only eight miles away (opposite and two miles below the mouth of the Rosebud) after having seen no hostiles for a week. But on May 21st his scouts were driven back across the river; on May 22nd his hunters were fired on and three were killed the next day; that afternoon hostiles demonstrated on the bluffs and on the 24th a spy penetrated the soldier camp. This close surveillance then abruptly stopped, whence we infer that the village moved a safer distance upstream on May 25th.

The lack of Indian references to these raids on Gibbon's camp is surprising. Wooden Leg says that at the next camp rumors came that Crow scouts had been seen and they prepared to go after them, but the rumors proved false and they merely moved upstream. We suspect that this actually applied to this first camp on the Rosebud, that the rumors were true, and that the move was prompted by a desire to get further away. It was at this first camp that Charcoal Bear, the chief medicine man of the Cheyennes arrived with the Sacred Buffalo Hat. In line with other additions, we assign ten lodges to this group.

The move for safety· was made twelve miles upstream on the east bank to mile 19, a site with overwhelming confirmation. It was here that Bradley again sighted it on May 27th. He called it "immense," but Mitch Boyer counted about four hundred lodges on June 16th; a newspaper letter quoted a figure of five hundred. Reno's scout bivouacked at this point on June 18th and Custer's column noted it on June 23rd. Wooden Leg says they remained here but one night, although we shall shortly adduce evidence that they remained through the night of May 28th.

Wooden Leg says they next moved twelve to fifteen miles upstream to a painted peak called Teat Butte, where they remained one night. This is an error, for he says the next move was to Greenleaf Creek at mile 34. Teat Butte is not named on the map, but a personal tour (July, 1964) disclosed but one painted peak answering to the name, located at about mile 25. The error is thus one of mileage only, for Reno's scouts spotted this campsite from the Butte and camped on it on June 16th; reporter Howard also noted it on August 10th. We date this six mile move on May 29th, and accept it as a one-night stand.

The next move was to the mouth of Greenleaf Creek at mile 34. This is also well confirmed, for Reno halted here for six hours on June 17th. Godfrey mentioned three campsites between mile 10 and mile 42 on June 23rd, and Lt. Maguire's itinerary mentioned the same three in August. Wooden Leg says they remained here five or six nights, although he left it after only three nights. Presuming his

330

hunters would not have forsaken their lodge-fires in a blizzard, we date his departure June 2nd, which is confirmed by a datable event on his hunt. This indicates the village moved there on the 30th, a time fix that suggested the preceding move from mile 19 on the 29th. To fit future events, we leave the village at Greenleaf Creek through the night of June 4th.

Wooden Leg says that from this camp the Sioux went buffalo hunting to the west, while his own party went east; during his absence the village moved again to the famous sun dance camp. But we must first follow Wooden Leg's hunt, which he describes in sufficient detail to support a chronology, assuming they traveled twenty to thirty-five miles a day, depending on the luck of the hunt.

On June 6th the hunting party was moving westward from Powder River and approaching present Sheridan, Wyoming. This was the day Crook's column got lost and camped in a rain storm on Prairie Dog Creek, just east of Sheridan. That afternoon the hunting party spotted the troops, and after dusk went to observe the soldier camp-fires. On June 7th Crook marched down to camp for several days on Tongue River. After the soldiers left that morning the hunters found they had left some rain-soaked hardtack. They followed the army and watched it camp on the Tongue. The next morning they realized the troops were not moving farther, and so left to carry the news to the village. Traveling to and then down the Rosebud, they found the village on the morning of June 9th in camp ten miles below Busby at the mouth of Muddy Creek, having moved from the sun dance camp.

The village had moved to the sun dance camp, located on a flat at about mile 45 on the Rosebud, some eight miles below the mouth of Lame Deer Creek. Black Elk recalled that they selected the sun dance tree on the first day, erected it on the second, and danced on the third and fourth days. Stanley Vestal learned that Sitting Bull danced only a day and a night and the next moon experienced his prophetic vision of soldiers falling into camp. All agree that they moved the next day. Lt. Schwatka, who passed this camp with Crook's column on August 10th, noted not only the sun dance lodge, but that the tepees were ditched against rain, which fell on June 6th. From all this, we conclude that the sun dance camp was occupied for the nights of June 4-7, including the rainy June 6th. Then on June 8th it moved twelve miles up to the mouth of Muddy Creek at mile 57, to be in position there when Wooden Leg's hunters rejoined it on the 9th.

Wooden Leg mentioned the appearance of more Cheyennes at the Greenleaf Creek camp, but identified neither chief nor numbers.

331

This was undoubtedly the party which Black Elk accompanied. His family left Red Cloud in May and was joined by other Oglalas, including Jack Red Cloud, and some Cheyennes. They arrived at the Greenleaf camp, for Black Elk says the next move was to the sun dance camp. Assuming ten lodges each for the Oglalas and Cheyennes, the size of the sun dance camp becomes 466 lodges.

This total was more potential than realized at this date, however, for we have made no allowance for departures. It is true that Sitting Bull was using his camp soldiers to force reluctant lodges to remain, as reported by Kill Eagle and others. But on the other hand, trustworthy parties were sent out temporarily to hunt, steal ponies, and to trade for arms and ammunition. In mid-April it was reported from Standing Rock that Sitting Bull had dispatched scouts to keep watch on army posts along the Missouri. That same month Sitting Bull's nephew, White Bull, joined a sizeable party of Miniconjous and Hunkpapas for a horse-stealing raid to the Black Hills. At least twelve lodges of Hunkpapas came again to trade at Fort Berthold in late April, and others appeared at Fort Peck in late May.

It is reasonable that departures so matched arrivals over the period from mid-May to June 7th that the village remained static at about four hundred lodges. This conclusion is supported by direct evidence. On Reno's reconnaissance, Mitch Boyer examined the five deserted camp sites from the one at Garland on the Tongue to the sun dance camp. Yet he gave only *one* figure for the size of these camps. The inescapable inference is that no significant growth had been noted, for this would have been of crucial importance. As final proof, Godfrey's diary recorded the sun dance camp as "three to four hundred lodges" strong. This compels a highly significant conclusion: this village represented the consolidated winter roamers, and that even as late as June 7th, when the sun dance concluded, summer roamers had not yet joined in significant numbers.

When Wooden Leg's hunters brought news of soldiers on Tongue River to the village at Muddy Creek on the morning of June 9th, the Cheyennes promptly sent out another scouting party under Little Hawk to check further. Grinnell says they left the Muddy Creek village and rushed over to Tongue River hoping to steal cavalry horses, but when the troops thwarted them with a hail of bullets, they reappeared next morning at the village, which had not moved. This foray was made at good speed, for they attacked Crook at 6:30 p.m. of June 9th. We leave the village at this site for the nights of June 8-11, for it rained on the last three days, and Custer's Rees noted on June 24th that the lodges of this camp had also been well ditched against rain.

As Wooden Leg says, they next moved twelve miles up to present Busby at mile 69, where Custer's column noted it, and we leave it for three nights. Then on June 15th it moved another dozen miles up Davis Creek to camp near the divide, for only one night by all accounts. That evening Little Hawk led another party to scout the troops. The next afternoon, while hunting buffalo near the source of the Rosebud, they spotted Crook's force on its June 16th march. The party sped back that night to warn the village and found it had moved some eight miles down Reno Creek to its upper forks. All that night warriors streamed from the camp to attack the soldiers before they could threaten the village. The Battle of the Rosebud raged all morning and part of the afternoon of June 17th. That night and next morning the triumphant warriors swarmed back to the village. Because of battle deaths, the village moved that day, June 18th, leaving the body of a dead Sioux lying in state in a lone tepee.

Kate Bighead, Wooden Leg, and Little Hawk agree that this move took them down Reno Creek and then a short distance up the Little Big Horn, where they camped for six nights, June 18-23, celebrating their victory over Crook with dances. It is also probable, though unmentioned, that summer roamers arrived during this period in such numbers as to prolong the feasting and dancing as welcoming ceremonies. Although the village had intended to move farther upstream, reports of bountiful game downstream prompted a short move on June 24th down to present Garryowen station, at mile 17, on the west bank. There Custer's column surprised them the next afternoon.

Five Arapaho warriors joined just before the battle, as told by them and confirmed by Wooden Leg. He also mentioned the arrival of many Sioux and some Cheyennes. John Stands in Timber, the late Cheyenne historian, has related that a band of fifteen or twenty lodges, made up of Magpie Eagle's band of Cheyennes and a few Oglalas arrived on June 24th. We allow the Cheyennes thirteen of these lodges. Then on the evening of June 25th, the Cheyenne chief, Dull Knife, arrived with his band of seven lodges. The total of Cheyennes who participated in the two-day battle thus comes to 120 lodges, including the original fifty of winter roamers and seventy from the Red Cloud Agency who had joined later in small parties.

This detailed reconstruction of the movements of the gathering village of winter roamers reveals just where it was when the military columns were so eager to find and destroy it. Lt. Bradley was the first to locate and keep track of it, but Gibbon failed to report this invaluable intelligence and then with no concern whatever marched away from it. Terry's search for it on the Little Missouri was hundreds of miles off the mark. His first plan to catch it on the lower Rosebud in a pincers movement was utterly hopeless, a fact revealed to him by Reno's disobedience of orders. Crook's erratic marches found no village, but enabled the village to find him. When Custer attacked, it was in an awkward location and enormously swelled by the recent arrival of summer roamers.

Chapter 28
The Summer Migrations

The annual migration of summer roamers from the agencies to unceded territory was as familiar as reveille to every army officer on the frontier. For years they had missed no opportunity to complain bitterly of having to skirmish every summer with braves whom the Indian agents had fed, armed, and "coddled" all winter. Nevertheless, the army command in 1876 managed to discount this habitual phenomenon even though it had taken extraordinary measures to aggravate it.

Even the most trusting agency Indian read the arms embargo, imposed by the army, as an ominous threat. They knew all about the schemes to force a cession of the Black Hills and were most aware of its invasion by gold-seekers. They had been first to hear of the army moves to drive in the winter roamers. Reynolds' winter attack convinced them of the need to hoard ponies and arms to aid their jeopardized relatives. They faced the threat of witheld rations and removal to the Missouri or to the south. They knew from painful experience that when soldiers took the war path, the friendly agency Indians were the easiest to find and punish. It was both fear and resentment that drove the summer roamers out that year in unprecedented numbers.

Except for a few lodges, the major migration had to await the growth of new grass, so necessary for reconditioning winter-poor ponies. This year, the new grass sprang up in the last week of April. At that time many lodges began moving out from the inhospitable agencies to the greening prairies on the edge of the reservation. After a few weeks of good grazing the strengthened ponies were ready for the next move out to the unceded territory.

The peak of departure would thus come in mid-May, but between the agencies and the magnetic valleys of the Rosebud and Little Big Horn lay three hundred miles of plains. The trek could be made in two weeks of determined travel, or a more leisurely month with pauses to gather lodge poles and to hunt. The influx into the villages of the winter roamers would therefore not peak until after mid-June. As we have already shown, only a few lodges in the van had arrived before the sun dance of June 5-7. The main wave would not arrive until after the Rosebud Battle of June 17th.

There is direct evidence that the departures peaked in mid-May. As late as April 27th, Crook reported that although a few Cheyennes had slipped away, the Sioux still remained, but unless beef rations were promptly increased, they might be compelled to leave, too (O-28). Barely a month later, the scene had changed drastically. On May 17th, Captain Egan's Black Hills patrol had seen a hundred lodges of Sioux heading north, having just attacked a wagon train. By May 28th he learned at the agencies that 120 lodges of Oglalas and fifty of Brules had departed. The May newspapers carried a flood of reports detailing clashes between Indians and Black Hillers, still within the reservation boundaries. By mid-June, however, these stories disappeared.

There is also direct evidence for the congregation of these summer roamers on the edge of the reservation. On May 28th, Yellow Robe left a camp of 1800 (!) lodges on Rosebud Creek, preparing to set out for Powder River and anxious to fight (O-28). Since he reached the Red Cloud Agency in six days, this Rosebud Creek was not the far-distant branch of the Yellowstone, but the nearby branch of White River on the reservation.

The story was the same at the Missouri agencies, though the agents were reluctant to admit it. On May 5th, Edward Allison, the Sioux interpreter for the army post at Standing Rock, reported in Bismarck that many of the agency braves were moving out. Mrs. Galpin, a full-blooded Sioux widow who ran a trading store at the agency, reported that not five hundred braves had been present since May 15th. Louis Agard, an ex-army scout, reported on May 8th that 1500 (!) lodges had gathered on the western edge of the reservation at the junction of Box Elder Creek with the Little Missouri. John W. Smith, the sutler for the Dakota column, learned from Indian sources in the fall that on May 30th, when the Dakota column crossed to the Little Missouri, many Indians had gathered at these forks before striking for the Rosebud country to join the winter roamers (I-28).

More crucial than the date of departure is the time of arrival at the consolidated camp of winter roamers. The first group to arrive right after the sun dance was a band of 130 Two Kettles from the Cheyenne River Agency, led by Chief Runs-the-Enemy. Usher L. Burdick claimed that Gall and Crow King, prominent war chiefs of the Hunkpapas, did not arrive until after the Rosebud fight of June 17th, and ex-Indian agent James McLaughlin claimed that this battle was fought "before the union of the hostile forces."

We believe that the majority descended on the village between June 18th and 25th, when it was encamped on the Little Big Horn just *above* Reno Creek. The prolonged feasting and dancing that prevailed over this period affords one clue. To be sure, the celebration was triggered by the triumph over Crook, but mass arrivals in need of welcoming and eager to hear the details of the victory may well have prolonged it. Stronger evidence, however, lies in the findings of Custer's column when it marched above the sun dance camp on June 24th. Suddenly, they found the Rosebud valley crisscrossed by innumerable trails, judged to be but a few days old, overlaying the original trail.

Even this maze of trails did not reveal the route of all the arriving summer roamers. Other trails led down the Little Big Horn to the burgeoning village. In his diary for July 29th, Bourke recorded the story of a Shoshone scout who had accompanied the Crows when they left Crook's camp on June 18th. The Shoshone reported that they had stumbled on a big Sioux village near the head of the Little Big Horn, which they had to climb the mountains to avoid. It was probably this large village that left the recent heavy trail descending the Little Big Horn that Captain Ball's reconnaissance discovered on June 28th. And there were probably other trails that no one noted.

This sudden influx of reinforcements was heavy enough to drastically alter the soldier-warrior odds on the very eve of the Custer battle. We shall analyze the strength of the swollen village in the next chapter, but we furnish a clue at this time. Taking the Cheyennes as our reference, we have already found that seventy lodges of summer roamers joined the original fifty of winter roamers. If we apply this same ratio to the entire village, it swelled from about 400 to 960 lodges, an increase of 140%. This is well within the ceiling of 1216 lodges imposed by our absentee-returnee analysis. It was this unanticipated expansion of the hostile village that spelled disaster for Custer.

Fate seems almost to have conspired to conceal from Terry and Custer this ultimate strength of their foe. The latest and most direct evidence was Mitch Boyer's count of four hundred lodges, and this fit only too nicely with the estimate of winter roamers that Custer had picked up in Washington. Not until the day before the battle, after passing the sun dance camp, did the evidence abruptly change. And at that critical moment, Custer seems to have misinterpreted the signs to mean that the village was breaking up and fleeing.

A traditional misjudgement of the Indian nature undoubtedly fostered this fatal misinterpretation. Every experienced officer on the plains knew that it was hard to force Indians into a pitched battle. Cultural bias stereotyped this prudence as a coward's preference for running instead of fighting — an egregious error. The Indian placed little value on the exploitation of property and people that drives the white race to stubborn conquest and domination. Instead, the Indian sought the honors won by rash bravery in games of war; but such quests were properly postponable until tomorrow, when the signs, spiritual or physical, proved unfavorable today. Both races, however, placed equal value on the lives of their loved ones, and would fight with abandoned resolution for self-preservation.

What the command failed to appreciate was that the roving bands understood perfectly well that the white man, through the agency of the army, had marked them and their way of life for extinction. Under such circumstances they would not play at war games, but fight desperately for survival. And a profound religious experience, the sun dance, had marvelously inspired their hopes and resolution. Custer's Indian scouts could smell all this on the prairie breeze, but were powerless to communicate their perceptions to insensitive and sometimes contemptuous soldier-whites.

*   *   *

After vanquishing Custer, the forces acting on the victorious village abruptly changed from centripetal to centrifugal. It had gathered to repel invasion and had triumphed. The prophecy of Sitting Bull had been fulfilled. The people were not only grateful — they were satisfied. They could now adjourn to enjoy the peaceful pursuits of the summer season. They could easily evade the soldier maniacs, should they prove foolish enough to keep after them.

Why Chief Washakie of the Shoshones failed to perceive this shift in mood is inexplicable, but he converted Crook to the same error. The Crows, on the other hand, soon perceived the change. Their agent wrote Washington on August 5th:

> I will here report that the Crows believe that the Sioux will do but little more fighting. They say that they must have exhausted their ammunition, that their horses are very poor, and that they have thrown away their lodges, a sure indication that they have had about all the fighting they want and intend to run. The Crows obtained this information

The centripetal forces were material as well as spiritual. A village of a thousand lodges meant a thousand wood fires to fuel, seven thousand hungry mouths to feed, and countless ponies to graze and water. Yet the mere presence of the village drove away the sustaining buffalo, consumed the sparse wood on the treeless plains, cropped the parched grass, and fouled the diminishing streams. Distressing shortages of necessities, to say nothing of sanitation problems, compelled an early break-up. This is precisely what transpired, despite untenable claims to the contrary.

The spin-off of small parties began immediately. Several groups of Cheyennes, including Magpie Eagle's party are said to have separated right after the battle, heading ultimately for the Black Hills area. Other parties of Sioux departed as early. Some moved back to the Rosebud, for when Crook's column descended the stream to the Busby bend in August, his scouts reported many trails coming in from the west. Such departures, in groups large and small, continued for months. Their van began to turn up on the periphery of the reservations as early as mid-July, and some even surrendered soon thereafter. Most of these can be identified as summer roamers.

It is highly probably that all these early losses represented the less dedicated and cohesive summer roamers. Some had never intended to war against the whites. Others feared retaliation for the audacious victories over the troops. Parties of this mind fled to the more comfortable environs of the reservations. This left a steadily diminishing village, whose nucleus consisted of dedicated winter roamers, who clung more or less together until the fall hunts forced a break-up. They were so group-oriented as to have left little record of the invaluable support they had received from the fading summer roamers. We cannot, of course, trace the splinter groups, but it is possible to follow the movements of the main nucleus.

On the afternoon of June 26th, scouts warned the big village on the Little Big Horn that still another large soldier force (the Terry-Gibbon column) was rapidly approaching from the north. The village decamped rather precipitately, for it left packed lodges, lodge poles, and personal possessions for the soldiers to ransack. Wooden Leg says the caravan in moving south took the benchland on the west side of the valley. Pausing that night for only a brief rest, they continued until they had covered the sixteen miles to present Lodge Grass, Montana. Here Lodge Grass Creek (Wood Lice Creek to the Sioux) joins the Little Big Horn from the southwest, and Owl Creek (then called Ash Creek) joins from the southeast. They camped here

339

for only the night of June 27th to celebrate their second victory with dancing.

Indian claims that they moved the next morning are confirmed by the failure of Captain Ball's reconnaissance to find either the village or its outriders on June 28th, when it scouted thirteen miles up its trail. The advance certainly sighted this location, though none mentioned a camp site. Various accounts, however, mention a division of the trail, one diverging southeast up Owl Creek, one leading southwest up Lodge Grass Creek, and a third ascending the main stream. These diverging trails were also noted by the courier parties that Terry later sent Crook.

This evidence indicates a significant spin-off at this point on the morning of June 28th. The departing bands were summer roamers, but the main nucleus took the right hand trail up Lodge Grass Creek. This contradicts Wooden Leg, who said that they moved thirteen miles up the main stream to present Wyola, and then turned northeast to Rosebud Creek and on to the mouth of Powder River which they reached in sixteen days, the village still intact. Only the dedicated nucleus was intact, and his chronology is in error; it would take the village to the Yellowstone *before* the depot there was abandoned on July 21st. His itinerary also disagrees with most other accounts, which speak of a westward circuit and a much closer approach to the mountains.

Respects Nothing (Oglala) told Judge Ricker that the main camp moved up Lodge Grass Creek to the Big Horns, remaining several days in each of several camps. Both Two Moon (Cheyenne) and Feather Earring (Miniconjou) also imply a westward loop before returning to the head of the Little Big Horn. Gall and Mrs. Spotted Horn Bull (Hunkpapas) reported a stay of several days at the mountains. Black Elk (Oglala) claimed they spent a whole month there, but his later events contradict this. The adoption of this westward circuit corrects the major defect in Wooden Leg's account.

John Stands in Timber tells of how the Cheyennes moved into the Big Horns, where a Sheep-eater Indian slipped into their camp and killed three Cheyennes before being dispatched. Since this does not tally with Wooden Leg's story, it has been sometimes assumed that the Cheyennes had broken up by this time. But our correction of Wooden Leg's error removes the incompatibility and the evidence for a Cheyenne break-up.

There is direct corroboration of this longer sojourn at the foot of the mountains. On July 7th, Lt. Sibley's scouting party, as it rode toward the head of the Little Big Horn, found the country swarming with war parties. That afternoon they were forced into a skirmish

340

in the foothills, only three miles above the village, subsequently found to have been camped on the Little Big Horn where it debouches from the mountains. Three Sioux, Kill Eagle, Respects Nothing, and Feather Earring, mention this skirmish in which the Cheyenne, Tall Bear, was killed and all the soldier horses captured.

No Cheyennes mentioned this skirmish, unless Wooden Leg recounted it unwittingly. He tells of hunting near Sheridan, packing the meat, and then being frightened into a hasty flight back to the village by soldiers. He tells this story twice, the second time adding that the soldiers killed a Cheyenne named Tall Bear. The first telling coincides with the departure of the village for the Rosebud, but the second is timed in early fall, when no soldiers were present in the area. We believe these stories referred to a single event — the Sibley skirmish of July 7th.

From this array of evidence, we conclude that back on the morning of June 28th several sizeable parties of summer roamers turned south and east, while the main camp moved about thirteen miles southwest up Lodge Grass Creek to camp at the foot of the mountains. Undoubtedly some parties went up into the Big Horns to procure lodge poles. The village then worked southeast to the head of the Little Big Horn by July 7th. When Crook's scouts finally examined the site on August 1st, they found plenty of evidence that the villagers and their ponies alike had been faring very poorly.

Whether starving or not, the death of two Cheyenne warriors in the Sibley skirmish dictated a move the next morning. Grouard, on August 1st, scouted the departing trail, which led downstream to another campsite at Wyola, where Pass Creek joins the Little Big Horn. Much to Grouard's disgust, his biographer, Joe DeBarthe, invented a ridiculous story of Frank's wandering among the corpses of Custer's men on the night of June 25th. DeBarthe then had to omit Frank's actual scout of August 1st, because he had woven this material into the fabricated story. But this abused material clearly confirms the Wyola camp site. From there Frank traced it east toward the head of the Rosebud, exactly as Wooden Leg said. We thus find that the main village departed from the valley of the Little Big Horn at Wyola on the morning of July 9th. This was why Terry's soldier couriers found trails, but no village, when they ascended the stream two days later.

Although the main nucleus left Crook's front on July 9th, many others, mostly summer roamers, lingered behind. On finding the soldiers immobile and sticking close to camp, they turned to enthusiastic harrassment, firing into the camp at night, trying to stampede the animal herds, and burning off the grazing for miles around. This palled after a week or so and subsided, to be followed by prairie burnings to the northeast in the wake of their own withdrawal. By then, there were only thin patrols in the area, as Crook so belatedly discovered.

According to Wooden Leg, the main village camped at the very source of the Rosebud for the night of July 9th. The next day they moved down to a point a few miles below the site of the Rosebud fight, just above present Kirby. When Crook's force reached this point on August 7th, they mistook this camp site for that of the village which supplied the warriors for that fight, and which they had tried to find and attack. This error at least confirms the age of this deserted site.

Still finding game distressingly scarce, the village traveled rapidly each day down the Rosebud, as Wooden Leg says, to the mouth of Greenleaf Creek, where they turned east to Tongue River and down to the mouth of Beaver Creek at present Brandenburg. This entire route is confirmed by Crook's pursuit. The arrival at Brandenburg can be dated July 14th by a terrific thunder storm that struck that night, momentarily breaking a dry spell of weeks.

Kill Eagle's party had been soldiered into remaining with Sitting Bull, but he relates that with the help of the Cheyennes he escaped from a camp on Tongue River at Beaver Creek. Significantly he describes the escape as made under cover of a furious nocturnal rain storm. This fixes the date as July 14th, for no more rain fell for ten days, by which time he had reached his reservation. Speeded by fear, they fled desperately day and night to reach safety near Black Horse Butte on Grand River, about 75 miles from Standing Rock Agency office. Word of his return reached the agency on July 21st, but illness, fear, and negotiations delayed his formal surrender until September 14th.

The rapid travel of the village reveals that it had not yet found the much-needed buffalo herds. This prompted the break-up that occurred at Brandenburg and involved even the nucleus of winter roamers. Wooden Leg accompanied a smaller division that turned up Tongue River, although he mentions no separation. Black Elk and Respects Nothing accompanied the larger division that turned downstream. This break-up is confirmed by the Terry-Crook column, who found the deserted camp with a heavy trail leading down, a lighter one leading up, and another heading due east over the divide, such as Kill Eagle's fleeing band would have left. Apparently on breaking up, they arranged a future rendezvous on Powder River.

The large division that turned down the Tongue apparently found buffalo at last, for they abruptly slowed their pace. Godfrey

342

recorded eight camp sites along the forty-mile stretch between the mouths of Beaver and Pumpkin Creeks. Even though three represented camps occupied on the spring out-trail, the remaining five signal a leisurely rate of travel. That they lingered in the Tongue valley for at least two weeks is confirmed by Medicine Cloud, a Yanktonnais, who returned to Fort Peck on August 2nd. Agent Mitchell had sent him as an emissary to Sitting Bull back in May, but he had been soldiered to remain just like Kill Eagle. He reported that the Hunkpapa chiefs, Sitting Bull, Black Moon, and Four Horns had held a council to compose a message for him to deliver to the agent. He was then released from their camp at "White Ridge" on Tongue River on July 27th (O-18).

Further confirmation comes from Black Elk, who says that while they were still on Tongue River, scouts reported that the soldiers had left piles of corn and oats at the mouth of Powder River. Some braves then rode down and brought back some corn, having had one of their number killed by soldiers who landed from a steamboat. Black Elk does not mention that the village had moved when these foragers returned, but the *Far West* salvaged the oats and corn on August 2nd, its troop escort killing an Indian.

Even the rear guard must have left the Tongue Valley by August 1st, for on that day and the next observers at the mouth of the Rosebud noted heavy smoke from prairie fires in that direction. We suggest that by July 29th the village started up Pumpkin Creek, crossed the divide to the Mizpah ford and turned down the east bank of Powder River to camp just above Locate Creek on August 1st. The Terry-Crook column followed their trail by this route, and Terry himself noted a large camp site somewhere between Mizpah ford and Locate Creek, a few miles below which the trail broke up and scattered to the east. This was the rendezvous camp which the village occupied before the final, complete break-up occurred.

We now return to the smaller division, which included the Cheyennes and Wooden Leg. Still traveling rapidly in search of buffalo, they ascended the Tongue to present Ashland where they took Otter Creek up to the divide to Pumpkin Creek and on to Powder River above present Broadus. As a possible confirmation, eight Indians soon appeared at the Cheyenne River agency, reporting that their hostile village had been moving south before they left it on July 19th (O-4).

At this point Wooden Leg's itinerary becomes vague and confused. He says they traveled fast (still no buffalo?) down Powder River to a camp apparently some twenty-two miles above Locate Creek, where they remained four or five nights before the grand break-up occurred. The Cheyennes *then* went down to the Yellow-stone to find soldier corn, fire into a passing boat (the *Carroll* skirmish of July 24th?) and find the body of a scalped Sioux brave (killed in the *Far West* skirmish of August 2nd?). Kate Bighead adds that a pair of steamboats passed while they were there (the *Durfee* and *Josephine*, July 31st?).

We believe Wooden Leg reversed the order of the grand break-up and the Yellowstone sortie, and moved his party far too fast. We suggest that they finally found buffalo on Powder River and therefore descended it more slowly. Some, or all, proceeded to the Yellowstone, where they saw boats, forage, and bodies, and *then* returned upriver to the rendezvous camp just above Locate Creek. The grand break-up then followed, probably no later than August 5th.

Many small parties left this rendezvous camp to head for their reservations, hoping to sneak in to the agencies unobtrusively, but resigned to give themselves up if necessary. It was probably such a party that Crook's column stumbled on at Slim Buttes, a month later. The Cheyennes, traveling leisurely, seem to have moved far up Powder River. The Sioux apparently broke up into small hunting parties that turned eastward to Beaver Creek and the Little Missouri. Even their rear guard must have reached Beaver Creek by August 11th, for there the prairie burning stopped, quenched by the heavy rains that began on that date. These Sioux then re-grouped, not in one large village, but in a number of small ones, as was their usual habit.

Long Dog's Hunkpapa band crossed the Yellowstone near Glendive on August 22nd. Sitting Bull's larger band turned down the Little Missouri to hunt in the Killdeer Mountains by August 21st, when a splinter group tried to trade at Fort Berthold. Crazy Horse's followers turned south up the Little Missouri, where they were encamped not far from Slim Buttes by September 10th. By that time Terry had abandoned the campaign and Crook did the same the next day.

The foregoing reconstruction is sufficiently detailed and reliable to provide ample explanation for the dismal failure of the army's summer campaign. For want of keeping his scouts out, Crook did not launch his first stern chase until nearly a month after the hostiles had left his front. Although Terry knew that hostiles were thronging at the mouth of Powder River to the east, he started southwest to join Crook. When the two armies left the Rosebud in pursuit, their quarry had already scattered east of Powder River nearly a week before. It is no wonder that so belated a stern chase punished the

344

troops without glimpsing an Indian.

When they resumed the campaign on August 27th, the tribes were dispersed all over the plains. Terry's swing to the north unwittingly frightened off Long Dog's party, the only band north of the Yellowstone, but the troops arrived too late to catch him on the Missouri at Wolf Point. Crook resumed the blind chase, following an army road in lieu of a hostile trail. Neglecting what sign he finally found, he overshot his mark to the east. While heading south for supplies before his troops expired, a detachment struck a small village heading for their agencies to surrender. Then when Crazy Horse rallied to the rescue, Crook beat a retreat.

The summer campaign proved the obvious: to search for Indians with eyes closed is apt to be frustrating.

Chapter 29
The Strength of the Little Big Horn Village

One of the most baffling puzzles of the Battle of the Little Big Horn has been the strength of the village that so decisively defeated the 7th Cavalry. You may choose any number between one and forty thousand and find that it corresponds to someone's estimate of lodges, warriors, or persons. The discrepancies persist even if we focus on only one small tribe, the Cheyennes, for example. Such eminent authorities as George E. Hyde, George Bird Grinnell, Dr. Charles A. Eastman, and Dr. Thomas B. Marquis have cited figures ranging from 55 to 300 lodges of Cheyennes present for the great battle.

Recognizing that the citing of authorities, or the averaging of any number of baseless speculations could continue endlessly without bringing one iota of progress, Harry H. Anderson in 1960 introduced the idea of analysis. Concentrating on the Northern Cheyennes, he first attempted to establish the tribal population and then to work within this constraint. He found that the higher estimates exceeded the tribal population, and his own best judgement suggested the presence of only 70 Cheyenne lodges for the Custer fight (M-2). This pioneering effort represented a genuine breakthrough, capable, with extension and refinement, of reducing the uncertainty by some orders of magnitude.

In an earlier chapter we applied Anderson's approach to establish the constraints imposed by population as well as absentees from and returnees to the reservations for all the tribes involved. Although figures for the Cheyennes were included, their discussion was postponed. We now consider these figures and extend the analysis to yield estimates of Cheyenne strength on many crucial dates in 1876 and 1877. Then using a variety of independent methods, we shall attempt to establish the total strength of the Little Big Horn village.

The counts of Southern Cheyennes made at the Upper Arkansas Agency in the years 1872-76, before inflation became rampant there, and for 1886-90, when reliable censuses again became available, average 2125 and 2175 persons, respectively. This again confirms the static nature of the population. We choose a round population number of 2160, equivalent to 270 lodges. Counts of the Northern Cheyennes at Red Cloud Agency for the pre-inflation years from 1872 to 1874 average 1540. Censuses for 1889-90 at Pine Ridge and Tongue River Agencies average only 1400, lower because of heavy casualties and absorption into other tribes. We choose the round number of 1520, equivalent to 190 lodges for this tribe. This is somewhat higher than the single anomalously low count of 1200 chosen by Anderson.

Instead of merely determining absentees and returnees in 1876 for these bands, we have attempted to establish the geographic distribution of all 460 lodges of Cheyennes on nine significant dates in the years 1876-77, using all the available information, which is rather extensive. The results are presented in Table 1, which will serve as the focus of the discussion that follows.

All Cheyenne accounts agree that a small but significant number of Southern Cheyennes participated in the war in the north. In the fall of 1875, Agent John D. Miles of the Upper Arkansas Agency, reported some fifty lodges of this band absent in the north, and by August 31, 1876, twenty-two of these lodges were still absent. The number absent in March of 1876, when the first engagement of the war took place, is uncertain, but we incline to an estimate of thirty lodges. Many were at the Red Cloud Agency, while others were with the winter roamers.

The first critical date in Table 1 is March 17th, when General Reynolds' attack opened the war. At this time we post 240 lodges of Cheyennes at the Upper Arkansas Agency, leaving the other thirty lodges in the north. In accordance with Wooden Leg's account, we post forty lodges in the main camp that Reynolds struck and ten with Crazy Horse's village. This leaves 170 lodges at Red Cloud Agency, in contrast to Agent James S. Hasting's inflated count of 270 for April (O-36). This, incidentally, is the last of the exaggerated counts from this agency for the rest of our period.

Following this first battle, the Cheyennes began slipping away from the Red Cloud Agency in small parties, according to both Agent Hastings and General Crook. But on June 5th, the former

TABLE 1

Geographic Distribution of Cheyenne Lodges, 1876-77

LOCATIONS	POP.	1876						1877		
		3/17	6/5	6/17	6/26	7/25	11/25	1/8	5/7	9/10
AGENCIES										
Red Cloud	190	170	120	99	99	87	24	24	133	18
Upper Arkansas	270	240	240	241	241	244	251	270	270	394
Fort Keogh									38	38
subtotal	460	410	360	340	340	331	275	294	441	450
ABSENT										
Main band		40	100	100	120	103	173	156		
Crazy Horse		10					10			
Magpie Eagle				13		13				
Little Wolf				7						
Dull Knife						12				
Lame Deer									4	
In transit									5	
Killed						1	2	10	10	10
subtotal		50	100	120	120	129	185	166	19	10
GRAND TOTAL	460	460	460	460	460	460	460	460	460	460

reported that no more than fifty lodges had departed in this fashion (O-36). We have seen that Wooden Leg enumerated fifty lodges of agency Indians that had joined the Cheyenne circle in the main camp by this same date, that of the sun dance, in nice agreement with the agent. Our table, therefore, shows 100 lodges in the main camp at this time, leaving 120 still at the agency.

The next important date is June 17th, that of Crook's Rosebud fight. Captain William H. Jordan, commanding Fort Robinson on the Red Cloud Agency, reported that Chief Little Wolf had departed on June 15th with 125 lodges — a few more than we have cited as present. But Agent Hastings corrected the Captain's exaggeration by making a head count on June 19th that showed 99 lodges present (O-36). Thus by our reckoning, only 21 lodges had left since June 5th. We make one of these a returnee to the southern agency, leaving thirteen for Magpie Eagle's band, which had reached the Rosebud, and seven for Little Wolf's party, still in transit. Confirmation of seven lodges with Little Wolf comes from Lt. Col. Wesley Merritt's investigation of affairs at the agency in the preceding March. At that time one beef was issued to each 27 persons, and Little Wolf's group received two beeves, implying 54 persons, or seven lodges (O-26).

We thus find only 133 Cheyenne lodges available to participate in the Rosebud fight. Incidentally, there were probablay no more than 500 lodges of all tribes to confront Crook — equivalent to about 900 warriors, only a portion of whom sallied out from the distant village to engage in the fight.

On the evening of June 25th there were only 120 lodges of Cheyennes in the village on the Little Big Horn to vanquish Custer. Magpie Eagle had joined the main camp on the day before the battle, and Little Wolf on the evening of the first day. It should be noted that most of the Cheyennes had come out in *advance* of the main wave of Sioux, because of their reaction to Reynolds' attack.

The threat of an army take-over of the agencies, and the inspiring news of the victories in the north spurred another wave of Indian departures in mid-July. On the 15th the over-reactive Captain Jordan reported that 100 lodges of Cheyennes were leaving, again slightly more than the total present. This report, of course, negated the Captain's previous one, and substantiated the agent's correction of it. But this second alarm was destined to boomerang on the army. Colonel Merrittt, who had just marshaled the 5th Cavalry to reinforce Crook, then waiting impatiently on Goose Creek, delayed to drive these "800" Cheyennes back to the agency.

On July 17th Agent Hastings reported only 20 Cheyenne lodges at his agency, implying that 79 had left; but he added that they were already flocking back after encountering Merritt's force that morning (O-36). The Colonel reported on July 18th that the number of departures had been exaggerated, that he had driven only a few hundred back, and not more than 12 lodges had escaped, thus promptly restoring the agency population to 87 lodges (O-36). Hastings confirmed this on the 25th. The principal escapee at this time was Chief Dull Knife.

As of July 25th, therefore, we show 87 lodges at Red Cloud and three more than before at the southern agency, for Agent Miles reported in early August that a few of his Indians had returned from the north. We also post one lodge to represent the Cheyennes killed in the Custer fight. The main camp had already begun to split up, but since we can only identify the departure of Magpie Eagle, we can do no better than to leave 103 in the main village.

The next crucial date is November 25th, when General Mackenzie struck the consolidated Cheyenne camp under Dull Knife. This was by far the largest assemblage of the tribe during the period in question. The exodus from the Red Cloud Agency had continued, for in August Lt. Oscar Elting found only 40 Cheyenne lodges present. On November 8th, after the confiscation of arms and ponies, Lt. Frederick S. Calhoun made another exact count that yielded only 24 lodges (O-36). As early as September Agent Miles reported only 22 lodges of Southern Cheyennes still in the north; we have arbitrarily added three more returnees in the intervening month or so, making 251 at that agency. We have also added the equivalent of another lodge for the nine warriors killed in a Cheyenne attack on the Shoshones in early November. According to various sources, about ten lodges, as usual, were with Crazy Horse's camp in the north. All this leaves 173 lodges in the large Cheyenne camp that General Mackenzie destroyed. This is the precise number officially reported, an excellent check on our total reconstruction.

On January 8, 1877, General Miles attacked the camp of Crazy Horse and Dull Knife refugees on Tongue River. John Stands in Timber related that right after the Mackenzie fight about 18 lodges of Southern Cheyennes headed for their agency; although they may not all have arrived by January, we nevertheless post 270 lodges at that agency. Since 40 or more persons had been killed by Mackenzie and 14 or more others had died of exposure in the resulting flight, we now enter a total of 10 lodges for casualties. This leaves 156 Cheyenne lodges in the mixed village, which General Miles reported as totalling 500 lodges.

The mass surrenders began in the spring of 1877. We choose May 7th as our next date, because of General Miles' attack on Lame

Deer's small village of hold-outs on that day, and because nearly all the Cheyennes had turned themselves in by then. On April 23rd, 38 lodges were fortunate enough to surrender to Miles at Fort Keogh (O-39). But 109 lodges chose the Red Cloud Agency, swelling the roles there to 133 lodges.* Of the nine lodges still out, four had joined Lame Deer, leaving five others in transit somewhere.

On May 28th, 117 lodges of miserable Northern Cheyennes were escorted to the hated southern agency, leaving only 16 lodges at Red Cloud (O-36). By September 10th, the last of Lame Deer's survivors came in, three lodges reporting to Red Cloud and one to the southern agency. The five remaining lodges apparently also came in to the latter, for the military records there show a net increase of five persons over the winter, representing the excess of late returnees over deaths by sickness (O-30), the latter given as 41 by Dr. Grinnell. Hence, on our final date of September 10th, all 460 lodges of Cheyennes are accounted for as dead or present at the three agencies.

This attempt to account for the whereabouts of the entire Cheyenne population at nine crucial dates has uncovered a considerable number of confirmations and checks among a host of sources. At none of the dates was it necessary to strain the evidence to reach a full accounting. On the other hand, the results are not as perfect as the arithmetic. But figures carrying an error of plus or minus ten lodges make a gratifying reduction in the previous chaotic uncertainties.

The reconstruction provides strong support for the conclusion already drawn from Wooden Leg's account that the Cheyenne circle in the Little Big Horn village totalled about 120 lodges. Yet when this incredibly reliable Indian was questioned directly on this point, his estimates abruptly turned impossible. He made four separate statements that amount to estimates. The most direct one specified 300 lodges. Another claimed that all the Northern Cheyennes were present, which we must reckon at 190 lodges. Still another specified 300 warriors, which converts to 150 lodges. A final guess, made in conjunction with Dr. Marquis, came to 1600 persons, which converts to 200 lodges.

Wooden Leg was not alone in making such overestimates. Two Moons and other Cheyenne informants convinced Dr. Grinnell that 200 lodges were present. Why are all these high? We venture to suggest that these Indians were victims of a perfectly natural mis-

*Lt. W.P. Clark's report, Fort Robinson, May 24, 1877. Copy furnished by Harry G. Anderson.

take. They subconsciously felt that they had been strongest when they achieved their greatest victory. They therefore canvassed their memories for the size of the largest camp circle of that year — and came up with not bad estimates of their consolidated village of 173 lodges that Mackenzie destroyed in November, instead of the 120 lodges that vanquished Custer in June.

*   *   *

The reasonable figure now available for the Cheyenne strength in the Little Big Horn village provides leverage in attacking the problem of the total strength of all the tribes in that village. We have already mentioned that if the ratio of final strength to winter roamer strength (12 to 5) applies as well to the Sioux, it makes a tenuous estimate of about 960 lodges for the full village. Dr. Grinnell's informants gave the total as 1500 lodges, including 200 Cheyennes; they further stated that the six Sioux circles were each larger than the Cheyenne. It follows that the Sioux circles averaged 216 lodges each, only 8% larger than the Cheyenne. Since this would seem undetectable, we assume a more obvious 20% difference. Then using the reliable 120 lodges for the Cheyenne base, the total comes to 984 lodges.

Again it is Wooden Leg who provided the most careful estimates of the *relative* sizes of the camp circles. We give his comparative statements and add our translation into ratios in parentheses: the Hunkpapa circle (2.0) was twice the size of the Cheyenne (1.0); the Blackfeet (0.8) had a few less, and the Sans Arc (1.2) more; the Oglala (1.8) and Miniconjou (1.5) each had more than the Sans Arc. The sum of these ratios is 8.3, and applying it to the Cheyenne base of 120 yields a total of 996 lodges. Finally, Dr. Eastman, himiself a Sioux who served many years as physician at several Sioux agencies, spent years collecting information on this point from Indian informants as well as agency records. His total was 949 lodges, but included only 55 of Cheyenne (I-9).

We now have four estimates, based wholly or in part on Indian sources and utilizing different methods, which range narrowly from 949 to 996 total lodges. They are all reasonably within the 1216 lodges we have established as the ceiling by our absentee-returnee analysis. Can we do as well with white sources?

At first blush it would seem hopeless to make anything of the incredibly disparate estimates emanating from white sources. But two striking features of this disarray of numbers provide an entering wedge. First, the numbers escalate with time after the battle, beginning within hours. For example, Benteen estimated the warrior strength at 1500-1800 on the morning of June 27th, 2500 by that evening, 300 on July 4th, and 8-9000 in 1879! Second, the myriad of statements made by those not present have no value as evidence. They are usually grotesquely high, reflecting the chauvinistic bias that rejected any other explanation of the "massacre" of white soldiers by redskins. We can accept only *primary* estimates made by persons on the spot at the time and promptly recorded. Such primary estimates fall into two categories, one based on the sight of warriors in action on the field, and the other on the examination of the standing village or its deserted site. For reasons that will emerge, these categories must be treated separately.

We have found but one primary estimate of the size of the standing village. This came from William Cross, a halfbreed Indian scout, who circulated around a good deal in pursuit of Indian ponies, giving him the opportunity to view the village while standing. Having left that afternoon with the Ree scouts he had little opportunity and no reason to revise his original impression. On reaching the Powder River depot on June 28th, he was immediately debriefed, and Lieutenant B.A. Byrne included a transcript of the proceedings in a newspaper dispatch. In response to a direct question, Cross stated that there were 800 or 900 tepees in the village.

Several officers took pains to examine the deserted village site. Lieutenant Hare, detailed to burn the village debris on June 28th, tesitfied that he counted 40 lodges sites and estimated the total at 1500, with 500 wickiup sites. Lieutenant DeRudio also examined the area, testifying to an estimated 1200 to 1500 lodge sites, with no reference to wickiups. The next summer, Lieutenant Hugh L. Scott also studied the area while serving on the Sheridan-Nowlan exhumation party, counting 1500 lodge sites and numerous wickiup sites. As a manifestation of the escalation process, the officers had reached a concensus of 1800 lodge sites by the time of the Reno Inquiry. Our best figures, therefore, are 1500 lodges and 500 wickiups.

Taken at face value these figures grossly exceed the "ceiling" number for the maximum lodges off the reservation that year. But if one thing is certain, the number of deserted *sites* must exceed the number of *lodges* in the standing village. Numerous whites and Indians have recorded that in response to the attack, the village followed the standard practice of striking the lodges in preparation for the flight of women and children to safety. By the time the poles were packed, flight was unnecessary, and they turned out to watch the excitement. By the time Custer was annihilated and dark-

353

ness had called the seige on Reno Hill, it was late for re-erecting the lodges. Some prudent ones did so, not in their original positions, but on clean new spots, as many have recorded. Others were replaced by quick wickiups to provide shelter for the night, during which a light rain fell. The presence of so many wickiups is proof enough of this.

Much has been made of these wickiups because they were the structure used by braves on the war path. Everyone has assumed that they housed warriors who had fled the agencies to war on the soldiers. Since they would run four braves to the wickiup, they alone could account for 2000 warriors! Unfortunately, there is not one iota of evidence to suggest that the original village contained a single wickiup. On the contrary, there is proof that if there were any at all, they did not harbor family-free summer roamers.

The summer migration regularly included entire families, for the women and children enjoyed the outing as much as the men. Expecting to be out all summer, families insisted on being together. They went to procure lodge-poles and lodge-skins, and the women were the lodge-builders. They went to hunt buffalo and the women were the butchers and cooks. They wanted robes to trade and new clothes to wear, and the women were the tanners and tailors. The children needed education and the parents were the teachers. How could they learn Indian ways if banished from Indian life? The senile and decrepit may have been left at the agencies, but the women and children? Never!

There is conclusive proof of this. The good military censuses of those left on the agencies show no excess of women and children. The excellent counts of those who surrendered show no excess men. The idea of thousands of wickiup-sheltered agency war parties is an incredible myth. The wickiups sprouted in the drizzle on the night of June 25th!

If we now examine the primary evidence of the deserted camp-site, we find that if the original village had consisted entirely of lodges, numbering one thousand, and all of these were struck during the attack, but only half re-erected on new sites and the other half replaced by wickiups, the signs would have revealed 1500 lodge sites and 500 wickiup sites, precisely as noted by those who studied them. This evidence, therefore, is perfectly compatible with a standing village of one thousand lodges, in excellent agreement with all our preceding evidence.

Let us turn now to the primary evidence regarding the warrior force as seen in action. On the morning of June 27th, General Terry interrogated the surviving officers as to the strength of the hostiles.

Col. Robert P. Hughes, the General's aide, wrote: "The replies pivoted about the figure of 1500, and I can recall Col. Benteen's reply almost verbatim, which was as follows: 'I have been accustomed to seeing divisions of cavalry during the War, and from my observations I would say that there were 1500 to 1800 warriors.' No one in the group at that time put this estimate above 1800 (R-26)." Taking the "pivotal" figure of 1500 and allowing two warriors to each of the 120 Cheyenne lodges and 1.75 to each of the remaining Sioux lodges, the total comes to 960 lodges, in perfect agreement with all our previous estimates.

Why this primary estimate so quickly escalated is revealed by Col. Graham, a non-witness, who wrote about this same incident: "According to Captain E.W. Smith, Terry's adjutant, their estimates pivoted around the figure 1800. After they observed the immensity of the village site, however, these estimates increased, and properly so (M-22)." It would seem that Graham wrote this from slippery memory of Hughes' statement. But more important, he casually converted a ceiling into an average. Still worse, he believed this number required upward revision to correspond, not to the standing village, but to its deserted site, thus falling into the very trap we have exposed.

The rapidity with which the false evidence of the camp site misled the officers is revealed in General Terry's official dispatch written only a few hours later that same evening: "Major Reno and Captain Benteen, both of whom are officers of great experience, accustomed to seeing large masses of mounted men, estimated the number of Indians engaged at not less than 2500. Other officers think that the number was greater than this (O-39)." Assuming as many as two warriors to each lodge, this escalated figure converts to an impossible 1350 lodges! General Gibbon was only a little slower in riding the escalator, for he wrote in a private letter the next day that the Indians "were estimated at from 1800 to 2500 warriors (C-37)."

It should now be clear that a variety of independent methods, both of Indian and white origin, all converge convincingly on a common estimate of no more than a thousand lodges in the village on the Little Big Horn. Without pretending an equal accuracy, Table 2 presents a break-down of this total by tribes. The first column makes a compromise solution to the difficult problem of "camp circles" and their probable tribal composition. The next repeats the "ceiling" figures yielded by our absentee-returnee analysis. The next two present Wooden Leg's relative ratio estimates and Dr. Eastman's figures. The final column offers a "best guess"

Table 2
Tribal Distribution in the Little Big Horn Village

TRIBES	CEILING	LITTLE BIG HORN VILLAGE		
		WOODEN LEG	DR. EASTMAN	"BEST"
Cheyenne Circle	196	120	55	120
Hunkpapa Circle	262	240	239	260
Hunkpapa	237		224	235
Yanktonnais, Santee	25		15	25
Oglala Circle	264	216	240	240
Miniconjou Circle	186	180	190	150
Sans Arc Circle	131	144	85	110
Blackfeet Circle	177	96	140	120
Brule	125			68
Blackfeet	34			34
Two Kettle	18			18
TOTAL	1216	996	949	1000

resolution of the discrepancies, made to total 1000 lodges. The differences between ceiling and best guess columns reflect the numbers that left the agencies too late to participate in the Custer fight.

This village of one thousand lodges would have contained 7,120 persons, including only 1780 adult males. In response to an overwhelming threat to the women and children, older boys might have swelled the ranks of the defenders to as many as two thousand, but it is not clear that this degree of threat did in fact materialize on June 25th.

Is it possible that less than two thousand fighting Indians could have so soundly thrashed the 7th Regiment of U.S. Cavalry? There is absolutely no reason to doubt it. On June 25th the regiment, as we have seen, mustered only 566 enlisted men, no match in individual combat skills for the Indian warriors. And, as we have also seen, they were so divided in space and time as to have fought against even worse odds. There is no longer any excuse for grossly exaggerating the Indian strength in order to account for so decisive an outcome. The real marvel is that so large a village could have remained together long enough to be ready at the critical moment. It remained intact only briefly, but fate timed the encounter perfectly for the Indian.

A NOTE ON DOCUMENTATION

Convinced that the system of documentation that has become standard in the field of history is unnecessarily expensive, repetitious, and obtrusive, without achieving full usefulness, a special system has been devised for the present work.

In order to eliminate the expense of endlessly repetitive footnotes, a single master bibliography is provided below, divided into five significant categories. *Contemporaneous* accounts from participants, such as diaries, journals, letters, news dispatches, and interviews, are given the code-letter "C." *Reminiscent* accounts from participants are coded "R." *Indian* accounts from participants are designated "I." *Official* records, largely those of the army and Indian office from the National Archives, or in published government documents, are coded "O." Then there is the inevitable *miscelaneous* category, coded "M." Since the entries within each category are arranged alphabetically and then given a serial number, the resulting letter-number code identifies the address of every item. In the text, necessary references are made by this letter-number code, enclosed in parentheses. This immediately signals the significant category without interrupting the reader.

Within the three participant categories, the arrangement and style of entries has been designed for maximum usefulness; they are alphabetized according to the name of the *participant*. The entry then adds the procurement source, i.e., the book, periodical, newspaper, or depository where the item may be found, sometimes by a letter-code reference to another bibliographic entry. The entries also include the participant's role and the force he accompanied, as well as dates of diaries, letters, and dispatches. Besides thus providing important information customarily omitted, this scheme enormously reduces the need for code citations in the text. Frequently the name and category of an informant are as germane to the narrative as the information provided, in which case they are woven into the narrative, making a code reference redundant.

As its sole disadvantage, this system has not been elaborated to permit citations of particular pages or specific items in document collections, for the obvious reason that the general reader is not interested and the serious student wants to read thoroughly anyhow. If this be a defect, we trust that the considerable advantages in economy, unobtrusiveness, and extra usefulness will more than compensate.

Some essential newspaper references, used but once, are referenced in the text and therefore do not appear in the bibliography.

As a preliminary to composing the narrative, it was necessary to compile a chronological collation of information from all sources, sometimes twenty to thirty in number. Since the serious student can do no less, he needs no rash of code references following each phrase.

Even the present economical system does not permit the citation of all sources used. For example, repeated scourings of newspapers, both frontier and metropolitan, yielded thousands of squibs on persons, boats, arrivals, and departures, etc. Though essential to the reconstruction of movements and sequences, these minutia are left undocumented. The reader may be assured, however, that such information was taken from contemporaneous notices and not from fallible recollections.

With this system, we hope the general reader will welcome the apparent lack of annoying documentation, while the serious student will find it adequate and the bibliography more useful than most.

Bibliography

I. Contemporaneous Accounts from Participants

C-1 Anonymous (with Crook). Dispatches: In Camp, June 17-28, N.Y. *Times*, July 13; Owl Cr., Sept. 10, *idem*, Sept. 17.

C-2 Anonymous (with Custer). Dispatch: Mo. of Big Horn, July 5, N.Y. *Herald*, July 30.

C-3 Anonymous (with Gibbon). Letter: Mo. of Big Horn, July 4, Helena *Herald*, July 20.

C-4 Anonymous (with Moore). Letter: Yellowstone Depot, July 15, N.Y. *Herald*, Aug. 1 (see M-21).

C-5 Anonymous (with Terry). Dispatches: Mo. of Big Horn, July 3, N.Y. *Tribune* (see M-43); Bismarck, July 8, St. Paul *Pioneer-Press*, July 13; Bismarck, July 12, N.Y. *Herald*, July 26; Terry's Camp on Rosebud, Aug. 11, Chicago *Times*, Aug. 20; Terry's Camp on Yellowstone, Aug. 26 (clipping in C-7).

C-6 Benteen, Frederick W. (Capt. Co. H, 7 Cav., with Custer). Letters: July 2-30 and July 4 (see M-21); Interview: N.Y. *Herald*, Aug. 8 (see M-21).

C-7 Bourke, John G. (1 Lt. 3 Cav., Aide to Crook). *Diary, 1876*. West Point Library (microfilm from Bell & Howell).

C-8 Bradley, James H. (1 Lt. 7 Inf., Gibbon's Chief of Scouts). *Journal* (Mar. 17 - June 26). *Mont. Hist. Soc. Contr.*, 2:140, 1896. Interview: Helena *Herald*, July 15. Letter: Helena, July 25, *idem*, July 25.

C-9 Brisbin, James S. (Maj. 2 Cav., with Gibbon). Unsigned dispatch: Custer's Battlefield, June 28, N.Y. *Herald*, July 8.

C-10 Brown, Alexander (Sgt. Co. H, 7 Cav., with Custer). *Diary* (July 1 - Sept. 10). Mss. Minn. Hist. Soc.

C-11 Brown, Edwin M. (Tptr. Co. B, 5 Inf., with Miles). "Memoranda of Sioux Expedition" (July 12 - Dec.). Mss., Mont. Hist. Soc.

C-12 Burleigh, Walter (Clerk on *Far West*). *Log of Far West* (June 26 - July 6). Excerpts in "Sitting Bull Wanted a Navy," *Sunshine Mag.*, Sept. 1930.

C-13 Burt, Andrew S. (Capt. Co. H, 9 Inf., with Crook). Dispatches: Goose Cr., July 15, Chicago *Tribune*, July 16 and Cincinnatti *Commercial*, July 16; Pumpkin Cr., Aug. 14 and Mo. of Powder R., Aug. 23, Cincinnatti *Commercial*,

Sept. 11; Heart R., Sept. 5, *idem*, Sept. 14; Rabbit Cr., Sept. 9 and Owl Cr., Sept. 10, *idem*, Sept. 17; Whitewood Cr., Sept. 13, *idem*, Sept. 19.

C-14 Byrne, Bernard A. (2 Lt. Co. C, 6 Inf., QM with Moore). Unsigned dispatches: On Yellowstone, June 1 and Powder R., June 10, N.Y. *Times*, June 27; Powder R., June 23-4, *idem*, July 11; Powder R., July 4, *idem*, July 13; Powder R., July 18, *idem*, July 29; Rosebud Cr., Aug. 2, *idem*, Aug. 13; Rosebud Cr., Aug. 4, *idem*, Aug. 18; Rosebud Cr., Aug. 7, *idem*, Aug. 21; Glendive Cr., Sept. 6, *idem*, Sept. 16.

C-15 Capron, Thaddeus H. (1 Lt. Co. C, 9 Inf., with Crook). *Diary and Letters* (May 23 - Oct. 1). Mss., U. of Wyo.

C-16 Carland, John (1 Lt. Co. B, 6 Inf., with Terry). Dispatches: Mo. of Little Big Horn, June 29, N.Y. *Herald*, July 14; Glendive Cr., Sept. 2 and Sept. 5, *idem*, Sept. 13.

C-17 Carr, Eugene A. (Lt.Col. 5 Cav., with Merritt). Letters: James T. King. *War Eagle, A Life of Gen. Eugene A. Carr*. Lincoln, 1963.

C-18 Carroll, Matthew (Freighter with Gibbon). *Diary* (May 15 - Sept. 12). *Mont. Hist. Soc. Contr.*, 2:229, 1896.

C-19 Clark, W. Philo (1 Lt. 2 Cav., with Crook). "Memo of a Voyage from Benson's Landing . . . to Mouth of Powder R." (Aug. 6-17). Mss., Mont. Hist. Soc.

C-20 Clifford, Walter (Capt. Co. E, 7 Inf., with Gibbon). "The Yellowstone Campaign of 1876" (a journal, Mar. - Aug.), serialized in the *Rocky Mountain Husbandman*, 1879. Dispatches: Custer's Battlefield, June 26-7, N.Y. *Herald*, July 13; Mo. of Big Horn, July 16, *idem*, July 29. All of the above are reprinted in the *Chicago Westerners Brandbook*, Dec., 1969, Jan., 1970, Jan., 1971, and Aug., 1972.

C-21 Cross, William (Ree scout with Custer). Interview: July 4, Powder R., with Lt. B.A. Byrne (?), N.Y. *Times*, July 13.

C-22 Crow Scouts (with Crook). Interview: Bozeman *Times*, July 6.

C-23 Custer, George A. (Lt.Col., 7th Cav.). Dispatches: Little Missouri, May 30, N.Y. *Herald*, June 19; Mo. of Powder R., June 12, *idem*, June 27; Mo. of Rosebud, June 22, *idem*, July 23. Letters: see M-14 and M-54.

C-24 Daniels, Zed H. (Scout with Terry). Dispatches: Crook City, June 6, Bozeman *Times*, July 6; Bismarck, July 21, *idem*, Aug. 10; Glendive Cr., Sept. 2, *idem*, Sept. 28.

C-25 Davenport. Reuben B. (reporter with Crook). Dispatches: Goose Cr., June 11, Chicago *Tribune*, June 19; Goose Cr., June 15, N.Y. *Herald*, June 21; Goose Cr., June 19, Chicago *Tribune*, June 27; Goose Cr., June 20; N.Y. *Herald*, July 6; Camp Cloud Peak, July 12, Chicago *Times*, July 18; Camp Cloud Peak, July 12, N.Y. *Times*, July 17; Goose Cr., Aug. 4, N.Y. *Herald*, Aug. 18; Owl Cr., Sept. 10 and Crook City, Sept. 12, *idem*, Sept. 17; Deadwood, Sept. 15, *idem*, Oct. 2.

C-26 DeRudio, Charles C. (1 Lt. Co. A, 7 Cav., with Custer). Dispatch: Mo. of Big Horn, July 5, N.Y. *Herald*, July 30 (see M-21).

C-27 DeWolf, James M. (Act. Ass. Surg., with Custer). "The Diary and Letters of Dr. James M. DeWolf" (Mar. 10 - June 24), edited by Edward S. Luce, *No. Dak. Hist.*, 25:35 and 41, Apr. and July, 1958.

C-28 Diehl, Charles S. (reporter with Terry). Dispatches: Ft. A. Lincoln, Aug. 1, Chicago *Times*, Aug. 9; Ft. Buford, Aug. 5, *idem*, Aug. 16; Ft. Buford, Aug. 15, *idem*, Aug. 19; On *Josephine*, Aug. 20, 22, and 23, *idem*, Aug. 26; On *Josephine* at Powder R., Aug. 25, and Camp on Yellowstone, Aug. 26 and 27, *idem*, Sept. 5; Deer Cr., Aug. 30, *idem*, Sept. 7; Glendive Cr., Sept. 2

and 5, *idem*, Sept. 12; Glendive Cr., Sept. 6, *idem*, Sept. 16; Ft. Buford, Sept. 10, *idem*, Sept. 20.

C-29 Dolan, John (Sgt. Co. M, 7 Cav., disch. at Powder R.). Interview at St. Paul, N.Y. *Herald*, July 23.

C-30 Edgerly, Winfield S. (1 Lt. Co. D, 7 Cav., wtih Custer). Letter: July 4 (see M-5).

C-31 English, William L. (1 Lt. Co. I, 7 Inf., with Gibbon). "Field Diary of Lt. William L. English" (Mar. 17 - Sept. 5), ed. by Barry C. Johnson, *English Westerners Brandbook*, July and Oct., 1966. Unsigned itinerary for Co. I: "From Ft. Shaw to the Yellowstone" (Mar. 17 - July 3). Mss., Mont. Hist. Soc.

C-32 Finerty, John F. (reporter with Crook). *War Path and Bivouac*. Chicago, 1890.

C-33 Flynn, Richard (Pvt. Co. D, 4 Inf., with Crook). "Journal of Richard Flynn" (Aug. 3, 1876 - Jan. 18, 1877). Mss., Custer Battlefield Nat. Mon.

C-34 Forsyth, James W. (Lt. Col., 10 Cav., Mil. Sec. to Sheridan). Interview: St. Paul, Aug. 10, Chicago *Inter-Ocean*, Aug. 11.

C-35 Foster, James E.H. (2 Lt. Co. I, 3 Cav., with Crook). Journal: May 29 - June 18, Chicago *Tribune*, July 5; May 28 - June 19, Cincinnatti *Commercial*, July 17; Goose Cr., June 26, Chicago *Tribune*, July 11; Goose Cr., July 12, *idem*, Aug. 1; Crook City, Sept. 19 and Custer's Park, Sept. 26, *idem*, Oct. 10.

C-36 Freeman, Henry B. (Capt. Co. H, 7 Inf., with Gibbon). "Diary of Capt. Henry B. Freeman" (Mar. 21 - Sept. 25). Mss., Custer Battlefield Nat. Mon.

C-37 Gibbon, John (Col. 7 Inf., comdg. Distr. of Mont.). Letter: June 28. *Mont. Hist. Soc. Contr.*, 4:285, 1903.

C-38 Gibson, Francis M. (1 Lt. Co. H, 7 Cav., with Custer). Letter of July 4: Katherine Gibson Fougera. *With Custer's Cavalry*. Caldwell, 1942.

C-39 Godfrey, Edward S. (1 Lt. Co. K, 7 Cav., with Custer). *The Field Diary of . . .* (May 17 - Sept. 24). Ed. by Edgar I. and Jane R. Stewart. Portland, 1957.

C-40 Grouard, Frank (scout with Crook). Interview: Red Cloud Agency, Sept. 17, N.Y. *Times*, Sept. 19.

C-41 "Hardtack" (with Gibbon). Dispatches (some unsigned): Ft. Pease, May 9, Bozeman *Times*, May 18; Below Baker's Battleground, May 29, *idem*, June 8; Above Powder R., June 9, and Below Rosebud Cr., June 15, *idem*, June 29; Camp on Little Big Horn, June 28, *idem*, July 6.

C-42 Hare, Luther (2 Lt. Co. K, 7 Cav., with Custer). Letter: July 3, Denison (Tex.) Daily *News*, July 15. Reprinted in *Chicago Westerners Brandbook*, Jan., 1969.

C-43 Herendeen, George A. (scout with Gibbon). Dispatch: Bismarck, July 7 (Sic! Mo. of Big Horn, July 3), N.Y. *Herald*, July 8. (See M-21).

C-44 Howard, James W. ("Phocion") (reporter with Terry). Dispatches: Aboard *Carroll*, July, Aboard *Carroll*, Powder R., July 29, and Camp Rosebud, Aug. 1, Chicago *Tribune*, Aug. 11; Camp Rosebud, Aug. 5, *idem*, Aug. 15; On Rosebud Cr., Aug. 8-9, *idem*, Aug. 18; Mizpah Cr., Aug. 15 and Mo. of Powder R., Aug. 18, *idem*, Sept. 9; Mo. of Powder R., Aug. 27, and Bismarck, Sept. 4, *idem*, Sept. 5; Bismarck, Sept. 4, *idem*, Sept. 9.

C-45 Johnson, Alfred B. (2 Lt. Co. I, 7 Inf., with Gibbon). Letter: July 4, St. Paul *Pioneer-Press*, July 22.

C-46 Kellogg, Mark H. (reporter with Terry). *Diary* (May 17 - June 9). *Mont. Hist. Soc. Contr.* 9:213, 1923. Dispatches: Ft. Lincoln, May 14, Bismarck *Tribune*, May 17; Heart R., May 17, *idem*, May 24; Expedition, N.Y. *Herald*, May 24; Rosebud Buttes, May 29, Bismarck *Tribune*, June 14; Mo. of Powder

R., June 12, *idem*, June 21; Mo. of Rosebud, June 21, N.Y. *Herald*, July 11.

C-47 "Long Horse" (with Gibbon). Dispatches: L. Prickly Pear, Mar. 20, Helena *Herald*, Mar. 23; Tongue R., May 28, *idem*, June 15; Tongue R., June 6, *idem*, July 6; Near Rosebud, June 14, *idem*, June 29.

C-48 Lounsberry, Clement A. (editor, Bismarck *Tribune*). Compilation, Bismarck *Tribune*, extra of July 6, and regular of July 12.

C-49 Luhn, Gerhard L. (Capt. Co. F, 4 Inf., with Crook). "Diary and Letters" (May 29 - Oct. 30). Mss., U. of Wyo.

C-50 McGillicuddy, Valentine T. (Act. Asst. Surg., with Crook). "Diary of Yellowstone and Big Horn Expedition" (May 26, 1876 - Apr. 10, 1877). *Denver Brandbook*, 9:279, 1953.

C-51 MacMillan, Thomas C. ("Mac") (reporter with Crook). Dispatches: Ft. Fetterman, May 27, Chicago *Inter-Ocean*, June 7; Ft. Fetterman, May 29, *idem*, June 8; Ft. Reno, June 2, *idem*, June 29; Mo. of Prairie Dog Cr., June 10, *idem*, June 16 and June 27; Goose Cr., June 15, *idem*, June 21 and June 27; Rosebud Cr., June 17, and Goose Cr., June 19, *idem*, June 24; Powder R., June 24, *idem*, June 27.

C-52 McCormick, Paul W. (sutler with Gibbon). Interview: Bozeman, Bozeman *Times*, June 8. Letter: Mo. of Big Horn, June 29, *idem*, July 6.

C-53 Mannion, James (with Moore). Letter: Mo. of Powder R., July 5, Chicago *Inter-Ocean*, Aug. 4.

C-54 Marsh, Grant (Capt. of *Far West*). Letter: On *Far West*, near Powder R., Aug. 29, St. Paul *Pioneer-Press*, Sept. 9.

C-55 Miles, George M. (clerk with Miles). "Notes of a Trip from Westminster, Mass., to Montana, in 1876" (July 11 - Dec. 27). Mss., *Mont. Hist. Soc.*

C-56 Miles, Nelson A. (Col. 5th Inf., with Terry). Letters in Virginia M. Johnson. *The Unregimented General*. Boston, 1962.

C-57 Mills, Cuthbert (reporter with Merritt). Dispatches: Goose Cr., Aug. 3, N.Y. *Times*, Aug. 17; Tongue R., Aug. 4, *idem*, Aug. 18; Rosebud Cr., Aug. 9, *idem*, Aug. 27; Mo. of Powder R., Aug. 23, *idem*, Sept. 12; Beaver Cr., Aug. 30, *idem*, Sept. 14; Belle Fourche R., Sept. 13, *idem*, Sept. 28; Custer City, Sept. 22, *idem*, Oct. 12; Custer City, Sept. 25, *idem*, Oct. 11.

C-58 O., J.W. (with Gibbon). Letter: Ft. Pease, Apr. 23, *Rocky Mountain Husbandman*, May 11.

C-59 O'Kelly, James J. (reporter with Terry and Miles). Dispatches: Rosebud Cr., Aug. 2, N.Y. *Herald*, Aug. 7; Rosebud Cr., *idem*, Aug. 8; Camp on Yellowstone, Aug. 3, *idem*, Aug. 11; *Far West*, Powder R., Aug. 15, *Far West*, Powder R., Aug. 17, and *Far West*, Glendive Cr., Aug. 18, *idem*, Aug. 24; Powder R., Aug. 24, *idem*, Sept. 12; Powder R., Aug. 26, and O'Fallon's Cr., Aug. 27, *idem*, Sept. 5; Deer Cr., Aug. 30, *idem*, Sept. 8; Glendive Cr., Sept. 4-5, *idem*, Sept. 12; Ft. Lincoln, Sept. 21, *idem*, Sept. 21.

C-60 Omohundro, John B. ("Texas Jack") (scout with Terry). Dispatch: Mo. of Powder R., Aug. 23, N.Y. *Herald*, Sept. 17. Interview: New York, *idem*, Sept. 30.

C-61 Paulding, Holmes O. (Asst. Surg., with Gibbon). "Dr. Paulding and his Remarkable Diary" (Apr. 1 - Nov. 17), ed. by Barry C. Johnson. In Francis B. Taunton, ed. *Sidelights of the Sioux War*. English Westerners Society, London, 1967. Letters of July 8 and July 15, in Dean Hudnutt, "New Light on the Little Big Horn", *Field Art. J.*, 26:347, 1936.

C-62 Pickard, Edwin H. (Pvt. Co. F, 7 Cav., with Custer). Letter: Aug. 1, Bangor (Me.) *Whig and Courier*, Aug. 16. Reprinted in Little Big Horn Associates *Newsletter*, April, 1968.

C-63 Porter, Henry R. (Act. Asst. Surg., with Custer). Interview, N.Y. *Herald*, July 11.

C-64 Reno, Marcus A. (Maj. 7 Cav., with Custer). Dispatch, unsigned: July 4, *Spriit of the Times*, July 29. Reprinted in *Chicago Westerners Brandbook*, Aug., 1965. Interview: N.Y. *Herald*, Aug. 8 (see M-21). Letter: July 30, *idem*, Aug. 8 (see M-21).

C-65 Reynolds, Charles A. (scout with Custer). "Diary of Charles A. Reynolds" (May 17 - June 23). Mss., Minn. Hist. Soc.

C-66 Roe, Charles F. (2 Lt. Co. F, 2 Cav., with Gibbon). Letter: Little Horn R., June 28 (see M-60).

C-67 Schuyler, Walter S. (1 Lt. 5 Cav., aide to Crook). Letter: Nov. 1, (see M-61).

C-68 Schwatka, Frederick (2 Lt. Co. M, 3 Cav., with Crook). Dispatches: Goose Cr., July 23, Chicago *Inter-Ocean*, Aug. 3; Wyoming, Aug. 4, *idem*, Aug. 16; Rosebud, Aug. 10, *idem*, Sept. 11; Mo. of Powder R., Aug. 18, *idem*, Sept. 26; Whitewood Cr., Sept. 16, *idem*, Oct. 4.

C-69 Sheridan, Phillip H. (Lt. Gen., cmdg. Div. of Mo.). "Sheridan Papers". Mss., Library of Congress.

C-70 Smith, Edward W. (Capt. 18 Inf., Adj. to Terry). Unsigned dispatches: Ft. Lincoln, May 14, St. Paul *Pioneer-Press*, May 19; Big Mudddy, May 20, *idem*, May 27; Little Missouri, May 30, *idem*, June 15; Powder R., June 8, *idem*, June 24; Powder R., June 15, and Tongue R., June 20, *idem*, July 9; Mo. of Big Horn R., July 1, *idem*, July 7; Battlefield Map and Notes, *idem*, July 12; Mo. of Rosebud, July 30, *idem*, Aug. 2; Mo. of Rosebud, Aug. 5, *idem*, Aug. 11; Mo. of Rosebud, Aug. 7, *idem*, Aug. 15; On Rosebud, Aug. 10, *idem*, Aug. 22; No. Bank of Yellowstone, Aug. 27, *idem*, Sept. 5; Glendive Cr., Sept. 5, *idem*, Sept. 12.

C-71 Smith, W.H. (teamster with Terry). Interview, St. Paul *Pioneer-Press*, Aug. 13.

C-72 Stanton, Thaddeus H. (Maj., Paymaster, with Reynolds). Dispatches: Cheyenne, Feb. 24, N.Y. *Tribune*, Feb. 28; Ft. Fetterman, Feb. 28, *idem*, Mar. 9; Journal, Mar 7-15, *idem*, Apr. 14; In Camp, Mar. 18 and Old Ft. Reno, Mar. 21, *idem*, Apr. 4; Old Ft. Reno, Mar. 22, *idem*, Mar. 27; Cheyenne, Apr. 1, *idem*, Apr. 7; Letter: Red Cloud Agency, Oct. 27, Omaha *Herald*, Nov. 3 (see C-7).

C-73 Strahorn, Robert E. ("Alter Ego") (reporter with Crook). Dispatches, series 1: Cheyenne, Feb. 23, *Rocky Mountain News*, Feb. 24; Ft. Fetterman, Feb. 27 and 29, *idem*, Mar. 5; So. Cheyenne R., Mar. 3, *idem*, Mar. 23; Crazy Woman's Fk., Mar. 7, *idem*, Apr. 6; Tongue R., Mar. 13, *idem*, Apr. 4; Otter Cr., Mar. 16, *idem*, Apr. 5; Powder R., Mar. 18, *idem*, Apr. 7; Ft. Reno, Mar. 21, *idem*, Mar. 26; Cheyenne, Mar. 3-1, *idem*, Apr. 1; Denver, Apr. 11, *idem*, Apr. 12; Cheyenne, Apr. 24, *idem*, Apr. 25; Cheyenne, May 1, *idem*, May 2; Cheyenne, May 21, *idem*, May 23; Ft. Fetterman, May 29, *idem*, May 30; Sage Cr., May 29, *idem*, June 6; Tongue R., June 8, *idem*, June 27; Tongue R., June 11, *idem*, June 16; Goose Cr., June 19, *idem*, June 24; Cloud Peak, June 20, *idem*, July 4; Cloud Peak, June 28, *idem*, July 11; Cloud Peak, July 12, *idem*, July 25.

Dispatches, series two (to the Cheyenne *Sun*, available only as clippings in C-7): Ft. Reno, June 2; Ft. P. Kearney, June 5; Tongue R., June 10; Goose Cr., June 11; Goose Cr., June 19; On *Far West*, Aug. 22; Crook City, Sept. 13.

Dispatches, series three: Goose Cr., July 23, Chicago *Tribune*, Aug. 2; Goose Cr., Aug. 4, *idem*, Aug. 9; Goose Cr., Aug. 4, *idem*, Aug. 16; Heart R., Sept.

5, *idem*, Sept. 9; Slim Buttes, Sept. 9, *idem*, Sept. 17.

C-74 Taylor, H.M. ("Muggins") (scout with Gibbon). Interviews: Bozeman *Times*, July 6; Helena *Herald*, July 23.

C-75 Terry, Alfred H. (Maj. Gen., comdg. Dept. of Dak.). "Diary of the Expedition of 1876" (May 17 - Aug. 22). Mss., Library of Congress. Letter: see M-60.

C-76 Thompson, Richard E. (2 Lt., 6 Inf., Terry's Com. of Sub.). Letters: In the field, May 20, and Mo. of Big Horn, July 1-4, N.Y. *Times*, July 9.

C-77 Varnum, Charles A. (2 Lt., 7 Cav., Custer's Chief of Scouts). Letter, July 4 (see M-21).

C-78 Wasson, Joe ("Jose") (reporter with Crook). Dispatches: In Camp, May 30, *Alta California*, June 26; Fks. of Tongue and Prairie Dog Cr., June 9, *idem*, July 6; So. Fk. Tongue R., July 22, *idem*, Aug. 1; Junction of Yellowstone and Powder R., Aug. 18, *idem*, Sept. 26; Little Missouri R., Sept. 4, *idem*, Sept. 17.

C-79 White, William H. (Pvt. Co. F, 2 Cav., with Gibbon). "Diary of . . ." (Jan. 1 - July 23). Mss., Custer Battlefield Nat. Mon.

C-80 Williamson, John (scout with Gibbon). Interviews: Bozeman, June 22, Bozeman *Times*, June 29; Stillwater, June 21, Helena *Herald*, July 6.

II. Reminiscent Accounts from Participants

R-1 Adams, Jacob (Pvt. Co. H, 7 Cav., with Custer). Accounts: Horace Ellis, "A Survivor's Story . . .," *J. Am. Hist.*, 3:227, 1909; George R. McCormack, "Man Who Fought Custer," *National Republic*, 21:14, Mar. 1934; Jacob Adams, *A Story of the Custer Massacre*, pam., n.d., Vincennes.

R-2 Arnold, Ben (courier with Crook). Lewis F. Crawford. *Rekindling Campfires*. Bismarck, 1926.

R-3 Benteen, Frederick W. "Narrative, 1890" (see M-21). "The Benteen-Goldin Letters" (see M-21).

R-4 Berry, George C. (Pvt. Co. E, 7 Inf., with Gibbon). "Experiences" (see M-9).

R-5 Bourke, John G. *Mackenzie's Last Fight with the Cheyennes*. Ann Arbor, 1966.

R-6 Bourke, John G. *On the Border with Crook*, N.Y., 1891.

R-7 Brinkerhoff, Henry M. (Pvt. Co. G, 7 Cav., with Custer). "True Story of Battle of Little Big Horn," clipping in *Custer Battle Scrapbook*, Billings Public Library. Letter, July 8, 1928, to Albert W. Johnson, in *Dustin Papers*, Custer Battlefield Nat. Mon.

R-8 Brisbin, James S. Letter, Jan. 1, 1892, to E.S. Godfrey (see M-9).

R-9 Burkman, John (Pvt. Co. L, 7 Cav., with Custer). Glendolin D. Wagner. *Old Neutriment*. Boston, 1934.

R-10 Cody, William F. (scout with Merritt and Terry). *The Life of Hon. William F. Cody*. Hartford, 1879.

R-11 Coleman, James (sutler's clerk with Terry). "Statement" (see R-47).

R-12 Curly (Crow scout with Gibbon and Custer). Interviews: with Lt. Charles F. Roe, *Army and Navy J.*, March 25, 1882; with Gen. Hugh L. Scott, Aug. 25, 1919 (see M-21); with Joseph K. Dixon, 1909 (see M-17). Statement: (see M-65).

R-13 Daly, Henry W. (packer with Crook), "The War Path," *American Legion Monthly*, April, 1927.

R-14 Edgerly, Winfield S. Letter to Mrs. Custer, Oct. 10, 1877 (see M-54). Interview, Leavenworth *Times*, Aug. 18, 1881 (see M-21). "Narrative, 1883," (see M-5). "Narrative, 1892-95," in *W.J. Ghent Papers*, Library of Congress.

R-15 Gerard, Frederick F. (Ree interpreter with Custer). Accounts: see M-35 and R-47.

R-16 Gibbon, John, "Last Summer's Expedition Against the Sioux," continued as "Hunting Sitting Bull," *Am. Catholic Quart. Rev.*, April and October, 1877.

R-17 Godfrey, Edward S., "Custer's Last Battle," (see M-21). Albert J. Partoll, "After the Custer Battle," in *Frontier Omnibus*, ed. by John W. Hakola and H.G. Merriam, Helena, 1962.

R-18 Goes Ahead (Crow scout with Gibbon and Custer). Statements: see M-65, R-47, and M-17.

R-19 Goldin, Theodore W. (Pvt. Co. G, 7 Cav., with Custer), "Carried Custer's Last Message to Reno," Milwaukee *Journal*, Oct. 27, 1929. Accounts: see M-7 and M-9.

R-20 Grouard, Frank. Joe De Barthe. *Life and Adventures of Frank Grouard*. Norman, 1958.

R-21 Hairy Moccasin (Crow scout with Gibbon and Custer). Statements: see M-65 and M-17.

R-22 Hammon, John E. Interview with C.E. Deland, Feb. 28, 1898, in *Dustin Collection*, Custer Battlefield Nat. Mon.

R-23 Herendeen, George A. Letter of Jan, 4, 1878, N.Y. *Herald*, Jan. 22, 1878 (see M-21).

R-24 Hetler, Jacob (Pvt. Co. D, 7 Cav., with Custer). Account in *Winners of the West*, Nov. 30, 1935.

R-25 Horner, Jacob. (Pvt. Co. K, 7 Cav., with Custer). See Roy P. Johnson, "Jacob Horner of the 7th Cavalry," *No. Dak. Hist.*, April, 1949.

R-26 Hughes, Robert P. (Capt., 3 Inf., aide to Terry), "The Campaign Against the Sioux," *J. Mil. Serv. Inst.*, Jan. 1896 (see M-22).

R-27 Hynds, Hugh A. (Sgt. 20 Inf., with Gatling Battery and Terry). Account, June 25, 1926. Copy in Custer Battlefield Nat. Mon.

R-28 Jackson, William (Ree scout with Custer). Letter, July 24, 1899 (see M-68). Interview with James Willard Schultz, 1888 (see M-63).

R-29 Johnson, Francis (Pvt. Co. I, 7 Cav., with Custer). Statement, about 1900, to Albert W. Johnson. *Dustin Collection*, Custer Battlefield Nat. Mon.

R-30 Kanipe, Daniel A. (Sgt. Co. C, 7 Cav., with Custer). Accounts in *Mont. Hist. Soc. Contr.*, 4:277, 1903, and in M-21.

R-31 King, Charles (1 Lt. Co. K, 5 Cav., with Merritt). *Campaigning with Crook*. N.Y, 1890.

R-32 Korn, Gustave (Pvt. Co. I, 7 Cav., with Custer). Note, May 21, 1888, on back of photo of Comanche, in *Winners of the West*, Jan, 30, 1936. See also, article by Roy P. Johnson, Fargo *Forum*, Jan. 30, 1949.

R-33 Larsen, Ole (crewman of *Far West*). Interview with C.E. Deland, Mar. 7, 1907, in *Dustin Papers*, Custer Battlefield Nat. Mon.

R-34 Leforge, Thomas H. (Crow interpreter with Gibbon). Thomas B. Marquis. *Memoirs of a White Crow Indian*. N.Y., 1928. Also statement in M-65.

R-35 Lemly, Henry R. (2 Lt. Co. E, 3 Cav., with Crook). *Battle of the Rosebud*. Pam. Copy supplied by Harry H. Anderson.

R-36 Martin, John (Tptr. Co. H, 7 Cav., with Custer). See W.A. Graham, "Custer's Battle Plan," *Cav. Jour.*, July, 1923 (in M-21).

R-37 Miles, Nelson A. *Personal Recollections*. Chicago, 1897.

R-38 Mills, Anson (Capt. Co. M, 3 Cav., with Crook). *My Story*. Washington, 1918.

R-39 Morris, William E. (Pvt. Co. M, 7 Cav., with Custer). Letters: to C.T. Brady, Sept. 21, 1904 (see M-7); to Robert Bruce, May 23, 1928, copy in Custer Battlefield Nat. Mon.

R-40 Newell, Daniel (Pvt. Co. M, 7 Cav., with Custer). Account in John P. Everett, "Bullets, Boots, and Saddles," *Sunshine Mag.*, Sept., 1930.

R-41 Nugent, William D. (Pvt. Co. A, 7 Cav., with Custer). "Near the Custer Battlefield," *Winners of the West*, June 24, 1926; "From Memory's Store," tyescript, Custer Battlefield Nat. Mon.; see also "Wm. O. Taylor's Notes," Coe Collection, Yale U.

R-42 O'Neill, Thomas (Pvt. Co. G, 7 Cav., with Custer). "A Thrilling Escape," (see M-9).

R-43 Pickard, Edwin H. (Pvt. Co. F, 7 Cav., with Custer). Account of 1923 in Edgar I. Stewart, "I Fought with Custer," *Montana Mag.*, Summer, 1954.

R-44 Pigford, Edward A. (Pvt. Co. M, 7 Cav., with Custer). Interview with Earle R. Forrest, Washington (Pa.) *Observer*, Oct. 3-19, 1932.

R-45 Plenty Coups (Crow scout with Crook). Frank Linderman. *American*. N.Y., 1930.

R-46 Porter, Henry R. Interview, Bismarck *Tribune*, May 24, 1878.

R-47 Ree Scouts (with Custer). O.G. Libby. *The Arikara Narrative. No. Dak. Hist. Coll.* v.6, 1920.

R-48 Reno, Marcus A. Narrative, about 1886, in "Brief Biography of Major M.A. Reno," *Americana*, March and April, 1912.

R-49 Roe, Charles Francis, "Custer's Last Battle," (see M-60).

R-50 Rutten, Roman (Pvt. Co. M, 7 Cav., with Custer). Letter, April 21, 1911, in Wm. O. Taylor's *Notes*, Coe Collection, Yale U.

R-51 Ryan, John (Sgt. Co. M, 7 Cav., with Custer). Account in Hardin *Tribune*, June 22, 1923 (see M-21).

R-52 Sellow, William (teamster with Terry). Account in Dupuyer *Acantha*, July 15, 1899 (see M-68).

R-53 Sivertsen, John (Pvt. Co. M, 7 Cav., with Custer). Account in M-65.

R-54 Slaper, William C. (Pvt. Co. M, 7 Cav., with Custer), "A Trooper's Account of the Battle," in M-9.

R-55 Smith, John Henry (Pvt. Co. I, 6 Inf., with Moore). "A Soldier's Report of the Custer Massacre . . ." Mss., Custer Battlefield Nat. Mon.

R-56 Taylor, William O. (Pvt. Co. A, 7 Cav., with Custer). "Wm. O. Taylor's Notes," Coe Collection, Yale U. Also, letter to E.S. Godfrey, Feb. 20, 1910 (see M-21).

R-57 Thompson, Peter (Pvt. Co. C, 7 Cav., with Custer). Account in J. Brown and A.M. Willard. *The Black Hills Trails*. Rapid City, 1924.

R-58 Towne, Phineas (Pvt. Co. F, 3 Cav., with Crook). Account in M-7.

R-59 Varnum, Charles A. Undated Statement in R-26.

R-60 White, William H. See Thomas B. Marquis. *Two Days Before the Custer Battle*. Pam., 1935.

R-61 White Man Runs Him (Crow scout with Gibbon and Custer). Interviews: with J.K. Dixon, 1909 (see M-17); with Gen. Hugh L. Scott, Aug. 25, 1919 (see M-21). Statement in M-65.

R-62 Wilber, James (Pvt. Co. M, 7 Cav., with Custer). Account in M-65.

R-63 Windolph, Charles (Pvt. Co. H, 7 Cav., with Custer). Accounts: John P. Everett, "Bullets, Boots and Saddles," *Sunshine Mag.*, Sept. 1930; also see M-36.

III. Indian Accounts

I-1 Bighead, Kate (Cheyenne). Thomas B. Marquis. *She Watched Custer's Last Battle*. Pam., 1933.

I-2 Black Elk (Oglala). John G. Neihardt. *Black Elk Speaks*. Lincoln, 1961.

I-3 Brother of Bull Eagle (Miniconjou). Interview with Lt. Geo. Ruhlen, Cheyenne R. Agcy., April 19, 1876 (see O-9).

I-4 Charger, Samuel (Sioux), "Chronology of the Sioux," *Sunshine Mag.*, Dec. 1928.

I-5 Clark, W. Philo. Report, Sept. 14, 1877, to Adj. Gen., Dept. of the Platte (from Indians surrendering at Red Cloud and Spotted Tail Agencies). Copy supplied by Harry H. Anderson.

I-6 Crazy Horse (Oglala). Interview with C.S. Diehl, Camp Robinson, May 24, 1877, Chicago *Times*, May 26.

I-7 Crow King (Hunkpapa). Interview, Fort Yates, July 30, 1881 (see M-21).

I-8 Eagle Bear (Oglala). Interview, 1938 (see M-36).

I-9 Eastman, Charles A. (Santee), "The Story of the Little Big Horn," *Chautauqua Mag.*, v.31, No. 4, 1900.

I-10 Feather Earring (Miniconjou). Interview with Gen. H.L. Scott, Poplar, Mont., Sept, 9, 1919 (see M-21).

I-11 Flying Hawk (Oglala). M.I. McCreight. *Chief Flying Hawk's Tales*. N.Y., 1936.

I-12 Gall (Hunkpapa). Interviews: Custer Battlefield, June 25, 1886 (see M-21); Fort Custer, July 14, 1886 (see M-21).

I-13 Grinnell, George B. *The Fighting Cheyennes*. N.Y., 1915.

I-14 Horned Horse (Oglala). Interview, May, 1877 (see R-6).

I-15 Hump (Miniconjou). Interview, Fort Yates, July 30, 1881 (see M-21).

I-16 Iron Hawk (Oglala). Interview, May 12, 1907, in *Judge Ricker Papers*. Mss., Neb. St. Hist. Soc.

I-17 Iron Thunder (Miniconjou). Interview, Ft. Yates, July 30, 1881 (see M-21).

I-18 Kill Eagle (Blackfoot Sioux). Statement, Standing Rock Agcy., Sept. 17, 1876 (see M-21).

I-19 Low Dog (Oglala). Interview, Ft. Yates, July 30, 1881 (see M-21).

I-20 Left Hand (Arapahoe). Interview, 1920 (see M-21).

I-21 One Bull (Hunkpapa). Interview with John P. Everett, "Bullets, Boots an Saddles," *Sunshine Mag.*, Sept. 1930.

I-22 Rain in the Face (Hunkpapa). Accounts: Thomas W. Kent, "The Personal Story of Rain in the Face," (see M-7); Charles A. Eastman, "Rain in the Face, the Story of a Sioux Warrior," *Outlook*, Oct. 27, 1906.

I-23 Red Cloud, Jack (Oglala). Interview, 1909 (see M-17).

I-24 Red Horse (Miniconjou). Statements of 1877 and 1881 (see M-21).

I-25 Respects Nothing (Oglala). Interview, Nov. 9, 1906, in *Judge Ricker Papers*, Mss., Neb. St. Hist. Soc.

I-26 Runs the Enemy (Two Kettle). Interview, 1909 (see M-17).

I-27 Sitting Bull (Hunkpapa). Interview, Oct. 17, 1877 (see M-21).

I-28 Smith, John W., "The Sioux War," (information from Standing Rock Indians), Bismarck *Tribune*, Nov. 7, 1876.

I-29 Spotted Horn Bull, Mrs. (Hunkpapa). Accounts: 1883 (see M-17); see also M-51.

I-30 Stands in Timber, John, and Margot Liberty. *Cheyenne Memories*. New Haven, 1967.

368

I-31 Two Bulls (Yanktonnais). Edward A. Milligan. *High Noon on the Greasy Grass*. Pam., 1972.

I-32 Two Moon (Cheyenne). Hamlin Garland, "Gen. Custer's Last Fight as seen by Two Moon," (see M-21). Interview, 1909 (see M-17). -

I-33 Waterman (Arapahoe). Interview, 1920 (see M-21).

I-34 Weasel Bear (Cheyenne). Interview, 1938 (see M-36).

I-35 White Bull (Miniconjou). Stanley Vestal, *Warpath*. Boston, 1934.

I-36 Wooden Leg (Cheyenne). Thomas B. Marquis. *Wooden Leg, A Warrior Who Fought Custer*. Lincoln, 1957.

IV. Official Records

O-1 Belknap Inquiry. Index to Reports of House Committees, 44 Cong., 1 Sess., 1875-6.

O-2 Board of Indian Commissioners. *Annual Reports*, 1875-6. Washington.

O-3 "Certain Concessions from the Sioux," Sen. Ex. Doc. No. 9, 44 Cong., 2 Sess.

O-4 Cheyenne River Agency, *Letters Received* from, 1876-7. M234, Roll 129. RG 75, NARS.

O-5 Commissioner of Indian Affairs, *Annual Reports*, 1865-90.

O-6 *Congressional Record*, 1876.

O-7 Crow Agency, *Letters Received* from, in Montana Superintendency, 1876, M234, Rolls 504-5, RG 75, NARS.

O-8 Dakota, Dept. of. *General and Special Orders*, 1876. Booklet in NARS.

O-9 Dakota, Dept. of, *Letters Received*, 1876. RG 98, NARS.

O-10 Daley, H.W. *Manuel of Pack Transportation*. Washington, 1917.

O-11 Fort Abraham Lincoln, *Letters Sent*, 1874-7. RG 98, NARS.

O-12 Fort Abraham Lincoln, *Medical History* of, 1872-6. RG 94, NARS.

O-13 Fort Berthold Agency, *Letters Received* from, 1875-6. M234, Roll 295. RG 75, NARS.

O-14 Fort Buford, *Letters Sent*, 1876. RG 98, NARS.

O-15 Fort Buford, *Post Returns*, 1876. RG 98, NARS.

O-16 Fort Buford, *Medical History* of, 1876. RG 94, NARS.

O-17 Fort Buford, *Document File*, 1873-7. RG 98, NARS.

O-18 Fort Peck Agency, *Letters Received* from, in Montana Superintendency, 1870-6. M234, Rolls 490-505. RG 75, NARS.

O-19 Graham, W.A. *The Reno Court of Inquiry* (Abstract). Harrisburg, 1954.

O-20 Hammer, Kenneth. *Men with Custer*. Fort Collins, 1972.

O-21 Heitman, Francis B. *Historical Register and Dictionary of the U.S. Army*. Washington, 1903.

O-22 Kappler, Charles J. *Indian Affairs: Laws and Treaties*. Washington, 1904.

O-23 Ludlow, William *Report of a Reconnaissance of the Black Hills*. Washington, 1875.

O-24 McClernand, Edward J., "Journal of Marches Made by the Forces under Colonel John Gibbon," (April 1 - Oct. 6) Ann. Rept., Chief of Engineers, 1876, Appendix PP.

O-25 Maguire, Edward, "Report of Expedition Against Hostile Indians in the Summer of 1876," (May 17 - Sept. 7), Ann. Rept., Chief of Engineers, 1876, Appendix PP.

O-26 Merritt, Wesley, "Report on Red Cloud Indian Needs, March 17, 1876," Hse. Ex. Doc. No. 145, 44 Cong., 1 Sess.

O-27 "Military Expedition Against the Sioux Indians," Hse. Ex. Doc., No. 184, 44 Cong., 1 Sess.

O-28 Missouri, Division of, *Letters Received*, 1876. RG 98, NARS.

O-29 Missouri, Division of, *Letters Sent*, 1876. RG 98, NARS.

O-30 Missouri, Division of. *Record of Engagements with Hostile Indians*, 1868-82. Chicago, 1882.

O-31 Montana, District of, *Telegrams Sent*, 1876. RG 98, NARS.

O-32 Otis, George A. *Transport of Sick and Wounded by Pack Animals.* Circular No. 9, Surg. Gen.'s Off. Washington, 1877.

O-33 Overfield, Loyd J. *The Little Big Horn* (Official Documents and Troop Rosters). Glendale, 1971.

O-34 Quartermaster Department, "Monthly Reports of Persons Hired," (Various commands, 1876). RG 92, NARS.

O-35 Red Cloud Agency, *Investigation of Affairs at*, July 1875. Washington, 1875.

O-36 Red Cloud Agency, *Letters Received* from, 1876. M234, Roll 720. RG 75, NARS.

O-37 *Regulations for the Army of the United States*, 1861. Washington, 1862.

O-38 *Reno Court of Inquiry, 1879, The Chicago Times Account.* Fort Collins, 1972.

O-39 Secretary of War. *Annual Reports*, 1874-7. Washington.

O-40 Seventh Cavalry. *Orderbook*, 1876. RG 393, NARS.

O-41 Seventh Cavalry. *Returns and Muster Rolls*, 1876. RG 94, NARS.

O-42 Sixth Infantry. *Returns*, 1876. RG 94, NARS.

O-43 Spotted Tail Agency, *Letters Received* from, 1875-7. M234, Rolls 840-1. RG 75, NARS.

O-44 Standing Rock Agency, *Letters Received* from, 1875-7. M234, Rolls 846-7. RG 75, NARS.

O-45 Stanton, Williams S., "Annual Report," (May 29 - June 21), in Ann. Rept., Chief of Engineers, 1876, Appendix PP.

O-46 *U.S. Statutes at Large*, vol. 9, Dec. 1875 - Mar. 1877. Washington.

O-47 Upper Platte Agency, *Letters Received* from, 1867. M234, Roll 892. RG 75, NARS.

O-48 Wallace, George D., "Report of," (June 22-25), in Ann. Rept., Chief of Engineers, 1876, Appendix PP.

O-49 Whittemore, James, and F.N. Heath. *Ammunition, Fuses, Primers . . .* Ordnance Memo. No. 21. Washington, 1878.

O-50 Wilson, James E., "Report of . . ." (on board *Far West*, June 24-29), in Ann. Rept., Chief of Engineers, 1876, Appendix PP.

V. Miscelaneous

M-1 Amaral, Anthony A. *Comanche, the Horse that Survived the Custer Massacre.* Los Angeles, 1961.

M-2 Anderson, Harry H., "Cheyennes at the Little Big Horn — A Study in Statistics," *No. Dak. Hist. Quart.*, 27:3, 1960.

M-3 Anderson, Harry H., "Indian Peace-Talkers and the Conclusion of the Sioux War of 1876," *Neb. Hist.*, 44:233, 1963.

M-4 Armes, George A. *Ups and Downs of an Army Officer.* Washington, 1900.

M-5 Bailly, Edward C., "Echoes from Custer's Last Fight," *Military Affairs,* 17:170, 1953.

M-6 Berthrong, Donald J. *The Southern Cheyennes.* Norman, 1963.

M-7 Brady, Cyrus T. *Indian Fights and Fighters.* N.Y., 1909.

M-8 Brady, Cyrus T. *Northwestern Fights and Fighters.* N.Y., 1909.

M-9 Brinninstool, E.A. *Troopers with Custer.* Harrisburg, 1952.

M-10 Burdick, Usher L. *The Last Battle of the Sioux Nation.* Stevens Point, 1929.

M-11 Burgum, Jessamine S. *Zezula, or Pioneer Days in the Smoky Water Country.* Valley City, 1937.

M-12 Chandler, Melbourne C. *Of Garryowen in Glory.* 1960.

M-13 Culbertson, Thaddeus. *Journal of an Expedition to the . . . Upper Missouri in 1850.* Bur. of Am. Ethnol. Bull. No. 147. Washington, 1952.

M-14 Custer, Elizabeth. *Boots and Saddles.* N.Y., 1885.

M-15 DeLand, Charles E., "The Sioux Wars," *So. Dak. Hist. Coll.,* vols. 25 and 27, 1930 and 1934.

M-16 *Dictionary of American Biography.*

M-17 Dixon, Joseph K. *The Vanishing Race.* Garden City, 1913.

M-18 Erlanson, Charles B. *Battle of the Butte.* Pam., 1963.

M-19 "Frederick F. Gerard," *No. Dak. Hist. Coll.,* 1:344, 1908.

M-20 Gilbert, Hila. *Big Bat Pourier.* Pam., Sheridan, 1968.

M-21 Graham, W.A. *The Custer Myth.* Harrisburg, 1953.

M-22 Graham, W.A. *The Story of the Little Big Horn.* Harrisburg, 1959.

M-23 *Grand Rapids and Kent County, Michigan.* 1900.

M-24 Gray, John S., "Arikara Scouts with Custer," *No. Dak. Hist.,* 35:442, 1968.

M-25 Gray, John S., "Frank Grouard: Kanaka Scout or Mulatto Renegade?" *Chicago Westerners Brandbook,* 16:57, 1959.

M-26 Gray, John S., "Bloody Knife, Ree Scout for Custer," *Chicago Westerners Brandbook* 17:89, 1961.

M-27 Gray, John S., "The Lame Deer Fight," *Chicago Westerners Brandbook,* 31:17, 1974.

M-28 Gray, John S., "Medical Service on the Little Big Horn Campaign," *Chicago Westerners Brandbook,* 24:81, 1968. (The present book corrects many errors in medical assignments in this article, which, however, names the wounded and their disposition.)

M-29 Gray, John S., "On the Trail of Lonesome Charley Reynolds," *Chicago Westerners Brandbook,* 14:57, 1957.

M-30 Gray, John S., "Peace-Talkers from Standing Rock Agency," *Chicago Westerners Brandbook,* 23:17, 1966.

M-31 Gray, John S., "The Reno Petition," *Chicago Westerners Brandbook,* 24:41, 1967.

M-32 Gray, John S., "Sitting Bull Strikes the Glendive Supply Trains," *Chicago Westerners Brandbook,* 28:25, 1971.

M-33 Hammer, Kenneth. *The Springfield Carbine on the Western Frontier.* Pam., 1962.

M-34 Hanson, Joseph M. *The Conquest of the Missouri.* N.Y., 1946.

M-35 Holley, Frances C. *Once Their Home.* Chicago, 1892.

M-36 Hunt, Frazier and Robert. *I Fought with Custer.* N.Y., 1947.

M-37 Hyde, George E. *Spotted Tail's Folk.* Norman, 1961.

M-38 Hyde, George E. *Red Cloud's Folk.* Norman, 1936.

M-39 Innis, Ben. *Bloody Knife, Custer's Favorite Scout.* Fort Collins, 1973.

M-40 Johnson, Barry C., "Custer, Reno, Merrill and the Lauffer Case," *English Westerners Brandbook,* July and Oct., 1970.

M-41 Johnson, Barry C., "George Herendeen, Montana Scout," *English Westerners Brandbook,* April and July, 1960.

M-42 Johnson, Virginia M. *The Unregimented General.* Boston, 1962.

M-43 Johnson, W. Fletcher. *Life of Sitting Bull.* 1891.

M-44 Jones, Brian, "Those Wild Reshaw Boys," in Francis B. Taunton, ed., *Sidelights of the Sioux Wars.* English Westerners Society, London, 1967.

M-45 King, James T. *War Eagle, A Life of Gen. Eugene A. Carr.* Lincoln, 1963.

M-46 Kingsbury, George M. *History of Dakota Territory.* Chicago, 1915.

M-47 Lass, William E. *A History of Steamboating on the Upper Missouri.* Lincoln, 1962.

M-48 Lounsberry, Clement A., "A Story of 1876," *The Record,* Jan. 1897.

M-49 Luce, Edward S. *Keogh, Comanche and Custer.* St. Louis, 1939.

M-50 McConnell, Ronald C., "Isaiah Dorman and the Custer Expedition," *J. of Negro Hist.,* 33:344, 1948.

M-51 McLaughlin, James. *My Friend the Indian.* Boston, 1910.

M-52 McLemore, Clyde, "Fort Pease, the First Attempted Settlement in Yellowstone Valley," *Mont. Mag.,* Jan. 1952.

M-53 Manypenny, George M. *Our Indian Wards.* Cincinnatti, 1880.

M-54 Merington, Marguerite. *The Custer Story.* N.Y., 1950.

M-55 Merrillat, Louis A. and Dalwin M. Campbell. *Veterinary Military History of the U.S.* 2 vols. Chicago, 1935.

M-56 Nevins, Allan. *Hamilton Fish.* N.Y., 1936.

M-57 Nye, Elwood L., "Marching with Custer," *Veterinary Bulletin* (Supplement to *Army Medical Bulletin*), 35:114, April 1941.

M-58 Olson, James C. *Red Cloud and the Sioux Problem.* Lincoln, 1965.

M-59 Powell, Peter J. *Sweet Medicine.* 2 vols. Norman, 1969.

M-60 Roe, Charles F. and Charles F. Bates. *Custer Engages the Hostiles.* Fort Collins, 1973.

M-61 Schmidt, Martin F. *Gen. George Crook, His Autobiography.* Norman, 1946.

M-62 Scott, Hugh L. *Some Memories of a Soldier.* N.Y., 1928.

M-63 Seele, Keith C., ed. *Blackfeet and Buffalo.* Norman, 1962.

M-64 Strong, W.E. *A Trip to Yellowstone National Park.* Norman, 1968.

M-65 *Tepee Book,* 1916.

M-66 Vaughn, J.W. *The Reynolds Campaign on Powder River.* Norman, 1961.

M-67 Vaughn, J.W. *With Crook at the Rosebud.* Harrisburg, 1956.

M-68 Vaughn, Robert. *Then and Now.* Minneapolis, 1900.

M-69 Vestal, Stanley. *Sitting Bull, Champion of the Sioux.* Norman, 1932.

M-70 Whittaker, Frederick. *A Complete Life of Gen. George A. Custer.* N.Y., 1876.

MAPS

373

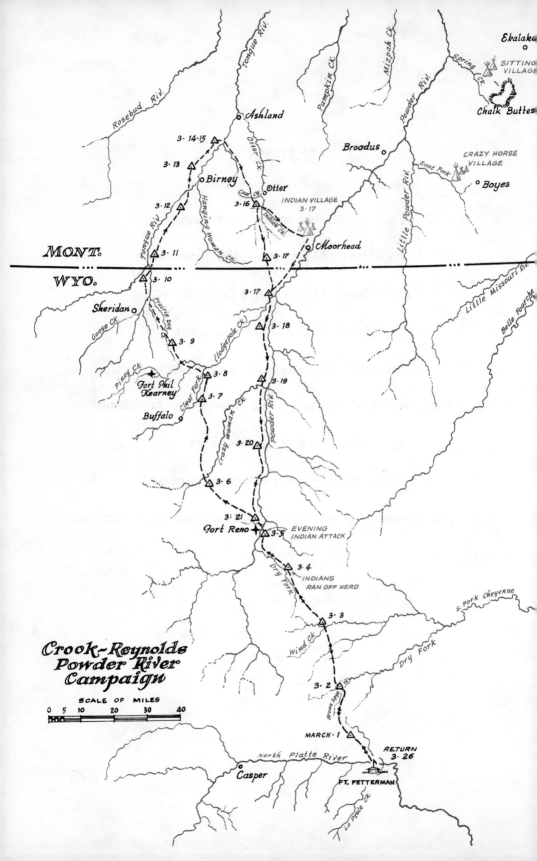

Ekalaka

SITTING
VILLAGE

Chalk Buttes

Rosebud Riv.

Tongue Riv.

Pumpkin Ck.

Mizpah Ck.

Powder Riv.

Spring Ck.

Ashland

3·14-15

3·13

Birney

Otter Ck.

Otter

Broadus

CRAZY HORSE
VILLAGE

East Fork

Boyes

Little Powder Riv.

3·12

Coal Ck.

3·16

INDIAN VILLAGE
3·17

Hanging Woman Ck.

Tongue Riv.

MONT.

WYO.

3·11

3·10

Sheridan

Goose Ck.

Prairie Dog

3·9

Piney Ck.

Fort Phil
Kearney

Buffalo

Clear Fork

3·8

3·7

Crazy Woman Ck.

(Clodgepole Ck.)

Moorhead

3·17

3·17

3·18

3·19

3·20

Powder Riv.

Little Missouri Riv.

Belle Fourche

3·6

3·21

Fort Reno

3·5

EVENING
INDIAN ATTACK

3·4

Dry Fork

INDIANS
RAN OFF HERD

S. Fork Cheyenne

3·3

Wind Ck.

Dry Fork

Crook~Reynolds
Powder River
Campaign

SCALE OF MILES

0 5 10   20   30   40

3·2

Brown Spg Ck.

MARCH·1

North Platte River

Casper

RETURN
3·26

FT. FETTERMAN

Lo Prele Ck.

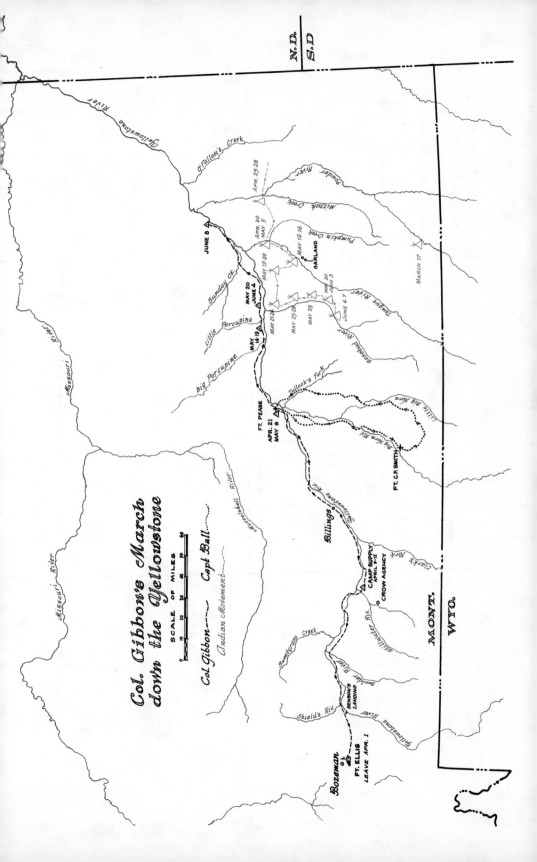

Col. Gibbon's March
down the Yellowstone

Col. Gibbon———— Capt Ball.............
Indian Movement———

SCALE OF MILES
0   10   20   30   40   50

N.D.
S.D

Yellowstone River

O'Fallon's Creek

APR. 25 28

Powder River

Mizpah Creek

Pumpkin Creek

MAY 12-16

GARLAND

MARCH 17

APR. 30
MAY 5

MAY 17 20

JUNE 8

Sunday Ck.

Little Porcupine

MAY 20
JUNE 4

MAY 14 19

Big Porcupine

MAY 21 24

MAY 25 28

MAY 29

Tongue River

MAY 30
JUNE 3

JUNE 4-7

Rosebud River

Tullock's Fork

FT. PEASE
APR. 21
MAY 9

Little Big Horn

Big Horn Riv.

FT. C.F. SMITH

Missouri River

Musselshell River

Billings

Yellowstone Riv.

Clark's Fork

CAMP SUPPLY
APRIL 9-12
CROW AGENCY

Stillwater Riv.

MONT.
WYO.

Sweetgrass Creek

Boulder River

BENSON'S LANDING

Shield's Riv.

Yellowstone River

Bozeman

FT. ELLIS
LEAVE APR. 1

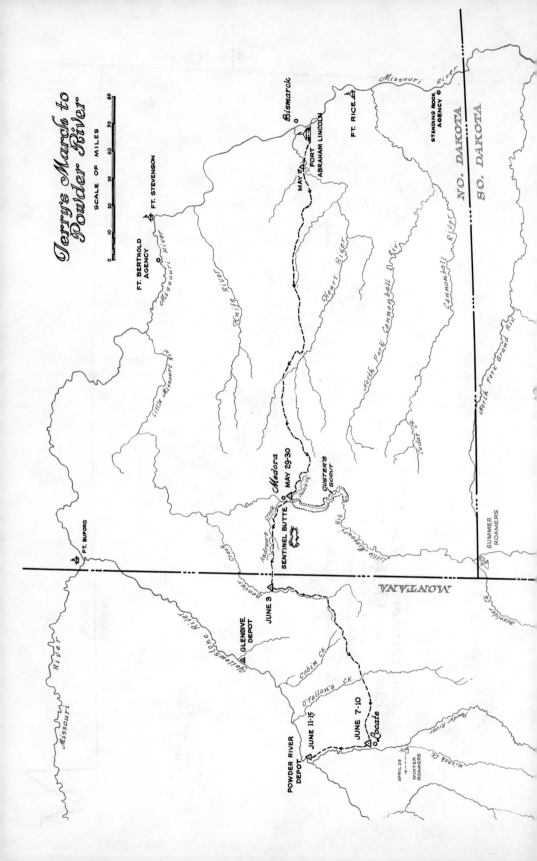

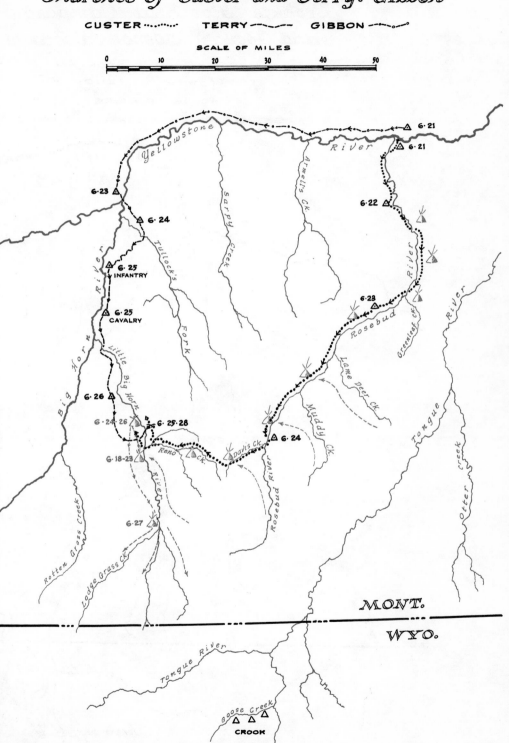

Marches of Custer and Terry=Gibbon

CUSTER ········ TERRY ——-—— GIBBON ——o——o

SCALE OF MILES

0   10   20   30   40   50

Yellowstone

River

6·21

6·21

6·22

6·23

6·24

6·25 INFANTRY

6·25 CAVALRY

6·23

6·26

6·24·26

6·25·28

6·18·23

6·24

6·27

Big Horn River

Little Big Horn

Tullock's Fork

Sarpy Creek

Arnell's Ck.

Rosebud

Greenleaf Ck.

River

Lame Deer Ck.

Tongue

Otter Creek

Muddy Ck.

Rosebud River

Reno Ck.

Davis Ck.

Rotten Grass Creek

Lodge Grass Ck.

River

MONT.

WYO.

Tongue River

Goose Creek

CROOK

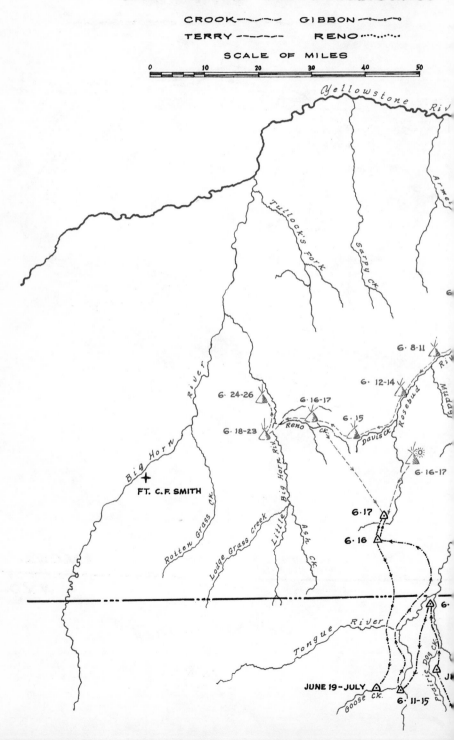

Crook's Rosebud Campaign and Reno's Reconnaissance

CROOK ―∿― GIBBON ―o―o―o
TERRY ―――― RENO ·····

SCALE OF MILES

0   10   20   30   40   50

Yellowstone Riv

Armel

Tullock's Fork

Sarpy Ck.

6· 8·11

6· 12-14

Rosebud

Muddy

6· 24-26   6·16-17

6· 15

Reno Ck.

6· 18-23

Davis Ck.

6· 16-17

Big Horn River

FT. C. F. SMITH

Big Horn Riv.

6· 17

6· 16

Rotten Grass Ck.

Lodge Grass creek

Little

Ash Ck.

6·

Tongue River

JUNE 19-JULY

J.

Prairie Dog Ck.

6·

Goose Ck.

6· 11-15

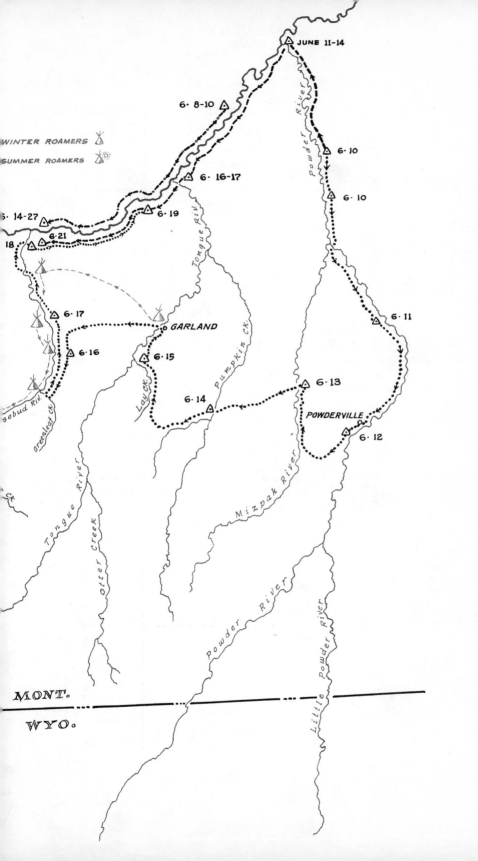

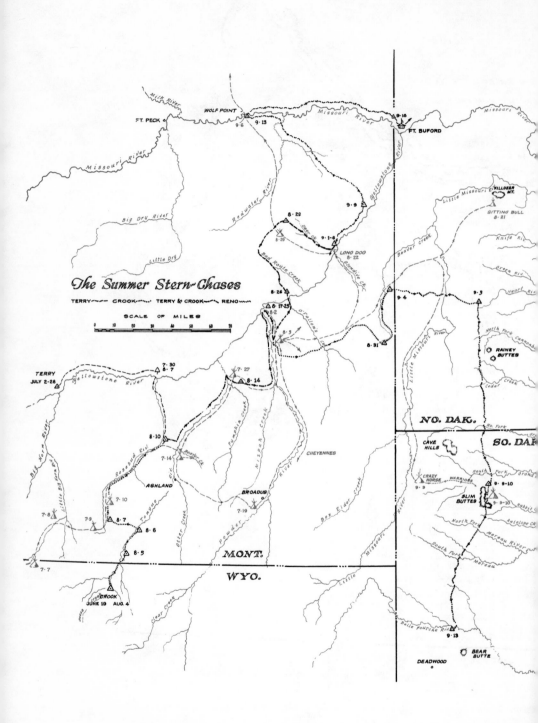

The Summer Stern-Chases

TERRY ——— CROOK ········· TERRY & CROOK ═══════ RENO ·······

SCALE OF MILES

0   10   20   30   40   50   60   70

INDEX

Bloody Knife, 86, 98, 152, 154, 160, 166, 168
Blue Earth Creek, 325
Blue Earth Hills, 56, 325
Blue Mountains, 325
Blue Mud Hills, 325
Boone, Albert G., 261
Booth, Lt. Charles A., 202
Bostwick, Henry S., 73, 77, 78, 185, 190, 191, 194, 195, 201
Bourke, Lt. John G., 27, 44, 46, 47, 49, 51-53, 55, 57, 92, 93, 110, 114, 115, 118, 200, 206, 213, 216, 225, 228, 229, 239, 240, 244, 322, 337
Bovard, Pvt. James, 275, 276
Box Elder Creek, 90, 336
Boy Chief, 158
Boyer, Michael (Mitch), 73, 76, 81, 82, 109, 125, 126, 131-135, 143, 154, 156, 164, 167-169, 176-178, 316, 329, 330, 332
Boyes, Montana, 323
Bozeman, Montana, 19, 40, 41, 72, 83, 113
Bozeman *Times*, 74, 117, 223
Bozeman Trail, 10, 12, 15, 47, 93, 113
Bradley, Lt. James H., 74-84, 103, 107, 108, 131-133, 135, 138, 143, 146, 154, 185, 186, 188-190, 192, 201, 203, 275, 329, 333
Brainerd, Minnesota, 271
Brandenburg, Montana, 342
Bravo, Bernard (Barney), 74, 79, 82, 107, 189, 190, 214, 215
Bridger, Jim, 73, 316
Brinkerhoff, Pvt. Henry M., 160
Brisbin, Maj. James S., 41, 42, 72, 106, 108, 140, 144, 145, 147, 149, 184, 185, 188, 196, 229
Broadus, Montana, 343
Brockmeyer, Wesley, 201, 210, 211
Bronson, Lt. Nelson, 102, 108
Brown, Charles C., 98, 102
Brown, Edwin M., 210
Bubb, Lt. John W., 245-247, 251-253
Buffalo Bill, *See* Cody, Buffalo Bill
"Buffalo Chips", *See* White,

Jonathan
Buffalo Rapids, 222, 224, 228, 235
Bulis, Henry C., 261
Bull, 167, 168
Bull Eagle, 322, 323, 325
Burdick, Usher L., 337
Burke (Courier), 223
Burleigh, Walter "Bub", 227, 281, 282
Burnett, Lt. Levi F., 74, 187, 188, 203, 215
Burt, Capt. Andrew S., 113, 117, 118, 212, 227
Busby Bend of Rosebud, 119, 120, 134, 135, 141, 142, 149, 156, 160-163, 213, 331, 333, 339
Byrne, Dr. Charles C., 229
Byrne, Lt. Bernard A., 88, 102, 208, 211, 353

Cabin Creek, 104, 239, 267
Calhoun, Lt. Frederick S., 350
Calhoun, James, 154
Calhoun, Margaret, 98
Callahan, Cpl. John J., 272, 274, 276, 292
Cameron, J.D., 256
Camp Baker, 72
Camp Brown, 93, 118
Camp Cloud Peak, 198, 199
Camp Hancock, 272
Camp Robinson, 91-93, 264, 265, 349, 351ff
Camp Supply, 73, 75, 82
Campbell, Dave, 211
Canning, Pvt. Matthew, 275
Capron, Lt. Thaddeus H., 111, 115, 116, 238-240
Carland, Lt. John A., 86
Carlin, Lt. Col. William P., 312, 325
Carr, Lt. Col. Eugene, 212, 228, 239, 240, 245, 248-250, 253
Carr, Sgt. John A., 93
Carrington, Col. Henry B., 10
Carroll (Steamer), 209, 210, 227-229, 232, 235, 237, 344
Carroll, Matthew, 75, 82, 107, 184, 211, 293
Cassidy, Pvt. John H., 211

384

385

191, 195-199, 201, 202, 204, 206-208, 234, 279, 280, 283, 299, 304, 305, 333, 336, 337, 339-341
Little Big Horn Valley, 304
Little Face, 187, 189
Little Hawk, 115, 120, 332, 333
Little Missouri River, 32, 37, 48, 87, 89, 90, 97-100, 102, 107, 125, 207, 219, 224, 227, 236, 239, 241, 243, 249, 267, 334, 336, 344
Little Porcupine River, 79-81, 135
Little Powder River, 323
Little Pumpkin Creek, 132
Little Sioux, 158
Little Wolf, 349
Livingston, See Benson's Landing
Locate, Montana, 104
Locate Creek, 218, 231, 343, 344
Lodge Grass Creek, 194, 204, 339-341
Lodge Grass, Montana, 339
Lodgepole Creek, 53
Logan, Capt. William, 75, 76
Long Dog, 233, 236, 242, 249, 344, 345
Long Fork, 194
Lord, Surgeon George E., 88, 154, 274, 276, 292
Lorentz, Pvt. George, 276
Lounsberry, Clement A., 60
Low, Lt. William H., 97, 147, 185, 196
Lower Brule Agency, 31, 259, 264, 314
Luce, Col. Edward, 291
Luhn, Capt. Gerhard L., 111, 115

Mack, Pvt. George B., 293
Mackenzie, Col. Ranald S., 260, 264, 266, 350, 352
Macmillan, Thomas B., 110, 116, 198
Madden, Pvt. Michael, 279, 280
Magpie, Eagle, 119, 120, 333, 339, 349, 350
Maguire, Lt. Edward, 98, 151, 187, 218, 330

Manypenny, George W., 27, 28, 261
Marquis, Dr. Thomas B., 74, 346, 351
Marsh, Capt. Grant, 19, 87, 102, 105, 108, 128, 187, 195-197, 222, 235, 282
Marsh, Professor Othniel C., 24
Martin, Trumpeter John, 177, 179, 305
Mathey, Lt. Edward G., 152, 172, 277, 299
McClay & Company, 76
McClernand, Lt. Edward J., 75, 76, 135, 186, 219
McCormick, Paul W., 40, 41, 73, 78, 79, 106
McDougall, Capt. Thomas M., 172, 177, 277, 299, 300, 306
McGillicuddy, Valentine T., 198, 252, 310, 313, 316
McIlhargy, Pvt. Archibald, 174
McIntosh, Lt. Donald, 182, 192
McKinney, Dr. J.A., 229
McLaughlin, James, 157, 269, 337
McWilliams, Pvt. David, 273, 282
Medical Service, 270-283
Medicine Cloud, 343
Medicine Tail Coulee, 177
Medora, South Dakota, 89, 90, 99
Meeker, Ralph, 60, 65, 66
Meinhold, Capt. Charles, 111, 112
Merrill, Lewis, 63-65, 68
Merritt, Lt. Col. Wesley, 91, 200, 205, 207, 253, 349, 350
Michaelis, Capt. Otto E., 234
Middle Fork of Reno Creek, 299, 304
Middleton, Asst. Surgeon J.V.D., 271, 274, 283
Miles, George M., 210
Miles, Agent John D., 347, 350
Miles, Gen. Nelson A., 204, 210, 216, 218-229, 232, 234, 237, 267, 268, 350, 351
Milk River, 95, 310
Milk River Agency, 311
Mills, Capt. Anson, 55, 115, 122, 198, 213, 245, 247, 248, 251, 252
Mills, Cuthbert, 212, 226, 239, 244

387

Missouri River, 12, 16, 35, 91, 95, 236, 242, 261, 265, 266, 268, 282, 316, 335, 345
Mitchell, Pvt. John, 174, 227, 231, 234
Mitchell, Agent Thomas J., 343
Mizpah Creek, 126, 128, 132, 219, 328, 343
Montana Road, *See* Bozeman Trail
Moore, Cpl., 51
Moore, Capt. Alexander, 54, 55, 57
Moore, Maj. Orlando H., 87, 88, 102, 103, 125, 127, 129, 208-210, 222, 235, 237, 242, 274
Moore, Thomas, 110, 245
Moorehead, Montana, 322
Moreau River, 247
Morgan, George W., 203, 209-211, 222
Morris, Charles R. (Sandy), 201, 202
Mounts, Matthew (Cy), 222-224
Moylan, Capt. Myles, 154, 203
Muddy Creek, 158, 159, 161, 163, 268, 331, 332
Mulligan, George P., 88, 102, 222
Munn, Dr. Charles E., 54, 55
Munson, Capt. Jacob F., 244

Newell, South Dakota, 252
New York *Graphic*, 212
New York *Herald*, 21, 25, 44, 60, 61, 65, 66, 70, 98, 106, 110, 123, 127, 128, 138, 145, 146, 209, 292
New York *Times*, 212
New York *Tribune*, 18, 44
Nickerson, Capt. Azor H., 122
North, Maj. Frank, 258
Northern Pacific Rail Road, 9, 15, 16, 23, 43, 44, 73
North Fork of Reno Creek, 299
North Platte River, 14, 44, 47
Nowlan, Lt. Henry J., 86, 209, 220, 286, 353
Noyes, Capt. Henry E., 54, 55, 113, 122

O'Dell Creek, 52, 53
O'Fallon's Creek, 104, 105, 131, 219, 224, 226, 232, 235, 325
O'Kelly, James J., 209, 211, 223, 225, 235, 236, 242
Old Crow, 117
Omohundro, Texas Jack, 231, 232, 236, 242
O'Neil, Pvt. Thomas, 182
Otis, Lt. Col. Elwell S., 209, 210, 217, 241
Otter Creek, 52, 53, 118, 329, 343
Owl Creek, 118, 204, 247, 339, 340

Palmer, Pvt. Charles, 272, 274, 281
Pandtle, Pvt. Christopher, 272, 274, 276, 281, 282
Pass Creek, 206, 341
Paulding, Surgeon Holmes O., 75, 81, 83, 84, 107, 108, 130, 191-193, 196, 275, 276, 279, 281
Pease, Fellows D., 40
Peno Creek, 114
Pickens, Charles, 232
Pine Ridge Agency, 310, 314, 347
Piney Creek, 51
Piquet, Pvt. Charles, 232
Platte River Agency, 314, 316
Platte River, 9, 12
Plenty Coups, 120
Pompey's Pillar, 201
Porter, Surgeon Henry R., 126, 154, 156, 179, 192, 193, 196, 211, 272-275, 276, 277, 279, 281-283
Portugee Philips, 45
Pourier, Big Bat, 48, 49, 92, 110, 112, 113, 117, 118, 198, 199, 227, 244, 248
Powder River, 12, 13, 36, 37, 46, 48-54, 56, 57, 72-74, 76, 88, 89, 93, 103-106, 108, 109, 111, 113, 125-128, 132, 196, 201, 203-206, 208, 210, 211, 215-224, 227, 229-232, 234, 235, 238, 240, 241, 244, 253, 258, 259, 272, 274, 288, 321-323, 325, 328, 336, 340, 342-344, 353
Powder River Hospital, 273
Powderville, 132

388

389

390

Taylor, N.G., 11

Teat Butte, 133, 134, 154, 330

Terry, Gen. Alfred H., 11, 17, 26, 31-33, 36-43, 59, 62, 66-73, 75-78, 81, 84, 86-90, 94, 95, 97-109, 115, 125-131, 133-153, 158, 161, 164, 165, 173, 181-191, 193-198, 200-205, 207-243, 258, 259, 266, 267, 271, 272, 274, 276, 279-282, 286, 290, 292, 329, 334, 337, 339-345, 354, 355

"Texas Jack", *See* Omohundro, Texas Jack

Thayer, John M., 91, 92

Thompson, Benjamin, 224

Thompson Creek, 322

Thompson, J.D., 60

Thompson, Capt. Lewis, 81, 82, 130, 131

Thompson, Pvt. Peter, 133, 134

Tongue River, 19 36, 41, 44, 46, 49, 51-53, 79-82, 84, 103, 105-109, 114-116, 118-120, 126, 128, 129, 132-136, 142, 147, 149, 201, 204-207, 210, 213-215, 217-219, 222-224, 231, 234, 235, 237, 241, 244, 258, 259, 266, 268, 274, 321, 325, 328, 329, 331, 332, 342, 343, 350

Tongue River Agency, 347

Tongue River Cantonment, 325, 267

Tracy, Hospital Steward Steve, 275

Trail Creek, 120

Tullock's Fork, 130, 131, 140, 142, 144, 148, 149, 156, 159, 162, 163, 165, 168, 184-186, 190, 202, 209

Turtle Mountains, 236

Two Kettle, 337

Two Moon, 325, 328, 340, 351

Ucross, Wyoming, 51

Union Pacific Rail Road, 9

Upham, Maj. John J., 251, 253

Upper Arkansas Agency, 313, 347

Van Vliet, Capt. Frederick, 93, 111, 112

Varnum, Lt. Charles A., 97, 100, 101, 132, 159, 161, 164-168, 180, 215, 279

Vestal, Stanley, 325, 331

von Leuttwitz, Lt. Adolphus H., 246-248

Voss, Trumpeter Henry, 173, 304

Wagoner, John C., 98, 100, 132

Wallace, Lt. George, 152, 155, 158, 160-163, 165, 166, 172, 173, 193, 298, 300, 301

Washakie, 200, 205, 206, 227, 338

Wasson, Joseph, 111

Watkins, Erwin Curtis, 28, 30, 198

Watkins Report, 27, 28, 31, 32

Weir, Capt. Thomas B., 99, 180, 277, 292, 306

Weston, Lt. John F., 39

Whipple, Bishop Henry B., 261, 263

Whelan, Lt. James N., 82, 107

Whistler, Lt. Col. J.N.G., 231-235

Whistler's Trail, 101

White Bull, 321, 332

White Cloud, 222

White, Jonathan, 212, 248

White-Man-Runs-Him, 162, 167, 169, 174, 189, 299, 301

"White Ridge", 343

White River, 336

White, Sgt. William H., 75, 293

White Swan, 189, 277, 282

Whitewood Creek, 252, 253

Williams, Dr. John W., 102, 185, 187, 193, 196, 272-274, 276, 279-282

Williams, Pvt. Robert F., 275

Williamson, John W., 41, 73, 85, 102, 105, 107, 143, 201, 214, 222, 223

Wilson, Sgt. James E., 187, 188, 276, 280

Wind River Reservation, 118, 123

Wolf Mountains, 79-81

Wolf Point, 242, 345

Wolf Rapids, 222, 225, 227, 229, 232-235

Woodbridge, Lt. Francis, 222, 223

Wooden Leg, 114, 115, 133, 134,

CUSTER
HILL

Little Big Horn River

Medicine Tail Coulee

WEIR
POINT

RENO HILL

North Fork Reno Creek

Reno Creek

LONE
TEPEE

Little Big Horn River

Long Otter Creek

South Fork Re